Source and Summit

Source and Summit

Commemorating Josef A. Jungmann, S.J.

Joanne M. Pierce and Michael Downey
Editors

Foreword by Balthasar Fischer

Joanne M. Pierce
Kathleen Hughes, R.S.C.J.
Gerard Austin, O.P.
John F. Baldovin, S.J.
John Allyn Melloh, S.M.
Thomas P. Rausch, S.J.
Nancy A. Dallavalle
Karen B. Westerfield Tucker
Kenneth Stevenson
Peter E. Fink, S.J.
Marjorie Procter-Smith
Nathan D. Mitchell
Don E. Saliers
Michael Downey
Mark E. Wedig, O.P.
John K. Leonard
Regis A. Duffy, O.F.M.

A Liturgical Press Book

THE LITURGICAL PRESS
Collegeville, Minnesota

Cover design by Greg Becker

1   2   3   4   5   6   7   8

Library of Congress Cataloging-in-Publication Data

Source and summit : commemorating Josef A. Jungmann, S.J. / Joanne M. Pierce . . .
   [et al.] ; Joanne M. Pierce and Michael Downey, editors ; foreword by Balthasar Fischer.
      p.   cm.
   Includes bibliographical references and index.
   ISBN 0-8146-2461-8 (alk. paper)
   1. Catholic Church—Liturgy—History—20th century. 2. Catholic
Church—Liturgy. [1. Jungmann, Josef A. (Josef Andreas),
1889–1975.] I. Pierce, Joanne M. II. Downey, Michael.
BX1975.S68   1999
264'.02'0092—dc21   99-20800
                                                                              CIP

Contents

14. Spirituality

15. Art and Architecture

16. Music

17. Liturgy and Culture

Foreword

The unexpected news of a *Festschrift* planned by American authors to appear for the year 2000 to honor the twenty-fifth anniversary of the death of Josef A. Jungmann was greeted with pleasure by his students, friends, and readers on this side of the Atlantic. Understandably, that pleasure is especially keen for one who was the co-editor of the two *Festschriften* that honored Jungmann during his lifetime (one for his sixtieth birthday in 1950, with a second edition in 1953, namely *Die Messe in der Glaubensverkündigung,* and the other, entitled *Paschatis Sollemnia,* honoring his seventieth birthday, appearing in 1959).

Now comes the third Jungmann *Festschrift,* this time from the New World. That would be quite agreeable to the honoree, now twenty-five years parted from us. Josef A. Jungmann, thanks to his many American students in the department of theology in Innsbruck, always had an open ear for the United States. When Fr. Michael A. Mathis, C.S.C. (1885–1960), invited him to be visiting professor at the Notre Dame summer school in 1949, he at first hesitated, but eventually accepted the invitation, and he never regretted it. Those lectures in the summer of 1949 yielded the sole original English book by Jungmann (appearing only eight years later in German): *The Early Liturgy to the Time of Gregory the Great* (Notre Dame, Ind.: University of Notre Dame Press, 1958).

Experience shows that it is always good for a *Festschrift* to have self-imposed restrictions. That is certainly true of the thematic specificity of this American *Festschrift,* which focuses on one of the Innsbruck liturgist's many essays, in which he described "The Defeat of Teutonic Arianism and the Revolution in Religious Culture in the Early Middle Ages" in the *Zeitschrift für Katholische Theologie* in 1947 [Editorial note: This article was reprinted in English in the collection *Pastoral Liturgy,* 1962.]. Those who were intimately familiar with the milieu of Jungmann's thought know that the editors have made a brilliant choice: in fact, none of Jungmann's many articles was as important as this one.

The choice seems to me especially fortunate because Jungmann's lifelong engagement with his favorite idea, here reaching its mature form—namely, the role of Christ's mediatorship in Christian prayer—reveals the extraordinary flexibility of this Tyrolean scholar (though his literary opponents called him stiffnecked!) throughout the course of a long life. It was a long road from the first scholarly contributions of the young professor on the role of Christ in Christian prayer to his ultimate insights on that subject. The research of his student Rudolf Pacik has brought to light an amazingly one-sided statement from his diary for the year 1914: "Only prayer to the Father through Christ is prayer in the strict, true, original sense" (*ZKTh* 111 [1989] 346). At the end of that long road we find the mature knowledge in his last book, *Christliches Beten im Wandel und Bestand* (Munich, 1969). In that book the old master acknowledged the rightful place of prayer to Christ, rooted in the New Testament, alongside prayer through Christ in the presidential prayers of the Roman liturgy. Here the great liturgist left us his ultimate wisdom on the theme of Christian prayer, the outgrowth of much patient research and certainly much more of his own prayer.

Trier, September 8, 1998   Balthasar Fischer

Introduction

This volume of essays marks the twenty-fifth anniversary of the death of the Austrian Jesuit liturgical scholar Josef Andreas Jungmann (1889–1975). It is almost impossible to overestimate the impact that Jungmann and his work have had on the liturgical reforms which flowed from the work of the Second Vatican Council, both in preparing the way for these reforms as well as in implementing the directives of the council's documents; happily, he did indeed live to see the fruits of his long labor. At the time of his death at the age of 85, on January 26, 1975, the council had been adjourned for ten years, and the reformed *ordo missae* of Paul VI had been published and celebrated throughout the world for five years. Jungmann's reputation as an expert in liturgical history and theology had been firmly established before the convocation of the council, and his presence there as a *peritus*, and later, as a member of the Consilium, "the commission entrusted with the implementation of the Constitution on the Sacred Liturgy," was an influential one, although he "exercised great influence . . . almost despite himself [and his diffidence and shyness]."[1]

The editors of this volume judged it fitting to mark the twenty-fifth anniversary of Jungmann's death by inviting a number of scholars active in the broad area of pastoral liturgy, each with a different specialization, to reflect on the importance of Jungmann's work and on developments that have taken place during the years since his death. Since Jungmann's publications are so numerous, we selected what we considered to be the most influential of his many essays as a common starting point for each author's reflections. This key essay is "The Defeat of Teutonic Arianism and the Revolution in Religious Culture in the Early Middle Ages," which was published in English as the lead article in Jungmann's important collection *Pastoral Liturgy* (1962).[2] Unfortunately, this essay is no longer in print. Instead of

---

[1] Robert Peiffer, "Josef Jungmann: Laying a Foundation for Vatican II," in Robert L. Tuzik, ed., *How Firm a Foundation: Leaders of the Liturgical Movement* (Chicago: Liturgical Training Publications, 1990) 59.

[2] Josef Jungmann, *Pastoral Liturgy* (New York: Herder and Herder, 1962) 1–101, also published in Great Britain by Challoner (1962); the German original was published as *Liturgisches Erbe und pastorale Gegenwart. Studien und Vorträge*, 1960. The article itself was first published in German as "Die Abwehr des germanischen Arianismus und der Umbruch der religiösen Kultur im frühen Mittelalter," in *Zeitschrift für katholische Theologie* 69 (1947) 36–99.

reprinting the essay (impossible because of its great length), Joanne Pierce has summarized its main points, which the other contributors address more fully in different ways. Therefore, this summary essay stands at the beginning of the collection to provide both a starting point and a point of reference for the rest of the essays, and, in many ways, serves as an introduction to the volume.

Overall, we have grouped these essays into four general categories, which reflect four governing concerns: Jungmann's own context; historical and theological considerations; diverse perspectives; and present and future implications. While there may in fact be some overlap among the essays, they are distinguished by the different approach taken by each author. The first two groups of articles address the context out of which Jungmann's essay (and the whole of his work) emerges, either theologically or historically. Thus, the essential article by Kathleen Hughes which discusses Jungmann's influence on Vatican II serves as a kind of "gateway" essay for the entire collection, and for the second group in particular. The other essays in the second cluster cover various areas or topics which form a part of Jungmann's immediate historical and theological horizon: Gerard Austin on liturgical history; John Baldovin on Eucharist; John Melloh on preaching; Thomas Rausch on ecclesiology; and Nancy Dallavalle on Trinity.

The third cluster of essays takes a different tack. These authors were asked to reflect on Jungmann's work from a particular perspective which was not Jungmann's own. These essays provide a spectrum of reflection from different denominational or methodological "lenses" which serve to expand on Jungmann's immediate horizon: Karen Westerfield Tucker offers Protestant perspectives; Kenneth Stevenson, Anglican perspectives; Peter Fink, Eastern Catholic perspectives; and Marjorie Procter-Smith, feminist perspectives. Finally, the fourth and last cluster of essays provides another approach. These authors deal with more theoretical ramifications of Jungmann's thought and work, critical ramifications which extend beyond that initial context and point to the liturgical future. Here, Nathan Mitchell reflects on liturgical theology, Don Saliers on liturgy and ethics, Michael Downey on spirituality, Mark Wedig on art and architecture, and John Leonard on music. The final essay of the volume, Regis Duffy's discussion of liturgy and culture, provides a compelling conclusion to the movement of the collection as a whole, and serves as a kind of "capstone" essay. A bibliography of Jungmann's major publications in English closes the volume.

We would like to express our thanks to each of the authors for contributing to this volume, as well as to those who have offered encouraging words to one or both of us along the way: Phyllis Pierce and Janice Pierce; Mary Ann Hinsdale and Alice Laffey of the Department of Religious Studies at the College of the Holy Cross; the Cistercian Community at Mepkin Abbey in South Carolina; Thomas X. Davis, O.C.S.O., Abbot of New Clairvaux in Vina, California; Roger Cardinal Mahony, Archbishop of Los Angeles; Gladys Posakony; and Michael Naughton, O.S.B, and Mark Twomey of The Liturgical Press. Above all, we here acknowledge the delight we have both taken in working together as coordinators and co-editors of a project that we hope will be of service to the liturgical and pastoral life of the churches.

The title of this volume derives from the Second Vatican Council's Constitution on the Sacred Liturgy, which described the liturgy as the source and summit of the Church's life.[3] It is our hope that this Jungmann commemorative volume will honor the memory of one of the greatest liturgical scholars of the twentieth century, not just by reflecting on his past achievements, but by highlighting the trajectories of his influence on the life of the churches twenty-five years after his death, and into the next century.

Joanne M. Pierce
Michael Downey
Advent 1998

---

[3] CSL no. 10.

I. JUNGMANN IN CONTEXT

1. Important Features of Jungmann's "The Defeat of Teutonic Arianism and the Revolution in Religious Culture in the Early Middle Ages"

"Christocentric" and "Corporate": Heretical Reverberations and Living Reform in Western Christian Liturgy

Joanne M. Pierce

Introduction

Josef Jungmann, S.J., produced a remarkable list of published works during his life.[1] However, if one had to name a single essay which captured the essence of his many books and articles, it would be "The Defeat of Teutonic Arianism and the Revolution in Religious Culture in the Early Middle Ages."[2] It is for this reason that each contributor to this commemorative volume was asked to read this essay and begin his or her reflections using it as a starting point. However, this important essay is found in English only in the rather scarce volume of Jungmann's collected essays entitled *Pastoral Liturgy*. Unfortunately, because of its great length (101 pages), the text cannot be reprinted here in full. For these reasons I have undertaken the task of preparing a comprehensive summary of this single article to serve as the lead essay in the present collection.[3]

The Text

Sources and Context of the Christological Struggle
(Sections one through four)

Jungmann divides this rather lengthy essay into eleven sections of unequal lengths, headed by a short introduction. He begins by noting that in a history of

---

[1] See the bibliography of his works in English at the close of this volume.

[2] Josef Jungmann, *Pastoral Liturgy* (New York: Herder and Herder, 1962) 1–101. This translation is a revised and updated version of the article, originally published as "Die Abwehr des germanischen Arianismus und der Umbruch der religösen Kultur im frühen Mittelalter" in *Zeitschrift für katholische Theologie* 69 (1947) 36–99.

[3] References to page numbers will be included in the body of the text in parentheses, for the convenience of the reader.

Christian spirituality by Pierre Pourat, a key period of Church history, from Gregory the Great to Bernard of Clairvaux (approximately the years 600 to 1100), remained essentially unexamined, a lacuna made even more regrettable since, in his opinion, "no period has ever seen a greater revolution in religious thought and institutions" (1). Therefore, he proposes an on-going "task," which is "to illuminate, within the period mentioned, the history of the kerygma against the backdrop of the history of dogma"; the essay which follows provides only an "outline" which, Jungmann envisions, will be fleshed out by other, more "specialized essays" (1). This more "detailed" analysis of a broad range of sources will, he hopes, "serve a higher theological purpose: the discernment of what is an essential possession in religious life, and what is the passing fashion of an age" (2).

The first section of the article, entitled "The contrast between early Christian and early medieval religious culture" (2–9), is devoted to an overview of the key elements, which, in Jungmann's opinion, differentiate Christianity in antiquity and the early medieval period. He draws the contrast along two different lines: liturgy and art. Early Christian liturgy is characterized by several important concepts and practices: it is clearly "corporate public worship"; theologically it is "dominated by the *Easter motif*"; and its prayer is "addressed to the Father and presented 'through Christ'" (2–4). In the early Middle Ages, Christian liturgy has undergone a number of changes. First, the priest-presider is "consciously" detached from the congregation, a detachment expressed by the silent Canon, the exclusive use of Latin, the increased distance of the altar from the nave, and the decrease in frequency of lay communion (2–3). Easter themes are slowly overtaken by the parallels of the Christmas cycle, while Sundays become more and more oriented toward the "glorification of the Holy Trinity" (3). Finally, liturgical prayers addressed directly to Christ and the Trinity are introduced, e.g., the *Suscipe sancta Trinitas* series at the offertory of the Mass (4).

Christian art also provides evidence of these changes over time. In antiquity, Christian art is symbolic, with an "eschatological quality"; events in the Old Testament history of salvation are depicted as fulfilled "in the redemptive work of the new"; and this salvation "in Christ" is expressed in images of the "glorified" and "triumphant" Christ (4–5). Early medieval art, on the other hand, shows different characteristics. The separation of Old Testament and New Testament pictorial narratives shows that the "historical perspective of salvation is reduced," as does the growing frequency of the appearance of the image of the crucified Christ over that of the "glorified" Christ of earlier centuries. Its use "in isolation" is accompanied by other elements, which parallel liturgical shifts: the "stark realism" of various events of the Passion, and increased appearance of images of the Trinity (5–6).

For Jungmann, these liturgical and artistic shifts are evidence of "an increasing emphasis on the individual and upon what is subjective, and the beginnings of the break-up of the basic Easter motif" (6). In support of this contention, he uses the earlier work of Ildefonse Herwegen concerning this historical period.[4] For Herwegen, "mystery predominates" in early Christianity; it is "objective" and "corporate," and focuses on "grace." However, in medieval Christianity, the focus is on "human action" and "moral accomplishments"; it is "subjective" and "individual" (7). Jungmann notes Herwegen's contention that this "shift" is due to the "transition" of Christianity from the Mediterranean to the "Teutonic peoples" and culture, thus, a shift from "objective . . . universal 'being' filled with abundant life" to "the subjective, individual flux of becoming."[5] Therefore, across a broad "range" of "religious thought and life . . . the objective and permanent" gives way to the "subjective, temporal, mutable and historically transitory" (8). This process continues to later eras (e.g., Gothic, Romantic) and can be seen in other developments, for example, the sequences of Notker, the *traditio instrumentorum* in ordination rites, and certain customs at marriage (8–9).

Section two, "Greek influences and parallels" (9–15), deals with Greek influences on early medieval Europe. Jungmann notes Greek influences on the Gallican liturgy of the fourth century, and other Eastern elements (e.g., the *Kyrie eleison,* certain Marian feasts, the Creed) some of which appear in sixth-century Rome and then "the whole of the West" (9–10). However, this influence alone does not account for the medieval mutations in western Christian culture; indeed, Jungmann asks why Eastern Christianity departs "so far from the spirit of a more ancient Christianity" (10). In his opinion, the same "factor" influences the evolution of both Eastern and Western Christianity: "the reverberation of the Christological disturbances, which the Greek Orient suffered" (10). The remainder of the section is devoted to an analysis of various sources to demonstrate the effect of this reverberation in Byzantine Christianity. Byzantine liturgical prayer texts begin to reflect "individual sinfulness and nothingness," and some are addressed to "Christ our God" and refer to the "Godbearer" and adoration of "'the most holy Trinity'" (11). He contends that "homiletic literature" reveals "meditations on Christology" and on Marian themes. "Doxologies" are also evidence of the "anti-heretical attitude of Greek piety" (11), especially the formulation "Glory to the Father with (μετά) the Son along with (σύν) the Holy Spirit" defended by both Basil and John Chrysostom (12). These Greek Fathers also "stressed . . . fear . . . with regard to the Eucharist" as well an "intense reverence of Christ," now both eucharistic "High Priest" and "Consecrator" so that his "humanity lost sight of" (12–13). This stress on Christ's divinity leads to a "lack of [theological] balance" which would later result in Monophysitism and Monothelism. Marian theology, too, provides a site for battle, as the title *Theotokos* becomes almost a password for orthodoxy; this tendency eventually leads to her image as a mediator to Christ in Byzantine liturgical prayer (14–15).

The third section, "Battle-grounds and Spheres of Influence in the West" (15–22), carries the same line of analysis to Western Christianity. While noting

---

[4] Ibid., 7, note 17: I. Herwegen, *Kirche und Seele. Die Seelenhaltung des Mysterienkultes und ihr Wandel in Mittelalter* (Münster 1926).

[5] Ibid., 7, and note 21.

that there is no "simple transference"[6] of the Eastern process into the West, Jungmann still holds that "a whole series of phenomena" are the same, e.g., the increasing predominance of the Trinity over "Christ as Mediator" and the strengthening of the role of Mary (16). The West, like the East, became a site of struggle against Arianism, not only in "a regulative" role in contrast to the reactionary Christological pendulum swings of Eastern theology (e.g., Nestorianism and Monophysitism), but also as the "Teutonic peoples" converted to Arian Christianity and overran the old Roman Empire in the West (16). According to Jungmann, the "physical resistance" to Arianism, which was finally defeated in the political arena with the conversion of the Visigoths to Catholicism in the late sixth century, was paralleled by ongoing *"spiritual and intellectual resistance* as well" (17).

Jungmann then turns to an examination of the struggle in a specific geographical location: Spain. Noting the duration of Arian influence in Spain,[7] where it lasted until the end of the sixth century, Jungmann traces the influence of "anti-Arian" elements from Spain (the "tutor of the West") to France, and then, to the rest of the West (18). The influence of the Carolingian Empire, its liturgy, theology, and other elements of religious culture, become "normative" in Italy and "all of the West" (18–19). However, the source of that Carolingian culture lies in the intense "intellectual life" of Spain and its theologians of the sixth and seventh centuries.[8] "Bridges" between Spain and the continental West included Toulouse and, more importantly, Britain. Jungmann here cites the classic identification of "Spanish symptoms" in "Scoto-Irish" culture and liturgy made early in the twentieth century by Ludwig Traube and Edmund Bishop, and refers to examples from Irish-British liturgical texts (e.g., Stowe Missal, Book of Cerne) as examples of this link from Spain, to Ireland, to Anglo-Saxon Britain, and finally, to France and the rest of Europe.[9] He also briefly discusses use of the Nicene-Constantinopolitan Creed at Mass as another example of the Spanish-British-Carolingian connection. For Jungmann, this analysis

> proves the possibility, at least, that the explanation of the contrast between the religious culture of the rising Middle Age and that of the Patristic age is to be found to some extent in the handing down and the spread of forms of devotion which were created in the theatres of anti-Arian warfare. (22)

The fourth section of the essay is entitled "The Defensive Battle against Teutonic Arianism and its Immediate Reaction" (23–32). Here, Jungmann defines the basic Arian doctrine under discussion: that the Son is "only *like* the Father" and that the "relationship" between the Son and the Holy Spirit is "similar," which leads to the possi-

---

[6] Ibid., 15; he uses as an artistic example the Eastern Christian use of the Christ-*Pantocrator*, and as a liturgical example, the strength of the theme of eschatology in Eastern liturgy.

[7] Although he notes the same struggle in various parts of France, largely in the fifth and early sixth centuries; see 19.

[8] For example, Isidore of Seville, see 19–20.

[9] Ibid., 20, especially note 15, and 21.

bility of the Holy Spirit being considered "a creature." This, in Jungmann's view, leads to a kind of scripturally based, monotheistic "Ditheism" or "Tritheism" (23). Next, Jungmann summarizes the debate over the Catholic theological "defense" of orthodoxy through a "defense" of "various divine attributes" of the Son, in the controversy over doxological (and other eucharistic) formulations (24–25). As he notes, "the central issue" is the scriptural "proof" of the doctrine of *homoousios* (ὁμοούσιος), as seen in fourth- and fifth-century examples from theological and other literature. Jungmann also underlines the "danger of Priscillianism" with its "Modalist" tendencies, especially in Spain (25–26). "Against Arianism they [Spanish synods] stress the unity of divine Being: against Priscillianism, the Trinity of Persons" (26).

The "zeal" with which Arianism is "condemned" in sixth-century Spain leads to expansive and sharply directed "antithetical" language, which finds its way into the liturgy and "devotional life" (27). The cited example of the Council of Toledo (583) serves to underline Jungmann's point: the focus is "to ensure that equal honour and adoration is given to all three Persons in the Trinity" (27). The Mozarabic liturgy likewise shows evidence of this "zeal," when its earliest levels (using phrasing congruent with "the prayer-language of the early church") are compared with later compositions, for example, many of the prefaces, whose language reflects the "new viewpoint." Many phrases imply or "refer" to "Christ as Lord and God," including the embolism between preface and Sanctus, which now infers that "the Sanctus is thus seen as an adoration of Christ" (28-29). In the *Missale Mixtum* (1500), Jungmann finds evidence of "Trinitarian statements" being "transferred" to Christology, a kind of "arbitrariness" in address (God/Christ/Trinity) which Jungmann finds "characteristic of Mozarabic liturgy" (29). Thus, even in later centuries the "bellicose attitude" of Catholicism against Arianism is reflected in prayer texts as well as an "inner mentality," the "structure of faith's awareness" which lingers in writings of the seventh century (30). Jungmann contents that no other churches (e.g., Rome) show evidence of this anti-Arian struggle "outside the Spanish-Gallic sphere"; and even in the Gallican texts, there is "less definition,"[10] although the Gallican *Salvator mundi* doxology is cited as one of a few examples of the Gallican "preference[s] for Trinitarian symbolism" (32).

Medieval Repercussions in Liturgy and Theology
(Sections five through eight)

The next section, *"Fides Trinitatis"* (32–38), continues Jungmann's analysis of the effect of "anti-Arian piety" on the Carolingian period (32). From a restatement of the nature of medieval Christian faith ("as *fides Trinitatis*"), both East and West, Jungmann moves to an examination of liturgical texts and structures which reflect this understanding: "What is new is a manner of speech which seems to identify the

[10] Ibid., 31–32. Interestingly, he proposes that the interplay of Roman and Spanish "influences" in contemporary Britain (e.g., Bede) would be a rewarding study.

substance of Faith with the doctrine of the Blessed Trinity, and to mention this holy mystery very frequently" (33–34). By the year 800, the trinitarian emphasis has become pronounced in Frankish liturgy; in the tenth century this included a feast of the Trinity which was not accepted in Rome until the twelfth century, and made universal in the fourteenth (35). The ninth-century addition of the *Suscipe sancta Trinitas* prayer series at the offertory (and the *Placeat tibi sancta Trinitas* prayer after Mass) are clear examples of this tendency, and the three-form *Kyrie* is also given this trinitarian "interpretation."[11] Other liturgical examples (e.g., the three-fingered gesture used in blessing) and some homiletic material support Jungmann's argument; and it is from these "living germs" of trinitarian focus that Jungmann sees a "blossom[ing] out into even more elaborate forms" (36–37) in later medieval liturgical practice, theological attention, and artistic expression (37–38).

The next three sections discuss the logical consequences of these anti-Arian "repercussions" in the Western Christian tradition. Section six, "Christ our God" (38–47), and section seven, "*Christus Secundum Carnem*" (48–58), both sketch out the implications of this trinitarian/christological ambiguity in the preaching, prayer, and art of the medieval church, while section eight, "Christ, the Church, and the Sacraments" (58–63) examines the "effect" on two other "spheres of faith . . . ecclesiology and the sacraments" (58).

The focus on the Trinity and the anti-Arian discussion of the "subordination" of Christ in his "human nature" led to the "impression" in orthodox Christianity that the "divine nature of Christ . . . predominates." This "impression," combined with the slant of "Teutonic spirituality" and what Jungmann describes as "sketchy instruction," causes in "carolingian catechetical writings" an "intermingling" of "God and Christ" (39–43). This is problematic, in Jungmann's view, on a "kerygmatic" level, since the earlier "suppression of Christ's humanity" now continues to shape "the style of medieval piety," resulting in an important problem: "Christ's mediation became more difficult to grasp" (44). Liturgically, the effect on concluding doxologies is apparent, as is the corresponding "development of the veneration of the saints" to fill this mediatorial role, to become the "bridge to God" (44). In art, the increase in the appearance of the crucifix and "images of the saints" became more pronounced, as did the "zeal . . . for relics . . . and shrines" (44–45). Theologically, the effect was an "almost Modalist" use of language about God and Christ, whose "earthly appearance" is interpreted now as only "the point of God's operation," as contemporary literature (e.g., the *Heiland*) and homiletics seem to indicate (45–46). For instance, one finds references to "God's Passion" through the sixteenth century, while, in art, the corresponding depiction of the Father "in human form" becomes more common.[12]

Jungmann treats the theme of "Christ according to the flesh" also according to liturgical and artistic expression. Theologically, as the "ascended Christ" be-

---

[11] By Amalarius; see 35–36.

[12] As opposed to the "hand from a cloud," see 47–48.

comes "merged in [the glory] of the Trinity," this theme becomes "more strongly emphasized" (48). Thus, Jungmann notes that several "moments" in Christ's earthly life become focal points for theological and liturgical attention. One prominent "moment" is the Incarnation, especially in reference to the *Theotokos* debate, the cult of Mary, and the development of Christmas (and Advent) especially in the West. Other liturgical examples can also be cited, for example, the reference to the Incarnation in the Roman Canon, the development of "Marian Mass formularies, Offices, vesicles at the canonical Hours and Cluniac chapels (49–51). The literary and artistic attention paid to Mary with "her divine Child" (e.g., Nativity plays, discussion of the childhood of Jesus) also supports Jungmann's argument. The point that Jungmann makes is that the "focus" shifts to the "events" of salvation history, rather than "the angle of its own consummation" (49).

The second "moment" accorded a real preeminence is the Passion. Here, Jungmann notes the shift from the "Cross of glory" to the "sufferings" Christ endured in the Passion. Again, attention is focused on separate historical "events," a consideration of the Passion "in every detail," rather than seeing it all in the light of the "glory of the Resurrection." The appeal is to "our compassion" (53). Thus, liturgical attention is centered on this theme of suffering: the feast of the Circumcision, the elaboration of the rite of Veneration of the Cross, the "burial ceremonies" which become part of medieval Holy Week (54–55). Poetry and art, too, seek to evoke "feeling" for the suffering of Christ, so that artistic depictions of the Passion, the Crucifixion, "bear more the character of vanquished suffering than the beginning of glory" (55). This medieval "'Jesus piety'" in the West, an indirect reverberation of the christological controversies of late antiquity, can be understood as a consequence of "so much stress on the divine nature of Christ" (57). The human nature of Christ is viewed in ways which "appeal to sense and arouse feelings of compassion, of amazement, of thanksgiving and repentance," but these perspectives reveal that "the meaning of the human nature for redemption . . . was . . . lost to view" (57–58). Jungmann can simply state that, while "primitive Christianity" emphasized "Christ's divinity," medieval Christianity's "devotion to the humanity of Christ was" could be understood, in a qualified way, as "great innovation" (56).

The next section turns to a consideration of these shifts in relation to ecclesiology and the sacraments. The understanding of the nature of the church was indeed affected by these repercussions: "It is well-known how little the thought of the Church as the Body of Christ flourished in the Middle Ages" (58). The predominant medieval concept of the church seems rather to hang on a kind of "moral cohesion," seen, for example, in the history of the "image of Church as Mother" (58). The ecclesiological birth and nurture themes in antiquity, of which the font is an example, mutate into "juridical-hierarchical" authoritarian images in the medieval period, for example, the depiction of the Church as a bishop on a throne in liturgical art (59). The "sharp distinction between clergy and laity" is one consequence, supported by (and resulting in) many other elements: clerical/liturgical use of Latin, "Teutonic class structures," sacrificial theology of the priesthood, silent Canon, altar further removed from the nave.[13] "The Church begins to be represented chiefly by the clergy" (60). The relationship between Church and State seems, in Jungmann's view, to mirror the shifts ("blending") in the relationship between God and Christ, and the relationship between the two natures of Christ. "The temptation becomes ever stronger, to combine the two entities in a single theocratic system" (60). Liturgical structures also supported this tendency, e.g., the rite for the coronation of a king, in which the king is given a kind of christic anointing.

The sacraments were the venues by which the laity participated in the "spiritual nature of the Church" (62). However, that participation is tinged by a personal "negative attitude," which finds expression in prayer texts redolent with "self-accusation" and "confession of personal unworthiness and sin." The "share in Christ's holiness" granted to all Christians in baptism seems not to be a part of medieval Christian self-image, replaced by a "clinging to moral goodness" which places "this world . . . to the fore" (62). Jungmann's major liturgical example, to which he will return in the next section, is the "attitude to the Eucharist." This sense of unworthiness seems to lead to the decrease in the "frequency of communion"; the "daily bread" of antiquity is now the object of adoration: "not the *use* of the Sacrament but its *cult* . . . a deviation from the original meaning of the Sacrament"[14] due to the unbalanced "state of Christological thought" (63).

Transitions to the Contemporary Situation (Sections nine through eleven)

The ninth section of the article, "The State of Liturgical Life on the Eve of the Reformation" (64–80), is a crucial component of the whole piece. Here, Jungmann discusses the liturgical life of the late Middle Ages, "a time of decline, of decay, to be followed by an extensive collapse" (64), with an eye toward noting points of stagnation and fragmentation. He does not begin with unequivocally negative comments; indeed, at this period one characteristic of Christian liturgy in the West was its "great splendor," thoroughgoing observance of the Sundays and feast days of the year (some fifty or so) in both church and wider society. The primacy of the cathedral, the lively activity of parish and monastic churches, the numerous "collegiate churches" with their communities of canons dedicated to daily public celebration of Mass and Office, all speak of a "liturgical profusion" clearly part of the daily life of the ordinary person (64–65). This "zeal" is also inferred from the size and number of church buildings in the late Middle Ages.

But Jungmann also notes "the onset of liturgical hypertrophy" in the large proportion of clergy to laity,[15] and the concurrent "clerical nature" of liturgical

---

[13] See also 2–3.

[14] However these practices might be an "enrichment of a Eucharistic piety derived from another source, and ultimately capable of integration with it;" 63.

[15] Leading to a "mass-produced and decadent" liturgical life; 66.

celebration" (65–66). This "more or less broad gulf" leads, in Jungmann's view, to a "tension between clergy and the people" resulting from clerical "immense wealth" and "privileges" (66–67). The clerical nature of the liturgy can be seen in architecture; the use of rood-screens and the placement of a remote "high altar" at the end of a long choir necessitated the placement of another altar in front of the rood-screen ("a so-called people's altar or Crucifix altar") for the laity (67). Professional choirs and liturgical Latin contributed to the mute "observation" of worship by the laity, and numerous "side altars" especially proved to be "obstacle[s] in the way of a truly corporate divine worship" (68). "Solemn but remote," the liturgy had become, in Jungmann's opinion, a "lifeless civil act" (68–69).

However, lay participation in Christian worship was not completely lost. The role of the sermon in late medieval worship is an important one, as "a vestige of lay participation," with vernacular singing as a component (augmented by "vernacular interpolations" in sequences) and the remains of a *"prayer of the faithful"* in the intercessions which often formed its conclusion (69–70). Offertory processions also took place on occasion, especially at "great festivals . . . [and] Nuptial and Requiem masses" (70). And while the frequency of communion was much reduced, the popular "urge to contemplate" leads to a focus on the "elevation of the Host at the Consecration" (70–71). The desire to gaze at the host was also transferred to the relics of saints; thus, expositions of both relics and the Blessed Sacrament were an important element of popular worship. Eucharistic devotion can also be measured in frequency of processions, "Holy Hours," and "confraternities . . . all that can be called in general 'Corpus Christi devotion'" despite the threat of "dangerous and superstitious ideas" surrounding eucharistic adoration (71). "The threatening evil was that men would indeed venerate the Sacrament, but would see in it first and foremost the source of temporal blessing," in an "automatic" way, for example, protection from illness or age (71). Jungmann notes in this shift the twisting of the notion of the Eucharist as gift: the gift of sacrifice, and of communion, is "disregarded" in favor of "gifts and benefits" received *"through* it from God [emphasis mine]" (72).

Jungmann next moves to the concept of memorial as another "more positive way" in the later medieval understanding of the Eucharist, seen most clearly in the allegorical interpretations prevalent "to provide meditation on the life of the Lord, especially on his Passion." Following Kolping, he notes that this is not a "unitive amnesis" but a "disintegration" of *the* Mystery into "a multiplicity of mysteries," scattered among the various historical events of the Passion.[16] This kind of diffusion and fragmentation does "violence to the *sacramentality* of the liturgy," which is the "making present of the work of salvation . . . into which we ought to enter deeper and deeper" (73). Even the lively celebrations of the feasts of the liturgical year, marked by the various Mystery Plays, are but a "pseudo-presence" despite the strength of the "religious themes [which] deeply . . . imbued the spirit of the

---

[16] Ibid., 72–73, especially 72, note 12.

age."[17] The same is true of the veneration of saints, whether during feast days, in baptismal names, or as patron saints of guilds, businesses, institutions, and "specific needs . . . situations" or states and ranks of social life (75–77). Other offices were also marked by "a special accompaniment of the Church's blessing," such as rituals of knighthood or bestowal of ecclesiastical office on kings or emperors (77).

But for Jungmann (following Huizinga), all of this activity is "the flowering of autumn . . . a mighty façade, and behind it—a great emptiness" (78). The key point is the medieval "loss of understanding of the sacramentality of the liturgy;" because of this "the liturgy . . . lies unused" (78). The "presence of the Christian Mystery" must "continually penetrate and transform Christianity" especially through the sacraments. The true mystery and nature of the sacraments, and thus of the Church, remains obscured because of the fundamental Christological issue: the "absorption" of the resurrected Christ "in the Divinity, in the Blessed Trinity," and the "interchangeability" of God and Christ, for example, in speaking of "God's corpse, God's Passion" (78). The concept of "the Church as the mystical Body of Christ," of which Christ is "the living Head" must be "rediscovered" by us "in our own time."

Ironically, the great devotional movements of the later Middle Ages show less and less of a connection with the Church (e.g., mystics, *Devotio Moderna*), now viewed as an "earthly, sociological entity" (78–79). In setting the stage for the Reformation and Luther's "blow" not only to abuses but to the "very heart of the liturgy," the late Gothic period in both architecture (numerous side chapels for different interest groups) and legislation (separation of the Sunday Mass obligation from the local parish setting) expresses this "loss" of the sense of Church as "communion of the Faithful," and the resultant focus on "the fragments of faith, peripheral things" (79–80). On the eve of the Reformation, "subjectivism is on the ascendant" marked by "a growing insecurity and many-sided discontent" (79).

Section ten, "Liturgical Life in the Baroque Period" (80–89), covers the subsequent development of these later medieval tendencies. Jungmann notes the context of Tridentine liturgical reform and "religious revival" in the "definition and reform of abuses" (80). The new liturgical books must have been seen in this light, a light cast by the Congregation of Rites (1588), as well as the reforming bishops and new religious orders of the era. The "reconquest" of some Protestant eras of Europe also contributed to the "sense of triumph" which was a major mood of the Baroque era (81). Liturgically, this was both a time of "persistent uniformity . . . [governed by] the law of stability" like "no other period in the history of the liturgy," as well as a time marked by the "culture of the festival," and a "resurgence of festival celebrations" (81). Jungmann notes music in particular as an important area of activity (echoed architecturally by organ and choir lofts), but remarks that

[17] Ibid., 73–74. Likewise, the artistic depictions of the events of the Passion, (in "great detail of suffering)," and of the Resurrection, as "a past event."

much of this liturgical expression is really only "presented" to the laity. "Liturgical creativeness" in terms of lay engagement really finds expression in eucharistic processions, as well as in vernacular hymnody and the development of "evening devotions" (81–82). Supported by earlier traditions of liturgical procession and group representation of the events of "salvation history" (e.g., mystery plays), Corpus Christi processions (and others, e.g., Holy Thursday, and other feasts or special days) allowed all ranks, classes, and categories of persons a chance to participate in celebrating "the sacramental presence of the Body of Christ, as the *nearness* of the Lord," marked out by dress and music (82–84). The Baroque is "the age of processions" with the Sacrament as "the focal point"; in these devotions the "Eucharistic devotions of the late Middle Ages enjoyed their full blossoming."[18]

This focus had an effect on other devotional developments as well. Evening devotions are capped by Benediction; architecturally, the tabernacle and monstrance are stressed. The cult of Mary undergoes expansion and development (e.g., the veneration of Mary under various "titles," almost as separate "cults"), and combined with devotion to the Blessed Sacrament, becomes almost a hallmark of the piety of the era.[19] Jungmann notes that Blessed Sacrament devotion has trumped or subsumed earlier relic-oriented devotion, as Mary now has almost subsumed the wider devotion to the saints, and that, in an interesting way, both "laity and clergy are at a distance" from the liturgy, the one by the language barrier, the other as rubricism leaves them "unmoved by the Spirit" (87). Liturgy is law "to be observed" but not "lived." Neither preaching not reception of communion by the people take place during Mass, but as "independent devotional act[s] . . . split off from [their] liturgical context" (88). Time is, in a sense, frozen: "Medieval devotions continue, but people do not look back to their origins" (88). The "exclusive" focus on "the Real Presence" obscures "truly sacramental thinking," and the arrested attention on the "events of salvation history" is only a "substitute for the continuance of the story of Redemption in the *action* of the sacrament [italics mine]" (88–89). Despite some "isolated approaches," Jungmann emphasizes that "it was quite some time before anything happened to force religious life right back to ultimate sources"; the "rich life" of the Baroque was drawn from "secondary channels" (89).

The eleventh, and final, section serves as a conclusion and attempts to apply some of the results of Jungmann's lengthy analysis to his contemporary liturgical situation. Appropriately, it is entitled "Conservation and Change in the Liturgy" (89–101). He characterizes the more recent past (some "fifty years ago") as a time of "liturgical antiquarianism," influenced perhaps by post-Enlightenment interest and "fresh enthusiasm toward the Middle Ages" (89–90). The sense of the liturgy as "a precious vessel," or "a sacred heritage" tended to emphasize its clerical nature

---

[18] Ibid., 85–86; and which, he notes, are "slowly vanishing today," 86.

[19] Ibid., 86–87; note his comment about the Jesuit novice St. John Berchmans and his application of these two hallmarks to the lives of the saints in general.

and the need to preserve its "even more precious contents" (90–91). However, lay participation was still very much confined to the "peripheral sphere" (e.g., private devotions), not the "esoteric sphere," resulting in the "risk" of identifying liturgical act as "an aesthetic show-piece" or "a work of art from the past" (90–91).

Jungmann notes the "necessary" characteristic of liturgy: the "law of continuity" and its "conservative" nature (rooted, as he sees it, in the unchanging nature of God and Revelation). However, this "disinclination" to make changes in liturgical forms must also be balanced by considering another analogy: "like every living organism, the liturgy has to adapt itself to the present conditions of life" (92). While this change does not always move at the same pace (from "standstill" to "rapid advance"), the two extremes are the immediate context of the mid-twentieth century experience. The "wild unhealthy profusion" of the late Middle Ages was countered by the era of the Tridentine reform, in which "a period of standstill was inaugurated" (92). The period of scrupulous rubricism[20] was ended by Pius X, but real change could only be made by more pulses or "jerks" of reform after so long a time of stasis and minimum understanding of "the meaning of traditional forms" (92–93).

Here Jungmann locates the need of the contemporary church: a better understanding of early Christian liturgical structures to "invite us once more to enter more deeply into their meaning," and which can support a response to the contemporary demand for "forms of Church life such as will be found in a meaningful, corporately celebrated liturgy" (93). One must take into account the needs of a population both "estranged" from Christian "naïve, habitual piety" and "educated" beyond the level of passive, superficial, or "second-rate" practices, the "substitute forms and little out-houses on the fringe of the sanctuary" (93). The responses of the nineteenth century to the problem of augmenting lay participation (lay missals, "prayer and song-Mass") strengthen, in Jungmann's view, the "sense of the 'we' of the liturgy . . . the 'holy priesthood' of the laity" (94). This leads into the twentieth-century "renewal of the liturgy," which, in Jungmann's view, will call for deeper changes (using the image of thawing something that is frozen): "the liturgy itself is on the move," and not everyone is pleased (94).

A number of changes had already been made by the time Jungmann wrote this article, as the result of a number of scholarly influences. He describes Pius XII's encyclical *Mediator Dei* (1947) as real "recognition" of the "development of liturgical forms" and the field of liturgical studies itself which has unearthed and charted this development. Liturgical journals (especially *Ephemerides liturgicae*), as well as international liturgical conferences, have provided sketches of "the coming shape of the liturgy" (95). And he isolates one key issue common to all of this discussion: "the question of the liturgical language."

[20] "'nothing was to be added or taken away or changed' . . . an order, not to be binding forever, and itself introducing a novelty which could only have been possible after the invention of printing;" see 92.

Jungmann devotes some time to a discussion of the use of the vernacular in the liturgy. He cites H. Schmidt in interpreting the "seeming insurmountable obstacle" to use of the vernacular in liturgy raised by the decisions of the Council of Trent, as raising no "theological reason" why this must be forbidden in a post-sixteenth century context when Latin is no longer the language "of all educated people" (96). He next moves to a consideration of some few exceptions made to this rule in Europe in this century, and then a longer treatment of the use of the vernacular in Easter Catholic rites (Byzantine, Melchite, etc.). Many of these groups were permitted to continue using their vernaculars in the liturgy after reuniting with Rome, even into the 1930s (96–98).

Jungmann then follows Baumstark in identifying the "deeper problem" behind the use of the vernacular: "How to make palatable to modern man the religious modes of thought and manners of speech which were crystallized 1500 years ago" (98). This is precisely the point of both scholarly study of liturgical history and theology, "clarifying and enlivening of liturgical forces," as well as of homiletics, "preaching of the Faith which matches the spirit of the liturgy" (98). Here is Jungmann's central theme: "Liturgy must become pastoral" and "intelligible," both so that the Catholic layperson can indeed take an "active part," and so that it becomes "the support of a joyful awareness of Faith and of a Christian life in the harsh everyday world" (98–99). This "goal" has already had "significant" effects, especially in the area of Church music (not without some "crisis" due to the tension between the "established" structures and "rebuilding the edifice"). The structure of the liturgy, especially the Mass, has already undergone some modification, and will, in Jungmann's view, undergo more. "The construction of the Mass ought to be made more obvious" (99), with specific suggestions listed, including the "enrichment" of the "scripture reading" through a multi-year "cycle" (100). The liturgical year, Divine Office, and "evening devotions"[21] have already seen changes and reform, and will see more even though "many years will have to pass." More preparatory work must be done, both on the scholarly and on the popular level: "pastoral work . . . must prepare the way for a revival of the liturgy, using as its tools teaching and preaching" (100–101).

Jungmann's concluding sentences speak eloquently to his ultimate vision of what a reformed and revived liturgy should be: a locus of "redemptive powers," characterized by a "transparent Christocentricity and profound sense of corporate life."[22] Through preaching and catechetics:

> We must reach a situation where the *Ecclesia orans* is no longer a mere ideal of liturgical books, partially realized by the celebrating clergy. It is the whole believing people who make up the *Ecclesia* which approaches God in prayer through the liturgy (101).

---

[21] Jungmann notes especially the "softening" of the "violent contrast . . . between popular devotions and liturgical Vespers," see 101.

[22] Which "must come alive in preaching as well," see 101.

Conclusion

In this essay, Jungmann sets forth a sweeping analysis of the major factor which, in his view, has shaped the Christian liturgical context of the West: the repercussions, both immediate and more distant, of the Christological controversies which marked the fourth and fifth centuries of Christian theological history. These repercussions, echoing as they did across a temporal, geographical, and cultural divide as Christianity moved from its ancient Mediterranean and Hellenistic context into the Northern European, "Teutonic" worldview, had profound and lasting effects on the outer forms and inner "spirit" of the liturgy. Jungmann finds these effects to be largely detrimental, obscuring original "understandings" and participation and forcing the energy of the "popular life" of worship into secondary channels. Liturgical life in the late Middle Ages, as well as in the Baroque period, carries these tendencies to what he sees as rather logical (or at least, comprehensible) conclusions. The stasis introduced and maintained by the Tridentine liturgical books maintains these conditions until the late nineteenth- and twentieth-century periods, which see the increasing awareness, on both scholarly and popular levels, of the need for a new direction, a renewal and revitalization of liturgical celebration. On pastoral, ecclesiological and sacramental grounds, the ideal of simplicity and clarity, to enhance full, conscious, and active participation by all (seen most clearly at this point in the issues of music and vernacular liturgical language) is truly the foundation for Jungmann's notion of pastoral liturgy: a liturgy which embodies a living faith, interactive with and supportive of life in the increasingly complex interweaving of human cultures and societies as the twentieth century turned toward its second half and the end of the second millennium.

2. Jungmann's Influence on Vatican II

Meticulous Scholarship at the Service of a Living Liturgy

Kathleen Hughes, R.S.C.J.

Jungmann's Contribution to the Reforms of the Council: An Overview

It is impossible to overestimate the contribution of Josef Jungmann to the Second Vatican Council, above all, to the pastoral renewal of the liturgy—to the momentum for reform which had been gathering energy for decades, to the climate within which it unfolded, to its preparations, inner workings, implementation and reception around the world. By the time the council was announced Jungmann was already the elder statesman of the liturgical movement whose writing, teaching and preaching had formed a generation of scholars and pastors.[1] His world-wide recognition as an astute historian of the liturgy had been established decades earlier in the publication of his magisterial *Missarum Solemnia*. This comprehensive history of the evolution of the Mass of the Roman Rite provided a scientific apparatus for future liturgical reform, amply illustrating how to "make the minutiae of historical study serve a higher theological purpose: the discernment of what is an essential possession in religious life, and what the passing fashion of an age."[2]

Jungmann further stimulated twentieth century liturgical scholarship through his participation in a series of International Congresses of Liturgical Studies[3] during

---

[1] One thinks, among others, of Balthasar Fischer of the Liturgical Institute at Trier, chief architect of the council's Rite of Christian Initiation of Adults, of Johannes Hofinger, S.J., who kept alive Jungmann's kerygmatic catechetical method, and of Erie's bishop Donald Trautman, intrepid chair of the Bishops' Committee on the Liturgy during the critical discussion and vote on the revised Sacramentary. Jungmann taught at the University of Innsbruck from 1925–1952 (when he reached the age of compulsory retirement) and was one of a handful of European scholars invited by Michael Mathis to teach at the University of Notre Dame during the early days of its summer institute in liturgy.

[2] Such was Jungmann's explicit challenge to younger scholars in his essay "The Defeat of Teutonic Arianism and the Revolution in Religious Culture in the Early Middle Ages," *Pastoral Liturgy*, trans. Ronald Walls (Worcestershire, Great Britain: Challoner Publications, 1962) 2.

[3] These meetings took place at Maria Laach (1951), Ste. Odile (1952), Lugano (1953), Mont César (1954), Louvain (1955), Assisi (1956), Monserrat (1958) and Munich (1960). Many of the participants were later appointed to the liturgical Preparatory Commission and thus the schema on the liturgy had a certain coherence not yet present in the earliest drafts of schemata of other commissions.

the 1950s in which he and a few dozen other scholars, mostly from Europe, discussed and debated a wide variety of liturgical issues. In the process of these meetings there developed a growing consensus about specific principles of liturgical renewal and concrete proposals for the reform of the church's sacramental life. In particular, Jungmann's contribution to the Assisi Conference of 1956, "The Pastoral Idea in the History of the Liturgy,"[4] galvanized participants, including some of Rome's officialdom. There he argued for the lifting of the "Fog Curtain"[5] which separated the liturgy from the people whose worship it was meant to express, for liturgy is the very "life of the Church with her face towards God."[6] At all times, he concluded, "the purpose of the liturgy has been to bring the faithful together, so that they might stand before God as the Church, as the people of God. But the liturgy has also intended more than this: it has aimed to lead the faithful to a *conscious Christian faith.*"[7] In Jungmann's view it was *conscious participation*, denied to the assembly for centuries, which supported and sustained *conscious Christian faith*. Reform of the Church's sacramental life would be justified to the extent that participation was thereby enhanced.

Jungmann was a key player in the council itself.[8] He was appointed a member of the Preparatory Commission on the Liturgy and later became an influential *peritus* during the council and a consultor to the post-conciliar Consilium. As *relator* (chair) of the subcommission on the Mass it was Jungmann who personally drafted the second chapter of *Sacrosanctum Concilium*, "The Most Sacred Mystery of the Eucharist," and who, subsequently, prepared the corresponding chapter in *Inter Oecumenici*, the first Instruction for the orderly implementation of the Constitution.[9] Though a gentle, even reticent man, he was not above politicking among the Council Fathers, especially among the Austrians and the Germans, to garner support for the liturgical reforms which he most earnestly desired for the good of the church.[10]

Finally, after the Constitution on the Sacred Liturgy had been approved and promulgated, Jungmann offered a number of commentaries on its general principles and particular details which also give insights into their author's liturgical predilections, never far removed from his earlier catechetical convictions: "The

---

[4] Josef Jungmann, "The Pastoral Idea in the History of the Liturgy," in *The Assisi Papers*: Proceedings of the First International Congress of Pastoral Liturgy (Collegeville: The Liturgical Press, 1957) 18–31.

[5] Ibid., 30.

[6] Ibid., 19.

[7] Ibid., 23.

[8] Jungmann's several official appointments are noted in Annibale Bugnini's *The Reform of the Liturgy 1948–1975*, trans. Matthew J. O'Connell (Collegeville: The Liturgical Press, 1990).

[9] Both *Sacrosanctum Concilium* and *Inter Oecumenici* may be found in *Documents on the Liturgy 1963–1979: Conciliar, Papal and Curial Texts* [DOL] ed. International Commission on English in the Liturgy (Collegeville: The Liturgical Press, 1982) as DOL:1 and DOL:23.

[10] Jungmann's arts of persuasion were described for me by Msgr. Frederick McManus, himself a *peritus* who served on the liturgical preparatory commission and throughout the council.

Christian message can find a response only if it is proclaimed with a new lucidity and clarity, especially in the assembly of the faithful Sunday by Sunday—that is, in the liturgy."[11]

Clearly Jungmann had a central role in the liturgical movement prior to the council, throughout the development of the Constitution on the Sacred Liturgy, and in interpreting its meaning in the immediate post-conciliar period. Three aspects of his contribution will occupy the remaining pages of this essay: his meticulous scholarly method oriented to the pastoral life of the church; some fundamental principles in the Constitution derived from his work; and the special emphasis on the assembly's participation which we find in the section of the Constitution that Jungmann drafted.

Jungmann's Essay as Harbinger of Conciliar Method

This book is concerned with a particular essay of Josef Jungmann, published during the preparatory phase of the council, and so we must ask: What more specific contribution to Vatican II is revealed through the lens of his brilliant study "The Defeat of Teutonic Arianism and the Revolution in Religious Culture in the Early Middle Ages"?[12] Is it significant that the collection of which this essay[13] is cornerstone appeared in print just after the council was announced? Was Jungmann offering a kind of summary of the fruits of his life-long research just on the eve of the council in order to make a case for the pastoral liturgical reforms so dear to his heart? Was he offering a kind of blueprint for the restoration of earlier, simpler patterns of prayer?

The obvious approach to such questions about Jungmann's influence at Vatican II is to place his essay side by side with the Constitution on the Sacred Liturgy and to note the one to one correspondence of so many key facets of liturgical theology and pastoral practice, emphases perhaps lost or diminished for more than a thousand years but now able to be embraced again: the restored emphasis on the paschal mystery as axial to liturgical theology and celebration; the essentially communal nature of the liturgy; the role of the assembly as co-offerers; the recovery of the centrality of Easter in the conception of an annual liturgical cycle; the renewed appreciation for the ancient liturgical structure of word and sacrament; the importance of a comprehensible liturgical language; and so on. In fact, there can be no doubt that much of

---

[11] "Constitution on the Sacred Liturgy," *Commentary on the Documents of Vatican II*, ed. Herbert Vorgrimler, trans. Lalit Adolphus (New York: Herder and Herder, 1967) 1. See also "The Most Holy Mystery of the Eucharist: Preface," *The Commentary on the Constitution and on the Instruction on the Sacred Liturgy*, ed. A. Bugnini and C. Braga, trans. V. Mallon (New York: Benziger Brothers, 1965) 135–137.

[12] See note 2 above.

[13] It was originally published as "Die Abwehr des germanischen Arianismus und der Umbruch der religiösen Kultur im frühen Mitelalter," in *Zeitschrift für katholische Theologie* 69 (1947) 36–99. The revised and updated article was translated and reprinted in the collection *Pastoral Liturgy*.

what Jungmann illuminates in this essay—what he calls "the shifts of accent and changes of viewpoint"[14] in the liturgy over the centuries—provides a sure foundation for the conciliar winnowing of "immutable elements, divinely instituted, and of elements subject to change [which] not only may but ought to be changed with the passage of time if they have suffered from the intrusion of anything out of harmony with the inner nature of the liturgy or have become pointless."[15]

Jungmann played a far more significant role in the work of conciliar reform than simply suggesting a series of specific pastoral amendments of liturgical practice, whether by the addition, suppression, recovery, adaptation or development of individual liturgical forms and practices.[16] More than these specific reforms, Jungmann's essay illustrates ingeniously a *method* of liturgical scholarship undergirding the reform which was adopted by the council, both in the liturgy and elsewhere, a method that the Constitution makes explicit:

> That sound tradition may be retained, and yet the way remain open to legitimate progress, a careful investigation is always to be made into each part of the liturgy to be revised. This investigation should be *theological, historical, and pastoral.* Also the general laws governing the structure and meaning of the liturgy must be studied in conjunction with the experience derived from recent liturgical reforms and from the indults conceded to various places. Finally, there must be no innovations unless the good of the Church genuinely and certainly requires them; care must be taken that any new forms adopted should in some way grow organically from forms already existing [emphasis added].[17]

Jungmann's essay on "The Defeat of Teutonic Arianism and the Revolution in Religious Culture in the Early Middle Ages" brilliantly illustrates such an approach to liturgiology as mandated in the Constitution. His study is a careful, even painstaking interweaving of the development of the liturgy with the history of dogma and the rise of medieval culture. It is an essay which presents the mutations and transformations of the liturgy and the church's devotional life as the inevitable result of the interplay of various forces—ecclesial, political, and cultural. It examines the way church controversy, particularly the Arian struggle, played itself out when the community gathered for prayer. It explores the interaction of church life in Spain, Ireland, Britain, Rome, and France and its repercussions on the Roman liturgy when elements were borrowed, adopted and adapted.

Throughout his essay Jungmann seeks to explain the development of the medieval religious culture of Christianity through an historical study of the liturgy particularly in its relation to early doctrinal conflicts. He demonstrates, in the

[14] Ibid., 1.
[15] DOL 1:21.
[16] See John O'Malley's "Reform, Historical Consciousness and Vatican II's *Aggiornamento*" (*Theological Studies* 32 [1971] 573–601) for a fascinating discussion of the many methods of reform operative at Vatican II.
[17] DOL 1:23.

process, that while there were numerous legitimate developments, on the whole liturgical life suffered because of certain developments in the aftermath of the Arian heresies and their refutation, especially developments which led to a diminished sense of Christ's mediatorial priesthood and of the mystical body, head and members, as subject of the church's worship. When Christ's divinity was under attack, the community responded not only with credal statements but also with altered forms of liturgical prayer to underscore Christ's divinity. Yet typically in such instances as the controversy passed and the dust settled, patterns of worship remained shaped to meet an enemy long dead and genuine corporate worship whose dominant theme was that of the Easter mystery yielded to a more individualistic, even quasi-private worship of Christ crucified.

Specifically, Jungmann tracks the progressive movement of the liturgy away from the gathered assembly towards the solitary priest who offers the Eucharistic sacrifice as the people's role is reduced to that of passive observers and recipients. With this movement comes a more elaborate liturgical calendar in which the paschal mystery begins to lose its unique liturgical centrality and significance, a change in prayer-language from an emphasis on the mediatorial function of Christ in the divine economy to one which exalts the divine Christ, and the change in focus in religious art from the eschatological reality of the Risen One to the martyred body of Jesus hanging on the cross. By the high Middle Ages, all of these movements had produced a more subjective, individualistic popular piety, focused more on mystery plays and personal devotions—the Christmas crib, the rosary, veneration of the cross, even a burial ceremony for Jesus—than on the liturgy. Jungmann locates the beginning of these changes in the confrontation between "orthodox," trinitarian Christianity and Arianism, a confrontation that eventually led to patterns of worship which no longer reflected clearly the basic relationship of God and humankind in Christ, patterns of worship which progressively disenfranchised an assembly of believers and turned them into silent spectators at a drama enacted on their behalf.

Such is the careful interweaving of historical and theological exposition throughout this essay that one comes to its conclusion with a certain confidence about the pastoral task of reforming the rites while keeping in balance both sound tradition and legitimate progress, a task whose goal is to achieve, once again, the conscious and active participation of the faithful. Paragraph 50 of the Constitution on the Sacred Liturgy, a strategic paragraph almost certainly crafted by Jungmann himself, further elaborates the procedures to be followed:

> [T]he rites are to be simplified, due care being taken to preserve their substance; elements that, with the passage of time, came to be duplicated or were added with but little advantage are now to be discarded; other elements that have suffered injury through accident of history are now, as may seem useful or necessary, to be restored to the vigor they had in the tradition of the Fathers.[18]

[18] DOL 1:50.

This paragraph demanded an investigation of liturgical tradition both rigorous and discerning. What is noble simplicity and how will it be achieved? How does one determine the substance of each rite from its accretions? Duplications, of course, are simpler to spot—prayers, signs of the cross, feast days, and so on. But resolving what duplications and which additions to the rites were advantageous and which had but little advantage takes more careful analysis. And perhaps the most difficult of all the elements of this mandate is the charge to discover and restore elements of the tradition lost through injury or accidents of history.

These various pastoral tasks of the Concilium could only be completed on the basis of the kind of preparatory historical-theological investigation offered by Jungmann. While his essay is dense with historical detail and dogmatic definition, it is thoroughly pastoral in its orientation for its concern is with a living liturgy, then as now, a liturgy subject to the vicissitudes of history and yet never simply a matter of antiquarian concern. "It is not a question here of revising a rite according to some archeological or historical or aesthetic aspect," Jungmann stated, "but altogether according to its pastoral aspect."[19] Early patterns "invite us once more to enter more deeply into their meaning," in order to develop, for our day, "a meaningful, corporately celebrated liturgy."[20]

Besides a method, Jungmann also demonstrates an approach to the study and catechesis of the liturgy and to the continuing implementation of the reform agenda in our day. His essay investigates the liturgy dispassionately. He notes the transmutation of its forms, the effects of its cultural context, the influence for good and ill of doctrine and politics—and he accomplishes all of this with such a blend of scientific detachment and pastoral sensitivity and concern that he inspires trust in his reader for we are convinced by his thorough presentation that he is neither a liturgical archeologist (though he is conservative in the best sense of the word) nor is he promoting radical liturgical innovation (though he is a strong proponent of reform). He would be the first to say that "there must be no innovations unless the good of the Church genuinely and certainly requires them" and that "care must be taken that any new forms adopted should in some way grow organically from forms already existing."[21] Such organic development of the church's living liturgy as well as its ossification through loss, injury, accretion, and duplication is demonstrated again and again in "The Defeat of Teutonic Arianism and the Revolution in Religious Culture in the Early Middle Ages." The publication of this essay could not have been more timely in providing a sure grounding for the pastoral-liturgical task at hand.

[19] *The Commentary on the Constitution and on the Instruction on the Sacred Liturgy*, ed. A. Bugnini and C. Braga, trans. V. Mallon (New York: Benziger Brothers, 1965) 136.

[20] "The Defeat . . . ," 93.

[21] DOL 1:23.

Foundational Conciliar Principles

While written before the council, many of Jungmann's pastoral principles, drawn from his historical and theological study of the gradual transformation of the liturgy during the Middle Ages anticipate the foundational principles and concrete reforms suggested in the Constitution on the Sacred Liturgy. Most significant in his essay, of course, is its basic thesis, namely, that the christological controversies of the fourth and fifth centuries played themselves out in the liturgy for the next thousand years and were the chief cause for the loss of pastoral liturgy and the establishment of the Fog Curtain to which Jungmann referred at Assisi.

In its turn, the Council's reform of the liturgy also begins with its christological foundation. The heart of the liturgy, the Constitution states, is the celebration of the paschal mystery of Jesus Christ in whose life, death and rising the redemption of humankind was accomplished once and for all, and through whose passover the Church was born.[22] Every celebration of the liturgy is thus an exercise of the priestly office of Jesus Christ, head and members, for the greater glory of God and the sanctification of humankind, and all of us, baptized into Christ's priesthood, are thus co-presiders and co-offerers with Christ, the one and only high priest.[23]

The ancient eschatological emphasis of eucharistic theology and piety is also given lyrical expression:

> In the earthly liturgy, we take part in a foretaste of that heavenly liturgy celebrated in the holy city of Jerusalem toward which we journey as pilgrims, where Christ is sitting at the right hand of God, a minister of the holies and of the true tabernacle; we sing a hymn to the Lord's glory with the whole company of heaven; venerating the memory of the saints, we hope for some part and fellowship with them; we eagerly await the Savior, our Lord Jesus Christ, until he, our life, shall appear and we too will appear with him in glory.[24]

In a few short introductory paragraphs the Constitution on the Sacred Liturgy achieves an admirable balance between the human and salvific person and work of Christ and his divine Lordship, between Christ's high priestly mediation and the action of the community as his Body, between God's glorification and human sanctification. In Jungmann's essay he quotes Abbot Ildefons Herwegen's dictum that "the ideal mean is seen in equilibrium."[25] One can only marvel at the christological "equilibrium" achieved in the Constitution's foundational paragraphs which opens the way for the restoration of the community's active participation in the liturgy, the "summit toward which the activity of the Church is directed" and "fount from which all the Church's power flows."[26]

[22] DOL 1:5-6.
[23] DOL 1:7.
[24] DOL 8.
[25] "The Defeat . . . ," 7.
[26] DOL 1:10.

Active participation, too, is a foundational principle of the conciliar reform, flowing as it does from the christological vision of the opening paragraphs of the *Constitution* and demanded by the very nature of the church as Christ's Body. Participation demands, first of all, an opening of the liturgy to the people and a pastoral practice of liturgy which recognizes that active participation is called for by the very nature of the liturgy, the right and duty of Christians in virtue of their baptism: "In the reform and promotion of the liturgy, this full and active participation by all the people is the aim to be considered before all else. For it is the primary and indispensable source from which the faithful are to derive the true Christian spirit and therefore pastors must zealously strive in all their pastoral work to achieve such participation by means of the necessary instruction."[27] Such participation, of course, includes the use of the vernacular, "since the use of the mother tongue, whether in the Mass, the administration of the sacraments, or other parts of the liturgy, frequently may be of great advantage to the people. . . ."[28]

But active participation includes more than vernacular prayer. It includes the liturgical formation of the clergy in order that they be "imbued with the spirit and power of the liturgy and make themselves its teachers."[29] It includes: specialized training for those who teach the liturgy at every level; re-formation of curricula in seminaries and houses of study; continuing formation in the liturgy; and, above all, excellence of celebration as the best form of catechesis. While active participation is promoted by means of "acclamations, responses, psalmody, antiphons, and songs, as well as by actions, gestures and bearing,"[30] active participation is both internal as well as external[31] and is also nurtured by silence[32] so that the faithful might become "conscious of what they are doing, with devotion and full involvement."[33] "*Doing*," as in the preceding sentence, is the operative word of the reform. Active participation involves the entire community once again in the offering, in praise and thanksgiving, in meal, and in living out in deed, what has been enacted in word and ritual action, for the liturgy does not exhaust the activity of the church but sends the assembly "to be the light of the world and to glorify the Father in the eyes of all."[34]

Jungmann suggests that pastoral reform will restore the "we" of the liturgy and bring clergy and laity closer together in an order established by the altar around which they gather as one body with Christ as leader of prayer. Similarly, the council recognized that "liturgical services are not private functions, but are

---

[27] DOL 1:14.
[28] DOL 1:36.
[29] DOL 1:14.
[30] DOL 1:30.
[31] DOL 1:19.
[32] DOL 1:30.
[33] DOL 1:48.
[34] DOL 1:9.

celebrations belonging to the church, which is the 'sacrament of unity,' namely, the holy people united and ordered under their bishop. Therefore liturgical services involve the whole body of the church; they manifest it and have effects upon it, but they also concern the individual members of the Church in different ways, according to their different orders, offices, and actual participation."[35] Individualism and legalism associated with the liturgy of the high Middle Ages are thus overcome in a liturgy which is essentially communal and ordered according to baptismal dignity rather than hierarchical prerogative.

The question of "living liturgy" which Jungmann urges throughout his essay is a recognition that liturgy is not merely a matter of prayers and ceremonies handed down from another age but that liturgy is constantly in interaction with theological developments, popular piety and cultural diversity from place to place and from age to age. Surely it is "living liturgy"—a liturgy which both shapes and is shaped by its historical and cultural context—that is the focus of articles 37–40 in the Constitution, a series of paragraphs which deal with the adaptation of the liturgy to the culture and traditions of the peoples. "Respecting and fostering the genius and talents of various races and peoples" and allowing for "legitimate variations and adaptations to different groups, regions and peoples" promotes a living liturgy steeped in the mentality of peoples, their cultural giftedness and their particularity of time and place.

The Most Sacred Mystery of the Eucharist

Thus far we have examined Jungmann's method of doing pastoral liturgy as demonstrated in "The Defeat of Teutonic Arianism and the Revolution in Religious Culture in the Early Middle Ages" and suggested that his method of interweaving doctrinal and historical investigation to illuminate the pastoral development of a living liturgy was perhaps his greatest influence on the pastoral reform of the liturgy at Vatican II. Further, we have noted how some of the conclusions of his essay find their echo in the foundational section of the Constitution on the Sacred Liturgy, the chapter devoted to General Principles for the Reform and Promotion of the Sacred Liturgy.

Obviously, Jungmann's contribution is evident as well in the following chapter, The Most Sacred Mystery of the Eucharist, the chapter he himself drafted and refined. Perhaps even more telling than the concrete reform proposals of this chapter on the Mass—for example, more ample Scripture, the import of the homily, restoration of the prayer of the faithful, recovery of Word and Table as the principal parts of a single act of worship, reception of elements consecrated at the same Eucharist[36]—is the way in which each reform element is demonstrated to further

---

[35] DOL 1:26.
[36] DOL 51–56.

enhance the participation of the assembly, conscious participation as the avenue to conscious Christian faith.

Reflection on the Eucharist in chapter two begins with two paragraphs which give respectively the theological and pastoral foundations for the more concrete concerns which follow. A reformed eucharistic theology is one which will embrace the mystery of the eucharist under the aspects of sacrifice, sacrament, memorial and meal—the several strands of eucharistic theology which over the ages were sometimes lost, sometimes given exaggerated importance. Here they find careful balance and provide the substructure for what follows, namely, that in the celebration of the Eucharist, "a sacrament of love, a sign of unity, a bond of charity,"[37] images borrowed from Augustine, the Church is made present for in a very real way the Eucharist creates the Church. It is in the celebration of the Eucharist that the assembly of God's people is "formed day by day into an ever more perfect unity with God and with each other, so that finally God may be all in all."[38]

Eucharist is thus presented as the driving force of Christian life but not if the community remains as silent spectators. Here is the heart of the argument for active participation: a good understanding of the rites and conscious participation in the sacred event with devotion and full involvement leads to vigorous and active faith. It cannot be otherwise. The closer one comes to the mystery, the more adequate the opening of the word of God, the more nourishing the table of the Lord's body and blood, then the more engaged the assembly in the very action of Eucharist: praise, thanksgiving, offering and, ultimately, their own transformation.

Participation is above all interior. At the same time interior participation is both nurtured and expressed in exterior ritual actions. Thus, the reform of the order of Mass which follows this christological and ecclesial substructure includes quite concrete details of the celebration: a richer fare at the table of God's word will assure a biblically grounded and deepened spiritual life; a homily integral to the celebration will focus on the word of God as it touches this assembly gathered to give praise and thanksgiving; the universal prayer will be restored so that all in the assembly will experience their mediatorial role in the priesthood of believers; Communion under both kinds will communicate a more ample sign of the nourishment to which we are invited at the Lord's table; reception of Communion from the elements consecrated within the celebration will more forcefully demonstrate the importance of the whole eucharistic action of the gathered assembly; and all of this action, especially "parts belonging to the people" will achieve greater intelligibility because of the use of the mother tongue around the world.[39] Finally, the point of it all, according to the Constitution, was "in order that the sacrifice of the Mass, even in its ritual forms, might become pastorally effective to the utmost degree."[40]

[37] DOL 1:47.
[38] DOL 1:48.
[39] DOL 1:49-56.
[40] DOL 1:49.

Here we see the blend of scholarship and pastoral care. Here we see Jung-mann's method played out, an approach which is measured and careful. It becomes clear that his study of the christological controversies unleashed by Arianism is not simply speculative investigation in order to discover "gee whiz" esoteric facts about liturgical forms long dead. Rather his quest is to uncover the essential and enduring spirit of a living liturgy beneath its language and ceremonies and to make the fruit of that investigation available to those responsible for conciliar reform of the Church's liturgy. Behind historical developments, cultural modifications and doctrinal reinterpretations lies the Christ event, "making the work of our redemption a present actuality,"[41] enabling the heart of the Church's life together "with our face toward God."

Conclusion

It is significant to note that Jungmann's essay "The Defeat of Teutonic Arianism and the Revolution of Religious Culture in the Early Middle Ages" appeared in a book entitled, in English, *Pastoral Liturgy*. Its German title, *Liturgisches Erbe Und Pastorale Gegenwart*, more literally might have been translated "Liturgical Heritage and Present Pastoral Practice." Some reviewers actually faulted the English title suggesting that only in the final portion of the book was Jungmann concerned with pastoral issues. Such is hardly the case. His historical and doctrinal sections are thoroughly pastoral in their orientation and their goal. His pastoral conclusions and suggestions are thoroughly grounded in scholarship. It is all of a piece and it is all important to the continuing reform of liturgy.

The Church is filled with pastoral liturgists today who have lost their theological and historical moorings and have become liturgical dilettantes. Jungmann's method of doing pastoral liturgy challenges liturgists today to ground their convictions in meticulous research into the long and rich tradition of the Church's corporate prayer, and to recognize, at every step, the multiple factors which produced the liturgy in possession at the time of the council and the equally complex reality of the liturgy as it unfolds in the political and cultural context of our day.

Once Jungmann commented on a suggestion that a truly renewed liturgy for our day might actually be created *ex nihilo:*

> The well intentioned person who suggested that the Pope should call together the greatest artists and poets of the world and commission them to create an entirely new Mass liturgy was neither a good liturgist, nor a good theologian. No, the ideal Mass can never be something totally new; all that can—and must—be done is to aim at a form of celebration in which the best traditional structure and the divine content of the Mass such as Christ instituted it, find their fullest and most perfect expression.[42]

---

[41] DOL 1:2.
[42] "What the Sunday Mass Could Mean," *Worship* 37 (1962) 28.

This insight, in a way, sums up Jungmann's contribution to the conciliar liturgical reform. He kept in perfect tension the divine content and the best of traditional structures in championing conscious participation for the sake of more conscious Christian faith. It was his lifework, come to realization above all in his influence on Vatican II.

II. HISTORICAL AND THEOLOGICAL CONSIDERATIONS

3. Liturgical History

Restoring Equilibrium after the Struggle with Heresy

Gerard Austin, O.P.

Every victory is won at great cost. This is equally true whether of battlefields where soldiers kill or of wars of ideas hard fought and eloquently debated. Certainly the defeat of Teutonic Arianism so well described by Joseph A. Jungmann, S.J., in his famous essay is no exception.[1] Jungmann explains, "The Arianism of the Teutonic peoples was quite simply that which Wulfila and his Goths took over from Byzantium in the middle of the 4th century. . . . That the Son is less than the Father is the core of Arianism."[2] This heresy had to be combated, but the question must be asked whether in the long run the Church's reaction to Teutonic Arianism did not serve as a vehicle of changing the nature of the Church's liturgy, and indeed, the notion of the Church itself.

Jungmann poses the question, "What sort of modifications and changes did it (the ferment of anti-Arian piety) help to bring about in the form of medieval spirituality?"[3] His question will be expanded in this essay to include the effects upon modern or present spirituality as well.

In general terms, it can be said that the struggle against Teutonic Arianism in the West resulted in the shifting of emphasis from the humanity of Christ to his divinity. Jungmann puts it this way:

> On a foundation of pure Chalcedonianism which sharply separated the two natures in Christ and then set them simply side by side, the temptation was always present to lay so much stress on the divine nature that the meaning of the human nature for redemption, especially in its Easter consummation, all too easily was lost to view. But this was the form resistance to Arianism took in the West."[4]

This statement, however, needs careful nuance. Jungmann himself writes in his *Habilitationsschrift*:

---

[1] J. A. Jungmann, "The Defeat of Teutonic Arianism and the Revolution in Religious Culture in the Early Middle Ages," *Pastoral Liturgy* (London: Challoner Publications, 1962) 1–101.

[2] Ibid., 23.

[3] Ibid., 32.

[4] Ibid., 57–58.

The direction taken in the struggle against Arianism led in the course of time in different areas of the Church to room being made, even in the inner domain of the Mass, for the prayer-address to Christ. The common opinion that already in the fourth century the prayer to Christ had at once been seized upon as a weapon against the Arians of the time, so as to confront them with a loud confession of the divinity of Christ, is certainly incorrect. It would have been a blunt weapon. Even the Arians ascribed some kind of divinity to Christ. Indeed they prayed to him.[5]

Jungmann goes on to explain that it was not strictly speaking a question of the divinity of the Son, but of the identity and unity of substance with the Father. Thus, "To cherish belief in the Trinity, that is regarded as the first and last criterion of the true faith."[6]

While Rome was slow to cultivate what Jungmann calls the trinitarian theme in connection with the anti-Arian attitude, other areas of the Church, especially the Gallic-Spanish area, did so. There the position of Christ as mediator was allowed to fall more and more into the background. Jungmann explains:

Along with the concern for the Mediator formula, there vanishes also, however, the most important reason why the prayer in the liturgy had been directed up to now not to Christ, but always to God. Indeed, since the traditional liturgical prayer was frequently made to address, no longer simply God, but God the Father, it was easy to see the lack of a prayer to Christ as a gap which it was proper to fill. Thus there resulted, in places where the anti-Arian current was strongest, from this side also the custom of the address to Christ in the liturgical prayer.[7]

Finally, that custom extended itself to countries beyond Spain and Gaul and "became an important factor in the further history of the religious life in general in the West."[8] In another book, Jungmann explains how sometimes the anti-Arian tactics took root even in parts of the world that were not infected with Arianism. Ireland is an example. Jungmann argues:

A very brisk intercourse must have been maintained between Spain and Ireland . . . only thus can we explain the puzzle that in Irish piety a pronounced Anti-arian Christology and Anti-arian doctrine of the Trinity are in evidence, although Ireland had no truck at any time with Arians.[9]

The retort to Arianism was to put Christ on a par with the Father. This risked the obfuscation and even loss of awareness of the humanity of Christ—at least on many levels, and especially on the level of liturgical prayer. Ultimately this had dire consequences.

[5] Josef Jungmann, *The Place of Christ in Liturgical Prayer*, 2nd revised ed. (Staten Island, N.Y.: Alba House, 1965) 217–18.

[6] Ibid., 218.

[7] Ibid., 220–21.

[8] Ibid., 222.

[9] Josef A. Jungmann, *Christian Prayer Through the Centuries* (N.Y.: Paulist Press, 1978) 70.

In the early Church, emphasis during prayer had been on the communion of Christ with his people. Even the distinction between clergy and laity (at least in the earliest centuries) was primarily viewed from the point of view of what clergy and laity had in common: a share in the one priesthood of Christ their mediator. This emphasis on communion or unity was especially experienced at Eucharist, when the priest and faithful formed one Body with Christ who led them to the Father. But due to the Church's reaction to Teutonic Arianism with its stress on Christ's divinity at the expense of his humanity, the gulf between Christ and his people widened. Christ was no longer "one of them, their brother" taking them with him to the Father, but "God up there." Having lost Christ as mediator, the people began their search for someone to take his place. They found the saints, the Blessed Mother, and finally the priest.

This had great repercussions on an understanding of Eucharist. The movement of the Eucharist as the action of the *totus Christus* (head and members) being an acceptable offering to God (humanity's going to God through Christ) yielded to seeing the Eucharist as God's coming down to humans. David Wright describes this altered view:

> The concept of the Eucharist itself underwent a transformation. The conception of the Eucharist as the thanksgiving of the community of the faithful in which their gifts, themselves the sign of God's beneficence, became an acceptable sacrificial offering through the prayer of the priest and the means by which the faithful were united to their head, Jesus Christ, and to one another as members of his Body, yielded to a conception of the Eucharist as the *bona gratia*, the gift of God to mankind.[10]

Such a transformation in the understanding of Eucharist is the result of a shifting of roles of the actors involved in the Eucharist (people, priest, Christ), and in turn is something itself that brings about further changes in "religious culture" (as Jungmann puts it). This shift may be viewed from five different perspectives:

—Baptismal theology, Church as Body of Christ.
—Loss of Christ as mediator, search for replacement.
—Contrast between clergy and laity, priest as sacral figure.
—Eucharist as priest's affair, rise of the private Mass.
—Retrieval of baptismal consciousness, the entire assembly as the proper subject of the liturgical action.

Baptismal Theology, Church as Body of Christ

What is called ecclesiology today would have been contained within the area of baptismal theology in the early Church. Baptism and Eucharist were seen as the

---

[10] David F. Wright, *A Medieval Commentary on the Mass: "Particulae" 2–3 and 5–6 of the "De Missarum Mysteriis" (ca. 1195) of Cardinal Lothar of Segni (Pope Innocent III)* (Unpublished Doctoral Dissertation, University of Notre Dame, 1977) 9–10.

two premier sacraments. By baptism the Christian community is constituted as Church, as Body of Christ, as People of God. Some scholars believe that the First Epistle of Peter is taken substantially from an early Christian baptismal liturgy. Whether that is literally true or not, certainly it conveys a very early expression of the meaning of Christian baptism. The author says: "You, however, are a 'chosen race, a royal priesthood, a holy nation, a people he claims for his own to proclaim the glorious works' of the One who called you from darkness into his marvelous light."[11]

In early spirituality the Church was viewed as mother, who through the waters of the font, gives birth to new Christians. This Church-mother imagery in the waters of baptism was beautifully expressed by the fifth-century poem of Pope Sixtus III that is found on the walls of the baptistry of St. John Lateran, the cathedral of the city of Rome:

> Here a people of godly race are born for heaven;
> the Spirit gives them life in the fertile waters.
> The Church-mother, in these waves, bears her children
> like virginal fruit she has conceived by the Holy Spirit.[12]

This early baptismal theology viewed the baptized woman or man as the *alter Christus*. St. Augustine reminded the baptized of this: "Let us rejoice and give thanks: We have not only become Christians, but Christ himself. . . . Stand in awe and rejoice: We have become Christ."[13] This baptismal theology emphasized what all the baptized had in common: communion with Christ. It was based on the teaching of St. Paul that we form with Christ a single body, we are members of this body (Rom 12:3ff.; Eph 4:13 and 25ff.; Col 3:15ff.). Indeed, Paul says, "There does not exist among you Jew or Greek, slave or freeman, male or female. All are one in Christ Jesus" (Gal 3:28). Yves Congar explains that during the apostolic age and the earliest period of Christianity the Church is, in the first place, the Body of Christ. He writes:

> This immanence of the living Christ in the Church, his Body, is expressed by St. Paul in two very familiar phrases, each of which, ultimately, indicates the same thing—Christ in us, and us in Christ. The formula, "in Christ Jesus," which, counting equivalent expressions, occurs one hundred and sixty-four times, signifies being under his influence, receiving life and movement from him and, consequently, acting, as it were, under his auspices, performing actions that are really his and belong to the sphere which he animates; it amounts to saying, "in his Body." The corresponding formula, "Christ in us," represents his dwelling in us as our life, as an interior principle of action; it expresses the basis of all the Pauline mysticism of the Christian life as consisting in the imitation of Christ, in having in oneself the sentiments of Christ, the mind of Christ (1 Cor 2:16), and in Christ being formed in us (Gal 4:19). The two

---

[11] 1 Pet 2:9. (Biblical citations are from *The New American Bible*.)
[12] Translation taken from Cathedral baptistry, Brisbane, Australia.
[13] St. Augustine, *In Ioanne. Evang. Tract.* 21,8: *CCL* 36,216.

formulas express basically the same reality; what the Christian does as a Christian is an act of Christ, since the Christian is a member of Christ. Christians altogether, animated by the same spirit and acting in the name and under the impulse of the same Lord, form a single whole, the Body of Christ.[14]

This baptismal theology which saw the Church as the Body of Christ would not retain its prominence. Jungmann admits this. He writes:

> If the clouds which took the Lord away from His disciples up to heaven now, to some extent, hide the glorified God-man from the minds of the faithful, inasmuch as they have become accustomed to allowing His heavenly life to be swallowed up in the divine majesty in which He becomes one with the Father; so too that light by which the Church is seen as the Body of Christ grows dim also. For Christ can only be described as Head of the Church in His glorified humanity. It is only of His humanity that the faithful can become members through Baptism, so that they form one Body with Him, that they corporately become, indeed, His Body. It is well-known how little the thought of the Church as the Body of Christ flourished in the Middle Ages.[15]

It would seem that the Church's reaction to Teutonic Arianism contributed to this shift away from seeing the Church as the Body of Christ. By stressing the divinity of Christ, it becomes more and more difficult for the faithful to believe "you are Christ" because now Christ is a "distanced Christ." "Christ our God" expresses divine majesty and gradually assumes precedence over "Christ our brother" who is one like us, and with us. This took its toll on a baptismal theology that had seen the Church primarily as the Body of Christ. It also took its toll on the fundamental Catholic truth that Christ is our mediator, our Way to God.

Loss of Christ as Mediator, Search for Replacement

As noted earlier, the Church at Rome was much slower to address liturgical prayers to Christ than was the case for the Spanish and Gallican Churches. Roman practice remained loyal to the early tradition that the Eucharistic Prayer was directed to God the Father through the explicit mediatorship of Christ. In the *Veronense* and the *Gelasianum* even the *orationes* (collect, secret, post-communion) are addressed to God "through our Lord Jesus Christ" (*per* in the text), and this rule is not once broken.[16] Jungmann shows how the Roman Prefaces are true prayers of praise and thanks, in the center of which stands Christ—either as subject-matter (as the great gift for which God the almighty Father is offered thanks) or expressly as the High Priest through whom the acknowledgement is offered to God, or both together.[17]

---

[14] Yves Congar, *The Mystery of the Church* (Baltimore: Helicon Press, 1965) 26–27.

[15] Jungmann, *Pastoral Liturgy*, 58.

[16] See Jungmann, *The Place of Christ*, 114–15.

[17] See Jungmann, *The Place of Christ*, 105–23.

Jungmann says: "The uncertainty begins only in the *Gregorianum*. . . . With the old rule once broken, the number of Christ-addressed *orationes* in some Churches grew ever greater, albeit slowly and without a strict uniformity being observed as between different places."[18] As time goes on, many Roman *orationes* which were formerly considered simply as prayers to God which were offered through Christ, become Christ-addressed. Thus, as to Christ-addressed prayers, the Roman liturgy has in time resembled somewhat the practice of the Spanish and Gallican liturgy. Indeed, as regards the calendar, the Roman liturgy with its feasts of the Precious Blood, the Crown of Thorns, etc. has gone much further. Yet, as to the heart of the liturgy, the *anaphora* itself, the Roman liturgy stayed conservative, directing the prayer "to the Father through the Son."

This does not mean, however, that popular Roman piety did not shift the place of Christ in the Roman liturgy. Much more is shaped in this domain by the general liturgical ethos than merely by the words of the Eucharistic Prayer. "Appropriation" played a key role here. Appropriation, in the theological sense of the term is a device of the mind whereby attributes which in reality are common to the whole Trinity (since all God's operations *ad extra* pertain to the entire Trinity and are not proper to any one Person) are viewed in their particular relationship to one of the Persons, thus enabling a better understanding of the distinction of Persons in the Godhead.

Appropriation was common in the Gallican liturgy and writers. The writings of St. Caesarius of Arles (c. 470–542) provide an early Gallican example of a rather developed doctrine of what is called appropriation. He gives a long list at the end of his *Breviarium Adversus Haereticos* of operations and properties that are common to the three divine Persons. He quotes sacred Scripture to show that each of the operations listed is attributable to each of the three Persons, thus arguing to a perfect equality among the divine Persons in their operations, and thus finally to their consubstantiality.[19] St. Caesarius attributes creation most of the time to the Son. He appropriates the act of forgiving sins to the Holy Spirit, and indeed, uses this in turn to show the divinity of the Holy Spirit.[20]

The practice of describing Christ as Father was rather common in the Middle Ages, and occasionally appears even in earlier times.[21] In the *Missale Gothicum* there are examples of Christ being referred to as "Father."[22] Theologically speaking this is an acceptable way of speaking because the notion of fatherhood as regards creatures on God's part is common to the whole Trinity (since it is an *ad extra* ref-

[18] Jungmann, *The Place of Christ*, 115.

[19] *Sancti Caesarii Episcopi Arelatensis Opera Omnia* 2, *Opera Varia*, ed. G. Morin (Maredsous, 1942) 193.

[20] Ibid., 198.

[21] See L. E. Wels, "Lieber Vater Jesu, Vater Deiner Mutter!" *Theologische Streifzüge durch die Altfranzösische Literatur*, (Vechta, 1937) 33–44.

[22] *Missale Gothicum (Vat. Reg. lat. 317)*, ed. L.C. Mohlberg (*Rerum Ecclesiasticarum Documenta,* Series Major, Fontes 5) (Roma: Casa Editrice Herder, 1961).

erence); still, it is predicated primarily only of the First Person of the Trinity because the prime analogue of all fatherhood is the Father's eternally begetting His Son. Thus, a *Missale Gothicum* usage of directing the *Pater Noster* to the Son (#203, #204) is legitimate, but confusing in the light of the evangelical origin of the prayer, that is, as an example given by Christ as a prayer to the Father. This example in the *Missale Gothicum* is from the Mass for Palm Sunday. Jungmann states that this is the only example where the address to Christ is retained in a whole formulary: "Here it may well be said that the character of the feast, of which the theme is above all homage of Christ was a determining factor in the address."[23]

While legitimate, such appropriation is another strong factor in the loss of Christ's being viewed as mediator. Jungmann argues that even when the *per Christum* formula remains, "it has become an empty formula, the meaning of which is scarcely attended to any longer. It is as though the distance between God and man had become a sundering chasm which could no longer be bridged by a mediator but only in reference to God's mercy."[24] It was logical then, that in their search for a replacement for a mediator, people looked to the martyrs who had appeased God by shedding their blood, or to Mary under her title "Mother of Mercy."

Another secondary mediator gradually rises up to fill the void, and that is the priest. Earlier in the life of the Church the priest was seen as someone within the circle of the community, including his role as presider at Eucharist. Edward Schillebeeckx describes this situation:

> In the early church there is really an essential link between the community and its leader, and therefore between the community leader and the community celebrating the Eucharist. This nuance is important. It was essentially a matter of who presided over the community. . . . The figure who gives unity to the community also presides in the sacrament of church unity, which is the Eucharist.[25]

But as time went on, little by little the priest was seen as outside the circle of the community, not offering *with* the people, but *for* the people. This separation seems to have been caused, at least partially, by the priest's assuming Christ's vacant position as mediator. Peter Cramer, writing about the priest's role in the celebration of the sacrament of baptism, speaks of a shift in priestly function:

> The priest meanwhile, instead of being in dialogue with the assembly even at the heightened moment of the immersion itself, is now much more firmly represented as the broker of ritual power. This shift in priestly function, which is visible in the same period in the new rite of anointing the hands at ordination, marks an aloofness of

---

[23] Jungmann, *The Place of Christ*, 92.

[24] Jungmann, *Christian Prayer*, 70.

[25] Edward Schillebeeckx, *Ministry: Leadership in the Community of Jesus Christ* (New York: Crossroad, 1981) 49.

priest from people which will become important in the ecclesiological development of sacrament from the ninth to the twelfth century."[26]

Contrast Between Clergy and Laity, Priest as Sacral Figure

Jungmann describes the gradual separation of clergy and people:

> Only the priest is permitted to enter the sanctuary to offer the sacrifice. He begins from now on to say the prayers of the Canon in a low voice and the altar becomes farther and farther removed from the people into the rear of the apse. In some measure, the idea of a holy people who are as close to God as the priest is, has become lost. The Church begins to be represented chiefly by the clergy. The corporate character of public worship, so meaningful for early Christianity, begins to crumble at the foundations."[27]

The close connection between priest and people was regulated in the early Church by the prohibition of absolute ordination, that is, the practice of ordaining bishops and presbyters without attachment to any particular church. It was condemned by Canon 6 of the Council of Chalcedon in 451. Ordained ministry was by its very nature seen to be service to a particular church or congregation. Unfortunately, this view of defining ordained ministry essentially in ecclesial terms lost out, and absolute ordination became common in the Middle Ages.

Granted there are a number of factors at work in the process of the separation of clergy and people, still the loss of Christ as mediator seems to rank high. Yves Congar, in his classic study of the ecclesiology of the High Middle Ages, states that at the end of the eighth century, and then during the course of the ninth century, there were signs of two things: an accentuated distance between the priest and the people, and the role of the priest as mediator.[28] To the extent that the priest substitutes for the lost mediator, to that extent he is considered to be the holy one, the sacral figure. This expresses itself even in the different ways Communion was received by the priest and the people, that is, in the hand for the priest and in the mouth for adult laity. Jungmann writes that the practice of placing the host in the mouth, as opposed to in the hand, dates substantially from the ninth century: "The change of custom is contemporaneous with the transition from leavened to unleavened bread, and is probably related to it. The delicate pieces of thin wafer almost invited this method of distribution, since, unlike the pieces of unleavened bread formerly used, they easily adhered to the moist tongue."[29]

Pierre-Marie Gy disagrees with Jungmann on this. He argues that the change comes about due to an emphasis on the sacredness of the priest's hands, and thus

---

[26] Peter Cramer, *Baptism and Change in the Early Middle Ages, c. 200–c. 1150* (Cambridge Studies in Medieval Life and Thought, Fourth Series 20) (New York: Cambridge University Press, 1993) 142.

[27] Jungmann, *Pastoral Liturgy*, 60.

[28] See Yves Congar, *L'ecclésiologie du haut moyen-âge* (Paris: Les éditions du Cerf, 1968) 96.

[29] Joseph A. Jungmann, *The Mass of the Roman Rite: Its Origins and Development*, vol. two. (New York: Benziger Brothers, Inc., 1955) 382.

of the sacredness of the priest himself. Gy argues from a canonical collection of the early tenth century, *Libri de synodalibus* of Gegino of Prüm (c. 906) for the insistence that adult laity receive communion in the mouth (as opposed to the priest's receiving in the hand), and he says no similar legislation can be found before this time. Gy sees this as part of a new emphasis on the hands of the priest, and says it coincides with the rite of the consecration of the hands of priests which was universally adopted since the Carolingian era. It is during this same era that the anointing of the sick was reserved to priests. In general the Carolingian period was marked by a new emphasis on the role of the priest.[30]

Jungmann attributes part of the separation between clergy and laity to the higher education of the clergy: "Thus in the Carolingian empire the Mass-liturgy, so far as understanding its language was concerned, became a clerical reserve. A new kind of *disciplina arcani* or discipline of the secret had developed, a concealment of things holy, not from the heathen—there were none—but from the Christian people themselves."[31] Such a separation has far reaching effects and is of interest not just for the history of liturgy, but also for ecclesiology. Congar explains that it causes the concrete content of the word *ecclesia* to be affected. Starting with this period the list of witnesses who identify the Church principally with the clergy begins to multiply.[32] This in turn is symptomatic of a new way of viewing the Eucharist.

Eucharist as Priest's Affair, Rise of the Private Mass

This new way of viewing the Eucharist was the result of the loss of a corporate understanding of the Eucharist. Jungmann writes:

> Even though in the early days of the Church it was a fundamental principle that the Eucharist was to be celebrated only for the sake of the faithful and not as a personal devotion of one endowed with the powers of priesthood, still it was not seldom the case in this era when "they broke bread in this house or that" (Acts 2:20), that only a small domestic group gathered around the holy table. This domestic celebration of the Eucharist in the primitive Church was the forerunner of its later celebration in more or less private circles, and finally also of the private Mass."[33]

The shift in thinking from the communal to the individual approach can be dated especially from the beginning of the seventh century. According to Cyrille Vogel, little by little the Mass was seen as a "good work" to be performed for one's personal, individual salvation, whether that of the priest who celebrates it or that of the

[30] See Pierre-Marie Gy, "Quand et pourquoi la communion dans la bouche a-t-elle remplacé la communion dans la main dans l'église latine?" *Gestes et paroles dans les diverses familles liturgiques* (Conférences Saint-Serge, XXIVe semaine d'études liturgiques, Paris, 28 June–1 July 1977) (Rome: Centro Liturgico Vincenziano, 1978) 117–21.

[31] Joseph A. Jungmann, *The Mass of the Roman Rite: Its Origins and Development*, vol. one. (New York: Benziger Brothers, Inc., 1951) 81.

[32] See Congar, *L'écclesiologie du haut moyen-âge*, 98.

[33] Jungmann, *The Mass of the Roman Rite*, vol. One, 212–13.

layperson who requests its celebration. Influential in this view of the Eucharist was St. Isidore of Seville (d. 636). The Eucharist was no longer considered to be the corporate giving thanks of the community but a gift of grace given to the one who celebrates it or has it celebrated, by which one's salvation is effected and assured.[34]

The whole question of a "private" Mass is a complicated one due to the diverse and changing interpretations of "private" when applied to the Mass. The use of the term *missa privata* is very rare in the early Middle Ages. Indeed, Angelus Häussling would hold that it only occurs once during this period, namely, by Walafrid Strabo.[35] Häussling argues that the term "private" Mass is one celebrated not with the entire community present on Sundays with diverse ministers functioning, but one on ordinary days with a small group. Thus *privata* is opposed to *publica*.[36] For Häussling what is primary is the gradual change of emphasis until the intercessory aspect overshadows the building-up of the gathered community.[37] By the time of the Council of Trent, a private Mass is one where only the priest goes to Communion, regardless of the number in attendance. After Trent the private Mass gradually was understood to be a Mass celebrated by a solitary priest with only a server present.

The growing emphasis on the intercessory aspect to the detriment of the building-up of the gathered community aspect of the Eucharist had been long in coming. Jungmann comments:

> The personal devotion of the celebrant was not, however, whether in the monasteries or elsewhere, the only source of this increase in private Mass, nor was it even the strongest source. Stronger by far was the desire of the faithful for Votive Masses; that is to say, for Masses which took care of their earnest concerns (*vota*), not the least important of which was regard for the dead.[38]

While such concerns (*vota*) are understandable and indeed laudable, what is difficult to accept is the fact that the presence or absence of the donor was not viewed as that important. What was important was that the fruits of the Mass were applied by the priest according to the donor's intention.

The thesis that the private Mass was caused by the desire of the faithful for Votive Masses was argued especially by O. Nussbaum.[39] Schillebeeckx disagrees with this and argues for an earlier origin of the practice:

[34] See Cyrille Vogel, "Une mutation culturelle inexpliquée: le passage de l'eucharistie communautaire à la messe privée," *Revue des sciences religieuses* (54) 1980, no. 3, 231–50.

[35] See Angelus Häussling, *Mönchskonvent und Eucharistiefeier: Eine Studie über die Messe in der abendländischen Klosterliturgie des frühen Mittelalters und zur Geschichte der Messhäufigkeit* (Liturgiewissenschaftliche Quellen und Forschungen 58) (Münster: Aschendorff,1973) 246, n.336; 285, n.522.

[36] *Ibid.* Also see Vogel, "Une mutation," 234–36.

[37] See Häussling, *Mönchskonvent und Eucharistiefeier*, 251–55.

[38] Jungmann, *The Mass of the Roman Rite*, vol. one, 217.

[39] O. Nussbaum, *Kloster Priestermönch und Privatmesse* (Bonn: P. Hanstein, 1961).

In historical terms the veneration of relics is the first and decisive factor in the multi-plication of private masses, long before there was any question of masses for the dead or all kinds of votive masses, which according to Nussbaum mark the origin of the practice. This development encouraged the idea that only the priest was essential for the celebration of the eucharist. This gradually led increasingly to the conviction that he must have a very mysterious power.[40]

No matter which thesis is the correct one, the venerable belief in the corporate understanding of the Eucharist was lost. Congar judges that the sacrifice now appeared less to be offered by all the faithful (through the ministry of their priests) than by the priests for the people.[41]

One cannot help but wonder how much all this had been brought about, even indirectly, by the Church's reaction to Arianism. Had Christ not been so divinized, had a *communio* theology of Church as the Body of Christ (with emphasis on the unity of people, priest, and Christ) perdured, had the practice of Mass stipends never begun—would not the entire Christian community, including priest and people, have been seen as desirable and even necessary for the corporate celebration of the Church's liturgy?

Retrieval of Baptismal Consciousness, the Entire Assembly as the Proper Subject of the Liturgical Action

In the 1962 revised edition of his *Habilitationsschrift, The Place of Christ in Liturgical Prayer*, Jungmann notes:

Since the first appearance of this book, I have myself given detailed treatment to the change in the conception of the Eucharist in Western piety in several articles and lectures. . . . The return from the dominant *worship* of the Eucharist to the community *celebration* of the Eucharist has remained the principal theme of the liturgical renewal; it achieved an effective break-through at the Eucharistic Congress in Munich in 1960.[42]

It would reach its peak in 1963 at the Second Vatican Council with the signing of *Sacrosanctum Concilium*, the Constitution on the Sacred Liturgy: "The Church earnestly desires that all the faithful be led to that full, conscious, and active participation in liturgical celebrations called for by the very nature of the liturgy. Such participation by the Christian people as 'a chosen race, a royal priesthood, a holy nation, God's own people' (1 Pet 2:9; see 2:4-5) is their right and duty by reason of their baptism."[43] Many feel that the Second Vatican Council inaugurated an era that

[40] Edward Schillebeeckx, *The Church with a Human Face: A New and Expanded Theology of Ministry* (New York: Crossroad, 1985) 160.

[41] See Congar, *L'écclesiologie du haut moyen-âge*, 98.

[42] Jungmann, *The Place of Christ*, 256.

[43] *Constitution on the Liturgy, Sacrosanctum Concilium* 14: *Documents on the Liturgy 1963–1979 Conciliar, Papal and Curial Texts*, International Commission on English in the Liturgy. (Collegeville: The Liturgical Press, 1982), 8 (Conciliar citations are taken from this source).

will go down in history as "an era of baptismal consciousness." In an analysis of all the documents of Vatican II Schillebeeckx underlines in each what he considers to be truly new. He said of *Sacrosanctum concilium*:

> The fundamental gain of this Constitution is that it broke the clergy's monopoly of the liturgy. Whereas it was formerly the priest's affair, with the faithful no more than his clientele, the council regards not only the priest but the entire Christian community, God's people, as the subject of the liturgical celebration, in which each in his proper place is given his own particular, hierarchically ordered function—a theological view with all kinds of practical repercussions.[44]

The United States Bishops' Committee on the Liturgy stresses "that the liturgy is the action of the entire assembly of the faithful is basic."[45]

Such teaching is in harmony with the eleventh-century statement of Blessed Guerricus of Igny: "The priest does not consecrate by himself, he does not offer by himself, but the whole assembly of believers consecrates and offers along with him."[46] It is a return to the ecclesiology of communion of the early Church: the point of reference being what all have in common, a share in the priesthood of Christ. This ecclesiology of communion was dominant during the first millennium, but it sadly evolved into an ecclesiology of powers, based on the power (*potestas*) given through the sacrament of order whereby one member (the priest or bishop) governed the life of the Church and offered the sacrifice of the Eucharist. Hervé-Marie Legrand asks:

> How did such an evolution occur? It did not happen abruptly. For Congar it is to be explained by a passage from an ecclesiology of communion to an ecclesiology of powers which was effected in the beginning of the thirteenth century. "While for the ancients," Congar writes. . . . "it is existence in the body of the Church which makes it possible to perform the sacraments, after the twelfth century there emerged a theology of self-contained powers: if one personally possesses them, one can posit the sacraments."[47]

In this way of thinking, it was the bishops and priests who were thought to constitute the Church.

The Second Vatican Council reverses this thinking by retrieving the intimate relationship that exists between liturgy and ecclesiology. Liturgy and Church are presented as two inseparable concepts, and they are united by means of the Paschal

---

[44] Edward Schillebeeckx, *Vatican II: The Real Achievement* (London: Sheed and Ward, 1967) 27–28.

[45] Bishops' Committee on the Liturgy, *Newsletter* 14 (December 1978) 142.

[46] Sermon 5; *P.L.* 185.57.

[47] Hervé-Marie Legrand, "The Presidency of the Eucharist According to the Ancient Tradition," *Worship* 53 (1979) 435–36. Congar ref.: Yves Congar, *"L'ecclesia* ou communauté chrétienne, sujet intégral de l'action liturgique," *La Liturgie après Vatican II* (Unam Sanctam 66), eds. J.-P. Jossua and Y. Congar (Paris: Cerf, 1967) 241–82, esp. 261–67.

Mystery. *Sacrosanctum Concilium* states: "The liturgy is the summit toward which the activity of the Church is directed; at the same time it is the fount from which all the Church's power flows" (*SC* 10); "Liturgical services are not private functions, but are celebrations belonging to the Church, which is the 'sacrament of unity,' namely, the holy people united and ordered under their bishops. Therefore liturgical services involve the whole Body of the Church" (*SC* 26).

Conclusion

It would be naive to think that the Second Vatican Council has resolved all issues and restored total equilibrium. There is still a great deal of sorting-out to be done. In eucharistic theology and practice there is still too much of a dichotomy between priest and people. The Augustinian sense of Christ living in his Church, being present in his Church, is frequently overshadowed by a misinterpretation of the notion of the priest representing Christ and acting *in persona Christi* at the Eucharist. It would seem that a burning theological question that will remain in the forefront for a number of years to come is the inter-relationship of the baptismal priesthood and the ministerial priesthood.

Many of the liturgical changes we have examined in this essay have come about as a result of the Church's reactions to the heresy of Arianism. Still, we must be careful not to overstate the case. Jungmann wisely points out, "In their formation, anti-Arian feeling and popular custom could have worked together."[48]

Whatever the causes, battles have been fought. Much has been gained, but much has also been lost. In his book *The Early Liturgy* Jungmann concludes his chapter on the effects of Arianism on the liturgy with words that provoked a title ("Restoring Equilibrium After the Struggle With Heresy") for my own essay:

> So we must conclude that the struggle with heresy, though ultimately victorious, yet led in many points to losses. The conflict left its mark not only on the liturgy, especially in the East, but also on the peculiar character of oriental piety. This was probably unavoidable. But it is, and will always be, the task of the Church to do everything it can to restore equilibrium after the period of battle is over.[49]

I would argue that the West, too, developed a piety that was deeply affected by the struggle with Arianism. I would also suggest that a desired equilibrium is only in process of being restored.

[48] Jungmann, *The Place of Christ*, 225.

[49] Josef A. Jungmann, *The Early Liturgy: To the Time of Gregory the Great* (Liturgical Studies VI) (Notre Dame, Ind.: University of Notre Dame Press, 1959) 198.

4. Eucharist

The Body of Christ in Celebration:
On Eucharistic Liturgy, Theology, and Pastoral Practice

John F. Baldovin, S.J.

Few scholars can claim to have had as great an influence on the development of their field as Josef Jungmann. His magisterial *Missarum Sollemnia: The Mass of the Roman Rite* clearly set the agenda for the reform of the Eucharist at the Second Vatican Council.[1] A summary of his lifetime of liturgical scholarship was published posthumously (in English) as *The Mass* in 1976 and demonstrates his reflections in light of the reform following the council.[2] As we shall see, this last work reveals the complexity of Jungmann's thought on the Eucharist.

The purpose of the present essay is to analyze Jungmann's work on the Eucharist in light of scholarly, theological and pastoral developments of the past twenty-five years, especially through the lens of his essay "The Defeat of Teutonic Arianism and the Revolution in Religious Culture in the Middle Ages." This essay, published in English first in 1960 on the eve of Vatican II, synthesizes the major motifs of Jungmann's thought on the Eucharist and liturgy in general. It reveals the powerful sweep of his scholarship and grasp of the historical development of liturgy as a whole. Clearly the limits of the present essay allow little more than a survey of the enormous scholarly production on the Eucharist in the past twenty-five years. It is also clear, however, that the development of pastoral practice cannot

---

[1] Josef A. Jungmann, *Missarum Sollemnia: The Mass of the Roman Rite*, 2 vols., trans. F.A. Brunner (N.Y.: Benziger Bros., 1951/1955). The original German edition was published in 1949. On the extent of Jungmann's influence, see R. Peiffer, "Josef Jungmann: Laying a Foundation for Vatican II," in Robert Tuzik, ed., *How Firm a Foundation: Leaders of the Liturgical Movement* (Chicago: Liturgy Training Publications, 1990) 58–62 and Balthasar Fischer & Hans-Bernhard Meyer, eds., *J. A. Jungmann: Ein Leben für Liturgie und Kerygma* (Innsbruck: Tyrolia Verlag, 1975). It is not only through publication that Jungmann's influence has been felt. Two of his students, B. Fischer and H.-B. Meyer have served as mentor for another generation of liturgical scholars and—through them another generation. My own mentor, Aidan Kavanagh, O.S.B., worked under Fischer.

[2] J. A. Jungmann, *The Mass: An Historical, Theological, and Pastoral Survey*, trans. J. Fernandes, M. E. Evans, ed. (Collegeville: The Liturgical Press, 1976). The book had been published in German as *Messe im Gottesvolk: Ein nachkonziliarer Durchblick durch Missarum Sollemnia* in 1970.

be ignored. This may seem ironic in reflecting on Jungmann's essay which is so patently historical—until one comes to the end of the essay and realizes that the intent was fundamentally pastoral all along.[3]

The structure of the current essay will be as follows: (1) Jungmann's thesis: the Early Medieval Shift and its consequences, (2) Jungmann on the historical development of the eucharistic liturgy, (3) Jungmann on the Eucharistic Prayer, with special reference to the place of Christ in liturgical prayer, and finally (4) Jungmann's eucharistic theology and its pastoral consequences.

1. Jungmann's Thesis: The Early Medieval Shift

For several centuries the period that stretched between the end of antiquity and the High Middle Ages has been viewed as "the Dark Ages." To say the least "Dark Ages" is a misnomer for the Early Middle Ages, which were centuries of great ferment and crucial liturgical development. For Jungmann this period was crucial in the shift from a patristic piety to medieval piety. In this shift the reaction to Arianism, not only in the fourth and fifth centuries but especially in the transformation of the "Northern" Arianism of the Germanic tribes, holds the key to centuries of liturgical development ending only with the liturgical movement of the twentieth century. Anti-Arianism is accompanied by a massive cultural shift between antiquity and the Middle Ages, one which accommodated traditional Mediterranean Christianity to the spirit and culture of the North. Jungmann's insight into the significance of Germanic culture in the transformation of Christianity, especially with regard to the reification or objectification of Christian practices like the value of the Mass, has been recently confirmed by James Russell. [4] It is difficult to underestimate the significance of the shift to a reified notion of the Mass. One could say that liturgy went from being primarily celebration to primarily transaction. In all of this the loss of the celebrating assembly was crucial to Jungmann's understanding of the gradual decline of liturgy.

Recent writers have been critical of Jungmann's fundamental framework for understanding the historical development of the eucharistic liturgy. John Bossy certainly has Jungmann (among others) in mind when he writes:

---

[3] J. A. Jungmann, "The Defeat of Teutonic Ariansim and the Revolution in Religious Culture in the Early Middle Ages," in *idem.*, *Pastoral Liturgy* (New York: Herder and Herder, 1962). The original German essay was published in the *Zeitschrift für katholische Theologie* in 1947. That Jungmann saw historical research as the key to understanding the pastoral situation is evident from the German title of the collection—*Liturgisches Erbe und Pastorale Gegenwart* (The Liturgical Heritage and the Pastoral Situation of the Present). Only eight of the twenty-two essays collected in *Pastoral Liturgy* are explicitly pastoral, but the historical essays have a clearly pastoral thrust.

[4] See "Defeat," 7 and James Russell, *The Germanization of Early Medieval Christianity: A Sociohistorical Approach to Religious Transformation* (Oxford: Oxford University Press, 1994). See also Albert Mirgeler, *Mutations of Western Christianity* (Notre Dame, Ind.: University of Notre Dame Press, 1964) esp. 44–65 and Alexander Gerken, *Die Theologie der Eucharistie* (Munich: Kösel Verlag, 1977) 101–11.

Despite the complaints of liturgists and reformers, it was not a contradiction that mass should be offered by the priest alone, in a ritual language, largely in silence and partly out of sight, and yet embody or create the sense of collective identity.[5]

Bossy and other revisionist historians of the late Middle Ages continue to paint a far more cheerful picture of liturgical (especially eucharistic) practice in that period. It should be noted, however, that Jungmann himself was far from ignorant of the positive side of the liturgical situation of the late Middle Ages. He recognized that, at least quantitatively, there was much to be said for the practice of the period.[6] But he also clearly viewed the decline of active participation and consciousness of the assembled Church as the Body of Christ as a serious deficiency when compared to the situation prior to the early Middle Ages.

Another type of criticism has been launched by Thomas Day, who lays the blame for a destructive and ineffectual vision of liturgy at the door of Jungmann's influential *Mass of the Roman Rite*. According to Day, Jungmann and those who agree with him are similar to the "International Style" architects (e.g., van der Rohe, LeCorbusier, Gropius) who swept away "clutter" in the name of simplicity and function.[7] The criticism does have a point, at least with regard to those who took Jungmann's historical presuppositions and brought them to their logical conclusion. One can detect in Jungmann a certain nostalgia for the "noble simplicity" of the papal stational Mass described in the seventh century *Ordo Romanus Primus*.[8] Of course, the word simplicity applies only when one strips this form of the Eucharist of its court ceremonial and looks only to the structure of the liturgy. This seems to have been the case with those who prepared the reform of the eucharistic liturgy in the wake of Vatican II.[9] Perhaps, as Anscar Chupungco has argued, this streamlining of the Roman liturgy may serve to open the way for more profound inculturation.[10]

Even more important themes in Jungmann's classic essay on the defeat of Teutonic Arianism are, of course, the theological issues associated with the struggle against the Arian subordination of Christ and the triumph of trinitarian

---

[5] John Bossy, *Christianity in the West 1400-1700* (Oxford: Oxford University Press, 1985) 67. See also *idem.,* "The Mass as a Social Institution 1200–1700," *Past and Present* 100 (1983) 29–61.

[6] See "Defeat," 66ff.

[7] Thomas Day, *Why Catholics Can't Sing: The Culture of Catholicism and the Culture of Bad Taste* (New York: Crossroad, 1990) 88–94, 154.

[8] See MRR I, 67–74 for a description of this type of liturgy which became a kind of model. See also, "Defeat," 31 for the notion than the Roman liturgy was relatively "pure" of other Western European influence in the seventh century.

[9] See Annibale Bugnini, *The Reform of the Liturgy 1948–1975*, trans. M. J. O'Connell (Collegeville: The Liturgical Press, 1990) 337–42; also Johannes Wagner, "Liturgie auf dem Vaticanum II," in *Jungmann: Ein Leben*, 150–55. Jungmann (along with his former students J. Wagner and B. Fischer) was a member of the liturgical Consilium's study group #10 on the order of Mass.

[10] Anscar Chupungco, *Liturgies of the Future: The Process and Methods of Inculturation* (New York: Paulist Press, 1989) 7 and *passim*.

orthodoxy. While by no means denying the trinitarian orthodoxy of Nicea and the other early councils, Jungmann does see a dark side to an overemphasis on the divinity of Christ. Christ is now addressed directly in liturgical prayer.[11] The human mediatorial role of Christ as High Priest is lost in the process.[12] The Christ who is triumphant over sin and death in the patristic era becomes the Christ in judgement over the individual sinner in the Romanesque.[13] A static, more metaphysical, notion of God as Trinity replaces the dynamic theology of salvation found in the patristic era.[14]

All of these developments of the early medieval period ultimately have profound consequences for eucharistic practice. For Jungmann they lead in a relatively straight line to the distancing of the action of the Eucharist from the people, especially with regard to the frequency of Communion and the veneration of the Blessed Sacrament as an object only tenuously related to eucharistic celebration.[15]

The presuppositions behind Jungmann's classic essay "The Defeat of Teutonic Arianism" clearly demonstrate the main lines of Jungmann's treatment of the Eucharist. They show a preference for the liturgy (and theology) of the Patristic era, unencumbered by the factors that distanced Christ and the liturgy from the people in the early Middle Ages. Having discussed these, we can now turn to more specific aspects of Jungmann's corpus of writings on the Eucharist.

2. Historical Development of the Eucharistic Liturgy

Nowhere does Jungmann show his mastery of the history of the liturgy in the West as well as in *The Mass of the Roman Rite*. In those two volumes, written basically without a library during the Second World War, Jungmann was able to summarize and analyze one hundred years of scholarship on the history of the eucharistic liturgy in the West. In addition his grasp of the medieval sources of the Roman liturgy is breathtaking.[16]

---

[11] "Defeat," 13, 29–32; this was the subject of Jungmann's 1925 *Habilitationschrift*: *The Place of Christ in Liturgical Prayer* (Collegeville: The Liturgical Press, 1989)—from the revised German edition of 1962. This theme will be dealt with further in part three of this essay.

[12] "Defeat," 44; see also 16. This development began in the East with the transferring the reference of High Priest from the humanity to the divinity of Christ, 12–13.

[13] "Defeat," 5–6.

[14] "Defeat," 34–37.

[15] "Defeat," 62–63.

[16] The only comparable history in terms of breadth is Gregory Dix, *The Shape of the Liturgy* (London: Dacre Press, 1945). Dix covers more ground in terms of comparative liturgy and, as an Anglican, deals in great detail with the liturgies of the Protestant Reformation. He also set the agenda for a generation of liturgical scholars who argued for the recovery of his "four-fold" shape of the Eucharist. In terms of dealing with sources, however, Jungmann's is by far the more scholarly treatment. In recent years, the most comprehensive treatment of the Eucharist has been written by one of Jungmann's students, Hans Bernhard Meyer, *Eucharistie: Geschichte, Theologie, Pastoral (Gottesdienst der Kirche* 4) (Regensburg: Pustet, 1989). It is dedicated to Jungmann on what would have been his one hundredth birthday.

Many of Jungmann's insights, hypotheses, and judgements have stood the test of time and can still be considered valid today. In some other areas he laid the groundwork for further research. Given the sweep of his scholarship, only a few examples will be treated here: the development of the sacramentary tradition, the entrance rite, and the offertory procession.

The greatest part of the Western Sacramentary tradition received new editions only after the appearance of *The Mass of the Roman Rite*.[17] Nor did Jungmann have the benefit of the major studies on the Gelasian and Gregorian sacramentaries by Antoine Chavasse and Jean Deshusses.[18] For example, Jungmann recognized that the Gelasian Sacramentary was fundamentally Roman and that it lacked the stational notices (i.e., churches where the papal liturgy would be held on specific days). It was Chavasse, however, who argued that the Gelasian represented the tradition of the presbyteral (or titular) churches of Rome as opposed to the papal stational liturgy and that part of the collection could be traced to a single church, St. Peter's in Chains.[19] Moreover, against the scholarly consensus (which Jungmann supported) that the Gelasian originated in the sixth century, Chavasse argued persuasively that its origins were to be found in the seventh, partly because it shows the influence of Gregory the Great's additions to the Roman Canon and Communion rite.[20] Finally, prior to the work of Jean Deshusses it was commonly supposed that the supplement to the Gregorian had been written by Alcuin. Deshusses has argued that the Supplement and its prologue (*Hucusque*) were put together by the important ninth-century monastic reformer, Benedict of Aniane, especially for his abbeys.[21] Even though Jungmann's judgements on the sacramentary tradition have been surpassed in the last fifty years, one can still marvel at his mastery of the sources and secondary literature. This is one of the reasons that *The Mass of the*

[17] E.g., the Gelasian Sacramentary, C. Mohlberg et al., eds., *Liber Sacramentorum Romanae aecclesiae ordinis anni circuli* (Rome, 1960); the Gregorian Sacramentary, J. Deshusses, *Le Sacramentaire Grégorien (Spicilegium Fribourgense* 16) (Fribourg, 1971). For a complete review of the state of the question in sacramentary research, see Cyrille Vogel, *Medieval Liturgy: An Introduction to the Sources,* translated and edited by W. Story and N. K. Rasmussen (Washington, D.C.: Pastoral Press, 1986) 61–134; Jean Deshusses, "The Sacramentaries: A Progress Report," *Liturgy* (Gethsemani Abbey) 18 (1984) 13–60. Jungmann himself was well aware that new editions and studies of the various books were needed: "Some student to come will probably find much to supplement and, I am sure, much to straighten out, especially if later on the liturgical manuscripts in various countries (including, in part, Germany) are published, and critical editions of such important sources as the Roman *Ordines* are prepared." MRR I, vii. At the same time he recognized the need for further investigation by way of the comparative method of liturgical study.

[18] See Antoine Chavasse, *Le Sacramentaire Gélasien* (Tournai, 1958); for Deshusses, see note 16 above. For Jungmann's treatment, see MRR I, 60–66.

[19] Not without contest, however. See the argument for a Southern Italian origin to the book by C. Coebergh, "'Le sacramentaire gélasien ancien," *Archiv für Liturgiewissenschaft* 7 (1961) 45–88.

[20] See Vogel, 68–69.

[21] See J. Deshusses, "Le Supplément au Sacramentaire grégorien: Alcuin ou S. Benoit d'Aniane?" *Archiv für Liturgiewissenschaft* 9 (1965) 48–71; Vogel, 85–90.

Roman Rite became a reliable textbook for a generation of students of the liturgy as well as for medievalists.

Jungmann's major contribution to the historical understanding of the Roman Rite Eucharist, however, is not to be found in his general history of liturgical development (the greater part of volume I of *The Mass of the Roman Rite*) but rather in his careful investigation of the various liturgical units such as the *Kyrie* or the prayers at the Offertory. The German subtitle of his work reads: *Eine genetische Erklärung der römischen Messe* (a genetic explanation of the Roman Mass). He clearly saw the general historical survey as preparatory to the main contribution of his work—a careful analysis of the historical development of each part of the liturgy.[22] He was not, of course, the first scholar to investigate discrete liturgical units. Scholars like Capelle and Botte had also done so. But he was the first to provide so thorough an investigation of the entire eucharistic liturgy of the Roman Rite in all of its details and with such elaborate scholarly apparatus. In terms of analyzing liturgical units much of Jungmann's method has been adapted and refined by the leading historian of the Byzantine liturgy, Robert Taft.[23]

As we saw in part I of this essay, however, there is a bias underlying Jungmann's genetic analysis. He makes this bias clear in the Introduction to volume I of *The Mass of the Roman Rite*: "It is the task of the history of the liturgy to bring to light these ideal patterns of past phases of development which have been hidden in darkness and whose shapes are all awry." But he goes on to admit: "It is not the fact of antiquity that makes liturgical customs valuable, but their fulness of content and their expressive value. Even newer ceremonies, like the priest's blessing at the end of Mass, can possess a great beauty."[24] Contemporary research into the cultural and anthropological aspects of ritual should make it possible to avoid the idealization that can accompany a genetic explanation.

A good example of Jungmann's achievement can be found in his analysis of the structure of the entrance, offertory and Communion rites. All three rites are comprised of movement (entrance, Communion) or action (offertory). All three end with prayers: the opening prayer (or Collect), the Prayer over the Gifts (or Secret) and the Prayer after Communion. All three units are also accompanied by chants: the Introit, *Offertorium* and *Antiphona ad Communionem*. By means of his genetic analysis Jungmann was able to show how these units developed from actions which were covered by chants and concluded with prayer.[25] Thus he was able to demonstrate the very same basic structure for these disparate elements in the liturgy.

---

[22] See MRR I, 3–4.

[23] See Robert Taft, "The Structural Analysis of Liturgical Units," in *idem.*, *Beyond East and West: Problems in Liturgical Understanding* (Washington, D.C.: Pastoral Press, 1984) 151–66; and further his "How Liturgies Grow: The Evolution of the Byzantine Divine Liturgy," 167–92.

[24] MRR I, 5.

[25] See for example, with regard to the Introit, MRR I, 266. For a comparative analysis of the elimination of verses from the entrance chants, see Taft, "How Liturgies Grow," 173–76.

For Jungmann the opening prayer (or Collect) of the Eucharist concluded the *Kyrie eleison* litany which, after Gregory the Great, could be found in a simplified form; i.e., without the litanic petitions. It is not altogether clear that this is the case. In the first place, Paul DeClerck has shown that the *Kyrie,* as we know it in the medieval liturgy, entered the eucharistic rite as an independent chant; i.e. independent of the litany in which it had found its native home.[26] If this is so, then Jungmann's insistence that the Collect naturally concludes a (now pared-down) litany must be inaccurate. The popularity of stational processions must be sought as the reason for the introduction of the *Kyrie* into Sunday and feast-day liturgies.[27] While Jungmann has been superseded here, it should also be noted that he suggested the connections with Byzantine practice upon which much of the later research has relied.[28]

One of the enduring pastoral consequences of Jungmann's historical research has been the re-introduction of the procession of the gifts by the faithful in the Missal of Paul VI. On the basis of evidence on the importance of the people bringing their offering for the eucharistic sacrifice in the West, Jungmann formed an hypothesis with regard to an original (and now lost) offertory procession by the faithful in the East. Robert Taft has proven this hypothesis false by a thorough investigation of Byzantine and other Eastern sources.[29] Moreover, it appears that Jungmann's hypothesis of a similar procession in the Roman Rite rests on slender (or better, non-existent) evidence. He formed this hypothesis by analogy to offertory processions in the Gallican liturgy.[30] It may seem ironic, therefore, that such an important step was taken on the basis of little evidence, at least for "pure" Roman practice. The introduction of the offertory procession into the contemporary Roman Rite does, however, show the influence and importance of Jungmann's scholarly credibility.

A century from now the extent to which the current liturgical reform rested on unproven hypotheses will probably become clearer. One could argue even today

[26] Paul DeClerck, *La "Prairie Universal" days Les Liturgies Latins Ancienne: Témoignages patristiques et textes liturgiques (Liturgiewissenschaftliche Quellen und Forschungen* 62) (Münster: Aschendorff, 1977), 282–307; see also John F. Baldovin, *The Urban Character of Christian Worship: The Origins, Development and Meaning of Stational Liturgy (Orientalia Christiana Analecta* 228) (Rome: Pontifical Institute of Oriental Studies, 1987), 241–47.

[27] For the fuller argument, see Baldovin, *Urban Character*, 246–47, where I suggest that the litany followed rather than preceded the entrance psalm by analogy with the *synapte* of the Byzantine stational liturgy, which followed the antiphonal psalmody in processions.

[28] For example, see the method of analysis employed by Juan Mateos, *La Célébration de la Parole dans la Liturgie Byzantine: Étude historique (Orientalia Christiana Analecta* 191) (Rome: Pontifical Institute of Oriental Studies, 1971); see also, Robert Taft, *The Great Entrance: A History of the Transfer of the Gifts and other Preanaphoral Rites of the Liturgy of St. John Chrysostom (Orientalia Christiana Analecta* 200), (Rome: Pontifical Institute of Oriental Studies, 1975), xxiii.

[29] See Taft, *Great Entrance*, 12–52.

[30] See Joseph Dyer, "The Offertory Chant of the Roman Liturgy and Its Musical Form," *Studi Musicali* 11 (1982) 3–30; Richard Crocker & David Hiley, eds., *New Oxford History of Music: Vol. 2: The Early Middle Ages to 1300*, 2nd ed., (Oxford: Oxford University Press, 1990), 143–45.

that the reform rested heavily on historical-critical research with some theological development, but very little on sociological or anthropological study. To take another example, the Apostolic Tradition, attributed to Hippolytus of Rome, has had influence far beyond its dubious provenance, date, and authority.[31] All this to note that Jungmann's influence goes far beyond the study of history to the actual practice of the Roman Catholic Church. It would be too much to argue that the reform of the eucharistic rite depended entirely on his scholarship, but it is difficult to imagine the reform without it.

3. The Eucharistic Prayer

Jungmann's treatment of the Roman Canon amounts to 173 pages of the second volume of *The Mass of the Roman Rite*. After a general introduction to the history of the Roman Canon as a whole, Jungmann proceeds to discuss each element of the great prayer of the Church in great detail. For Jungmann the basic core of the Canon exists already at the end of the fourth century and has reminiscences of the Egyptian Eucharistic Prayers. Further than this he does not go into theories about the construction of Eucharistic Prayers.[32] This was left to a later generation of scholars who asked different questions of the history of the anaphora. Jungmann clearly regarded the role played by the institution narrative as the consecration without much further ado.[33] On the other hand, he emphasized what had been lost in the West when the Preface did not expand on motives for thanksgiving.[34] He understood the Roman Canon to combine offering and thanksgiving in a way that stressed the spiritual nature of the sacrifice.[35] In particular he emphasized the change in mentality during the Carolingian period signified by the insertion of the phrase *pro quibus tibi offerimus vel* (lit. "for whom we offer to you, or") into the *Memento* of the Living, which had previously only mentioned the offering made by the people (*circumadstantes*). What had once been an action of the faithful as a whole could now be performed by the priest.[36]

---

[31] See Paul Bradshaw, *The Search for the Origins of Christian Worship* (London: SPCK, 1992) 89–92; *idem.*, "Redating the Apostolic Tradition: Some Preliminary Steps," in N. Mitchell & J. Baldovin, eds., *Rule of Prayer, Rule of Faith: Essays in Honor of Aidan Kavanagh, O.S.B.* (Collegeville: The Liturgical Press, 1996) 3–17. For Jungmann's nuanced view of the importance of the Apostolic Tradition, see MRR I, 28–32.

[32] See MRR I, 49–57; MRR II, 101–274 for the treatment of individual aspects of the prayer.

[33] See below in part 4.

[34] MRR II, 115–24. See also, MRR II, 101: "A thanksgiving prayer rises from the congregation and is borne up to God by the priest; it shifts into the words of consecration, and then into the oblation of the sacred gifts, and this oblation, in turn, concludes with a solemn word of praise."

[35] MRR II, 149: "The Mass is a thanksgiving which culminates in the offering of a holy gift; it is an offering which is so spiritual that it appears to be only a thanksgiving."

[36] MRR II, 166–68; the same question is very important in "Defeat," 60: "The corporate character of public worship, so meaningful for early Christianity, begins to crumble at the foundations."

Subsequent scholarship has inquired more thoroughly into the questions of the origins of Eucharistic Prayers and, in particular, the role played by the institution narrative.[37] The tendency in contemporary research has been to question whether the institution narrative (in the form that we know it as a recital of the Last Supper) was part of the original core of the Eucharistic Prayer or whether other phrases (e.g., *Mal* 1:11) might have served the same function. If this were the case the notion of the role of the institution narrative as "consecration" would be transformed considerably. Bouyer and Mazza have confirmed Jungmann's suggestion that one can find Egyptian elements in the Roman Canon. In particular Mazza has argued that the prayer found in *Papyrus Strasbourg 254* provides a basis of comparison as well as an *Urform* of both the Anaphora of St. Mark and the Roman Canon.[38]

Finally, it is important to note that Jungmann's 1925 *Habilitations* thesis: *The Place of Christ in Liturgical Prayer* has had a significant impact on liturgical studies ever since—so much as to become "common opinion."[39] Jungmann's thesis that up until the middle of the fourth century liturgical prayer was addressed exclusively to God and that only in the wake of the Arian crisis was it addressed to Christ as God, has been seriously challenged by Albert Gerhards in his study of the Greek text of the Anaphora of Gregory of Nazianzus.[40] Gerhards argues that prayer addressed *per Christum* in early liturgical texts must be balanced by the more Johannine tradition that would easily address prayer to Christ. He does this on the basis of the address to Christ in the late fourth-century Anaphora of Gregory as well as on the history of doctrine and the (probably) third century East Syrian Anaphora of Addai and Mari, part of which is addressed to Christ directly.[41] Despite this refinement, one can agree with Balthasar Fischer:

---

[37] The bibliography here is enormous; suffice it to mention only several major contributions: Louis Bouyer, *Eucharist: Theology and Spirituality of the Eucharistic Prayer*, trans. C. Quinn, (Notre Dame, Ind.: Univ. of Notre Dame Press, 1968); Louis Ligier, "The Origins of the Eucharistic Prayer," *Studia Liturgica* 9 (1973) 161–85; Cesare Giraudo, *La struttura letteraria della preghiera eucaristica* (*Analaecta Biblica* 92) (Rome: Pontifical Biblical Institute, 1981); Enrico Mazza, *The Origins of the Eucharistic Prayer,* trans. R. Lane (Collegeville: The Liturgical Press, 1995).

[38] Mazza, 252–86.

[39] See Albert Gerhards, "Prière addresée à Dieu ou au Christ? Relecture d'une thèse importante de J. A. Jungmann à la lumière de la recherche actuelle," A. M. Triacca & A. Pistoia, eds., *Liturgie, Spiritualités, Cultures (Conférences S. Serge XXIX)* (Rome: Edizioni Liturgiche, 1983) 101.

[40] Albert Gerhards, *Die griechische Gregoriosanaphoa. Ein Beitrag zur Geschichte des eucharistichen Hochgebets*, Münster: Aschendorff, 1984; for a summary, see his "Prière," 101–14. For non-liturgical prayer addressed to Christ in the Ante-Nicene period, see Maurice Wiles, *The Making of Christian Doctrine* (Cambridge: Cambridge University Press, 1967) 62–93.

[41] See G. J. Cuming & R.C.D. Jaspers, eds., *Prayers of the Eucharist: Early and Reformed*, 3rd ed. (New York: Pueblo Publishing Co., 1987) 39–44; in addition see a similar address to Christ in the Maronite Third Anaphora of St. Peter, 45–51. Indeed the whole of this anaphora after the *Sanctus* is addressed to Christ. For original texts, see Anton Hänggi, Irmgard Pahl, eds., *Prex Eucharistica: Textus e variis Liturgiis Antiquioribus Selecti,* (= Spicilegium Fribourgense 12) 3rd edition, Fribourg, 1998.

> *The Place of Christ in Liturgical Prayer* represents what was a major breakthrough in liturgical theology, whose importance is not diminished by discovering that the total picture has turned out to be more nuanced than was supposed in the first flush of discovery.[42]

4. Eucharistic Theology and Pastoral Practice

Little attention has been paid to Jungmann's opinions as a theologian, perhaps because this was not the focus of his work—or perhaps because his last major work on the Eucharist betrayed a note of disappointment in the post-conciliar reform and revealed him as somewhat more traditional in eucharistic theology than his earlier work might have suggested. In this he is reminiscent of those biblical scholars who come to radical conclusions *vis à vis* the tradition and hesitate to draw any theological conclusions, since theology as such is not their bailiwick. Surely there is a note of Prufrockian "that is not what I meant at all" in *The Mass*. The work is intended as an update on *The Mass of the Roman Rite* in light of the post-Vatican II reform of the eucharistic liturgy. There can be little doubt that Jungmann followed without question what Edward Kilmartin has called the ordinary teaching of the Roman Church since the twelfth century, which centers on the consecratory power of the priest.[43] On the other hand, he was convinced enough by twentieth century eucharistic theology (in the writings of Anscar Vonier and Odo Casel) to insist that the Eucharist must be understood primarily as an action.[44] He also argued that not only the priest but the Church as a whole, understood as the actual gathered community, offered the sacrifice.[45]

It would have been difficult in the 1960s and '70s to predict how decisive the question of ministerial leadership of the Eucharist would become in the '80s and '90s. Among the pastoral and theological questions facing the Church with regard to the Eucharist today no question is as neuralgic. With increasing force questions have been raised not only about who can be ordained to the priesthood (e.g., women, married men) but also about what the precise role of the ordained minister is, especially with regard to the Eucharist. Among contemporary liturgical theologians, none has been more insistent on re-opening the question of the relation between priesthood and Eucharist than David Power. His incisive study of the Tridentine debates about eucharistic sacrifice has shown that the major unanswered question at Trent (and subsequently in Roman Catholic theology) was the role of the presiding minister at the Eucharist.[46] Here much hinges on the question

---

[42] Balthasar Fischer, "Foreword," in Jungmann, *Place of Christ*, x.

[43] Edward Kilmartin, "The Catholic Tradition of Eucharistic Theology: Towards the Third Millennium," *Theological Studies* 55 (1994) 405–57. See, *The Mass*, 106, 120–21, 126, 128–31.

[44] *The Mass*, 91–92. Jungmann acknowledges the work of Gregory Dix, *Shape* (see n.16). See *The Mass*, 20, 85.

[45] *The Mass*, 121–27.

[46] David Power, *The Sacrifice We Offer: The Tridentine Dogma and Its Reinterpretation* (New York: Crossroad, 1987).

of whether or not the priest acts *in persona Christi* (in the person of Christ). Jung-mann himself acknowledged that in ecumenical dialogue the issue of priesthood was "the most difficult question of all."[47] Elsewhere I have tried to demonstrate that this is a moot point if one begins by questioning the nature of the Eucharistic Prayer and particularly of eucharistic consecration.[48] These were issues that Jung-mann took for granted, as did the formulators of the Second Vatican Council's documents on the liturgy, Church, and priesthood. Given the widespread pastoral situation of the lack of priests, it is not likely that the question of the precise nature of the priesthood will be resolved in the near future.

By the same token Jungmann could hardly be faulted for not forseeing the cri-sis that the lack of priests would cause in so many areas of the world. Increasingly observers have noted that communities of faith have been deprived of the celebra-tion of the Eucharist, sometimes for years at a time.[49] At risk is the very participa-tion of the faithful in making eucharist that Jungmann's historical work showed had moved into decline in the Middle Ages.

Jungmann parted company with many contemporary liturgical scholars in insist-ing on the theological value of the offertory and insisted that Catholics and Protestants were still very much divided on the nature of the Eucharist as propitiatory sacrifice.[50]

As we saw above, Jungmann has been criticized for preferring a "modern" style liturgy after the fashion of twentieth-century functionalist architecture. Clearly this was one of the conclusions he reached at the end of "Defeat" when he wrote: "The construction of the Mass ought to be made more obvious."[51] In his last work, however, he wondered whether or not the ideal of rational clarity, the Liturgy Constitution's noble simplicity unencumbered by repetition has already (by 1970) been pushed to an extreme.[52] Once again one detects a "Prufrockian" note in Jungmann's last assessment of the eucharistic liturgy after Vatican II. Many liturgical scholars today would agree with him that "active participation" has been understood in a naive manner and that much more sophisticated tools of research into ritual are needed today in order to appreciate the nature of liturgical participa-tion.[53] On this issue Jungmann has proved to be prophetic. But his comments on

[47] *The Mass,* 277.

[48] John F. Baldovin, "Eucharist and Ministerial Leadership," in *Proceedings of the Catholic Theo-logical Society of America 1997.*

[49] See, for example, James Dallen, *The Dilemma of Priestless Sundays* (Chicago: Liturgy Train-ing Publications, 1994).

[50] With regard to the offertory, see *The Mass,* 126, 190 where he argues that the blessing formulas and the action of the priest constitute a gesture of offering. I interpret the actions as ones of simple placement of the gifts on the basis of the rubric that directs the priest to hold the gifts a little above the altar. For Protestant and Catholic theologies of sacrifice, see 150–52.

[51] "Defeat," 99; see also his comments on liturgy like architecture becoming "practical" (93).

[52] *The Mass,* 244.

[53] See, for example, the articles by Ronald Grimes, Aidan Kavanagh, Don Saliers and John Bal-dovin in Lawrence Madden, ed., *The Awakening Church;* also Mary Collins, "Liturgical Methodology

too facile an understanding of participation should be taken in the context of the fact that he also argued vigorously that the standard form of the liturgy is the "service for which the ecclesial community assembles on Sunday."[54] For him liturgy was anything but an historical curiosity, good for nothing but archeological interest.[55]

At the end of his life Jungmann also dealt cautiously with the issue of liturgical inculturation or adaptation. He could argue that the Church universal as such never celebrated the Eucharist, but only specific communities. At the same time, he was well aware that a tension obtains between "authenticity and order."[56] He was, after all, a master historian, who understood that the particular genius of each people had always left its mark upon eucharistic celebration, but warned: "[t]he special characteristics of a given group's spiritual and cultural heritage need not always be expressed precisely and literally in the form of a religious service, much less in the Mass."[57] The issue of liturgical adaptation and inculturation is the most difficult practical pastoral issue facing the world-wide Church today. One suspects that it will take many years for theologians and pastoral experts to be able to come up with commonly accepted judgements with regard to precisely what constitute "immutable elements, divinely instituted" as opposed to "elements subject to change," or the nature of the limits of "the genius and talents of various races and peoples" as opposed to the "substantial unity of the Roman Rite."[58] Precisely these questions form the 'battleground' over which the current liturgical war is being fought. At stake is the very nature of Christianity as a faith. Clearly Jungmann's program of streamlining the liturgy to essential elements was not sufficient to address this situation, but he was prescient enough to know that an ideal form, suitable to all, would never be found.[59]

As one of the architects of the liturgical reform, Jungmann favored the basic lines of the development of the liturgy after Vatican II. He remained, however, a relatively conservative theologian and was cautious about the actual unfolding of the reform itself. This comment by no means suggests that Jungmann did not have an enormous influence on the course of the reform itself. In so many areas of eucharistic liturgy, even in 1959, he advocated reforms that would shape contemporary practice and understanding of worship. For example, it is practically unthinkable today that Communion would not be distributed during the Communion of the

---

and the Cultural Evolution of Worship in the United States," in John May, ed., *The Bent World: Essays on Religion and Culture*, (Missoula, Mt.: Scholars Press, 1981) 127–47; Margaret Mary Kelleher, "The Communion Rite: A Study of Roman Catholic Liturgical Performance," *Journal of Ritual Studies* 5 (1991) 99–122.

[54] *The Mass*, 215.

[55] "Defeat," 91.

[56] *The Mass*, 228–29.

[57] *The Mass*, 266; see also 241.

[58] *Constitution on the Sacred Liturgy*, #21, 37–38.

[59] *The Mass*, 279.

Mass. But this is one of the reforms that Jungmann and others, like Bernard Botte advocated.[60] He saw the need for expanding the cycle of liturgical readings over a number of years as well as of introducing living languages into the Roman Rite. Similarly, Jungmann can be credited with a large share of the responsibility for introducing the *versus populum* altar, which is arguably the most significant change in the Post-Vatican II liturgy—after the introduction of the vernacular.[61] His scholarship abetted the revival of a procession by the faithful with the offerings, thus emphasizing his concern with the Eucharist as a communal activity. He put his massive scholarship to pastoral and theological effect by participating in all of the major committees before, during and after the Second Vatican Council.[62]

Conclusion

Josef Jungmann made his major contribution both with regard to scholarship and to the pastoral life of Roman Catholics in terms of his history of the Eucharist in the Roman Rite. No one before or since has been able to deal with as much evidence in making a case for the need for liturgical reform as well as to provide a clear vision of the Eucharist as a celebration of the community gathered in Christ's name and in his Spirit. If in certain areas of theology and historical research we may regard ourselves "ahead" of him today, we cannot pretend to have reached this point without his guidance.

Perhaps he should be best remembered for words written near the end of his last book:

> Accentuation of the Mass should not lead to a too narrow attitude toward the Eucharist, for the ultimate goal toward which all pastoral work is directed is not the presence of Christ's sacrifice upon the altar but the redemptive sacrifice itself as it was consummated once and as it now continues to be through all centuries *the sign of our hope and the guidepost for the proper orientation of our life.*[63]

[60] The author can remember a time in the early 1950s when the connection between the distribution of Communion, which took place just after the consecration, and the Communion of the priest was not at all discernible.

[61] Jungmann's historical arguments for and advocacy of the *versus populum* altar have not been with critics. See, e.g., Klaus Gamber, *The Reform of the Roman Liturgy*; see also, Jaime Lara, "*Versus Populum* Revisited," *Worship* 68 (1994) 210–21.

[62] See Bugnini, *Reform.*

[63] *The Mass,* 259 (emphasis in the original).

5. Preaching

A Prophet Vindicated: Proclaiming the Good News

John Allyn Melloh, S.M.

Pastoral Liturgy[1] appeared as an English translation in 1962, two years after the original German publication of *Liturgisches Erbe und pastorale Gegenwart.*[2] The dust-jacket of the English version states that Jungmann "writes not merely of liturgical texts and ceremonies; he is primarily concerned with the mentality which produced them, with the piety which was nourished by them, and with the culture which resulted from them." In truth this volume is concerned with the broad liturgical landscape—the religious cultural ethos that created or modified the shape of liturgical expression.

Clearly the centerpiece of the volume is the initial lengthy essay "The Defeat of Teutonic Arianism and the Revolution in Religious Culture in the Early Middle Ages,"[3] which in many ways is an epitome of Jungmann's insightful contributions to liturgical history and theology. This essay thus provides a way to access critical lines of thought of this prolific writer.

The title *Pastoral Liturgy* may strike the reader who is unfamiliar with Jungmann's corpus of writings as somewhat odd, when the reader peruses the table of contents. The three major divisions are respectively titled, "The Over-all Historical Picture," "Separate Historical Problems," and "The Fundamentals of Liturgy and Kerygma," and the term "pastoral" appears in only two of the thirty-two subdivisions. So on the one hand, the German title, literally *Liturgical Heritage and the Pastoral Present*, is more accurate, insofar as it focuses clearly on a liturgical tradition, on what has been inherited. On the other hand, "Pastoral Present" seems rather generic and unfocused. It appears that Jungmann, in titling the work, was putting "*Erbe*" in polaric tension with "*Gegenwart*." If that is so, then a free-rendering of the title[4] may be "The Richness of the Liturgical Inheritance in relation

---

[1] J. A. Jungmann, S.J., *Pastoral Liturgy* (New York: Herder and Herder, 1962).

[2] J. A. Jungmann, S.J., *Liturgisches Erbe und pastorale Gegenwart* (Innsbruck: Tyrolia-Verlag, 1960).

[3] J. A. Jungmann, S.J., "The Defeat of Teutonic Arianism and the Revolution in Religious Culture in the Early Middle Ages," in *Pastoral Liturgy* (New York: Herder and Herder, 1962) 1–101.

[4] I am grateful to my colleague, Robert A. Krieg, C.S.C., for this suggested title.

to Today's Pastoral Exigencies," surely a title that would please no publisher! Herein lies the genius of Jungmann: the insight that authentic pastoral work and praxis is rooted in and flows from solidly-grounded large-scale historical investigation reflected on theologically. A corollary follows, viz. that theological and historical study of the liturgy is directed toward the pastoral, the concrete liturgical act.[5]

The purpose of this essay is to reflect on "The Defeat of Teutonic Arianism" in relation to the topic of preaching. The task is rendered somewhat difficult since in the entire work there are fewer than ten specific references to preaching. Thus, what I propose to do is to consider first of all, significant "principles" from *Pastoral Liturgy* that relate both broadly and narrowly to preaching; second, to examine Jungmann's earlier work, *The Good News and Our Proclamation of the Faith*,[6] which stirred a theological controversy of no small proportion, centering around preaching and catechesis; third, to relate Jungmann's views on preaching to the Bishops' Committee document *Fulfilled in Your Hearing*,[7] the major document on preaching for the United States. It is my contention that the chief principles for preaching that Jungmann enunciated, initially viewed as controversial and roundly rejected by some theologians, have found a major and significant place in today's views of the preaching event. Jungmann's voice was prophetic for today's Church.

In the "Defeat of Teutonic Arianism" Jungmann begins with the assertion of two principles which are "particularly obvious." "In the early Christian age the liturgy is essentially *corporate public worship . . . .*"[8] and ". . . the celebration is dominated by the *Easter motif. . . .*"[9] These are the two lenses through which Jungmann views the historical unfolding of the Church's worship and theology. Likewise these two motifs—the corporate quality of worship and its paschal character—are the author's desiderata for continuing liturgical renewal: "We must reach a situation where the *Ecclesia orans* is no longer a mere ideal of liturgical books, partially realized by the celebrating clergy. It is the whole believing people who make up the *Ecclesia* which approaches God in prayer through the liturgy."[10] "Our kind of Christianity must once more become Easter Christianity."[11]

---

[5] Further considerations appear below.

[6] Josef Andreas Jungmann, S.J., *Die Frohbotschaft und unsere Glaubensverkündigung* (Regensburg: Verlag Friedrich Pustet, 1936). E.T. "The Good News and Our Proclamation of the Faith," trans. and abridged by William A Huesman, S.J., ed. Johannes Hofinger, S.J., *The Good News Yesterday and Today* (New York: W. H. Sadlier, 1962), published on the twenty-fifth anniversary of *Die Frohbotschaft*. Hereafter *Good News* or *Die Frohbotschaft*, where I modified the translation for either accuracy or style.

[7] The Bishops' Committee on Priestly Life and Ministry, *Fulfilled in Your Hearing. The Homily in the Sunday Assembly* (Washington, D.C., USCC, 1982).

[8] Jungmann, *Pastoral Liturgy*, 2.

[9] Ibid., 3.

[10] Ibid., 101. This quotation is from the last paragraph of the essay, "The Defeat of Teutonic Arianism." In the same essay "meaningful, corporately celebrated liturgy" is urged. Ibid., 93.

[11] Ibid., 416. This quotation is the last line of the essay "Easter Christianity," and the last sentence of *Pastoral Liturgy*. Jungmann contrasts the older versus the more modern approach to Easter, suggest-

An increasing emphasis on the individual as well as on the subjective are the critical issues identified as causes for the loss of genuine corporately-celebrated prayer and the loss of the centrality of the Easter motif. Approvingly, Jungmann quotes Abbot Herwegen who contrasts the spirit of early Christianity with that of the Middle Ages. In the early period "the world of grace, what is objective and corporate" is dominant; in a word, mystery predominates. As the Middle Ages unfold, "what is subjective and individual" moves to the foreground and more emphasis is then placed upon "human action and moral accomplishment."[12]

Jungmann himself nuances this opinion by noting that, although the reaction to Arianism produced a "shift of accent," there was additionally a "tendency to simplification and coarsening of the gospel message," a process which was evident where theological analysis of the "substance of Faith" and close contact with the "sources of Faith" was neglected.[13] Thus, "poor theologizing" led to "poor proclamation" which in turn led to an incorrect placement of emphases—a shift from mystery and grace to human action and behavior.

Another overarching insight that appears throughout is related to the break-up of primitive Easter spirituality, viz. the distancing of mystery. In discussing *Christus secundum Carnem*, Jungmann notes that Christian piety of any age must obviously focus on the person of Christ. If in the early medieval period the risen, ascended Christ recedes into the background because of absorption into the Trinity, then Christic devotion must find a different outlet. When "Christ according to the flesh" becomes a focal lens in the West, "Christ according to the spirit" recedes proportionally. As a result the mystery of the Incarnation, "Christ according to the flesh," receives significant attention, bringing the Christmas feast into prominence as well as Marian devotion and piety.

As an illustration of this phenomenon, Jungmann comments on typical Marian lyrical insertions, which migrated through the *Missale Gothicum* and the Bobbio missal into the Gelasian Sacramentary,[14] and states that

> [t]hese words ring with a quality we are accustomed to hear during the height of the Middle Ages. They express a pious meditation which no longer sees the whole scheme of salvation only from the angle of its own consummation, from the perspective of the exultation of Him who now sits at the Father's right hand; but which takes the contemplating soul back into the historical course of this story of salvation.[15]

---

ing that modern people tend to re-discover aspects of the life of the historical Jesus in the liturgical year and thus the feast "takes on a certain historical remoteness," rather than its being an entree into the "mysteries of the kingdom of God." Ibid., 409.

[12] Ibid., 7.

[13] Ibid., 47.

[14] The textual insertion from the Christmas Preface is: *Lacta mater cibum nostrum, lacta panem de coelo venientem, in praesepio positum velut piorum cibaria iumentorum.* . . .

[15] Jungmann, *Pastoral Liturgy,* 50.

So this shift in piety attends less to the reality of the presence of a world of grace, the presence of mystery as an on-going event and more to a recollection of historical events of grace. "No longer is the Christian mystery seen as something very much present, as the leaven which must constantly penetrate and transform Christianity. . . . It is seen almost entirely as an event of the past upon which to meditate more and more deeply. . . ."[16]

Related to the distanciation of mystery—of a failure to see the mystery as a present and active reality—is an obscuring of a Pauline theology of the Mystical Body. "Christ glorified, who lives on in His humanity as Redeemer, is hardly ever seen [in laudable devotions such as the Way of the Cross or the Rosary]. . . . He is no longer recognized as the living Head of the Church, who, through the Holy Spirit, gives life to the whole organism of the Church, and who goes on working through the mystery of the sacraments. Even amongst theologians, we will scarcely hear a mention of the Church as the Mystical Body of Christ. We in our own time must re-discover this fact. The Church in the late Middle Ages had become predominantly an earthly sociological entity. . . . Subjectivism is on the ascendant."[17]

If Jungmann's initial "principle" is that the liturgical act must become truly corporate, involving real participation of an active assembly of believers, he also sees preaching as an historical "vestige of lay participation,"[18] even at the end of the Middle Ages. Mendicant orders brought renewal to preaching and thus the sermon enjoyed a certain increase in importance.[19] Jungmann's own words, however, do not indicate that this was a flourishing renaissance: "The priest would *at least* relate some instruction, a few remarks about the meaning of the current feasts or the lives of the saints who were being commemorated, to the lessons from the liturgy of the Sunday and the days following."[20] Nor did this heritage of renewed preaching perdure to the present:

> The redemptive powers which are found in the mighty sweep of the liturgy with its transparent Christocentricity and profound sense of corporate life must come to live in preaching as well, if these powers are to produce their full effect; for they are contained first of all in the heritage of belief out of which the liturgy has grown.[21]

In his *Mass of the Roman Rite*, Jungmann notes that throughout Christian history, the sermon appears "almost as an indispensable part of public worship."[22] If the history of

---

[16] Ibid., 78.

[17] Ibid., 78.

[18] Ibid., 69.

[19] Jungmann further comments that "revival of the sermon during the height of the Middle Ages involved a separation from the liturgy, and also a departure from its homiletic character. It leaves the confines of the Mass in the form of a mission sermon of the new Orders." Rev. Joseph A. Jungmann, S.J., *Mass of the Roman Rite (Missarum Sollemnia)*, vol. one, trans. Rev. Francis A. Brunner (New York: Benziger Brothers, 1950), 460.

[20] Jungmann, *Pastoral Liturgy*, 69. Emphasis added.

[21] Ibid., 101.

[22] Jungmann, *Mass of the Roman Rite*, 456.

the liturgical sermon is mackled, the beginning of the medieval period saw a "strong return to the preaching of the word of God" and toward the end of the Middle Ages, in certain places in Germany the faithful were obliged "to attend Mass *and* the sermon on Sunday,"[23] when the sermon was becoming more and more separated from the liturgy itself. While Jungmann notes this tendency toward a separate preaching event, he clearly identifies a specific liturgical function of the sermon in a later work: "The homily should not be regarded as something extraneous just inserted into the liturgy as an interruption, but as a genuine constituent of the liturgy. . . ."[24]

Now clearly Jungmann recognizes the place and importance of the homily within public worship, yet he also holds out for another view of preaching, namely preaching as a part of pastoral work.

> Therefore, it is pastoral work which must prepare the way for a revival of the liturgy, using as its tools, teaching and preaching and all the other means which contribute to the formation of a full grasp of the Faith. Preaching the Faith and public worship should be related as statement to reply: the two would have to achieve complete congruence.[25]

Is Jungmann viewing the sermon as separate from the worship event? Might he be thinking of a Sunday afternoon service of preaching and Benediction? Is he considering preaching, even within the Sunday service, as an "extraneous" element? It seems that either preaching within the liturgy or outside the liturgy falls within the orbit. Yet the crux of his insight, I believe, relates to the question of "formation of a full grasp of the Faith." Immediately before the above-mentioned quotation, Jungmann asserts that "liturgical science" may prepare a way for reforming the liturgy and advance solid historical and theological proposals, but this scientific approach "cannot infuse life."

What infuses life is the proclamation of Christ as the "apex of our lost human race, making a way for us out of sin and guilt through the pain and darkness of this world to the glory of the Resurrection."[26] This sort of proclamation is necessary in an "age of hollowed-Christianity," since it serves as a "synthesis of what has been torn apart, a compendium of a heritage of faith which has been attenuated in diverse abstract concepts, now scarcely comprehensible."[27] Thus it is the proclamation of the Christ-event as a living reality which forms the core of formation in the faith, whether that be done in the context of preaching or teaching. Preaching the faith—in the liturgy or outside it—leads to public worship, as "statement to reply." Preaching or teaching the living Christ shapes the "proper atmosphere" for genuine liturgical celebration.

---

[23] Ibid., 456–7.

[24] Josef A. Jungmann, S.J., *Public Worship*, trans. Rev. Clifford Howell, S.J. (Collegeville: The Liturgical Press, 1957) 116.

[25] Jungmann, *Pastoral Liturgy*, 101.

[26] Ibid., 340.

[27] Ibid.

As a summary of Jungmann's thought, the following statement stands out:

> Liturgy must become pastoral. An increasing emphasis on pastoral concerns has been the mark of the liturgical movement in recent decades; and this emphasis is now reacting upon the liturgy itself. . . . The essential action of this should be so designed that it is intelligible to the Catholic Christian of average education, who should be able also to take an active part in it. . . . Public Worship must become both an invitation and a help to real adoration "in Spirit and in truth": it must become the support of a joyful awareness of Faith and of a Christian life in the harsh everyday world.[28]

The publication of *The Good News and Our Proclamation of the Faith*, Jungmann's 1936 work, focused on the then-current problems of catechetics and preaching, two distinct modes of communicating dogmatic and liturgical theology.[29] Anton Koch, S.J., wrote the following, which appeared on the dust-jacket of the original edition:

> At a time of decisive struggle about the significance and permanence of Christ's work on earth, an altogether singular importance should be attached to this book of reform—reform in the best sense of the word. Clear and decisive, yet at all times moderate, drawn from a mature knowledge of historical developments, it calls for a renewal arising from the essentials of the Christian proclamation, reveals the faulty developments of the past which are to be surmounted, and indicates the direction that liturgy, preaching, catechesis—in a word, ecclesiastical life and teaching—must take in order that Christ be brought anew into this new age.[30]

The book is divided into three inter-dependent and complementary sections, "The [Present] Situation," "Historical Reflections," and "Our Task," which form an organic whole. Historically and theologically grounded, it is, as Koch noted, a clear, decisive and moderate presentation, yet the work is also intended to be a clarion call for reform of the proclamation of the faith. It kindled the so called *Verkündigungstheologie*, or kerygmatic theology controversy. If the volume was not a "shot heard round the world," it surely reverberated throughout Europe.

Jungmann begins with an analysis of the faith-life of Christians and concludes that "Christianity is for so many not the Good News which one accepts joyfully, but a heavy law to which one submits to escape damnation."[31] Catholics lack a unified understanding of the faith and the major reason for that state of affairs is the manner in which the faith has been transmitted.

> . . . [I]t is not enough to show the necessity and reasonableness of the faith, nor enough to expound every point of doctrine and every commandment down to the very last division; but that it is singularly important to achieve first of all a vital

[28]   Ibid., 98–99.

[29]   Cf. footnote 5. Later *Die Frohbotschaft* was reissued under the title of *Glaubensverkündigung im Lichte der Frobotschaft.*

[30]   Quoted in Jungmann, *Good News,* vi.

[31]   Jungmann, *Die Frohbotschaft,* 3.

understanding of the Christian message, bringing together 'the many' into a consistent, unified whole that then there may be joyous interest and enthusiastic response in living faith.[32]

In arguing for a vital proclamation of living faith, Jungmann lays blame on both preachers and catechists for a wrong-headed presentation of the Good News of salvation. "The faithful actually live the kind of Faith they read about in their catechisms and hear in their Sunday sermons,"[33] an anemic and fragmented faith which radically contrasts with the proclamation and appropriation of the faith in the sub-apostolic period: "On one hand, a simple message, a graphic picture; on the other, a complicated edifice of concepts, divisions and distinctions."[34]

Further, the manner in which theology is taught in seminaries is another contributing factor. Seminary theology had neglected its pastoral and kerygmatic aspects and instead focused on historical problems and polemics or ivory tower speculations on revelation. Since preachers tend to pass on to the assembly the kind of religion internalized during seminary formation, the fallout is that preaching itself became a vulgarization of various theological tracts, generally unrelated to life.[35]

Preaching, for Jungmann, ought to be the proclamation of Good News,[36] not a popularization of theological treatises. "The meaning of Christianity is not knowledge, but life, not theology, but holiness."[37] Thus, "[d]ogma must be known; the kerygma must be proclaimed."[38] The distinction between theology and kerygma is elucidated:

> It is here, however, that one finds the real difference between theology and the proclamation of the faith. Theology is primarily at the service of knowledge; hence it investigates religious reality to the outermost limits of the knowable (*verum*) and struggles here for the last little piece of truth that can be grasped, without asking in each instance about the significance such effort may have for life. The proclamation of the faith, on the other hand, is entirely oriented toward life. Hence it considers this same religious reality wholly under the aspect of how it is a motivating goal of our efforts (*bonum*).[39]

---

[32] Jungmann, *Good News*, 6–7.

[33] Domenico Grasso, S.J., *Proclaiming God's Message. A Study in the Theology of Preaching.* (Notre Dame, UND Press, 1968) xxvii, commenting on Jungmann's *Good News*. Hereafter *Proclaiming God's Message*.

[34] Jungmann, *Die Frohbotschaft*, 53.

[35] "The meaning of this theological study, however, is not to be found in this, that they (candidates for ordination) should later give this theology back to the faithful in a more compendious form and less finished terminology." Jungmann, *Good News*, 31.

[36] "By kerygma, we understand the Christian doctrine as object of preaching, as foundation of Christian life, presented and put to the test in pastoral work." J. A. Jungmann, *Handing on the Faith. A Manual of Catechetics.* (New York: 1959) 376. Quoted in Grasso, *Proclaiming God's Message*, 234.

[37] Jungmann, *Die Frohbotschaft*, 61.

[38] Ibid., 60.

[39] Jungmann, *Good News*, 33.

The key theological insight expatiated throughout *Die Frohbotschaft* is that the center of Christian proclamation is the person of Christ. In the third section of the book, "Our Task," Jungmann reiterates the notion that focusing everything—in preaching and catechetics—on the person of Christ will contribute to a more vital understanding of the distinctive content of the message; additionally it will provide unity to the proclamation of the faith. As a result faith will not be an abstraction, but will connect with the life of the Christian person—the Christ-life of the baptized.[40]

This critical notion also appears as a theme in *Pastoral Liturgy*. The following is but one instance which expresses strong parallelism with *The Good News*:

> Here in Christ I embrace the sum total of all mystery. The separate dogmas which all seem so dark are but radiations from the one mystery which is contained in His person, emanating from the one mysterious decree that in Him God desired to draw all . . . to Himself in grace, through Him, through His sacraments, within the Church and by her authority. And it is here that I comprehend in a single glance the whole foundation of faith. For in the end Christ Himself is the great miracle in which God manifests Himself. He is God's eruption into human history, visible from afar, real as lightning which lights up the sky from East to West. . . .[41]

Domenico Grasso, S.J., whose fine commentary on *The Good News* has provided me a solid foundation, avers that Jungmann did not go further than to distinguish theology from kerygma, insist that preaching and catechetics be oriented toward the kerygma and argue that those who proclaim the Christian message be adequately prepared.[42] Other Innsbruck theologians demanded a special theology of proclamation of the faith (*Verkündigungstheologie*) as not only legitimate, but also necessary, seeking to justify such an approach with scholastic ontology.[43]

The so-called kerygmatic theology controversy ensued over several generations, spawned by Jungmann's work and the ideas of his colleagues. One of the fruits of the controversy is that Catholic theologians began to focus on the topic of preaching, a subject which had been largely ignored in the wake of the Protestant Reformation.[44]

Reaction to Jungmann's study was swift and incisive. Hans Urs von Balthasar saw in *Verkündigungstheologie* a way of bridging the chasm that divides theology from life, but he feared that this new approach would undermine the value of

---

[40] Ibid., 78.

[41] Jungmann, *Pastoral Liturgy,* 341.

[42] Domenico Grasso, S.J., "The Good News and the Renewal of Theology" in Jungmann, *Good News,* 203; hereafter "Renewal of Theology."

[43] Grasso, "Renewal of Theology," 204. The more notable supporters of *Verkündigungstheologie* were Hugo Rahner, J. B. Lotz and Lakner. Cf. Emil Kappler, *Die Verkündigungstheologie. Gottesword auf Lehrstuhl und Kanzel* (Freiburg, Switzerland: Paulusverlag, 1949), which contains a good bibliography.

[44] Grasso notes that before Karl Barth could accuse Catholic theologians of keeping "a very strict silence" on the subject of preaching, the silence had already been broken by Jungmann's *The Good News.* Grasso, "Renewal of Theology," 204.

speculative reasoning enlightened by faith.[45] Michael Schmaus contended that not holding to a strictly scientific point of view could lead to irrationalism.[46] Avelino Romero said that kerygmatic theology is just not necessary,[47] and even Jean Daniélou held that kerygmatic theology is "not admissible."[48] These three illustrations are typical and could be multiplied. Fundamentally theologians feared the development of a "double theology," a speculative scientifically-based theology vs. a practical theology (especially a theology of preaching).[49]

While there was critique, there was also a general agreement—and even among some critics—that theology must have a pastoral or kerygmatic component; and even Schmaus, one of the critics, noted that "[s]cientific theology must also be suited for preaching or it runs the risk of losing its scientific character."[50] Likewise von Balthasar affirmed Jungmann's christocentrism: ". . . God, the author of nature, has desired from all eternity that Christ be the true center and final truth of human nature and all forms of human thought."[51]

Because of the critical reactions, one might assume that *The Good News* was roundly rejected. That, however, was not the case, because in the end the cadre of theologians, even divided into different camps, agreed that theology must not ignore the problems and praxis of preaching. Almost two decades after the publication of *The Good News*, Jungmann replied to one critic:

> Theology must free itself from lifelessness, as Schmaus emphasized, that it may walk the path of history more resolutely—the path of salvation history which leads "to the historical Christ, who died, rose again and was glorified." That is Schmaus demands a Christocentric focus even for speculative theology. He introduces Christ into the very definition of theology, the proper object of which is not "God in Himself," but God "insofar as He has revealed Himself in Christ and insofar as His self-revelation is preserved in the Church and mediated by Her throughout all centuries." If theology is understood in this way, then the goal intended by the *Verkündigungstheologie* has actually been realized in its essentials, and the word might be dropped without further ado.[52]

[45] Hans Urs von Balthasar, "Théologie et sainteté," *Dieu Vivant* 12 (1948) 26. Quoted in Grasso, "Renewal of Theology," 204. Hereafter *Dieu Vivant*.

[46] Michael Schmaus, *Katholische Dogmatik* (München: Hueber, 1954) vol. II, preface. Hereafter *Dogmatik*. Quoted in Grasso "Renewal of Theology," 205.

[47] A. Avelino Esteban Romero, *Predicación viviente al día* (Madrid: 1956) 378. Quoted in Grasso, "Renewal of Theology," 205.

[48] "Parole de Dieu et mission de l'Eglise," in *Le prêtre ministre de la parole* (Paris: 1954) 48. Quoted in Grasso, "Renewal of Theology," 205.

[49] Cf. Grasso, "Renewal of Theology," 204–5; Grasso, *Proclaiming God's Message*, xxvii–xxix.

[50] Schmaus, *Dogmatik* preface. Quoted in Grasso, "Renewal of Theology," 205.

[51] Von Balthasar, *Dieu Vivant,* 27. Quoted in Grasso, "Renewal of Theology," 205.

[52] Josef A. Jungmann, S.J., *Katechetik. Aufgabe und Methode der religiosen Unterweisung.* (Wien: Herder, 1953) 302. Quoted in Grasso, "Renewal of Theology," 206.

Grasso comments that Jungmann's evaluation of the whole discussion, exhibited in his reply above, led him to return to his original premise, namely that in theology there needs to exist a vital, Christocentric, pastoral dimension, open to all questions of the Christian life.[53] The ideas for which Jungmann battled have won the day, because the pastoral and kerygmatic dimensions in theology are valued at least in theory, if not in actual practice.

It would be fatuous to hold that Jungmann longed for or anticipated the watershed events of Vatican II with its renewal of the liturgy and preaching. It would be equally foolish to look at contemporary documents and theological and pastoral works and conclude that "it's all in Jungmann." Nonetheless, the underlying theological principles that guide effective preaching which Jungmann held dearly are clearly enunciated as foundational principles for preaching today.

"The homily should not be regarded as something extraneous just inserted into the liturgy as an interruption, but as a genuine constituent of the liturgy . . ."[54] wrote Jungmann in *Public Worship* almost a decade before Vatican II asserted that "[t]he homily . . . is to be highly esteemed as part of the liturgy itself,"[55] a statement echoed seven years later in the *General Instruction of the Roman Missal*: "The homily is part of the liturgy and is strongly recommended, for it is a necessary source of nourishment for the Christian life."[56]

Scattered through the documents of Vatican II and post-Vatican II are seminal insights regarding the important place of preaching in the life of the Church. In 1982, however, under the auspices of The Bishops' Committee on Priestly Life and Ministry, a document entirely devoted to liturgical preaching was issued. *Fulfilled in Your Hearing*[57] (hereafter referred to as FIYH) has become the *vade-mecum* for today's preachers. It is my contention that crucial insights in FIYH can be discerned in Jungmann's writings and that the basic principles for preaching are similar, if not identical. Although from a historical point of view it may be more logical to examine Jungmann's writings and then compare them to FIYH, I shall proceed in the reverse direction, since the curious reader may wish to peruse the readily-available contemporary document.

First, the subtitle of the document is "The Homily in the Sunday Assembly," and after a brief introduction, the first chapter examines the liturgical assembly.

[53] Grasso, "Renewal of Theology," 206.

[54] Josef A. Jungmann, S.J., *Public Worship*, trans. Rev. Clifford Howell, S.J. (Collegeville: The Liturgical Press, 1957) 116.

[55] *The Constitution on the Sacred Liturgy*, par 52. *Vatican Council II. The Conciliar and Post Conciliar Documents*, ed. Austin Flannery, O.P. (Northport, N.Y.: Costello Publishing Co., 1975).

[56] *General Instruction of the Roman Missal*, par 41. *Vatican Council II. The Conciliar and Post Conciliar Documents*, ed. Austin Flannery, O.P. (Northport, N.Y.: Costello Publishing Co., 1975).

[57] The Bishops' Committee on Priestly Life and Ministry. National Conference of Catholic Bishops, *Fulfilled in Your Hearing. The Homily in the Sunday Assembly* (Washington, D.C., United States Catholic Conference, 1982).

Thus, this document is in line with the more contemporary approach to human communication, "receiver-oriented communication theory."[58] At its simplest, human communication concerns the sending of a message to a receiver. The "sender" needs to encode the message (e.g., in speech, writing, electronic signal, etc.) and the "receiver" must be able to decode it. Likewise, there must be some form of contact (e.g., physical contact for speech, etc.). Earlier in this century "sender-oriented" theory seemed to be regnant, that is, a high priority was placed on the "sender" and the role of encoding the message.[59] Today's theoreticians place a higher priority on the "receiver." Of course, actual communication takes place only if all the requisite components are working together.

FIYH notes that unless the preacher knows the congregation's needs, desires, and capabilities, "there is every possibility that the message offered in the homily will not meet the needs of the people who hear it," because what is communicated is not what is actually said, but rather is what is heard, and "what is heard is determined in large measure by what the hearer needs or wants to hear."[60] Additionally FIYH states that ". . . preachers [who interpret texts primarily to extract ethical demands to impose on a congregation] may offer good advice, but they are rarely heard as preachers of good news, and this very fact tends to distance them from their listeners."[61] This seems to parallel exactly Jungmann's own experience.

Jungmann's own pastoral work in the Tyrol provided him the opportunity to analyze the faith-life of his people and he found it wanting in joy and enthusiasm, because, he reasoned, the Christianity which had been inculcated was fundamentally submission to a "heavy law" to escape damnation, rather than the joyful acceptance of Good News offered through Christ Jesus.[62] The Christian faithful do not experience the freedom of sons and daughters of God, because moral and dogmatic precepts, threats and promises, as well as tasks and duties are seen as impositions.[63] And the reason why this is so is because the faith has not been presented in a manner both adequate to and appropriate for the hearer,[64] but rather in a manner geared toward the theological expert: "a complicated structure of concepts, divisions, distinctions."[65] In order to give the hearer an "orientation for life,"

---

[58] One may argue that this "contemporary" theory is not contemporary at all, but rather derived from the medieval dictum *Quidquid recipitur, recipitur per modum recipientis*, which seems to be a manualist rendering of Thomas Aquinas' actual statement *Omne quod recipitur in aliquo, recipitur in eo secundum modum recipientis* (S.T. III, q. 54, art. 2, ad 1).

[59] Some homiletics courses decades ago were titled "Sacred Eloquence" and concentrated on forms of encoding the message and styles of oral delivery.

[60] FIYH, 4.

[61] FIYH, 24.

[62] Grasso, *Proclaiming God's Message*, xxvii.

[63] J. A. Jungmann, "Le problème du message à transmettre ou le problème kerygmatique," *Lumen Vitae* 5 (1950) 272. Quoted in Grasso, xvii.

[64] Jungmann, *Good News*, 34.

[65] Ibid., 27.

Christian preaching follows not a theological ordering, but rather determines its presentation from the viewpoint of the hearer.[66]

Interestingly Jungmann notes that a "greater capacity of adjustment to the needs of his hearers"[67] should be a benefit acquired from the study of speculative theology. The

> study of dogmatic theology and the deepening penetration into its speculation should have led [the seminarian] to something positive—to that intellectual independence and security which would enable him to utilize the full treasure of eternal truth in a *thoroughly vital way* for the changeable needs of the time and the varying requirements of the community. In fact, the deeper the analysis has gone, the further it has penetrated to basic elements, the greater should be the freedom and flexibility with which the bearer of God's message brings forth from the store of doctrine that which can furnish the real answer to the questions and longing of the erring children [of the world].[68]

Second, FIYH boldly declares "A homily presupposes faith. Nor does the homily primarily concern itself with a systematic theological understanding of the faith."[69] The document recognizes that while the assembly share a common faith, rooted in baptism, this faith is "expressed in ways that extend from the highest levels of personal appropriation and intellectual understanding to the most immature forms of ritualism and routine."[70]

In *Die Frohbotschaft*, Jungmann expresses a parallel idea:

> Preaching of its nature is directed to an audience that is familiar with the content of Christian doctrine. It aims at recalling certain important points of doctrine to the minds of the faithful in order that they may be brought to a renewed joyous consciousness of their religious capital (*Besitz*) and thus be decisively orientated and properly stimulated once again to a full Catholic life."[71]

Yet this recollection of certain "points of doctrine," for Jungmann, means not a "theological disputation," but rather a substantive exposition of the faith,[72] presented in such a way that it becomes a life-giving orientation, a message of salvation. In commenting upon Jungmann's catechetical writings, Johannes Hofinger cuts to the heart of the matter, noting that Jungmann does not argue for a "better

[66] Jungmann, *Die Frohbotschaft*, 61. Jungmann notes that theology proceeds to arrange its material in an ontological order, but that preaching arranges it from a more psychological point of view. He notes that questions of God's inner life will come to the fore in preaching rarely; rather the economy of salvation will be an overarching theme.

[67] Jungmann, *Good News*, 32.

[68] Ibid. Emphasis added.

[69] FIYH, 17.

[70] FIYH, 6.

[71] Jungmann, *Good News*, 94.

[72] Throughout *The Good News* Jungmann insists on a substantive message in preaching, catechetics and indeed all pastoral work. E.g., "This does not mean, however, that kerygmatic knowledge must be superficial knowledge." Jungmann, *Good News*, 34.

method, but better understanding and a more relevant presentation of the *very core and substance* of the Christian message."[73]

As FIYH notes that effective preaching is not presenting a theological disputation, but is a proclamation of faith rooted in solid theology, Jungmann criticizes an "unwarranted and ill-advised use of such theology in the field of preaching,"[74] because the preaching became a "vulgarization of various theological tracts,"[75] rather than a deepening of the core of the Good News. "Theology," states Jungmann, "is primarily at the service of knowledge . . . The proclamation of the faith, on the other hand, is entirely oriented toward life."[76] The former is directed toward the *verum*, while the latter is geared toward the *bonum*.

Third, the *General Instruction of the Missal* notes that preaching should take into account the "mystery celebrated."[77] Although FIYH does not use the same *gatherum*, viz. "mystery," it expresses a similiar idea in these words: ". . . the homily is preached in order that a community of believers who have gathered to celebrate the liturgy may do so more deeply and more fully—more faithfully—and thus be formed for Christian witness in the world."[78] This is possible because the preacher, relying on God's scriptural word, interprets people's lives in such a way that they will be able to celebrate the sacrament.[79]

Jungmann criticizes the medieval development that no longer sees the Christian mystery "as something very much present, as the leaven which must constantly penetrate and transform Christianity—through the Sacrament. It is seen almost entirely as an event of the past upon which to meditate more and more deeply . . . ,"[80] whereas the Christian mystery ought to be seen and proclaimed as present and transformative.[81]

Fourth, addressed directly to preachers, FIYH asks: "Is it possible to say 'Look at the way in which God is present in your lives and turn to him with praise and thanksgiving?' Only if we recognize the active presence of God in our own lives, as broken and shattered as they may be, and out of that brokenness affirm that it is still good to praise him and even to give him thanks."[82] What the document is saying in so many words is that effective preaching holds human brokenness and wholeness in tension and can name both human experiences. Another way of

[73] Johannes Hofinger, S.J. "The Place of the Good News in Modern Catechetics" in Jungmann, *Good News* 173. Emphasis author's.

[74] Ibid., 176.

[75] Grasso, *Proclaiming God's Message,* xxvii.

[76] Jungmann, *Die Frohbotschaft,* 61. "The meaning of Christianity is not knowledge, but life, not theology, but holiness."

[77] GIRM, 41.

[78] FIYH, 17–18.

[79] FIYH, 20. "The homily is not so much *on* the Scriptures as *from* and *through* them."

[80] Jungmann, *Pastoral Liturgy,* 78.

[81] Ibid.

[82] FIYH, 27.

76   *John Allyn Melloh, S.M.*

putting it is that preaching always names sin and proclaims grace[83] or shows both the ignominy of the cross and the glory of resurrection.[84] The ideal preaching event is "an invitation to praise this God who wills to be lovingly and powerfully present in the lives of his people."[85]

Expressed differently, Jungmann holds a similar opinion:

> [Christ's] cross is the world's salvation: that remains the start and the finish of Christian preaching. But in the Cross we do not have to see *only* the Good Friday scene—the scene as it appeared to the impudent eyes of the mocking high-priests and scribes . . . . the believing heart cannot fail to see that the wounds radiate the glory of victory, and that the agony of death is swallowed up in the jubilant cry: 'It is consummated.'"[86]

And the last sentence of *Pastoral Liturgy* sums it up: "Our kind of Christianity must once more become Easter Christianity."[87]

Fifth, "Although we have received this good news," states FIYH, "believed in it and sealed our belief in the sacrament of baptism, we need to rediscover the truth of it again and again in our lives."[88] The gathered assembly awaits a word that will rekindle faith and enable the gathered to recognize the active presence of God in their lives. Such preaching will flow naturally out of the scriptural proclamation and into the subsequent liturgical action in the midst of a congregation ready to give thanks and praise.[89] "The preacher then has a formidable task: to speak from the Scriptures . . . in such a way that those assembled will be able to worship God in spirit and truth, and then go forth to love and serve the Lord."[90]

"Public Worship," which for Jungmann includes the sermon as integral, "must become both an invitation and a help to real adoration 'in Spirit and in truth': it must become the support of a joyful awareness of Faith and of a Christian life in the harsh everyday world."[91] The goal of preaching for Jungmann was essentially the renewal of the Christ-life of the faithful; only a full revitalization of the generally fragmentary and moralistic sermon could accomplish that end. Effective proclamation of the Good News, that is, a vibrant celebration of the Liturgy of the Word, would invite the Christian assembly to eucharistic worship "in Spirit

---

[83] Mary Catherine Hilkert, "Naming Grace: A Theology of Proclamation." *Worship* 60/5 (1986) 433–449. Cf. also her *Naming Grace. Preaching and the Sacramental Imagination* (New York: Continuum, 1997), *passim*.

[84] Cf. Hans Van Der Geest, *Presence in the Pulpit. The Impact of Personality in Preaching*, trans. Douglas W. Stott (Atlanta: John Knox Press, 1981) 69ff. for the *necessity* of proclamation of both sin/grace, law/gospel, death/resurrection.

[85] FIYH, 24.

[86] Jungmann, *Pastoral Liturgy*, 415–16.

[87] Ibid., 416.

[88] FIYH, 19.

[89] FIYH, 23, 19.

[90] FIYH, 19.

[91] Jungmann, *Pastoral Liturgy*, 98–99.

and in truth" at the table of the Lord. Nourished by both Word and Sacrament, the faithful could live with a joy-filled spirit even amid the trials of life.

In sum, Jungmann has argued for preaching a substantive, theologically-grounded message, fitting for the faith-levels of the hearers, which helps the faithful to recognize the present reality of the Christ-mystery so that in their lives they may worship "in Spirit and in truth." The message proclaims a word of life (Phil 2:16), of grace (Acts 14:3), of salvation (Rom 1:16), and of reconciliation (2 Cor 5:19).[92] The message is not a presentation of diluted theological abstractions, a vulgarization of theology, but of the living word of God, presented as the on-going mystery of salvation history. It invites the assembly into the reality of Christ dead and risen, celebrated at the table of the Word and the table of the Eucharist. This proclamation of Good News bears fruit in the lives of Christians through the animation of the out-poured Spirit. And these are precisely the crucial insights of FIYH. Briefly put, Josef Andreas Jungmann was a herald, announcing a prophetic vision for preaching in his day. While his views were not universally accepted at the time, the 1982 document, FIYH, stands as a vindication of his vision, arguing, as Jungmann did, for preaching as a realistic proclamation of the Good News of Christ Jesus!

[92] Cf. Grasso, *Proclaiming God's Message,* 236.

6. Ecclesiology

A Second Revolution: The Church and Its Ordained Ministry

Thomas P. Rausch, S.J.

Josef Jungmann's essay on the defeat of Teutonic Arianism charts a number of "shifts of accent and changes of viewpoint" in the five hundred years which separated the time of Gregory I (540–604) from that of St. Bernard (1090–1153), resulting in a revolution in religious culture which has left its mark down to our own time.[1] By contrasting early Christian with early medieval religious culture, Jungmann calls attention to a shift from an essentially communal understanding of the liturgy to one which has detached the priest from the congregation. At the same time, the understanding of the Church changed, from a spiritual notion, often imaged in symbolic, personal terms, to an emphasis on its juridical-hierarchical structure. As the Church was "secularized" into a sociologically determined institution, its pastoral office or ordained ministry was sacralized, so that the priest was increasingly seen as a sacred person. Though the Council of Trent clarified disputed points in doctrine, it also solidified these changed accents, making them to a considerable degree a matter of church doctrine.

Focussing on the ecclesial implications of Jungmann's study, I would like to sketch here a similar revolution in the self-understanding of the Catholic Church which has resulted from similar shifts and changes in Catholic theology, particularly as reflected in the ecclesiology of the Second Vatican Council. This new self-understanding has not yet been completely appropriated by the Church's faithful or fully expressed in its life or structure. But in the twenty-five years which have passed since Jungmann's death, it is safe to say that the Church has experienced at least three major shifts in the area of ecclesiology which have reversed to a considerable extent the "dissolution at the heart of ecclesiastical and liturgical life" which Jungmann's analysis had uncovered.[2]

---

[1] Josef Jungmann, "The Defeat of Teutonic Arianism and the Revolution in Religious Culture in the Early Middle Ages," in *Pastoral Liturgy* (New York: Herder and Herder, 1962) 1–101.

[2] Ibid., 79.

First, the Church has moved from a monarchical, institutional ecclesiology to one based on communion; second, its understanding of priesthood has changed from a sacral model based on the concept of sacred power to a representative, sacramental one. Finally, having rediscovered the communal character of the liturgy, the Church is struggling to find ways to move from a "priest-centered liturgy" to one which is "assembly-centered."[3] Leaving the third shift to the liturgists, we will consider the first two of them and then see what new issues must still be addressed.

I. From Church as Institution to Church as *Communio*

Particularly striking is Jungmann's remark about "how little the thought of the Church as the Body of Christ flourished in the Middle Ages."[4] No doubt the loss of this Pauline vision, with its sacramental implications, contributed to the juridical, sociologically conceived ecclesiology, the "institutional model" of church which prevailed in the Catholic Church from the end of the Council of Trent down to the Second Vatican Council.[5] The council challenged this ecclesial self-understanding with its emphasis in *Lumen gentium* on the Church as sacrament, as People of God, and particularly, with its collegial theology of the episcopal office. The council did not specifically describe the church itself as a *communio*, but it laid the foundations for an ecclesiology based on communion.

The ecclesial notion of *communio* (Greek, *koinonia*) was introduced by Ludwig Hertling in an essay first published in German in 1943; Jared Wicks refers to his work as a "seminal contribution in the development of ecclesiology."[6] In the years that followed, *communio* began to emerge as a central ecclesiological concept. Jerome Hamer showed how the mutual relations among Christians are founded on their participation in Christ and in the Spirit, so that to be Church is to be in relation with God and others.[7] Yves Congar explored the ecumenical implications of an ecclesiology of *communio*.[8]

The word *communio* "appears twenty-six times in *Lumen gentium* and twenty-five times it is used to express some kind of bond."[9] It is used in reference

---

[3] Cf. Bob Hurd, "Liturgy and Empowerment: the Restoration of the Liturgical Assembly," in Michael Downey (ed.) *That They Might Live: Power, Empowerment, and Leadership in the Church* (New York: Crossroad, 1991) 132.

[4] Jungmann, 58.

[5] Cf. Avery Dulles, *Models of the Church* (Garden City, N.Y.: Doubleday, 1974) 31–42.

[6] See Ludwig Hertling, *Communio: Church and Papacy in Early Christianity*, trans. with an introduction by Jared Wicks (Chicago: Loyola University Press, 1972) 4; Wick's translation is based on "Communio und Primat," *Una sancta* 17 (1962); an earlier version appeared in German in *Miscellanea historiae pontificiae* 7 (1943).

[7] Jerome Hamer, *The Church is a Communion* (New York: Sheed and Ward, 1964) 159–64.

[8] Yves Congar, "Notes sur les mots 'Confession,' 'Eglise,' et 'Communion,'" in *Irenikon* 23 (1950) 3–36; also *Diversity and Communion* (Mystic, Ct.: Twenty-Third, 1985).

[9] Ad Leys, *Ecclesiological Impacts of the Principle of Subsidiarity* (Kampen: Kok, 1995) 147.

to the bonds uniting the members (*LG* 4, 9, 13, 14), in describing the unity of the members of the episcopal college with each other and with the pope (*LG* 22), and added to the traditional bonds of faith, sacraments, and ecclesiastical government (*LG* 14). If the language of "communion of churches" is not used, it is clearly implied in the council's language of particular churches in relation to the universal Church: "In and from such individual churches there comes into being the one and only Catholic Church" (*LG* 23).

In the post-conciliar ecumenical dialogues the ecclesiology of *communio* has been increasingly used to explain the relationship between the one church and the many churches, and thus, as a way of understanding the unity of the Church. In 1985 the Roman Catholic Church made this ecclesiology officially its own when the report of the Extraordinary Synod of Bishops stated that the Church has fully assumed its ecumenical responsibility on the basis of the ecclesiology of communion.[10] Other communions have also moved in this direction. At the fifth world conference on Faith and Order, Cardinal Edward Idris Cassidy said that "the use of an ecclesiology of communion in many dialogues has been a key to unlocking the divergences between separated Christians and showing the bonds of communion that already exist between them."[11]

Finally, some theologians have seen the concept of *communio* implicated in the way authority is exercised in the Church. J. Robert Dionne's study of reception suggests that the Church involves elements of mutual dependence even on the level of its formulation of doctrine and dogma.[12] This means that in its fundamental nature, the Church is not an institution exercising authority from the top down, but rather it is a communion of interdependent members, ordained and unordained, faithful and hierarchy.[13]

Thus the ecclesiology of *communio* describes the Church as a communion of believers sharing in the divine life (*communio sanctorum*), as a communion of particular churches (*communio ecclesiarum*) linked by the bonds of communion joining their bishops (*communio hierarchica*), and as the wider but still imperfect communion of the all churches and ecclesial communities (*communio christiana*).[14] Finally, *communio* describes the Church itself in its inner nature as a communion of interdependent lay and ordained members.

---

[10] Extraordinary Synod of Bishops, "The Final Report," II,C,7; in *Origins* 15 (1985) 449; the synod stated that the ecclesiology of *communio* "is the central and fundamental concept in the documents of the Council," II,C,1; *Origins* 448.

[11] Edward Idris Cassidy "The Future of the Ecumenical Movement," in *On the Way to Fuller Koinonia*, Faith and Order Paper no. 166, ed. Thomas F. Best and Günter Gassmann (Geneva: WCC, 1994) 137.

[12] J. Robert Dionne, *The Papacy and The Church: A Study of Praxis and Reception in Ecumenical Perspective* (New York: Philosophical Library, 1987) 297.

[13] Ibid., 360–66.

[14] Cf. I. Riedel-Spangenberger, "Die Communio als Strukturprinzip der Kirche und ihre Rezeption im CIC/1983," *Trierer Theologische Zeitschrift* 97 (1988) 230–32.

II. From Sacral to Representative
Understanding of Priesthood

From the Middle Ages down to the Second Vatican Council, the Roman Catholic understanding of ordained ministry was dominated by a sacral model of priesthood, based on the concept of divine power (*sacra potestas*). Priesthood was defined in terms of the priest's relationship to the Eucharist, specifically, his power to consecrate.[15] From this perspective the priest too easily becomes not a minister but a sacred person who stands over the community, a mediator between God and the faithful marked by special powers and separated from them by obligatory celibacy, special privileges, and clerical dress. In the last ten to fifteen years however, a representational model of priesthood has moved to the fore; the priest is understood as acting in the person of Christ (*in persona Christi*) at certain moments in his ministry.[16]

The concept of the bishops and presbyters acting *in persona Christi* is an ancient one, based on the bishop's role as leader of the local church. Edward Kilmartin sees it developing from 1 Clement, whose author describes church leaders as successors of the apostles sent by Christ who in turn is sent by God.[17] According to Cyprian, the bishop acts in the place of Christ (*vice Christi*) as priest and judge (Ep. 59.5.1) and in presiding at the Eucharist (Ep. 63.14.1).[18] Medieval theology spoke of the priest acting *in persona Christi* at the Eucharist in virtue of the power of consecration received at ordination, while the bishop does so in virtue of his pastoral office.[19] One finds this view also in Aquinas.[20]

At the same time, scholastic theologians spoke of the priest as acting *in persona ecclesiae* in virtue of his role as president of the liturgical assembly. Peter Lombard argued that excommunicated priests were not able to confect the Eucharist because the celebrant offered the sacrament "*quasi ex persona Ecclesiae*,"[21] suggesting that the christic role was dependent on the ecclesial. The priest at the Eucharist represents both the Church and Christ who gathers the church together.

---

[15] See Edward Schillebeeckx, *The Church With a Human Face* (New York: Crossroad, 1985) 141–51; Thomas P. Rausch, *Priesthood Today: An Appraisal* (New York, Paulist, 1992) 15–22.

[16] See Edward J. Kilmartin, "Apostolic Office: Sacrament of Christ," *Theological Studies* 36 (1975) 243–64; Avery Dulles, "Models for Ministerial Priesthood," *Origins* 29 (1990) 284–89; David N. Power, "Representing Christ in Community and Sacrament," in Donald J. Goergen, *Being a Priest Today* (Collegeville: The Liturgical Press, 1992) 97–123; Susan K. Wood, "Priestly Identity: Sacrament of the Ecclesial Community," *Worship* 69/2 (1995) 109–27.

[17] Kilmartin, "Apostolic Office," 245.

[18] Richard Seagraves, *Pascentes cum Disciplina: A Lexical Study of the Clergy in the Cyprianic Correspondence* (Fribourg: Éditions Universitaires, 1993) 68; see also Hervé-Marie Legrand, "The Presidency of the Eucharist According to the Ancient Tradition," *Worship* 53 (1979) 424–25.

[19] Kilmartin sees this difference in function deriving from the change of emphasis from bishop as leader of the community to consecratory power of the presbyter; "Apostolic Office," ftnt 23, 246.

[20] *Summa Theologica* 3,82,1; see also Bernard D. Marliangeas, *Clés pour une théologie de ministère, In persona Christi, In persona Ecclesiae* (Paris: Ed. Beauchesne, 1978) 89–146.

[21] *Libri IV Sententiarum* D.XIII, c.i; see Marliangeas, 55–56.

However, with Aquinas a new distinction emerged between the actions performed *in persona Christi* and those performed *in persona ecclesiae*. David Power points out that Aquinas both distinguishes the instrumental acts of the priest from the other acts of ecclesial worship and sets the action and prayer of the priest in contrast with the action and prayer of the Church as a body of believers.[22] In the Tridentine Reform and after, the restricted sense in which the priest was seen as acting *in persona Christi* yielded to another; henceforth "there was a move to see the priest as one who had a special relation with Christ, operative not only in (all) his ministerial actions but also in his personal life."[23]

More recently, the phrase *in persona Christi* has been taken over by the magisterium. Pius XII adopted it in his encyclicals *Mystici corporis* (1943) and *Mediator Dei* (1947), extending it so that the priest is said to represent Christ in offering the sacrifice of the cross, and so represents the whole Church.[24] But this in effect makes the priest's acting *in persona ecclesiae* dependent on his acting *in persona Christi*. Vatican II described the priest as enabled by ordination to "act in the person of Christ the head" (*in persona Christi capitis*) (PO 2). There remains a division of opinion today as to whether the christic or ecclesial representation has priority, as we shall see below.

III. Unresolved Issues

The replacing of an institutional ecclesiology with one based on *communio* and the shift from a sacral to a representational model of priesthood have been an important part of the ecclesiological renewal brought on by the Second Vatican Council. But they have also led to new questions and sometimes new problems. Recognizing that these shifts in perspective have given the Church new resources for facing its contemporary challenges by recovering overlooked aspects of the tradition, I would like to briefly consider four "unresolved" issues. They are, first, the priority of priestly representation; second, the "iconic argument"; third, the renewal of the structures of authority; and finally, the question of apostolic succession. Here I can only indicate the direction of present scholarship and suggest where further research might be needed.

1. *The Priority of Representation.* Today many theologians argue that the priest is able to act *in persona Christi* precisely because he first acts *in persona ecclesiae*. Edward Kilmartin maintained that the priest or bishop is a sacrament of the Church and thus of Christ and the Spirit.[25] David Power says that the term *in persona Christi* was "applied to a variety of sacramental rites in order to underline

---

[22] Power, "Representing Christ in Community and Sacrament," 102.

[23] Ibid., 107.

[24] Pius XII, *Mystici corporis, AAS* 35 (1943) 232–33; *Mediator Dei, AAS* 39 (1947) 556.

[25] "The apostolic officer is *sacramentum* of the Church united in faith and love which in turn as *res* is also *sacramentum* of Christ and the Spirit"; "Apostolic Office," 260.

specific actions or words, indicating that these are the precise words or actions in which in the assembly Christ acts through the ordained minister."[26] Avery Dulles understands the representative role of the priest in terms of the Church as sacrament. The Church as the body of Christ represents Christ to the world. "But for the church to be a social and public reality in the world it is also necessary for Christ to be represented by the official actions of the church itself."[27] By their ordination bishops and priests become "ecclesiastical persons . . . public persons in the church."[28] This suggests that the christic representation flows from the ecclesial. Susan Wood takes a similar position, maintaining that the ordained minister recapitulates the ecclesial community as the *totus Christus*, head and members, and so "acts *in persona Christi capitis*."[29]

Two articles directed at Wood have challenged the position that the priest is able to represent Christ because he represents the Church. Both take as their point of departure the teaching of Vatican II on the priesthood. Sara Butler argues that the council establishes the ecclesiological dimension of the priest's identity in its christological foundation, in the priest's being "configured" to Christ the head of the Church through ordination.[30] Basing her argument on the council's *Acta synodalia* as well as its documents, she concludes that a development of doctrine has taken place.[31] Lawrence J. Welch takes a similar position, holding that priestly identity must be rooted in its sacramentalizing "a headship of Christ as the source of the Church."[32] He understands *LG* 10 as teaching that the ordained priest has a special participation in the mediatorship of Christ.[33]

The issue is not insignificant. The passing of the sacral model of priesthood and the substitution of the word "presider" for "priest" in reference to eucharistic leadership has contributed to a loss of identity for many priests. At the same time, it is not infrequently the case today that some communities will take it upon themselves to designate a presider who has not been ordained.[34] To maintain that the priest represents Christ because he represents the community, and therefore, the community can designate its own presider is to adopt a congregational theology that is clearly contrary to the Catholic tradition. The priest cannot be understood merely as a delegate of the community.

At the same time, it is important to avoid any suggestion that the priest is over the Church or prior to the Church rather than a part of it. David Coffey has criti-

---

[26] Power, "Representing Christ," 98.
[27] Dulles, "Models for Ministerial Priesthood," 288.
[28] Ibid.
[29] Wood, "Priestly Identity," 126.
[30] Sara Butler, "Priestly Identity: 'Sacrament' of Christ the Head," *Worship* 70 (1996) 303.
[31] Ibid., 293.
[32] Lawrence J. Welch, "Priestly Identity Reconsidered: A Reply to Susan Wood," *Worship* 70 (1996) 318.
[33] Welch, 311–12.
[34] Cf. Sheila Durkin Dierks, *WomanEucharist* (Boulder, Co.: WovenWord Press, 1997).

cized the notion that ordained priesthood can be understood immediately in christological terms by unpacking the pneumatological and ecclesiological aspects of both ordained and common priesthoods. He argues that Vatican II, following *Mediator Dei*, left the impression that the ordained priesthood was christological while the common priesthood was ecclesiological. But both priesthoods have christological and as well as ecclesiological reference, for the all the baptized are mystically united to Christ.[35] Seeing the common priesthood as "a dynamism of faith, of divine sonship or daughterhood," he identifies the ordained priesthood as "a charism, of official witness."[36] Because the council was unable to reconcile the two priesthoods in the person of Christ, it left in place "the popular impression of the priest as above the Church rather than as part of it."[37]

What is crucial is the question of sacramental authorization. By ordination into the order of presbyters, the priest is incorporated into the Church's pastoral office. Avery Dulles speaks of a "double empowerment" by which the ordained is enabled "to act in the name of the church and in the name of Christ as head of the church."[38] Thus a new relationship now exists between the priest and the Church, and consequently, a real (ontological) change has come about. But the priest must act as a member of the Church; as Kilmartin says, "pastoral office can only represent and act in the name of the Lord when it represents the life of faith of the Church. Outside the ecclesial context, apostolic office cannot represent Christ."[39]

2. *Iconic Argument*. Related to the assumption that ordained ministry should be understood immediately in christological terms is the so called "iconic" argument which in recent years seems to be emerging as the principal argument against the ordination of women. As it appears in *Inter insigniores*, the CDF document on the inadmissability of women to the priesthood, the argument has two parts. First, since the priest in celebrating the Eucharist represents Christ, the "natural resemblance" required for sacramental signs means that the priest should be a male. Second, the argument is sharpened by couching it in terms of the "nuptial analogy" which sees the priest at the Eucharist representing Christ as "bridegroom and head of the church."[40]

What can be said about this argument? First, it has little depth in the tradition. David Power notes that when the question of a minister's sex was raised by

[35] David Coffey, "The Common and the Ordained Priesthood," *Theological Studies* 58 (1997) 224–25.

[36] Ibid., 228.

[37] Ibid., 235; similarly Susan Wood maintains that "The ordained is configured to Christ as are the baptized, but the difference lies in the relationship to the ecclesial community"; "Priestly Identity," 126.

[38] Avery Dulles, *The Priestly Office: A Theological Reflection* (New York: Paulist, 1997) 35.

[39] Kilmartin, "Apostolic Office," 260; Kilmartin refers to scholastic discussions over whether a priest could consecrate the bread in a shopwindow to illustrate the theological consequences of separating the power of orders from the faith of the Church.

[40] Congregation for the Doctrine of the Faith, "Declaration on the Question of the Admission of Women to the Ministerial Priesthood" (*Inter insigniores*) art. 5; see *Origins* 6 (1977) 522.

Bonaventure or Aquinas, it was in regard to a particular understanding of gender differentiation, not resemblance to Christ; mention of a resemblance to Christ "is quite novel in the Church's teachings."[41]

Second, on the basis of Vatican II *Inter insigniores* says that the priest first represents Christ and because of this represents the church. As we have seen, David Coffey attributes this to the council's inability to reconcile both ordained and common priesthoods, leaving the impression that the ordained priesthood was christological while the common priesthood was ecclesiological.[42]

Finally, we should ask the question, does the representative role of the priest at the Eucharist and the nuptial argument require that the priest be a male?[43] It does not, at least according to David Coffey. The priest at the liturgy represents Christ primarily as head of the body, the Church; though Coffey admits that "allusion" is made to the second symbol of Christ as bridegroom of the Church, it is not possible for him to represent both at once.[44] What is at issue symbolically is not maleness but masculinity, with its donative characteristic. While donativity is in a general way associated with masculinity and receptivity with femininity, each is a clear distinguishing mark of men or women only at the physical level, since either can be appropriated by the other at the psychological and spiritual levels. Coffee observes that there is already an interchangeability of symbolism with regard to the priest within the liturgy:

> the priest represents Christ because he first represents the church; and a woman can represent the church better than a man; but a man can represent Christ better than a woman. In regard to their total representative ability, there appears to be little to choose between a man and a woman. Either can represent Christ and the church; neither does so perfectly.[45]

An analysis of priest-presider's role at the Eucharist illustrates this twofold representation, but does not bring into view any specifically nuptial imagery. In celebrating the Eucharist the community becomes more fully church, a local manifestation of the Body of Christ. The priest acts in the name of this community (*in persona ecclesiae*), addressing God in the first person plural in the presidential prayers and in giving thanks for the life, death, and resurrection of Jesus. Only in the recitation of institution narrative does the voice of the prayer change from first-person plural to first-person singular as the presider recounts Jesus' self-offering to the Father; "the 'we' of the community, the Body of Christ, becomes the 'I' of Christ the Head of his Body the Church."[46] But note John Baldovin's caution: to reduce the priest's

---

[41] Power, "Representing Christ," 120.

[42] Coffey, "Common and Ordained Priesthood," 235.

[43] See for example Sara Butler, "The Priest as Sacrament of Christ the Bridegroom," *Worship* 66 (1992) 498–517.

[44] David Coffee, "Priestly Representation and Women's Ordination," in *Priesthood: The Hard Questions*, ed. Gerald P. Gleeson (Newtown, N.S.W., Australia: E. J. Dwyer, 1993) 96.

[45] Ibid., 97.

[46] Robert Sokolowski, *Eucharistic Presence: A Study in the Theology of Disclosure* (Washington, D.C.: Catholic University of America, 1994) 17.

representation of Christ "either to the words of Christ at the institution narrative (thus misunderstanding the role of the narrative in the prayer) or to a specific moment of sacrificial offering (thus misunderstanding the sacrificial character of the Eucharist as a whole) would inevitably undermine the communal nature of the Eucharist."[47]

3. *The Renewal of the Structures of Authority.* An important implication of the ecclesiology of *communio* is that the Church can no longer afford to exercise authority as though it were an absolute monarchy; church government should be collegial in its form and the principle of subsidiarity should be honored in its practice.

Though there have been various protests in recent years against a recentralization of authority in the Church, one of the most significant was that of John Quinn, retired archbishop of San Francisco, in an address given at Oxford on June 29, 1996 entitled "The Exercise of the Primacy: Facing the Cost of Christian Unity."[48] Responding to Pope John Paul's request for assistance, "to find a way of exercising the primacy, which while in no way renouncing what is essential to its mission, is nonetheless open to a new situation,"[49] the archbishop observed that "Large segments of the Catholic Church as well as many Orthodox and other Christians do not believe that collegiality and subsidiarity are being practiced in the Catholic Church in a sufficiently meaningful way" (no. IX).

Quinn called for a number of specific reforms. Many of them, including the structural reform of the Roman curia, allowing bishops and episcopal conferences to exercise an active collegiality by having more say on doctrinal, liturgical, and disciplinary questions and to make pastoral decisions on particular issues facing their churches, providing for bishops to be selected by local churches, even granting the international synod of bishops to exercise—at least on occasion—deliberative power, could be accomplished within the present prescriptions of canon law.

Less clear is whether the principle of subsidiarity applies to the internal life of the Church. Though Quinn cites both Pope Pius XII and the Preface to the 1983 Code of Canon Law to argue that it does (no. IX), the issue was still unclear to the 1985 Extraordinary Synod which recommended that a study be made on its applicability.[50] After researching the question, Ad Leys, a former staff member of the Dutch Bishops' Conference, answered affirmatively.[51]

---

[47] John F. Baldovin in "*Accepit Panem*: The Gestures of the Priest at the Institution Narrative of the Eucharist," in Nathan Mitchell and John F. Baldovin, eds., *Rule of Prayer, Rule of Faith: Essays in Honor of Aidan Kavanagh, O.S.B.* (Collegeville: The Liturgical Press, 1996) 136. David Power makes a similar point in "Church Order: the Need for Redress," *Worship* 71 (1997) 301–04.

[48] The talk was published in *Commonweal* 123 (July 12, 1996) 11–20; also *Origins* 26 (1996) 113–27.

[49] John Paul II, *Ut unum sint*, no. 96; see *Origins* 25 (1995) 69.

[50] Extraordinary Synod of Bishops, "The Final Report" C,8; *Origins* 15 (1985) 449.

[51] Leys, *Ecclesiological Impacts of the Principle of Subsidiarity*, 209.

But Leys also argues that those relationships which constitute the church as a *communio*, the "tensile relationships" between pope and bishops, universal Church and particular churches, as well as church and individual believers, must be more clearly defined than they are in the new 1983 Code.[52] Indeed, he argues that the 1983 Code seems to accentuate the primacy even more than the 1917 Code did, to the effect that it "opens all the doors to a centralist exercise of primacy."[53] Though he does not specifically call for a reform of the Code, his study clearly implies that one is needed to safeguard the interdependent relationships implied by an ecclesiology of *communio*.

4. *Apostolic Succession.* The issue of apostolic succession in ministry has long been an obstacle to the reconciliation of ministries, and thus, to the restoration of the bonds of communion with other churches. Since the appearance of the WCC text, *Baptism, Eucharist and Ministry* in 1982, a broad consensus in regards to ministry has emerged.[54] Apostolic succession in the episcopal office is understood as a sign, not a guarantee, of the unity and continuity of the church (BEM, M no. 38). But if the ministry of bishops in a particular church is to be recognized by all parts of the universal Church, it must ordain its bishops in such a way as to invite this recognition.[55] With a fundamental consensus on faith and the sacraments, a process toward reconciliation could begin with a mutual recognition of ministries.

A number of churches are beginning to take concrete steps towards reconciliation.[56] But on the Catholic side, this emerging consensus on ordained ministry remains largely a consensus of theologians; the official Church has been slow to respond. Yet there may be some signs of movement. In 1991 Bishop Walter Kasper, now secretary of the Pontifical Commission for Promoting Christian Unity, delivered a bicentennial lecture at St. Mary's Seminary and University in Baltimore in which he pointed to the unresolved question of apostolic succession in episcopacy as that which particularly impedes progress towards eucharistic fellowship.[57]

Kasper's principal argument is that the apostolic succession needs to be discussed in its broader theological context rather than considered in isolation. Thus he specifically rejects a mechanistic, "pipeline" theory of apostolic succession through an unbroken line of ordinations, stretching back to an apostle, beneath which lurks the old argument of a uniquely transmitted sacramental power. Because of the inner unity of *successio* and *communio*, "it would be more correct to say that the individual bishop comes to be part of apostolic succession by becom-

[52] Ibid., 209–10.

[53] Ibid., 100.

[54] *Baptism, Eucharist and Ministry* (Geneva: World Council of Churches, 1982).

[55] *The COCU Consensus: In Quest of a Church Uniting*, (Princeton, N.J.: COCU, 1985) no. 48.

[56] Cf. John Hotchkin, "The Ecumenical Movement's Third Stage," *Origins* 25 (November 9, 1995).

[57] Walter Kasper, "Apostolic Succession in Episcopacy in an Ecumenical Context," *The Bicentennial Lecture*, ed. Rudi Ruckmann (Baltimore, Md.: St. Mary's Seminary & University, 1992) 1.

ing a member of the College of Apostles and of the College of Bishops, by being in *communio* with the whole *ordo episcoporum*."[58]

Among the consequences Kasper draws from his argument, two are particularly important to our concern here. First, he notes that "Vatican II merely talks about a *defectus* with regard to the full form of ministry, a lack, but not a complete absence. Thus a certain degree of recognition has been conceded."[59] Second, he sees promoting a greater understanding of the extent to which the true nature of the episcopal ministry is embedded in an ecclesiology of *communio* as a further challenge for the Catholic Church. This ecclesiology stresses that full ecclesial reality comes from being part of the *communio*: "The individual local Church is the true Church of Jesus Christ to the extent that it is in communion with all other local Churches."[60] Thus Kasper argues for a limited recognition of ministry in the Reformation churches and suggests that full ecclesial and ministerial reality is dependent, not on apostolic succession in the episcopal office considered by itself, but by integrating a given church into the communion of all the local churches. More recently, David N. Power has developed a similar view based on a theology of eucharistic communion. He argues that the question of ministry is not reducible to an issue of the power to celebrate, but to a lack of the fullness of visible communion.[61] Thus the movement beyond an understanding of priesthood based on sacred power and the emergence of an ecclesiology of *communio* has made possible a new evaluation of ministry in other churches and a rethinking of apostolic succession.

Conclusion

The Catholic Church in the third millennium faces two great challenges. First, it must complete the renewal of its own structures of authority so that the *communio* ecclesiology it has adopted might be more deeply expressed in its life. Second, it must take the steps necessary to restore the bonds of communion with other churches, so that the *ecclesia catholica* might again be a communion of all the churches and its own communion might be more truly "catholic." These two tasks are not unrelated; the second is dependent on the first.

The emergence of a *communio* ecclesiology and a representative model of ordained ministry have made possible a new approach to apostolic succession in the ordained ministry. But this is not the only obstacle to reconciliation today. The reform of the way authority is exercised is another. So is the ordination of women, for it is not clear how a church that does not recognize the ministry of ordained women can enter into eucharistic fellowship with others that do.

[58] Ibid., 8.

[59] Ibid., 12.

[60] Ibid., 15.

[61] David N. Power, "Roman Catholic Theologies of Eucharistic Communion: A Contribution to Ecumenical Conversation," *Theological Studies* 57 (1996) 609.

Moving towards a better expression of the Church's interdependent nature as a *communio* is not so much an issue of theology as it is of will; it demands not research but institutional renewal. The question of the ordination of women is much more difficult. If, as David Coffey among others suggests, Vatican II left the false impression that ordained ministry was christological while the common priesthood was ecclesiological, then further research on the question of priestly representation will be necessary. The last word on this question may not yet have been spoken.

7. Trinity

Fides Trinitatis:
Liturgical Practice and the Economy of Salvation

Nancy A. Dallavalle

Writing nearly fifteen years before the opening of the Second Vatican Council on the anti-Arian impetus for liturgical practice in the early middle ages, and the "liturgical hypertrophy" that too often characterized the late middle ages, Josef A. Jungmann, in his seminal essay "The Defeat of Teutonic Arianism and the Revolution in Religious Culture in the Early Middle Ages,"[1] certainly had somewhat more proximate problems in mind. "In our time," he observes in this ostensibly historical essay, "[h]uge sections of the people are estranged from the Church; others are perplexed with doubt and have no secure traditions; naive, habitual piety has withered before the biting blast of a scientific age."[2]

Jungmann's intent is to show that liturgical forms are clearly marked by social and cultural debate, and that these forms have changed in the past, and could and should change again so as to recapture the early Church's sense of a vital and corporate worship. For example, he buttresses his own concern for the use of the vernacular in Roman Catholic liturgy with the observation that the publication of the Roman Missal in 1570 was accompanied by a Bull declaring that "'nothing was to be added or taken away or changed,'" commenting wryly that such a charge was a "novelty which could only have been possible after the invention of printing."[3] Jungmann's point, of course, is that the uniformity imposed by Trent need not be seen as the last word, but rather as an historical innovation that reflected the concerns of its own time, an innovation, one must add, that could reasonably be considered "modernist." And, even as he wrote about the effects of anti-Arianism on the doctrine on the Trinity in the Middle Ages, trinitarian theology was, in the

---

[1] In *Pastoral Liturgy*, trans. Challoner Publications, Ltd. (New York: Herder and Herder, 1962) 1–101 (originally published as "Die Abwehr des germanischen Arianismus und der Umbruch der religiösen Kulture im frühen Mittelalter," *Zeitschrift für katholische Theologie* 69 [1947] 36–99).

[2] Josef A. Jungmann, *The Early Liturgy to the Time of Gregory the Great*, trans. Francis A. Brunner (Notre Dame, Ind.: University of Notre Dame Press, 1959) 93.

[3] Jungmann, "The Defeat of Teutonic Arianism," 92.

twentieth century, being shaken awake after a long relegation to the ether. In particular, Karl Rahner's own seminal essay would permanently reorient trinitarian theology, setting in motion a systematic project that continues to unfold. Jungmann's observations about the changing patterns of liturgical prayer in the early Middle Ages, reconsidered through the lenses of Karl Rahner's *Grundaxiom* and the trinitarian theology of Catherine Mowry LaCugna, prove to be a still-timely window into the mindset of the worshipping Church, and a key dialogue partner for continued scholarship in pastoral liturgy.

I. The Emphasis on the Trinity in the Middle Ages

Jungmann's argument was that the battle against Arianism, a conflict which continued long after Nicaea's embrace of the *homoousios*, reverberated strongly in liturgical language about the divinity of Christ, giving rise, in the early Middle Ages, to formulas emphasizing God's triunity so as to underscore the equality in divinity of the Son and the Father. Early patterns of liturgical prayer are directed to God through Christ, exemplified by Origin's dictum that prayer be directed to "the Father of all through Jesus Christ in the Holy Spirit."[4] This clearly subordinationist pattern was cited by Arian theology as decisively indicative of the distinction in status between the Son and the Father. While it was answered that the subordination was only of Christ's humanity, Eastern liturgical formulae began to reflect the conflict by defensively "flattening" the more complex pattern of divine self-gift and recapitulation (*exitus-reditus*) into one that offered glory "to the Father and to the Son and to the Holy Spirit." Later in the West a similar shift, first in Spain and Gaul, and finally in the Roman liturgies, was demonstrated by "the omission of *Per Dominum nostrum . . .* and the substitution for it of *Qui vivis et regnas . . .* as a termination"[5] to emphasize the equality in divinity among the trinitarian persons. Thus the Roman tradition gradually came to reflect the Gallic-Carolingian practice of closely paralleling Christ and the Father.[6]

Along with this anti-Arian polemic, was a tendency (with some basis in Scripture) to conflate "Christ" and "God." The person of Christ takes on an almost monophysitic cast, in which the Incarnation becomes an opportunity for "the adoring worship of the Son of God appearing on earth, clothed in human flesh."[7] Jungmann traces this tendency to a shift, in liturgical sensibility, from the communal to the individual and subjective, and to a shift from an Easter-centered liturgical year to a liturgical year almost equally marked by the Christmas cycle (and boasting a

---

[4] *De oratione* 33, cited in Jungmann, *The Place of Christ in Liturgical Prayer* (New York: Alba House, 1965) 157.

[5] Josef A. Jungmann, *Public Worship: A Survey*, trans. Clifford Howell (Collegeville: The Liturgical Press, 1957) 26.

[6] Jungmann, "The Defeat of Teutonic Arianism," 4.

[7] Ibid., 40.

new sprinkling of Marian feasts).[8] Moreover, this emphasis on the divinity of Christ in the early Middle Ages "heightened interest in all things connected with the Trinity."[9] Tracing the gradual crescendo of the τριαδικὴ ρίστις (the "threefold faith") in liturgical practice, Jungmann finds that the early defensive employ of trinitarian belief turned to a preoccupation with the doctrine itself after the turn of the millennium. "What is new," he observes, "is a manner of speech which seems to identify the substance of Faith with the doctrine of the Blessed Trinity," and a practice of gradually attaching trinitarian motifs and invocations to a wide variety of established liturgical forms.[10]

Yet another repercussion of the defensive emphasis upon Christ's divinity was that the mediation of Christ is now given over, in the popular mind, to the cult of the saints, to relics, and to various devotions. Such a focus on "the fringes of faith" and the mediation of the saints "could scarcely have gathered such momentum," Jungmann argues, had believers "been accustomed to view the Person of the Redeemer as much from the mediatorial and human side as from that of adoration of awesome divinity."[11] Liturgical action was best left, therefore, to the clergy, who acted for the laity with regard to a distant deity. In this perspective, the role of Christ's full humanity is dampened, as the pattern of prayer, and indeed, the pattern of the trinitarian life itself, is flattened.[12] The *Sanctus* may ring out thrice, but it is thrice in heaven.

These currents shape not only liturgical language but also visual representation, as stronger claims for the divinity of Christ required both concrete images of this glory as well as images of mediating figures, such as Mary. Thus in the late Middle Ages there was a growing emphasis on graphic images for the Trinity, which would firmly display for a largely unlettered public the co-equality of Son and Father. One image was the *Gnadenstuhl* (the "Mercy-Seat" or the "Throne of Grace") in which the Father is seated with the crucified Christ on his lap and the Spirit, usually in the form of a dove, hovering above. In these, Christ is not in resplendent glory, but suffering, yet the co-equal dignity of Father and Son is visually reinforced, often by color or form.[13] Another image, drawn from the story of the heavenly visitors to Abraham in Genesis 18, was that of the fifteenth-century iconographer Andrei Rublev which depicts the three persons of the Trinity as three co-equal human figures seated around a table.

A different approach to the same problem is observed in another visual image that gains in popularity: the crowning of Mary.[14] The title *Theotokos*, first confirmed

---

[8] Ibid., 3–6.

[9] Ibid., 38.

[10] Ibid., 34.

[11] Ibid., 45.

[12] Ibid., 23. This would suppress, for example, the notion of the monarchy of the Father.

[13] See the numerous plates and discussion in Fides Buchheim, *Der Gnadenstuhl: Darstellung der Dreifaltigkeit*, forward by Christian Schütz (Würzburg: Echter, 1984). I am grateful to Elizabeth Groppe for bringing this reference to my attention.

[14] Josef A. Jungmann, "Liturgy and Kerygma," in *Pastoral Liturgy*, 365.

against Nestorius to reinforce the unity of the divine and human in a single person, Jesus Christ, is now employed to counter the monophysitism which accompanied the emphasis on Christ's divinity. While the title is used as a doctrinal corrective, the image of the Mother of God becomes popular in and of itself, as the emphasis on Christ's divinity (sometimes expressed in formulae associated with Priscillianism[15]) leaves a vacuum in the created order which the Blessed Virgin is employed to fill.[16] While the icon of the *Theotokos* was already popular, the image of the crowning of Mary in the later Middle Ages shifted the focus from her as "Mother of God" (that is, vis-á-vis Jesus Christ) to her own mediating agency before God. As the "Mediatrix," Mary was seen as active in redemption, and was often presented in tandem with Christ or the Eucharist.[17]

It is not surprising to find that the medieval emphasis on Christ's distant divinity led to an emphasis on the Eucharist as a divine object rather than "daily bread." The *tremendum* with which the Eucharist was regarded gave rise to the celebration of the feast of Corpus Christi (promulgated by Pope Urban IV in 1264) and, paradoxically, to a drop-off in the reception of Communion. The fact that the laity had to be exhorted to receive Communion even on a yearly basis, Jungmann notes, was not due to a lack of interest in the Eucharist. On the contrary,

> [t]oo great a tension has been allowed to develop between the holiness and sublimity of what was received and the sinfulness and nothingness of him who received. . . At the same time, men do not abandon the Blessed Sacrament. A new relationship to the Eucharist arises, coming fully into evidence only at the turn of the 12th century. From then on, however, we can speak of a formal Eucharistic movement having as its object not the approach to the Blessed Sacrament but withdrawal from it. The Sacrament which men dare not receive is at least to be contemplated from a distance and devoutly adored.[18]

So too is the doctrine of the Trinity removed from earth to heaven, there "to be contemplated from a distance and devoutly adored."

---

[15] Jungmann, "The Defeat of Teutonic Arianism," 46.

[16] As "zeal for the honour of Mary" grew, Jungmann observes that it thus "becomes intelligible how in the liturgical prayer of the Byzantine liturgy, in the place where of old Christ stood as Mediator of self-offering to God, now Mary appears in such fashion that, commemorating her and all the saints, the congregation lay themselves in Christ's hands" (ibid., 15).

[17] See Jaroslav Pelikan, *The Christian Tradition 3: The Growth of Medieval Theology* (Chicago: University of Chicago Press, 1978) 66–80, 160–74. For a critical overview of several perspectives on the relationship between Mary and the divine, see Elizabeth A. Johnson, "Mary and the Female Face of God," *Theological Studies* 50 (1989). 500–26. In a recent and extreme example of the pairing of Mary and Christ, the call officially to bestow on Mary the title "Co-Redemptrix" over-emphasizes this pairing to such an extent that the hypostatic union itself is effectively (however unintentionally) undermined. See the collection *Mary Coredemptrix, Mediatrix, Advocate: Theological Foundations*, ed. Mark I. Miravalle (Santa Barbara, Calif.: Queenship Publishing, 1995).

[18] Jungmann, "The Defeat of Teutonic Arianism," 62–63.

II. The Contemporary Renaissance of Trinitarian Theology

To ask about Jungmann's contribution from the perspective of trinitarian theology is, of course, to ask about the work of his illustrious fellow Jesuit and faculty colleague at Innsbruck during the 1950s, the German theologian Karl Rahner (1904–1984).[19] A systematician, Rahner enters the debates about the relationship between nature and grace by positing a theology of divine self-communication in which the neo-scholastic plethora of graces and efficient causality are set aside in favor of an exposition of grace as God's self-gift (given through "quasi-formal causality"). Integral to this theology of divine self-communication is his formula (the *Grundaxiom*) that insists on the identity of the God of the economy of salvation and God's triune nature: "the Trinity of the economy of salvation *is* the immanent Trinity and vice-versa."[20] It is *as* triune, *as* Christ and the Spirit, that God reveals God's self in history, and it is precisely through the events of the Incarnation of the Word and the sending of the Spirit that the mystery of God is revealed as triune *in se*.

Rahner's axiom, based as it is on the conviction that the Incarnation and the sending of the Spirit represent two moments of God's self-communication, challenges the traditional distinction between the immanent and the economic Trinity. Rahner's declaration that "we may . . . confidently look for an access into the doctrine of the Trinity in Jesus and in his Spirit,"[21] is based on nothing less than the claim that "Jesus is not simply God in general, but the Son."[22] In the same manner, Rahner's description of grace as God's self-gift via "quasi-formal causality" struggles to make a similar claim for God's continued self-gift in the economy of salvation. This theology of divine self-communication represents, on Rahner's part, a turn away from what he saw as the speculative excesses of scholastic metaphysics, and a turn toward the economy of salvation as the locus of theological reflection.

This turn away from the "two-storey" universe and toward history as the site of the human encounter with God is central for Catholic theology in the mid-twentieth century. Although Jungmann's voice is consistently that of the liturgical historian and Rahner speaks as the systematic theologian, their work reflects a whole host of common ideas, texts, ecclesial perspectives and spiritual insights.

---

[19] Jungmann was professor of pastoral theology at Innsbruck from 1925–1975. Rahner began at Innsbruck in 1948 and left in 1964 (the years 1962–1964 were spent as a *peritus* to Vatican II) to succeed Romano Guardini, the great liturgical scholar, at Munich. At Innsbruck, Jungmann was editor of *Zeitschrift für katholische Theologie*, which continues to serve as a touchstone for Rahner studies.

[20] Karl Rahner, "Remarks on the Dogmatic Treatise 'De Trinitate,'" in *Theological Investigations*, vol. iv, trans. Kevin Smyth (Baltimore: Helicon, 1966) 87. Rahner also uses the formulation, "The 'economic' Trinity is the 'immanent' Trinity and the 'immanent' Trinity is the 'economic' Trinity," in *The Trinity*, trans. Joseph Donceel, with an introduction, index, and glossary by Catherine Mowry LaCugna (New York: Crossroad, 1997) 22.

[21] Rahner, *The Trinity*, 39.

[22] Ibid., 23. Rahner thus rejects the doctrine of appropriations.

Indeed, Jungmann's twentieth-century examination of the liturgical patterns in the early Middle Ages is paralleled by his colleague Rahner's appraisal of the impasse represented by neo-scholasticism. In this light, Rahner's constructive work may rightly be seen as something of a foil for the movement in the early Middle Ages Jungmann highlights. Whereas Jungmann traces the trinitarian effects of a doctrinal emphasis on the divinity of Christ, Rahner rethinks the doctrine of the Trinity by emphasizing the presence of divinity *in the humanity of Christ* and the fullness of God's self-gift in the historical life of grace.[23] Whereas Jungmann points to a renaissance of belief in the Trinity as an exalted threefold mystery, Rahner heralds the historical importance of the trinitarian life and, with this proclamation, rejuvenates trinitarian theology in the twentieth century.[24] Thus, unlike the anti-Arian emphasis on the complete co-equality of the trinitarian persons in the inner life of God, Rahner's focus on the economy restores the *taxis* [τάξις, the inner order] of the trinity (immanent and economic), as the two missions are the focus of the divine self-communication of the Father.

Rahner will therefore favor a trinitarian model that reflects the monarchial Father of Scripture and the Greek fathers over the scholastic model that begins with the divine nature in itself.[25] Certainly this perspective is due to the fact that he shares his colleague Jungmann's appropriation of the fruits and sensibility of the retrieval of Scripture and the writings of the early church found in the *nouvelle théologie*, scholarship which so enlivened the liturgical movement of the mid-twentieth century. And, while no one would accuse Rahner's work of being overly mired in historical detail, he does support the notion, cited by Jungmann, that "in the New Testament ὁ Θεός signifies the First Person of the Trinity," to whom prayer is offered through Christ.[26]

---

[23] Karl Rahner, *Foundations of Christian Faith: An Introduction to the Idea of Christianity*, trans. William V. Dych (New York: Seabury, 1978) 212–28.

[24] While bringing the discussion on the Trinity to a certain focus, particularly as he directly addressed the immanent/economic distinction, Rahner was hardly alone in this emphasis. Thirty years before the publication of Rahner's work on the trinity Karl Barth suggests that God's triunity is revealed in the economy of salvation (in his *Church Dogmatics* I/1, trans. G. T. Thomson [Edinburgh, T. & T. Clark, 1936] 479). For a discussion of the contemporary flowering of trinitarian theology, see John Thompson, *Modern Trinitarian Perspectives* (New York: Oxford University Press, 1994).

[25] Rahner, employing a typology sketched by Théodore de Régnon, describes the difference between the "Greek" and "Latin" models thus: "The latter proceeds from the unity of God's nature (one God in three Persons), so that the unity of the divine nature is a presupposition of the whole doctrine of the Trinity; while the former begins with the three Persons . . . or better, with the Father, who is the source from which the Son, and through the Son the Spirit, proceed, so that the unity and integrity of the divine nature is conceptually a *consequence* of the fact that the Father communicates his whole nature" ("*Theos* in the New Testament," in *Theological Investigations*, vol.1, trans. Cornelius Ernst [Baltimore: Helicon, 1961] 146). The over-dependence of Rahner and other trinitarian theologians on de Régnon's rather facile distinction is criticized by Gregory Havrilak, "Karl Rahner and the Greek Trinity," *St. Vladimir's Theological Quarterly* 34 (1990) 77; and more extensively by Michel Barnes, "Augustine in Contemporary Trinitarian Theology," *Theological Studies* 56 (1995) 237–50.

[26] Rahner, "*Theos* in the New Testament," 126–27. This essay is well-summarized in Robert Warner, "Rahner on the Unoriginate Father," *The Thomist* 55 (1991) 571–72.

While Rahner was also aware of Jungmann's observation of this pattern in the early Church, his own reasons for citing the pattern of prayer through Christ are explicitly systematic, to support the *Grundaxiom's* assertion of the mutual implication of immanent and economic Trinity in the work of salvation history. With this as the framework, prayer to God through Christ tends not to conflate Christ and God, but to see Christ as the self-gift of God.[27]

A full-blown exposition of the intersection of trinitarian theology and liturgical practice is advanced in the work of Catherine Mowry LaCugna.[28] LaCugna draws on both Jungmann[29] and Rahner, developing Rahner's thought in two important ways that support Jungmann's program. First, in reflection on the *Grundaxiom* she draws the concepts "the Trinity of the economy of salvation" and "the immanent Trinity" even closer by asserting that the distinction between the two is not ontological, as Rahner tried to hold, but epistemological.[30] For LaCugna, the world is the arena of God-with-us, such that the self-communicating God is found in the depth of the economy of salvation, an economy which is suffused with the ineffable God.[31] Secondly, she takes from Rahner the *taxis* of the self-communication found in the economy, a pattern of redemption and deification that reflects the pattern found in the New Testament *oikonomia*:

> In general, then, "economy" refers to the plan made known in the coming of Christ. Economy is the actualization in time and history of the eternal plan of redemption, the providential ordering of all things. A certain order (*taxis*) marks the economy that expresses the mystery of God's eternal being (*theologia*).[32]

---

[27] Moreover, recent scholarship reveals a more complex christological situation in the early Church than Jungmann indicates. Albert Gerhards, for example, points out that Jungmann's assertion of prayer to the Father neglected that the *per Christum* also indicated Christ's role as mediator to us. Thus one finds in the same chapter of John both "He who has seen me has seen the Father" (14,9), and "the Father is greater than I" (14,28) (in "Zu wem beten: die These Josef Andreas Jungmanns über den Adressaten des Eucharistischen Hochgebets im Licht der neueren Forschung," *Liturgisches Jahrbuch* 32 [1982] 229).

[28] Catherine Mowry LaCugna, *God For Us: The Trinity and Christian Life* (San Francisco: HarperSanFrancisco, 1991).

[29] LaCugna draws particularly on Jungmann's very early *The Place of Christ in Liturgical Prayer*, originally appearing in 1925 as *Die Stellung Christi im liturgischen Gebet*.

[30] For a fuller discussion of LaCugna's appropriation of Rahner, see Nancy A. Dallavalle, "Revisiting Rahner: On The Theological Status of Trinitarian Theology," *The Irish Theological Quarterly* 63 (1998) 133–50.

[31] This discussion invites comparison with the distinction in Orthodox theology between the divine essence and energies. See LaCugna's presentation of the distinction maintained as a limit of the Palamite model (in her *God For Us*, 181–205), and contrast this with Ralph DelColle's laudatory observation that Orthodox theology is able to accomplish what Rahner intends with the *Grundaxiom* while maintaining a strong distinction between theology and economy (in his *Christ and the Spirit: Spirit-Christology in Trinitarian Perspective* [New York: Oxford University Press, 1994] 12–16).

[32] LaCugna, *God For Us*, 25.

LaCugna's assertion that the mystery of the triune life is the mystery that indwells the sweep of all creation is not a reduction of the *ad intra* life of God to God's life *ad extra*, but rather a profound appropriation of the gospel claim that identifies Jesus and the Father, an appropriation which claims this insight *as gospel.*[33]

Drawing on Jungmann's description of the prayer formulae that defeated Arianism, LaCugna argues that the shift away from a pattern that reflects God's action in salvation history led to the sundering of soteriology and theology, and thus, particularly in the manuals of neo-scholasticism, to the marginalizing of the doctrine on the Trinity—in LaCugna's mind, to its "defeat."[34] God's triunity is not the most speculative of doctrines, but the most practical, as its focus is the saving presence of God in human history.[35] In an article titled, "Can Liturgy Ever Again Become a Source for Theology?" LaCugna argues that liturgy is indeed intimately intertwined with theology but, more importantly, that both properly proceed from doxology, "the living language of faith in which praise is offered to God for the abundance of God's generous love."[36] For LaCugna, a life that is characterized by right relationship to self, others and God is the first moment of doxology, a moment which in turn gives rise to liturgical speech or theological reflection.[37] Thus, doxology is always rooted in the economy of salvation, as its impetus is God's life with us. Indeed, LaCugna claims, doxology "is the precondition of theological speech, particularly any speech about God."[38] Seen in this light, the language of liturgy and theology has no choice but to reflect the pattern of redemption: "Theology in the mode of doxology forces the Christian doctrine of God to remain christological and pneumatological."[39] It is as Christ and the Spirit that God is with us and thus it is through Christ in the Spirit that our praise is given to God. For LaCugna, the claim that liturgical prayer must "remain christological and pneumatological" refers not to human finitude, but to the plenitude of God with us, not to the distance of God but to God's unfathomable immanence.

[33] LaCugna cites John 17, 20–21, in *God For Us*, 228.

[34] LaCugna notes that this characterization is found also in D. Wendebourg, "From the Cappadocian Fathers to Gregory Palamas: The Defeat of Trinitarian Theology," *Studia Patristica* 17 (1982) 194–97.

[35] In Roger Haight's words, "The point of the doctrine of the Trinity is therefore soteriological. . . . The doctrine is not intended to be information about the internal life of God, but about how God relates to human beings. It is a formula that guarantees that the salvation experienced in Jesus and the Spirit is really God's salvation" ("The Point of Trinitarian Theology," *Toronto Journal of Theology* 4 [1988] 199).

[36] LaCugna, *God for Us*, 5. LaCugna's antecedent for this is Daniel Hardy and David Ford, *Praising and Knowing God* (Philadelphia: Westminster, 1985). Christopher Cocksworth takes LaCugna's insight as a starting point for a discussion of liturgy that uses a "doxological hermeneutic" and takes seriously the experience of charismatic worship (in his "The Trinity Today: Opportunities and Challenges for Liturgical Study," *Studia Liturgica* 27 [1997] 61–78).

[37] LaCugna, *God For Us*, 342–50.

[38] Catherine Mowry LaCugna, "Response to John R. Sachs," *CTSA Proceedings* 51 (1996) 43.

[39] LaCugna, *God For Us*, 362.

III. Trinitarian communion: three observations

Jungmann contrasts the world of the early Church with the world of medieval Christianity by noting that:

> As long as Christianity was primarily intent on overcoming the world, as long as the light of Christianity stood opposed to heathen darkness, it presented the Christian idea as the *good news of salvation*; come alive for us in Christ. But now [in the middle ages], when faith in the mysterious inter-relation of the divine Persons has become threatened, the true Faith is seen as *fides Trinitatis*.[40]

In other words, every age calls forth a different lens on the complex mystery of the Christian faith. In an age of doubt, for example, Rahner emphasized the genuine self-communication of God in the economy of salvation in response to the tendency of neo-scholasticism to emphasize the distance of God at every turn. Writing as modernity shows the signs of age, LaCugna continues this trajectory by employing an ontology of relation to respond to criticisms of modernity's anthropology of rugged individualism. Similar responses are still taking shape and maturing in theological reflection, but their maturity will also depend on the consideration of other factors of contemporary sensibility—factors which are critical to, though not determinative of, genuinely pastoral liturgy.[41] Of primary importance is the fact that, for much of the industrialized West, contemporary Christian faith responds not to a world ignorant of Christ, but to one jaded from Christianity's hegemony; not to a specific doctrinal conflict, but to the sense that doctrine itself is, in a relativized world, supremely irrelevant. Contemporary Christian faith must therefore ask about its relevance to the world with a sense of "second naivete"; as a thoughtform that, for the industrialized West, has come and conquered—and been co-opted—and now must reassert itself, as Karl Barth would say, against itself. The explosion and continued interest in trinitarian theology stems from the growing appreciation of the centrality of the doctrine on the Trinity, standing as it does at the crossroads of anthropology, christology, pneumatology and ecclesiology. We may consider some of this wealth, particularly as relevant to pastoral liturgy, under three headings: the necessity of trinitarian order for trinitarian communion, the notion that ecclesial life is the life of the economy, and the need for a renewed consideration of the activity of the Spirit.

---

[40] Jungmann, "The Defeat of Teutonic Arianism," 33.

[41] In his vice-presidential address to the North American Academy of Liturgy in 1983, Mark Searle described one task of pastoral liturgical studies as that of evaluating critically the cultural milieu: "It will rely on sociocultural studies of contemporary society to identify the dominant features of our age, but it will then proceed to subject them to theological criticism, particularly with a view to their possible impact on contemporary celebration." Mark Searle, "New Tasks, New Methods: The Emergence of Pastoral Liturgical Studies," *Worship* 57 (1983) 303.

1. The doctrine of the Trinity and the τάξις of communion

In the wake of the explosion of interest in the Trinity, Edward Kilmartin's description of the sacraments illustrates how deeply the language of renewed trinitarian scholarship has permeated contemporary theological sensibilities:

> What sacraments manifest and realize is the Church in its deepest being, namely the communion of life between the Father and humankind in Christ through the gift of the Holy Spirit, which entails [a] sharing of [the] life of faith between those who participate in the mystery of the shared Trinitarian life.[42]

While this statement captures well the *taxis* of the Christian life, much reflection that employs the recent recovery of the doctrine on the Trinity tends to emphasize the "communion of life" to which Christians are called, and to highlight its horizontal characteristics. Part of this tendency reflects a concern for social justice, manifested as a concern that the divine life be one that repudiates all forms of oppressive power and hierarchy. For example, the language of *perichoresis* has become popular. This term reflects the mutual self-gift that characterizes the sharing of divinity among the trinitarian persons, a sharing now presented as one of "mutuality" and "equality in dignity," and thus an image of community to which all Christians are called. All of these qualities are sorely needed and are certainly the fruits of a life ordered to doxology. Indeed, many sources—philosophical, psychological, and sociological—have been instrumental in revitalizing the now common understanding of person as a self-in-relation, a self which is realized precisely in community.

For Catholic theology, much of this relational-social emphasis emerged in reaction to two things: neo-scholasticism's overly positivistic account of grace and the divine life, which emphasized the singularity and distance of God, and the individualistic anthropology of early modernity. Often it should be noted, these two very different perspectives became fused as a common "old" way of seeing the believer before God—that is, the rational individual of modernity was sometimes read back into the description of God, emphasizing characteristics such as the divine aseity (for example, over-reading the fact that the *Summa Theologiae* begins with an exploration of *De Deo Uno*) and downplaying relational themes. Against this model of theology and anthropology, the development of a more relational concept of the person emerged in contemporary theology along with God-models that emphasized the sociality of the trinitarian life[43] as well as God-models that emphasize relationality and communion as central to the trinitarian life.

---

[42]   Edward J. Kilmartin, "Sacraments as Liturgy of the Church," *Theological Studies* 50 (1989) 527.

[43]   For a critical survey of social models for the trinity, see John O'Donnell, "The Trinity as Divine Community: A Critical Reflection upon Recent Theological Developments," *Gregorianum* 69 (1988) 5–34; and John L. Gresham, "The Social Model of the Trinity and its Critics," *Scottish Journal of Theology* 46 (1993) 325–43. The social model is generally exemplified, in Protestant theology, by the work of Jürgen Moltmann (particularly his *The Trinity and the Kingdom: The Doctrine of God*, trans. Margaret Kohl [San Francisco: Harper & Row, 1981]). In Catholic thought, the social model is associated

But yet another development, from both within and without theology, causes further nuance to this trend: the raising on all fronts of the postmodern question of otherness and difference. While the model of the divine life as a lively communion of person-constituting giving and receiving works well for anthropological concerns about mutuality and equality, the divine life in abstraction from God's life with us seems to lack a basis for the differentiation that characterizes the human experience of persons-in relation. Moreover, unreflective claims for solidarity among persons that would mirror the "solidarity" among the trinitarian persons now comes under fire, as marginalized persons are suspicious of models of equality that don't also allow for real difference, and merely "include" the other under their hegemonic sway. Mark Searle refers to a similar problem in a concrete vein when he observed that "pastoral liturgical studies cannot lend themselves to the agenda of implementing official liturgical reforms, for its task must include a critical evaluation both of the official reforms and of their mode of implementation."[44]

Postmodern theology, with its critique of large narrative schemes and the foundational truths they purport to unfold, must consider how liturgical celebration can reflect Christian practice in this new climate. The assertion of a communion of transparent mutuality, based on an understanding of undifferentiated relationships within the immanent trinity and divorced from the *taxis* of the Trinity of the economy of salvation, will not adequately account for the complex identities of Christian believers and their communities.

2. Ecclesial life as life in Christ and the Spirit

Indeed, in itself ecclesial life is "trinitarian life" not because it mimics "the Trinity," but because it draws us into the economy of Christ and the Spirit which is always lived *ad Patrem*. Consider a brace of articles in a recent issue of *The Tablet*.[45] In the first, Paul Wilkes offers two nautical models of leadership in parish life: the sailing ship, open to the winds of the Spirit, but not without a rudder; and the rowboat, in which all labor under a single head in a fixed round. The former is desirable, and rare, the latter impoverished and all too common. Such a situation is precisely the premise for the second article, in which Alain Woodrow reflects on the enthusiasm which greeted John Paul II in his recent visit to Paris. Woodrow suggested that while there is little "audience" for the day-to-day parish life in Europe, young people are nonetheless drawn to large, enthusiastic mass meetings, or to movements headed by charismatic figures (such as Mother Teresa), even those whose ideals they reject. This dovetails nicely, Woodrow continues, with John

---

with process theology (see the recent collection by Joseph A. Bracken and Marjorie Hewitt Suchocki, eds., *Trinity in Process: A Relational Theology of God* [New York: Continuum, 1997]).

[44] Mark Searle, "New Tasks, New Methods," 305.

[45] Alain Woodrow, "A Love Affair in Paris," and Paul Wilkes, "That's the Spirit," *The Tablet* (August 30, 1997) 1088–89; 1092–93.

Paul's personal charisma. "The Pope believes in a powerful, visible, and obedient Church . . . [in which] public expression is monopolized by the hierarchy, often represented by the Pope alone." Such a "muscular Christianity," Woodrow adds, has no place for "the dissenter, the maverick, the enquiring theologian or the committed worker-priest, in a Church where uniformity is prized above all."[46]

Observations like these reveal the considerable distance between the now fairly common language of communion in academic theology and the ecclesial reality "on the ground." Once the metanarrative that effectively enjoined Christians to participation in church life was destroyed by the explosion of modernity and its aftermath, the rowboat model no longer compelled attendance. Lacking many instances of "the sailing ship," the only attractive alternative is the unidimensional attachment to a cult of personality. But, while the experience of communion is, of course, a social experience, the presence of others, however numerous and diverse, is not in itself a guarantee of communion. Certainly a strong spirit of fellowship emerges among those at such a gathering, but the parallel is less like the spirit of *Mystici Corporis* and more like the spirit of a Baroque Corpus Christi procession. Such an experience, however it may bond a smaller group of fellow-travellers, does not replace the working give-and-take of the life of trinitarian communion, precisely because it does not have any internal ordering, ordering which is found in the pattern of salvation history and not simply in the assertion of undifferentiated mutuality among the divine persons *ad intra*.[47]

And integral to that internal ordering is the pattern of liturgical prayer, as that prayer reflects the trinitarian life and thickens the internal ordering by placing such praise in the context of the entire economy of redemption. If liturgical practice offers praise not "to the Father and the Son and the Holy Spirit," but rather offered praise to the Father "through Christ in the Spirit," what shape would it take? It would be practice that reflected not only the equality and mutuality of community but also the variety and spontaneity of life in the Spirit, a liturgical practice that was not merely Christ-conformed, but Spirit-enlivened. Christians are called to "follow Christ," but this call is found in the ongoing life of the Spirit, which blows anew in every age. Neither Christ nor the Spirit is found outside of its ordering to the other. For those who fear for the sailing ship in the grip of a powerful wind, Catherine LaCugna reminds, "The Spirit moves freely, but moves always as God. The Spirit cannot act in any but a Godly way, since the Spirit is the Spirit of God."[48] Liturgical practice that takes seriously God's life with us will express the

[46] Woodrow, 1089.

[47] Against this, Bryan Spinks argues that the Eucharistic Prayer must more fully state as a foundational belief the *homoousios* of Father, Son and Spirit, and direct prayer to each. Contra Jungmann, he suggests that "public prayer to the Son and the Spirit has a much older and more orthodox pedigree than Jungmann wished to acknowledge" (Bryan D. Spinks, "Trinitarian Theology and the Eucharistic Prayer," *Studia Liturgica* 26 [1996] 221).

[48] LaCugna, *God For Us*, 299.

assertion that we cannot know Christ except in the Spirit, and will reflect this ordering in prayer formulae, in larger patterns of worship, and in the constitution of the community and the order of its ministry.

3. Postmodernity and the need for a fully realized pneumatology

In one of a series of lectures on early Christianity given at Notre Dame in 1949, Jungmann observed that the fight against Gnosticism led to liturgical practices that stressed the realism of Christian faith. He cites Ignatius of Antioch's imperative to those in a docetic milieu:

> Be deaf when anyone speaks to you apart from Jesus Christ, who was of the race of David, the son of Mary, who was truly born and ate and drank, who was truly persecuted under Pontius Pilate and was really crucified, and died in the sight of those in heaven and on earth and under the earth. Moreover, He was truly raised from the dead."[49]

To emphasize the christological point, the bringing of gifts becomes a focal point of Christian worship, gifts that were brought to a then newly-central altar. While *Eucharistia* is the understanding of this worship in the first and second centuries, the confrontation with gnosticism leads to an understanding of worship in which the language of oblation and sacrifice predominate. This understanding forces the reality of God-made-human to the forefront, and supports a liturgical practice that brings forward the materiality of the proceedings.

Such an emphasis seems no longer possible, in fact it is to state the obvious to say that our postmodern age has an uneasy relationship with the material, grasping one moment, diffident the next. Indeed, one could say that this age is plagued with a contemporary form of gnosticism in its excessive preoccupation with the surface of things and its forgetfulness of creation.[50] Not unlike the groups against whom Ignatius writes, we have a *de facto* disdain for the material which, in our own era, manifests itself in obsessive cycles of abstinence and slavery—whether the material in question is technology or consumer goods or food or flesh. And, like the early Christian gnostics, our culture tends to prize private over public knowledge, to the extent that all criteria can be relegated to "the personal," obliterating the possibility of genuine dialogue.

In the early Church, Christians raised high the public character of the Gospel in response to the gnostics' whispered cosmology, and insisted on the reality of the human Jesus as the Word incarnate. Can it be that, in recognizing that we face a renewed and peculiarly postmodern divorce of nature and spirit, the Christian claim that we cannot come to Christ without the Spirit calls for a renewed reflection on the Spirit's distinctive role in the economy of salvation? In the tradition, the Spirit

---

[49] Jungmann, *The Early Liturgy*, 113–14.

[50] For a discussion of the charge of "gnosticism" in the contemporary milieu, see Colin Gunton's *The One, The Three and the Many: God, Creation and the Culture of Modernity* (New York: Cambridge University Press, 1993).

has always been the self-effacing one, the bond of love that holds substantial others together. Even in LaCugna's insistence that christology and pneumatology are the starting point for theology, the Holy Spirit yields to Christ: "The Holy Spirit is always the means to God but never the end in itself, which is why it is impossible to specify what the spirit is in itself."[51] Unfortunately, such a proper differentiation of the work of Christ and the Spirit has often been incorrectly understood in a dualistic sense: Christ as the masculine, public, and concrete; the Spirit the feminine, private, and non-specific. This understanding of Christ too readily hardens into the totemic; this understanding of the Spirit too readily collapses into spiritualism.

Given these problematic understandings of the self-gift of God in Christ and the Spirit, it is clear that any reflection on the meeting of God and humanity in Christ now requires a concomitant articulation of the work of the Spirit. Particularly for Christians in the industrialized West, saturated in material goods, in images, and in realities that are merely virtual, the Spirit is crucial to an understanding of the material (including the material of humanity!) as *creation*. Michael Welker, for example, insists that the Spirit's work is making God *known*, "the charisms . . . are not simply individual postures and attitudes, but forms of participation and of inclusion in public powers."[52] His teacher, Jürgen Moltmann, grounds the experience of the Spirit in bodily experience.[53] The Spirit's work, according to Colin Gunton, is that of sustaining creation in relation to divinity, maintaining "the concreteness of things in their particular configurations in space and time: in their *haecceitas*" (that is, in their specificity).[54] These are just a few examples of an increasing body of reflection on the Spirit (interestingly, Welker, Moltmann and Gunton are Protestant theologians), which explore what an active embrace of the economic turn initiated by (the Catholic) Rahner and advanced by LaCugna might mean to a postmodern milieu and its concrete worship formulae.

Conclusion

Jungmann's observations about the liturgical implications of medieval anti-Arianism exemplify well the relationship between the worship and belief. Further explorations in this relationship will require a sustained collaborative effort between liturgical historians and systematic theologians. In particular, the "rediscovery" of the doctrine on the Trinity calls for this collaboration for, while this doctrine is quite appropriately exploited by contemporary sensibilities that seek social equality while prizing human differences, some caution in this direction is warranted.

[51] LaCugna, *God For Us*, 362.

[52] Michael Welker, *God the Spirit*, translated by John F. Hoffmeyer (Minneapolis: Fortress Press, 1994) 242.

[53] Jürgen Moltmann, *The Spirit of Life: A Universal Affirmation*, trans. Margaret Kohl (Minneapolis: Fortress Press, 1992) 17–38.

[54] Gunton, *The One, The Three and the Many*, 201.

Thus, the liturgical historian warns, with Jungmann, against any overly-facile embrace of the pieties of a given era. And the systematic theologian will need to explore the theological ramifications of claims for similarity and dissimilarity between the doctrine of God and theological anthropology.[55]

Certainly such theological analysis was set in motion by Karl Rahner's *Grundaxiom*. Rahner's turn to the economy as a starting point for trinitarian theology—and LaCugna's embrace of the economy of salvation as the realm of trinitarian theology—are, as extraordinarily fruitful theological insights, open to many readings, each with somewhat different liturgical implications. Indeed, the rise of the undifferentiated offer of praise "to the Father and to the Son and to the Holy Spirit" is of interest not only for its doctrinal origins, but also for its effects, as the "collapse" the intra-trinitarian distinctions had the effect of removing the whole from history. The twentieth-century reclamation of the doctrine on the Trinity is a reclamation of theology for the life of praise, as this move has rejected an understanding of the Christian life as one oriented toward a distant mystery and opted instead for an understanding of the Christian life as one caught up in life-giving *taxis* of Christ and the Spirit. In particular, this understanding of the Christian life requires a new recognition of the distinctive and public work of the Spirit. For the contemporary believer, the believer that rejects the unidimensional cult of authority for the *taxis* of redemption, the pattern of Christian prayer—through Christ, in the Spirit—is central because it is the way God is with us as we, in worship, plunge deeply into the incommensurable complexity of the economy of salvation, that is, into the trinitarian life of God.

[55] A full treatment of this question is found in Miroslav Volf, "'The Trinity is Our Social Program': The Doctrine of the Trinity and the Shape of Social Engagement," *Modern Theology* (1998) 403–23.

III. DIVERSE PERSPECTIVES

8. Protestant Perspectives

"Praise God from Whom All Blessings Flow": Trinitarian Euchology in the Churches of the Reformation

Karen B. Westerfield Tucker

In "The Defeat of Teutonic Arianism" and more fully in *The Place of Christ in Liturgical Prayer*, Josef Jungmann theorized that ongoing concerns to preserve the *homoousios* against Arian and other subordinationist claims eventually produced a shift away from long-held understandings about Christ's humanity and his mediatorial function as the Incarnate Son.[1] Emphasis was instead placed on the Son as the Second Person of the eternal Godhead who himself is worthy of worship. According to Jungmann, euchological formulae provide abundant testimony to this change, shown by the diminishing frequency of compositions such as the simple *per Jesum Christum Dominum nostrum* ("through Jesus Christ our Lord") or the ascription *Patri per Filium in Spiritu Sancto* ("to the Father, through the Son, in the Holy Spirit") in favor of the ascription *Patri et Filio cum [et] Spiritu[i] Sancto* ("to the Father and the Son with [and] the Holy Spirit") or the more elaborate expression of trinitarian co-equality *per eundem Dominum nostrum Jesum Christum, qui tecum vivit et regnat Deus in unitate Spiritus Sancti per omnia saecula saeculorum* ("through the same Jesus Christ our Lord, who liveth and reigneth with thee in the unity of the Holy Spirit, God, world without end"). An increase from the fourth century in the number of collects and other liturgical prayers addressed to Christ (e.g., *Domine Jesu Christe, Christe Deus*) or to the Trinity supplies further evidence. Despite this fixation on the divinity of Christ (if Jungmann's thesis is accurate), the western church was kept from Monophysitism; and, following a recovered appreciation of the humanity especially of the suffering Christ in the later Middle Ages, a further corrective rebalancing was asserted by the Reformation's soteriological stress on *solus Christus* which accentuated the importance of the redemptive work of "Christ Jesus, himself human" as the "one mediator between God and humankind" (1 Tim 2:5).

---

[1] Josef A. Jungmann, "The Defeat of Teutonic Arianism and the Revolution in Religious Culture in the Early Middle Ages" in *Pastoral Liturgy* (New York: Herder and Herder, 1962) 1–101, and *The Place of Christ in Liturgical Prayer* (Collegeville: The Liturgical Press, 1989).

The style of prayer, and quite often actual texts, were taken over from the Latin West by sixteenth-century Protestants, though prayers directed to Christ and especially to the Trinity met with some discomfort given the paucity of prayers addressed to Christ in Scripture (e.g., Acts 7:59; 2 Cor 12:8) and the total absence there of prayers to the Trinity. Prayer in the first century of Protestantism is almost exclusively directed to the Father. Some Latin prayers with implied address to the Son (as evident from the concluding formulation *qui vivis et regnas*, "who livest and reignest") are recast as prayers to the Father; the collect for the third Sunday of Advent in the *Book of Common Prayer* of 1549 and 1552 shows such alteration.[2] Gradually prayers to Christ become more common in Protestant euchology, but these are not primarily directed as worship to the eternal Son. Christ's divinity is assumed, but prayer rather is offered to Christ on the basis of his role as the high priest through whom humanity is enabled to draw near to the Father (Heb 2:11-18; 6:19-20; 7:25). Such a petition to Christ as mediator is used by Richard Baxter in the Eucharistic Prayer of *The Reformation of the Liturgy* (1661), also known as the Savoy Liturgy:

> Most merciful Saviour, as thou hast loved us to the death, and suffered for our sins, the just for the unjust, and hast instituted this holy Sacrament to be used in remembrance of thee till thy coming; we beseech thee, by thine intercession with the Father, through the sacrifice of thy body and blood, give us the pardon of our sins, and thy quickening Spirit, without which the flesh will profit us nothing. Reconcile us to the Father: nourish us as thy members to everlasting life.[3]

To affirm and reinforce Christ's mediatorial work in prayer and thanksgiving, the construction "through Jesus Christ our Lord" and its variants are commonly used to end classical Protestant prayers both liturgical and devotional, formulaic and extemporary. Doxological conclusions lauding the consubstantiality of the Godhead are only occasionally so employed. This being the case, and given the Protestant preference to address prayer to the Father, there is risk once again of a potential subordinationist misreading of Christ's mediation. Therefore, it is necessary to ask if the coinherence of the Triune God has been expressed at other points within Protestant worship and devotion. If the liturgy is truly a school of faith—the

---

[2] The Latin prayer "Aurem tuam quesumus domine precibus nostris accomoda: et mentis nostrae tenebras, gratia tuae visitationis illustra. Qui vivis . . . ." was translated and revised to "Lord, we beseech thee, give ear to our prayers, and by thy gracious visitation lighten the darkness of our heart, by our Lord Jesus Christ." See F. E. Brightman, *The English Rite* (London: Rivingtons, 1921) 1:208.

[3] Richard Baxter, *The Reformation of the Liturgy* (London, 1661) in *Reliquiae Liturgicae*, vol. 4, ed. Peter Hall (Bath: Binns and Goodwin, 1847) 69–70. This prayer constitutes the middle section of a tripartite prayer, the first section of which is addressed to the Father, the third part to the Holy Spirit. An unwitting successor to this prayer, also addressing each Person of the Godhead in sequence, is the 1948 Eucharistic Prayer of the German Methodist Church (Order A, *Liturgie der Methodistenkirche*, Hrsg. auf Anordnung der Zentralkonferenz der Methodistenkirche in Deutschland [Frankfurt a.M.: Anker-Verlag, 1948]).

Church's worship the place where persons are formed in faith as Christians—what has been proclaimed in Protestant worship about the One God in Three Persons?

The service of the Lord's Supper could be identified as one possible locus, though not all Protestants have used an established anaphora (save, perhaps, for rehearsal of the Words of Institution), and some texts lack overt reference to the Holy Spirit, thus suggesting binitarianism. And, for most Protestants, historically and at present, recitation of the Eucharistic Prayer occurs only occasionally since the Lord's Supper has functioned as a special feast rather than a weekly meal. Given, however, the structural and substantial importance of congregational song in Protestant worship, there is, perhaps, a not-so-surprising source for Protestant formation in trinitarian theology: the repeated liturgical and devotional use of the "Lesser Doxology" (the *Gloria Patri*), other short doxological ascriptions, hymns on the Trinity, and trinitarian hymns.

1. The Lesser Doxology And Other Short Doxological Ascriptions

The *Gloria Patri* migrated into Protestant worship as the trinitarian conclusion to the versicles at the opening of the office, to psalms and canticles, and even to the sermon. When placed after an Old Testament psalm or canticle, it allowed Christian revelation to influence the reading of that text. Lutherans and Anglicans embraced the *Gloria Patri* in the vernacular; among the latter, a metrical *Gloria* based upon the Latin text was composed for each of the different meters utilized in the English metrical psalters. However, Calvinists, especially the Puritans, rejected the use of the *Gloria* as a conclusion for their metrical psalms, finding it unscriptural: even though the *Gloria* is recognizably rooted in the Lord's commission to baptize (Matt 28:19-20), nowhere in the Bible is specifically found the form *Gloria Patri et Filio et Spiritui Sancto: Sicut erat in principio, et nunc, et semper, et in saecula saeculorum.* The doxology was also deemed "Romish," particularly in its use as a penance after private confession and priestly absolution, and an example of the "vain repetitions" that Christ himself deplored (Matt 6:7).

Calvin's eighteenth-century descendant, the Independent Congregationalist Isaac Watts, parted from his Reformed ancestors by finding a theological benefit in concluding his "christianized" psalm paraphrases in *Hymns and Spiritual Songs* (1707)—themselves a means of offering worship to the Father in the name of Christ[4]—with a metered *Gloria Patri*:

> I Cannot perswade my self to put a full Period to these Divine Hymns, till I have address'd a special Song of Glory to God the Father, the Son, and the Holy Spirit. Tho'

[4] Isaac Watts, "A Short Essay toward the Improvement of Psalmody: Or, An Enquiry how the Psalms of David ought to be translated into Christian Songs, and how lawful and necessary it is to compose other Hymns according to the clearer Revelations of the Gospel, for the Use of the Christian Church," *The Works of the Late Reverend and Learned Isaac Watts*, vol. 4 (London: Printed for T. and T. Longman et al., 1753) 283.

the *Latin* Name of it, *Gloria Patri*, be retain'd in our Nation from the *Roman* Church; and tho' there may be some Excesses of superstitious Honour paid to the Words of it, which may have wrought some unhappy Prejudices in Weaker Christians, yet I believe it still to be one of the noblest Parts of Christian Worship. The Subject of it is the Doctrine of the Trinity, which is that peculiar Glory of the Divine Nature, that our Lord *Jesus Christ* has so clearly revealed unto Men, and is so necessary to true Christianity. The action is Praise which is the most compleat and exalted Part of heavenly Worship. I have cast the Song into a Variety of Forms, and have fitted it by a plain Version or a larger Paraphrase, to be sung either alone or at the Conclusion of another Hymn. I have added also a few *Hosannas*, or Ascriptions of Salvation to *Christ*, in the same manner, and for the same end.[5]

Watts adhered to the substance of the Latin form of the *Gloria Patri* in his single and multiple-stanza, multi-meter doxologies: Christ is praised in his divinity and his co-equality with the Father and the Holy Spirit. For hymns in long meter, Watts provided:

To God the Father, God the Son,
And God the Spirit, Three in One,
Be Honour, Praise and Glory giv'n
By all on Earth, and all in Heav'n.

Or, in a reversed pattern, for common meter:

Honour to thee, Almighty Three
And Everlasting One;
All Glory to the Father be,
The Spirit, and the Son.

The trinitarian "prooftext" provided in Psalm 33:6 is echoed in another doxology which lauds the economic Trinity:

The God of Mercy be ador'd,
Who calls our Souls from Death,
Who saves by his Redeeming Word,
And new-creating Breath.
To praise the Father and the Son
And Spirit all Divine,
The One in Three, and Three in One,
Let Saints and Angels joyn.

Watts also framed stanzas, in different meters, acknowledging that the Three Persons, known individually and each meriting praise, are yet to be known by a single Name:

All Glory to thy wond'rous Name,
Father of Mercy, God of Love,

[5] Isaac Watts, *Hymns and Spiritual Songs*; reproduced in Selma L. Bishop, *Isaac Watts: Hymns and Spiritual Songs, 1707–1748; A Study in Early Eighteenth Century Language Changes* (London: Faith Press, 1962) 376–77.

Thus we exalt the Lord, the Lamb,
And thus we praise the heav'nly Dove.

To God the Father's Throne
Perpetual Honours raise;
Glory to God the Son,
To God the Spirit Praise:
    And while our Lips
    Their Tribute bring,
    Our Faith adores
    The Name we sing.[6]

Watts' hymns and psalm paraphrases—and the doxologies that concluded them—were written at a time when the Enlightenment philosophy of Rationalism and its theological expression in Deism were on the rise in Britain and elsewhere. Arianism and Unitarianism, both ultimately symptoms of Deism, had surfaced in Britain by the late seventeenth century,[7] and would find liturgical expression in the eighteenth century in unofficial revisions of the *Book of Common Prayer*, most notably those proposed by Samuel Clarke (author of the anti-Nicene treatise entitled *Scripture-Doctrine of the Trinity* [1712], his annotated Prayer Book was later published by Theophilus Lindsey as *The Book of Common Prayer Reformed According to the Plan of the Late Dr. Samuel Clarke* [1774]), and by William Whiston (*The Liturgy of the Church of England, Reduc'd Nearer to the Primitive Standard* [1713]).[8] Whiston, whose Arianism was grounded in a particular reading of Scripture and Christian antiquity, used both these classical determinants of Anglican doctrine against the bishop of London when the latter was attempting to squelch the proliferation of "new forms of doxology" similar to those of ancient heretics and enjoin an adherence to the patterns of Scripture and the earliest centuries. The bishop had informed "the Incumbents of all Churches and Chapels in his Diocese" that they should not be "seduced . . . by the strong Delusions of Pride and Self-conceit" into denying "a Trinity of Persons in the Unity of the Godhead" found in the historic faith of the Church if they should hope to "obtain Mercy from God the Father, through the Merits of Jesus Christ our Lord, and by the Sanctification of the Holy Ghost, Three Persons and One God Blessed for ever." Whiston thanked the bishop for his advocacy of pre-Nicene phraseology, and then accused the bishop himself of creating a "new" form by allowing that both Christ and the Holy Spirit are worthy of worship equal to the Father.[9] Such a climate undoubtedly encouraged

---

[6] Ibid., 380–82, 385 (Book 3, nos. 32, 35, 30, 33, 40).

[7] For a study of the "rise and fall of British Arianism," see Maurice Wiles, *Archetypal Heresy: Arianism through the Centuries* (Oxford: Clarendon, 1996) 62–164.

[8] Other Arian and Unitarian Prayer Book revisions are accounted for in A. Elliott Peaston, *The Prayer Book Reform Movement in the XVIIIth Century* (Oxford: Basil Blackwell, 1940).

[9] *Mr. Whiston's Letter of Thanks to the Right Reverend the Lord Bishop of London, For His Late Letter to His Clergy Against the Use of New Forms of Doxology, &c.* (London: Printed for J. Senex at the Globe in Salisbury-Court and W. Taylor at the Ship in Pater-noster-Row, 1719).

Watts to continue his poetic expression of trinitarian orthodoxy, a theological conviction which he stated in prose as well.[10]

Watts' trinitarian praise continued to be published well into the nineteenth century in numerous reprintings of his hymn books and in books which supplemented Watts' hymnic output with new material. Selections from his doxologies were also joined with other doxological compositions in nineteenth-century hymn collections produced in Britain and America, and in the official hymn books of numerous Protestant denominations of the nineteenth and twentieth centuries. Often these doxologies, in various quantities, were placed in a separate section of the hymn or psalm book. Though they still were used as conclusions to a hymn or psalm, they more commonly were sung as free-standing, single-stanza trinitarian tributes of praise. This practice proved to be highly popular at evangelical revivals and camp meetings because the song was short, easily memorized, and gave witness to the fullness of God's being. Single-stanza doxologies, as a genre, perhaps should be acknowledged as a predecessor of the praise choruses acclaimed in the so-called "contemporary worship" of the late twentieth century, though the newest form typically lacks the theological strength and the trinitarian boldness of its forebear.

In each generation, new translators and poets contribute doxologies to worship, most of which testify to the historic faith of the Church. Some are versified versions from the Latin, among which stand the superb translations of John Mason Neale (1818–66) which were vital to the Oxford Movement and the publication of *Hymns Ancient and Modern*, and which have, selectively, filtered into Protestant hymnals. Neale's work, which also includes translations from the Greek Fathers, provides in English the variety of nuances in doxological formulation. In translating a number of office hymns attributed to Ambrose of Milan, Neale phrases the doxology in a way that the Latin Church adopted when, with Ambrose's help, it rejected the Arian interpretation of mediatorial language:

> Almighty Father, hear our cry
> Through Jesus Christ our Lord most High,
> Who, with the Holy Ghost and Thee,
> Doth live and reign eternally.

Similarly, in a medieval text by Peter Abelard, Christ is described as the consubstantial divine mediator:

> Low before Him with our praises we fall,
> Of Whom, and in Whom, and through Whom are all;
> Of Whom, the Father; and in Whom, the Son;
> Thro' Whom, the Spirit with Them ever One.[11]

---

[10] For example, Watts' *The Christian Doctrine of the Trinity: Or, Father, Son, and Spirit, Three Persons and One God, asserted and prov'd, with their divine rights and honors vindicated by plain evidence of Scripture without the aid or incumbrance of human schemes* (London: Printed for J. Clark et al., 1722).

[11] *Hymns Ancient and Modern for Use in the Services of the Church* (London: Novello, Ewer and Co., 1869) 7–8, 331 (nos. 7–9, 343).

These examples from Neale also illustrate another source for doxologies: the final doxological stanza of a larger hymn. The most widely-used example, often functioning as a sung thanksgiving at the collection of monies, is the concluding stanza shared between the three hymns for the hours in Anglican Thomas Ken's *A Manual of Prayers for the Use of the Scholars of Winchester College* (1695 ed.). Known in many Protestant communities as *the* Doxology, this ascription praises the Three Persons in unity as the source of all good gifts:

Praise God, from whom all blessings flow,
Praise Him, all creatures here below;
Praise Him above, ye heavenly host,
Praise Father, Son and Holy Ghost.

Another category of doxologies comprises newly-inspired single-stanza texts and doxological acclamations that originally concluded a hymn, though that hymn is no longer extant. In many cases the original author is not known. Various theological emphases are stressed within the section of a hymnal devoted to doxologies, though the predominant theme is praise to the eternal, consubstantial Three. One text by an unknown author hints at the trinitarian ascription offered by Thomas Ken, but adds an English-language paraphrase of the final section of the Latin *Gloria Patri*:

Praise the Name of God most high;
Praise him, all below the sky:
Praise him, all ye heavenly host—
Father, Son, and Holy Ghost:
As through countless ages past,
Evermore his praise shall last.[12]

A doxology by English Congregationalist Josiah Conder (1789–1855) is found in several nineteenth and twentieth-century denominational hymn books inside and outside England and offers thanksgiving for the Triune God's economy of salvation:

Praise the God of all creation!
Praise the Father's boundless love!
Praise the Lamb, our Expiation,
Priest and King, enthroned above!
Praise the Fountain of salvation,
Him, by Whom our spirits live!
Undivided adoration
To the One Jehovah give![13]

In German-speaking Protestantism, there is a rich tradition of trinitarian doxologies that is taken up in the North-Elbian Lutheran Church edition of the current

---

[12] Cited from *Hymns for the Use of the Methodist Episcopal Church*, rev. ed. (New York: Nelson & Phillips, 1849; Cincinnati: Hitchcock & Walden, 1849) 682 (no. 1139).

[13] Cited from *Congregational Church Hymnal*, ed. George S. Barrett (London: Congregational Union of England and Wales, 1887) 589 (no. 734).

Evangelisches Gesangbuch (1994). Numbers 645–65 constitute a whole block of them ("*Gloria-Patri*-Strophen"), all basically in the coordinated form:

> Ehr sei dem Vater und dem Sohn
> und auch dem Heilgen Geist,
> wie es im Anfang war und nun,
> der uns sein Gnade leist!

The last line takes a soteriological turn ("who gives us his grace") that can become quite elaborate in other cases:

> Lob, Ehr und Preis in süssem Ton
> Gott Vater hoch im Himmelsthron
> von Herzen sei gesungen.
> Dem Heiland Christus, seinem Sohn:
> der lehr uns Gottes Willen tun,
> so ists uns wohlgelungen.
> Lob sei dem Heilgen Geist zugleich,
> der stärk uns in das Himmelreich
> und bring uns recht zusammen,
> dass wir Christus, den Gnadenschatz,
> finden zum Heil in Gotts Gesetz.
> Wer das begehrt, sprech: Amen.

Those two examples date from a Strasbourg collection of 1545, but the same kind of praise and prayer for salvation is found in several others borrowed from a Hanover collection of 1953. Thus:

> Lob, Ehr sei Gott im höchsten Throne,
> der uns als Vater je und je geliebt.
> Lob sei auch Christus, seinem Sohne,
> der sich für uns am Kreuz zum Opfer gibt.
> Lob sei allzeit dem werten Heilgen Geist,
> der uns in Nöten Trost und Hilf erweist.[14]

These doxologies are intended to be used either independently or attached to a hymn; at the conclusion of the hymn book (no. 961) a list of sixty-eight hymns is given that either end already with a trinitarian doxological stanza or may have one added to them.

2. Hymns On The Trinity And Trinitarian Hymns

Two types of hymns used in Protestant worship that glorify the Triune God may be differentiated: hymns on the Trinity—hymns written intentionally to delin-

---

[14] *Evangelisches Gesangbuch: Ausgabe für die Nordelbische Evangelisch-Lutherische Kirche* (Hamburg: Wittig, 1994; Kiel: Lutherische Verlagsgesellschaft, 1994) nos. 645, 648, 655.

eate trinitarian doctrine in verse, frequently laid out in four stanzas with each stanza in succession addressing the Father, Son, Holy Spirit, and the Triune Godhead; and trinitarian hymns—hymns which focus upon other dogmatic themes and only incidentally articulate trinitarian theology. An example in the latter category is a hymn by the eighteenth-century Anglican/Methodist hymnwriter Charles Wesley which has been in continuous use by British Methodists since the first publication of the text in 1746. In this hymn, glorification and sanctification are intermingled: praise is given to the Father who offered the remedy for human sin by the "sprinkled blood" of the Son; their mercy and efficacious work continue by the gift of the Spirit of "life, and power, and love."

> Father of everlasting grace,
> Thy goodness and thy truth we praise,
> Thy goodness and thy truth we prove;
> Thou hast, in honour of thy Son,
> The gift unspeakable sent down,
> The Spirit of life, and power, and love.
>
> Send us the Spirit of thy Son
> To make the depths of Godhead known,
> To make us share the life divine;
> Send him the sprinkled blood t'apply,
> Send him our souls to sanctify,
> And show and seal us ever thine.
>
> So shall we pray, and never cease,
> So shall we thankfully confess
> Thy wisdom, truth, and power, and love,
> With joy unspeakable adore,
> And bless, and praise thee evermore,
> And serve thee as thy hosts above.
>
> Till added to that heavenly choir
> We raise our songs of triumph higher,
> And praise thee in a bolder strain,
> Out-soar the first-born seraph's flight,
> And sing, with all our friends in light,
> Thy everlasting love to man.[15]

Hymns on the Trinity typically have been composed not only as doxology, but also as catechesis or apology. Anglican and Lutheran poets are predominantly the authors of these hymns; Presbyterians, Baptists, Methodists and other Protestants readily incorporated the Anglican and Lutheran texts into their respective hymn books, while their own hymn writers focused their hymns upon other themes. In

---

[15] *The Works of John Wesley,* vol. 7: *A Collection of Hymns for the Use of the People Called Methodists,* ed. Franz Hildebrandt and Oliver A. Beckerlegge (Nashville: Abingdon Press, 1983) 535 (no. 366).

addition to various trinitarian hymns, Charles Wesley produced two independent collections of hymns exclusively on the Trinity. The first, *Gloria Patri, &c. or Hymns to the Trinity* (1746), contains twenty-four hymns; twelve of the total are single-stanza tributes, several of which are reproduced in the doxology section of later Protestant hymnals. Wesley's second collection, *Hymns on the Trinity* (1767) is much larger—136 hymns with an addendum of fifty-two "Hymns and Prayers to the Trinity"—and was structured in four parts ("The Divinity of Christ," "The Divinity of the Holy Ghost," "The Plurality and Trinity of Persons," "The Trinity in Unity") following the organizing scheme of William Jones of Nayland's anti-Arian *The Catholic Doctrine of the Trinity* (1756).

Other Christian poets have been less prolific than Wesley in producing hymns on or to the Trinity; but some have included at least one distinctive Trinity hymn in their corpus of writings. Among nineteenth-century hymns must be counted Anglican bishop Reginald Heber's "Holy, Holy, Holy, Lord God Almighty," first published in 1827. Heber's text, originally composed as a hymn for Trinity Sunday, quickly became a Protestant standard. However, except for the phrase repeated in the last line of the first and fourth stanzas ("God in Three Persons, blessed Trinity!") and the thrice "holy" that begins each of the four stanzas (suggesting a trinitarian reading of the Sanctus), nothing else in the hymn distinguishes it as a hymn on the Trinity: the Persons are not named; their interrelationship is not defined; neither is their work confessed. Perhaps this was the key to its popularity; the Trinity as a Christian concept was affirmed in a hymn of praise, but the technicalities of doctrinal specificity are not attempted, thereby permitting a broad interpretation. Even the Unitarian Universalist Association found a place for Heber's hymn in their 1964 *Hymns for the Celebration of Life*, with the sole change that the overtly trinitarian concluding line is adjusted to "Who wert, and art, and evermore shalt be."

3. Ancient Heresies Revived?

In the twentieth century, short trinitarian doxologies and hymns on the Trinity have continued to be produced despite the concern in some quarters that advocacy of the doctrine of the Trinity creates a stumbling block in the dialogue between Christians and members of other world religions. Hymns articulating trinitarian belief, though not numerous, have been written especially after the 1970s, possibly for several reasons: as a reaction to the plethora of social gospel and social justice hymns that had been produced earlier in the century; and as a lyrical response to the rediscovery of the doctrine of the Trinity facilitated by the groundwork in neo-orthodox theology and carried out in the worship reforms encouraged by the Liturgical Movement. A hymn of four stanzas written in 1981 by Canadian Presbyterian Margaret Clarkson deliberately reexposes the soteriological significance of the economic Trinity:

> Praise, praise the Father, God of our salvation,
> Author of life, Creator of the spheres,

wellspring of love and fountainhead of mercy—
praised be his name throughout eternal years!

Praise, praise the Savior, God the Son incarnate,
sent to redeem a world by sin enslaved;
he gave his life that we might know salvation—
through Christ we break sin's bondage and are saved.

Praise, praise the Spirit, life of God within us,
Christ's gift to all who trust his saving Word;
he seals us sons, subdues our sinful natures,
makes us to grow in likeness to our Lord.

Praise, praise the Godhead, three in one supernal,
Maker, Redeemer, Power that makes us new;
come, sing to him glad songs of adoration—
give to the Lord the praise that is his due!

> Coda:We praise the Father, the Son, the Spirit,
> who loved us, bought us, made us his own;
> and when we see him face to face in glory
> we'll sing his praise before his holy throne![16]

But Clarkson's hymn, with its specificity regarding sin and redemption, and its explicit use of Father, Son, and Spirit, is unusual among late twentieth-century doxologies and hymns. The twentieth century has also given birth to theologies for which the starting point is God's actions of justice and liberation offered to the world and society. While the Social Gospel movement favored the address of "Father" as connoting the divine care for the entire human family, the perception by some Christians that the biblical and traditional Name for the First Person of the Godhead is a gendered term implying a male deity—thus suggesting females are not made in the *Imago Dei*—has caused a movement away from the use of "Father" in prayer and praise. The most pressing trinitarian problem thereby raised is the ambiguity resulting from the substitution for "Father" of the words "God" (as a simple synonym) or "Mother" (as a "balance" or "equivalent" to "Father"), or the use of a non-gendered metaphor. Admittedly, "God" can be used in the New Testament specifically for "the Father of our Lord Jesus Christ";[17] and "God" was used in lieu of "Father" in an eighteenth-century doxology attributed to Christopher Smart:

> To God, with the Lamb and the Dove,
> all honor and praise we commend.
> As is, was in truth, and in love,
> and shall be the world without end.[18]

---

[16] *100 Hymns of Hope* (Carol Stream, Ill.: Hope Publishing Company, 1992) no. 98.

[17] Karl Rahner, *"Theos* in the New Testament," *Theological Investigations*, vol. 1, trans. Cornelius Ernst (Baltimore: Helicon Press, 1961; London: Darton, Longman & Todd, 1961) 125-48.

[18] Cited from *Hymnal: A Worship Book* (Elgin, Ill.: Brethren Press, 1992; Newton, Kans.: Faith and Life Press, 1992; Scottdale, Pa.: Mennonite Publishing House, 1992) no. 125.

But in the late twentieth century, such a practice is becoming so common that the risk arises that "God" will be taken as designating *only* the First Person, thus making the Second and Third Persons less or other than "God"—Arianism redivivus!

Other doxological phrasings done to avoid the use of "Father" are also unwittingly reopening the door to theological interpretations once debated—and rejected—in the early centuries. The *Gloria Patri* regularly used at the Duke University Chapel, for example, in its functionalism smacks of Sabellianism:

> Glory be to our Creator,
> praise to our Redeemer Lord,
> glory be to our Sustainer,
> ever Three and ever One.
> As it was in the beginning,
> now and evermore shall be.

Protestant doxology is at a crossroads. Like the hymn writers of the past, Protestant poets today are willing to nuance the theological expression of doxology to meet the constraints—and opportunities—of conforming their text to a particular meter. But such a willingness to make changes in doxological formulation also sets up the possibility for theological misinterpretation. The words sung in Christian worship shape (or misshape) experience and belief. How, then, should trinitarian belief be expressed in an age of hypersensitivity to victimization and exploitation? One interesting attempt has been made through reliance on what was for Nicaea the secondary terminology of "light":

> God Almighty, Light creator,
> to thee laud and honor be;
> to thee, Light of Light begotten,
> praise be sung eternally;
> Holy Spirit, Light-revealer,
> glory, glory be to thee;
> mortals, angels, now and ever
> praise the Holy Trinity.[19]

Although the language of light derives from the Bible (Gen 1:3-5; John 1:4-5; 8:12; 1 Tim 6:16; cf. Heb 1:3), it is doubtful whether such hymnological use can remain genuinely scriptural and Nicene in the absence of the primary biblical and baptismal Name that Nicaea intended to clarify.[20]

---

[19] Cited from *A New Hymnal for Colleges and Schools*, ed. Jeffery Rowthorn and Russell Schulz-Widmar (New Haven and London: Yale University Press, 1992) no. 328.

[20] For a fuller discussion of the theological implications, see Geoffrey Wainwright, "The Doctrine of the Trinity: Where the Church Stands or Falls," *Interpretation* 45 (April 1991) 117–32; and Kathryn E. Greene-McCreight, "When I Say God, I Mean Father, Son and Holy Spirit: On the Ecumenical Baptismal Formula," *Pro Ecclesia* 6 (Summer 1997) 289–308.

9. Anglican Perspectives

"Somewhere Behind the World of Sensible Appearances": The Liturgy as Contextual, Devotional, Trinitarian, and Baptismal

Kenneth Stevenson

"Our theme concerns changes which have taken place somewhere be-hind the world of sensible appearances, but which are revealed both in cultural and artistic forms."[1]

In 1948, Jungmann published a lengthy review—just over seven pages—of Gregory Dix's masterpiece, *The Shape of the Liturgy*, which was published in 1945.[2] It is a sobering read, as one scholar evaluates the work of another across considerable distances of formation and allegiance. The Austrian Jesuit is clearly captivated by the work of the Anglican Benedictine. The reader only has to get as far as the second paragraph to realise that Jungmann grasped the significance of Dix's work; he distinguished between the Dix who is ready to explain evolution of the eucharist across the centuries, and the Dix who is at pains to address himself to the debates about liturgical revision going on in the Church of England at the time.

Since then, of course, a great deal has happened. Roman Catholic and Angli-can worship have changed—almost beyond recognition. The Second Vatican Council inaugurated a revision of the services of the Catholic Church, and a whole welter of service books have been issued throughout the worldwide Angli-can Communion, and many other churches as well. In many ways, Jungmann and Dix represent similar generations and temperaments, the only difference being that Dix himself died of cancer at the age of 51 in 1952, whereas Jungmann died of a ripe old age in 1975 and was therefore able to take part in and see the results of the great ferment in liturgical study that has been so much part of the twentieth century.

---

[1] J. A. Jungmann, "The Defeat of Teutonic Arianism and The Revolution in Religious Culture in the Early Middle Ages," in *Pastoral Liturgy* (London: Challoner 1962) 2.

[2] Gregory Dix, *The Shape of the Liturgy* (London: Dacre, 1945); reviewed by Jungmann in *Zeitschrift für Katcholische Theologie* 70 (1948) 224–31; see also Kenneth Stevenson, *Gregory Dix—25 Years On* (Grove Liturgical Study 10) (Bramcote: Grove, 1977) 23–35.

Both Jungmann and Dix grasped that liturgy cannot properly change "from above." As Dix himself remarked at the end of his book, "the depth and breadth and allusiveness of the classical rites come just from this, that their real author is always the worshipping church . . . not any individual however holy and gifted, any committee however representative, or any legislator however wise . . . the good liturgies were not written; they grew."[3] Such a remark complements Jungmann's own conviction that "liturgical science . . . may well prepare the way for reforming, may advance proposals well grounded in history and theology, but it cannot infuse life."[4]

It is the purpose of the following brief reflections to extrapolate from Jungmann's essay four important aspects of worship and theology and apply them to the Anglican Prayer Book inheritance in the first instance and then more briefly to look at the recent era of liturgical renewal. These are: the environment of the celebration of the Eucharist, the role of devotional prayer in the liturgy, the Trinity and the baptism of Christ, and what Jungmann himself describes as "appreciation of baptism."

1. The Environment of the Eucharist

One of the developments that fascinates Jungmann is the change from the corporate "basilican" Eucharist of the patristic era into the Carolingian side-altar Mass. He concentrates on this (with approbation) in his review of Dix, although he does not wholeheartedly endorse Dix's theory of the development of the Eucharist in the famous "three strata."[5] Nevertheless, it is accepted that for the majority of worshipping Christians throughout the later Middle Ages, the normal eucharistic diet was this low Mass, whether or not embellished by a sermon or vernacular devotions.

In the first English Prayer Books, we see a more composite dynamic at work.[6] In 1549, the celebrant is assisted by ministers who are, effectively, deacon and subdeacon, and who read the gospel and the epistle. The three are to stand at the altar, arrayed in some of the traditional vestments, namely alb and chasuble (or a cope is allowed instead), and alb and tunicle. The 1549 rite has all the marks of a revision, not of the low Mass, but of the high Mass. It is celebrated with the ministers facing eastward, after the recitation of morning prayer. There is an *introit* psalm. And the traditional chants of the ordinary of the Mass are to be sung by the clerks, i.e. the choir. There are many indications of the Reformation, not least that the service is in the mother tongue, that the liturgy of the Mass is considerably simplified and altered, and that there must be a sermon.

---

[3] Dix, *The Shape of the Liturgy,* 718f.

[4] Jungmann, 101.

[5] Dix, *The Shape of the Liturgy,* 434ff.

[6] See comparative texts in F. E. Brightman, *The English Rite* (vol. II) (London: Rivingtons, 1915) 638ff; see also Horton Davies, *Worship and Theology in England; from Cranmer to Hooker, 1534–1603* (Princeton: University Press, 1970) 165ff; and Davies, *Worship and Theology in England: from Andrewes to Baxter and Fox, 1603–1690* (Princeton: University Press, 1975) 286ff., 329ff.

When it comes to 1552, a more radical series of changes takes place. The environment of the eucharist is no longer that of a reformed capitular Mass in English. Now there is one clergyman, habited only in a surplice, and standing at the north side of a table set up in the chancel, around which the communicants gather; and the service is said throughout. Moreover, that Reformation corrective which placed emphasis on faithful reception of the sacrament finds expression in the order in which the eucharistic part of the service is framed. The communicants receive the bread and the wine immediately after the words of Christ are recited, for the eucharistic prayer which had survived into 1549 is now divided up into thanksgiving, prayer of approach, consecration, act of Communion, Lord's prayer, and prayer of self oblation or prayer of thanksgiving.

Many have been the attempts to discern what Cranmer thought he was doing. From an environmental point of view, the shift from Latin Mass to 1549 through to 1552 is a clear one. 1549 is indeed an adapted capitular Mass but 1552 is by contrast the low Mass, now audible and aggressively corporate, and—something unheard of in the Middle Ages—requiring communicants with the priest. It was this latter stipulation that really went against the grain of occasional lay communion at the time. It resulted in infrequent Eucharists, so that many Sunday morning services consisted of the Prayer Book Morning Prayer followed by the first part of the Eucharist, often called "Ante-communion, except where there was a definite drive towards the weekly Eucharist, as (for example) after the Restoration in 1660.

The tug-of-war between the more conservative ethos of 1549 and the more Protestant one of 1552 is a complex story in Anglicanism.[7] By the time of the 1662 Prayer Book, much water had flowed under the liturgical bridge. What we have in the 1662 service is the 1552 rite, but with careful editorial touches to indicate that important drift in sacramental theology among the seventeenth century divines— some of whom we shall look at later on—which insisted that the Anglican Eucharist was indeed a Reformed Catholic liturgy, in which the bread and the wine are consecrated, and the sacrifice of praise and thanksgiving offered through Christ, the great High Priest.[8] King James I and King Charles I did their best through loyal archbishops and bishops to move those communion tables back against the east end of their churches and to rail them off, thus demarcating the sanctuary as sacred space.

The Restoration of the monarchy in 1660 saw a perceptible drive towards greater reverence and frequency of the sacrament of the Eucharist, not just in cathedrals, and this can be seen in the architecture of the period. For after the Great Fire of London in 1666, new churches were built which give due prominence to the centrality of the altar at the east end, whilst at the same time acknowledging the

---

[7] See G. J. Cuming, *A History of Anglican Liturgy* (2nd. edn.) (London: Macmillan, 1982) 45ff; and see C. O. Buchanan, *What Did Cranmer Think He Was Doing?* (Grove Liturgical Study 7) (Bramcote: Grove, 1976).

[8] See Kenneth Stevenson, *Covenant of Grace Renewed: A Vision of the Eucharist in the Seventeenth Century* (London: Darton Longman and Todd, 1994).

place of the pulpit and reading desk and lectern, often built together in what is sometimes called the "three-decker" style. Those responsible for the production of the 1662 Prayer Book were perhaps unable (or not minded) to bring back the actual text of the 1549 book, but in environmental terms, their Eucharist bears all the signs of that collegiate celebration, with vested clergy, and a laity nourished by such manuals of devotion as Simon Patrick's *Mensa Mystica*.[9]

2. Jungmann Makes Much of the History of Prayer Addressed to Christ[10]

Whilst some of his conclusions have been questioned, there can be no doubt that devotional prayers to Christ became more frequent in the liturgy and outside it, as the Middle Ages progressed. For Jungmann, it is the ascended Christ who recedes from the scene as the Middle Ages progress, because the Trinity takes over the glory of the ascended Christ, and devotion to the crucified figure in his passion moves on to centre-stage.[11] But it is Dix who identifies this "third stratum" of devotional prayers which provide the liturgical background for the celebrant at the side-altar Mass; and this genre of piety is also reflected in the vernacular devotions, such as (in England) Langforde's Meditations, which date from the fifteenth century.[12]

How far the Reformation was continuous and how far discontinuous with the Middle Ages has long been a matter of debate. There is, however, one particular prayer written by Thomas Cranmer directed to be recited by the priest before communion which owes a great deal in *genre* both to the devotional prayers of the priest and to the vernacular devotions of the congregation. Here is the text:

> We do not presume to come to this thy Table (O merciful Lord) trusting in our own righteousness, but in thy manifold, and great mercies. We are not worthy so much as to gather up the crumbs under thy Table. But thou art the same Lord, whose property is always to have mercy; grant us therefore gracious Lord, so to eat the flesh of thy dear son, Jesus Christ, and to drink his blood, that our sinful bodies may be made clean by his body, and our souls washed through his most precious blood, and that we may ever more dwell in him, and he in us.[13]

The prayer is full of biblical allusions, particularly from the encounter between Jesus and the Canaanite woman: "yes, Lord, yet even the dogs eat the crumbs that fall from their master's table" (Matt 15:27). But where did Cranmer find inspira-

[9] On Simon Patrick, see Stevenson, *Covenant of Grace Renewed*, 149ff; see also Stevenson, "*The Mensa Mystica* of Simon Patrick (1626–1707); A Case Study in Restoration Eucharistic Piety," in Nathan Mitchell, John F. Baldovin, S.J., eds., *Rule of Prayer, Rule of Faith: Essays in Honor of Aidan Kavanagh, O.S.B.* (A Pueblo Book) (Collegeville: The Liturgical Press, 1996) 161–99.

[10] See, for example, Balthasar Fischer's Foreword to the second English edition of J. A. Jungmann, *The Place of Christ and Liturgical Prayer* (London: Chapman, 1989) ixf.

[11] Jungmann, 48.

[12] See above n.5.

[13] See text in Brightman, *The English Rite*, 691; see p. 700 for the 1549 text, which was felicitously edited in 1552.

tion for this prayer? As Archbishop of Canterbury and a lover of history he will have known well the prayers of his predecessor St. Anselm, which had a wide circulation throughout the later Middle Ages. In Anselm's "prayer before receiving the body and blood of Christ," there is a central section which was without doubt Cranmer's main source:

> Lord, acknowledge that I am far from worthy to approach and touch this sacrament: but I trust in that mercy which caused you to lay down your life for sinners that they might be justified, and because you gave yourself willingly as a holy sacrifice to the Father. A sinner, I presume to receive these gifts so that I may be justified by them. I beg and pray you, therefore, merciful lover of men, let not that which you have given for the cleansing of sins be unto me the increase of sin, but rather for forgiveness and protection.[14]

Subtle shifts of eucharistic theology are discernible from the Anselm original to Cranmer's new composition. But the liturgical styles are indeed similar. Anselm's prayer was written as a private devotion, probably for use when he himself was the celebrant. Cranmer's prayer, on the other hand, was written to be said aloud, by the priest, on behalf of the communicants. In historical terms, Anselm could have done none other than write a private prayer for himself, and Cranmer could only have written a corporate prayer in that style. But both prayers demonstrate the importance of "affective" piety, which does not fit into any of the set rules of the classical prayers of the patristic period. However, that must not disqualify either composition from the euchology of the Church Catholic.

3. The Baptism of Christ and the Trinity

Jungmann makes much of the doctrine of the Trinity and its effect on liturgy and piety. At the end of the eighth century, Alcuin of York wrote the prayers for the Mass of the Trinity which were the germ of the much later Feast of the Trinity.[15] Jungmann even suggests that the baptism of Christ becomes perhaps the most frequent event in Christ's life for the work of the artist, but more to represent the Trinity than the baptism of Christ.[16] The Prayer Book tradition retains the Feast of Trinity Sunday, with Alcuin's Collect and the old preface translated into English.

The trinitarian theology of the Reformers has been a long neglected area of study.[17] This is no less true of liturgy; for example, Luther's hymn on the baptism

---

[14] See *The Prayers and Meditations of St. Anselm with the Proslogion* (Translated with an introduction by Sister Benedicta Ward, S.L.G.) (London: Penguin Books, 1973) 100. I am indebted to Henry Chadwick for drawing my attention to this.

[15] On the development of the Feast of the Trinity, C. P. Browe, "Zur Geschichte des Dreifaltigkeitsfeste," *Archiv für Liturgiewissenschaft* 1 (1959) 65–81; see also Kenneth Stevenson, *Handing On: Borderlands of Worship and Tradition* (London: Darton Longman and Todd, 1996) 41ff., and 136 n.9.

[16] Jungmann, 38.

[17] See, for example, Christophe Schwöbel, "The Triune God of Grace: Trinitarian Thinking in the Theology of the Reformers," in James M. Byrne, ed., *The Christian Understanding of God Today:*

of Christ, *Christ unser Herr zum Jordan kam* takes an almost patristic view of the narrative of Christ at the Jordan, and from that starting point depicts the Trinity manifested there; but the hymn is essentially one about baptism.[18] Cranmer was not able to reintroduce the baptismal dimension of the Feast of the Epiphany; but the seventeenth century Anglican divines were sufficiently read in the Fathers to build on what Luther had begun and used the earlier traditions of the church to great advantage. For example, Lancelot Andrewes (1555–1626) as bishop of Ely preached before the court of King James I at Pentecost 1615 on the Lucan narrative of Christ's baptism (Luke 3:21-22). After a distinguished career at Cambridge, as a theologian and a preacher, Andrewes became dean of Westminster in 1601, and so took part in the funeral of Queen Elizabeth I and the coronation of King James I. He was probably the most brilliant preacher of his age. The sermon is a rich iconographic sweep in which there is no doubt whatever that the scene of Christ's baptism is *our* baptism as well. One of Andrewes' devices near the start of some of his sermons is to draw the Trinity into the text if he possibly can. This sermon is no exception: ". . . for here is the whole Trinity in person. The Son in the water, the Holy Ghost in the dove, the Father in the voice." Only three years before in another Whitsun sermon, he used the same conceit, "the Father in the voice, the Son in the flood, the Holy Ghost in the shape of a dove." But perhaps his most vivid and overtly baptismal image comes in the 1621 Whitsun sermon: "the Father, the Fountain; the Son, the Cistern: the Holy Ghost, the Conduit-pipe, or pipes, rather (for they are many) behind through which they are derived down to us."[19]

Andrewes' influence on the seventeenth-century English scene was a considerable one. His sermons were collected and published after his death. They have been read and sifted in the period since. Nicholas Lossky, the Russian Orthodox theologian, has made a significant ecumenical contribution to the study of Andrewes and likens him to the patristic bishop-teacher of old.[20]

Of the great writers and preachers of the later seventeenth century two in particular stand in the Andrewes tradition. The first is Jeremy Taylor (1613–1667), whose *Great Exemplar* (1649) was the first devotional life of Christ of its kind ever published. Taylor was one of the most prolific devotional writers of his time, and

---

Theological Colloquium on the Occasion of the 400th Anniversary of the Foundation of Trinity College, Dublin (Dublin: Columba Press, 1993) 49–64.

[18] *Evangelisches Kirchengesangbuch* (Hannover) no.160.

[19] See *Ninety-Six Sermons by Lancelot Andrewes* (vol. 3) (Library of Anglo-Catholic Theology) (Oxford: Parker, 1841) 185, 242, and 361f. See also Kenneth Stevenson, *Covenant of Grace Renewed*, 39–66; Stevenson, *Handing On*, 66–82, and Stevenson, "Human Nature Honoured; Absolution in Lancelot Andrewes," in Martin Dudley, ed., *Like a Two-Edged Sword: The Word of God in Liturgy and History: Essays in Honour of Canon Donald Gray* (Norwich: Canterbury Press, 1995) 113–38. See also A. M. Allchin, "Lancelot Andrewes" in Geoffrey Rowell, ed., *The English Religious Tradition and the Genius of Anglicanism* (Wantage: Ikon Books, 1992) 145–64.

[20] See Nicholas Lossky, *Lancelot Andrewes The Preacher (1555–1626); The Origins of the Mystical Theology of the Church of England* (Oxford: Clarendon Press 1991).

became bishop of Down, Connor and Dromore in Ireland after the Restoration. His reflections on Christ's baptism are luscious and inclusive and at times read like an extended improvisation on Andrewes' 1615 Whitsun sermon! Christ's baptism and our baptism are the main priority and the Trinity appears in baptismal reality: "and this was the greatest meeting that ever was upon earth, where the whole cabinet of the mysterious Trinity was opened and shown, as much as the capacities of our present imperfections will permit. . ."[21]

Herbert Thorndike (1598–1672), Cambridge theologian who became a canon of Westminster Abbey at the Restoration, was a prolific writer who almost outstrips Taylor in regarding conciseness as a vice. Among the Thorndike manuscripts in the Muniment Room at Westminster Abbey is an incomplete sermon for the Feast of the Epiphany using the Lucan narrative of Christ's baptism as the text—as Andrewes did. It begins thus: "The Festival of the Epiphany, that is the manifestation of Christ Jesus in our flesh, in the glory of his Godhead, the most glorious manifestation of it is this, at his baptism. For the nature, honour and glory of his Father so appeared, when a voice was brought from the most excellent glory, saying "thou art my beloved Son in whom I am well pleased'. . ."[22]

In these three writers (and others like them), we can see a determination to bring the baptism of Christ into the forefront of trinitarian theology and experience through a creative use of tradition. Its corollary is, surely, the centrality of baptism itself. To that we must now turn.

4. The Appreciation of Baptism

Jungmann looks at the Christian past and laments the paltry place which baptism holds in the piety of ordinary people. "Appreciation of baptism . . . seems to have vanished. Men seem to be preoccupied with clinging to moral goodness, with attaining a moral heroism raising them well above the average."[23]

Things have changed little across the centuries! But the Prayer Book represents a significant attempt to redress this balance—at least in aspiration.[24] There are two baptism rites, public and private, which describe in contextual terms what the mediaeval rites described as the baptism of children and the baptism of the sick. The service should be administered on Sundays and other holy days "when the most number of people come together"; and so that "every man present may be put in remembrance of his own profession, made to God in his baptism." It was not

---

[21] *The Whole Works of the Rt. Revd. Jeremy Taylor* (ed. Reginald Heber) (London: Rivingtons, 1828) (Vol. II) p.185 (Section IX.iii). See also Henry McAdoo, *First of Its Kind: Jeremy Taylor's Life of Christ, A Study in the Functioning of a Moral Theology* (Norwich: Canterbury Press, 1994).

[22] See Westminster Abbey Th.MS.3/045 p.1; on Thorndike, see also Stevenson, *Covenant of Grace Renewed*, 139ff.; and Kenneth Stevenson, *The Mystery of Baptism in the Anglican Tradition* (Norwich: Canterbury Press, 1998) 139ff.

[23] Jungmann, 62.

[24] See comparative texts in Brightman, *The English Rite*, 724ff.

until 1662 that a further rite for the baptism of those "of riper years" was added, for use in the colonies (!), and to baptise those who had been discouraged from being brought forward during the Commonwealth.

But how were these new provisions actually reflected on and taught? Richard Hooker (1554–1600) is probably one of the founding fathers of Anglicanism, who was often held up as the model of the scholar country parish priest. In the fifth book of his *Laws of Ecclesiastical Polity*[25] he stresses again and again the importance of baptism in the life of the Christian; and although in the Prayer Book the Eucharist precedes baptism, Hooker reverses this order because for him the Christian life starts at the font. In combating Puritan objections to the Sign of the Cross—the *only* such sign left in the 1552 Prayer Book—he insists that it is a sign of Christian faith and a memorial of the central act of redemption in the life of the believer.

But it is perhaps George Herbert (1593–1633) who gives us the most pastoral dimension to baptismal teaching. Like Hooker, Herbert was also a country priest, who was best known for his poetry. However, in his *Priest to the Temple* (1632), which was one of the few handbooks for priests published during the seventeenth century, Herbert insists that the parson should be dressed in white—the white surplice—because of the importance of the occasion; we need to remember that *any* vestment had to be defended in the atmosphere of Puritan opposition. Baptism is to take place on Sundays or festivals because it is a corporate occasion. Names are to be chosen for serious reasons and should not be trivial or meaningless. The service should be prayed in a reverent manner; and in this connection, Herbert singles out the prayer in the service which gives thanks for the providence of God in bringing the congregation to the point of baptism. The priest "willingly and cheerfully makes the signing of the cross," because he sees some considerable point in the exercise. Godparents are to be instructed on their duties and they do so in God's presence, in the communion of saints, and in the strength which only God can give; they do not exist in isolation. Finally, "he adviseth all to call to mind their baptism often," because baptism is central and it marks the beginning of the Christian life. One of the ways of calling to mind one's baptism is to be present at someone else's and Herbert at this point repeats those three words, "their baptism often."[26]

Another important theological and devotional writer was Simon Patrick (1626–1707) who as a parish priest preached a sermon on baptism in 1658 which was subsequently expanded and published as his first work entitled *Aqua Genitalis*, and which continued to be reprinted, after he became a bishop in 1689.[27]

---

[25] Richard Hooker, *Laws of Ecclesiastical Polity* V 58–66; see also Stevenson, *The Mystery of Baptism in the Anglican Tradition*, 37ff.

[26] *The English Poems of George Herbert with A Priest to the Temple* (The Ancient and Modern Library of Theological Literature) (London: Griffith, Farran, Oakden and Welsh, n.d.) 212f; see also Stevenson, *The Mystery of Baptism in the Anglican Tradition*, 68ff.

[27] See Alexander Taylor, ed., *The Works of Simon Patrick D.D. Including His Autobiography* (Oxford: University Press, 1858) (vol. I) 65ff; see also Stevenson, *The Mystery of Baptism in the Anglican Tradition*, 125ff.

Patrick was writing during the time of the Commonwealth when the Prayer Book was proscribed, but it is easy to see the theology of the Prayer Book at work between the lines. Sacraments are important from a psychological point-of-view ("rhythms which make a pretty noise or jingle are sooner fixed in peoples' minds than words and prose"). But they are also important because of what they do for the divine economy (baptism is "the sacrament of regeneration, or the second birth"). His discussion of the symbolism of water would do justice to a modern anthropologist. Adapting the covenant theology which was increasingly popular in the seventeenth century, he states that "to be baptised expresses something on our part, and something on God's; both which put together make of it a federal rite, wherewith we and God enter into a covenant and agreement together. . ." But Patrick is clear that baptism is both an event and a process, for in baptism God "admits us into that covenant of grace which accepts of repentance instead of innocence, and of amendment of life instead of unerring obedience." Here is the real heart of any lasting discussion of baptism. Patrick and the other Anglican divines see the dangers for theology as well as piety in an understanding of baptism which is exclusively objective or subjective. The two belong together. The Church acts, and the believer faithfully receives.

But what of the present? None of the issues so far touched upon have evaded the Anglican agenda, nor (one suspects) other churches. We are still struggling with the need for an *environment* which is truly authentic. Jungmann looked back to a rich patristic past which had become overladen with an understanding of the liturgical experience which was increasingly individualistic. The Prayer Book inheritance both built on that late mediaeval scene and tried hard to construct a more corporatist and flexible approach. From the seventeenth century to the middle of the nineteenth, most Anglican celebrants stood at the north end of the altar, both presiding over the worship of God's people and inviting them to participate at the holy table.

Such a position survives still in parts of the Anglican world not only as a relic of the past but as an indication that the real celebrant of the Eucharist is not the priest but Christ himself. From the middle of the nineteenth century, there was an increasing tendency for the celebrant to adopt the traditional eastward position, which (after all) is what was laid down in the 1549 Prayer Book. That particular approach means that all God's people face the same way in offering the eucharistic memorial until the coming of Christ. Then in more recent years Anglicans have increasingly followed the fashion of celebrating from behind the altar, gathering God's people around the table together. Not as primitive as some of its protagonists would have us believe, this "ecumenical" approach has helped to draw different Christian traditions together in a way that would have been unthinkable fifty or sixty years ago.

But the precise position of the celebrant, important as it obviously is, cannot at the end of the day, be of ultimate significance. "Somewhere behind the world of sensible appearances" there are subtle moves that require significant adaptation for a Eucharist on the grand scale in a cathedral, or on a Sunday morning in a parish context, or in those important (and sometimes undervalued) side-altar Eucharists that continue to nourish the lives of many Christians today. [28] We need a religious imagination that grasps what needs to be grasped "behind the world of sensible appearances" and to do so with "reverence and godly fear" (to quote from the Prayer Book). Many modern rites function reasonably well but they start and end badly, largely because they do so abruptly and without engaging with the ordinary prayers of God's people. We cannot spend all our time constructing liturgies but we do need some rules of thumb about how to adapt authentically.

Secondly, the relationship between liturgical and popular piety has never been entirely straightforward and this is still true today, despite the welter of fine and laudable new service books. For example, the prayer which Cranmer wrote which begins "we do not presume to come to this thy table. . ." was directed to be said in the Prayer Book by the priest on behalf of the communicants. About forty years ago many clergy started to invite the whole congregation to recite this prayer; this has resulted in some understandable resistance on the part of the people of God to surrender a much-loved prayer in the face of those with high ideals who cannot seem to find a place for it in the slick, stripped down liturgies of today![29] Perhaps its proper place is immediately before Communion. But for all the fine Eucharistic Prayers that have been written this century, this particular prayer expresses what many Anglicans *feel* as they approach the altar of God.

Thirdly, much of the work in recent years by theologians on the doctrine of the Trinity has some important parallels among the Anglican divines.[30] Andrewes uses the narrative of the baptism of Christ in a way that draws the people of God into that story. Christ's baptism is *our* baptism, alongside all the people of God. Father, Son and Holy Spirit have distinct but overlapping functions but it is always the whole Trinity that relates to us. This is why Andrewes is so trinitarian in his theology, and he is followed by Jeremy Taylor and Herbert Thorndike. The Trinity is not a problem to solve or a difficult part of the inheritance with which the Christian Church is lumbered. It becomes a way of speaking about God in vivid and pictorial terms. Modern iconography of the Trinity—which is taken increasingly seriously by theologians—relies not only on the three angels visiting Abraham and Sarah as depicted by the famous Russian icon painter Rublev. We are also turning our attention to icons of the baptism of Christ. For example, a few years ago the

[28] See Kenneth Stevenson, "Soft Points in the Eucharist," in Michael Perham (ed.) *Liturgy for a New Century: Further Essays for the Revision of the Alternative Service Book* (London: SPCK, 1991) 29–44.

[29] See *The Alternative Service Book 1980,* 128, 188. Interestingly, it is only retained as optional in the traditional language version of the Eucharist in *The Book of Common Prayer* (New York: Church Hymnal Corporation, 1979) 337.

[30] See, for example, Kilian McDonnell, O.S.B., *Jesus' Baptism in the Jordan: The Trinitarian and Cosmic Order of Salvation* (Collegeville: The Liturgical Press, 1996).

parish of Holy Trinity, Guildford, which I served as rector, commissioned an 8ft. x 4ft. icon of the baptism of Christ to stand behind the font in a large, spacious eighteenth-century interior. The Anglican monk who made the icon—and the congregation who commissioned it—relied on Andrewes' famous dictum, "for here the whole Trinity in person. The Son in the water, the Holy Ghost in the dove, the Father in the voice."

Finally, the radical character of modern baptism rites—in some ways infinitely more innovative than those of the Eucharist—demonstrates that for many of the Churches today baptism is the sacrament which is becoming more and more central.[31] Anglicans and others have in recent centuries used one or other of the narratives of Jesus and the children as a warrant for baptism. But lectionaries nowadays provide a much greater choice. It is now possible to hear the narrative of Christ's baptism as *our* narrative also. Jeremy Taylor in his "underground" Commonwealth liturgy (1658) directs this narrative to be read at baptism and he is almost unique—even prophetic—in this.[32] Like many of the seventeenth century divines, so much liturgical renewal of our own time has sought to unlock the riches of the past and to *adapt* them to a different world. But we are still wrestling with the relationship between baptism as event and process—and rightly so.

Meanwhile, liturgies will continue to shift, change and evolve, and respond to different kinds of pressures, as men and women continue to reflect on how God and their lives meet. Jungmann knew the limitations of the science of liturgical studies and was a devout enough realist to accept that God is quite capable of acting in spite of as well as because of his Church, "somewhere behind the world of sensible appearances." Jungmann's genuine humility in the face of the inheritance of the past and the possibilities of the future—in all its cultural forms—is indeed a lesson that many may rightly heed today.

[31] The Literature on the subject is prodigious; see in particular Aidan Kavanagh, *The Shape of Baptism: The Rite of Christian Initiation* (New York: Pueblo, 1978).

[32] On the Armenian rite's use of the narrative see Gabriele Winkler, *Das Armenische Initiationsrituale* (Orientalia Christiana Analecta 217) (Rome: Pont. Institutum Studiorum Orientalium, 1982) 452.

10. Eastern Catholic Perspectives

Jungmann's Challenge and the Churches of the East

Peter E. Fink, S.J.

The work of Josef Jungmann which inspires the essays in this book is about defeat and revolution on the one hand, and about restoration and challenge on the other. "The Defeat of Teutonic Arianism," which his title announces, is about a radical shift in piety and religious culture from a time when worship was corporate and public to a time of silence, of mystery, of clerical control and of the withdrawal of the people from most, if not all, participation.[1] The challenge which it poses to the contemporary Church is a restoration, the return of worship to its proper nature as the Church gathered with Christ its Head in Christ's own worship of God and Christ's own saving action for the world.[2]

Jungmann's primary concern is the shift that took place in the West. His challenge, therefore, is primarily addressed to the West. His starting point is the enormous gap between the death of Gregory the Great (ca. 604 C.E.) and the time of St. Bernard (twelfth century). On the one hand, he recognized that during this sizeable gap "no important compendium of spiritual teaching appears to have been written."[3] On the other hand, he knew that "no period has ever seen a greater revolution in religious thought and institutions than that which took place in the five centuries between the close of the patristic age and the dawn of scholasticism."[4] He was particularly concerned how the early Christian liturgies, with their emphasis on the objective deeds of God, and especially the resurrection of Jesus Christ, had yielded to a more subjective and transient way of thinking. In the course of time the liturgy had become passively received, given over primarily to the priests while the people's own piety began to focus elsewhere than the liturgy. The populace was concerned with sin, human unworthiness, and the person of Christ the Divine One

---

[1] Josef A. Jungmann, "The Defeat of Teutonic Arianism and the Revolution in Religious Culture in the Early Middle Ages," in *Pastoral Liturgy* (New York: Herder and Herder, 1962) 1–101; here, 2–3.

[2] Constitution on the Sacred Liturgy, 7.

[3] Jungmann, 1.

[4] Ibid.

who has sacrificed all and saved us.[5] Jungmann's exploration of this shift is at the same time a source of challenge for the contemporary Church.

This particular essay stands somewhat on the fringe of Jungmann's own concern. He was exploring the revolution in the West and the challenge that is required in the contemporary West. The question here is with the Churches of the East. Simply put, does the challenge of Jungmann also apply here? A word from Vatican II might guide us: "Among these principles and norms there are some which can and should be applied both to the Roman rite and also to all other rites. The practical norms which follow, however, should be taken as pertaining only to the Roman rite, except for those which, in the nature of things, affect other rites as well."[6]

Jungmann made two major references to the East. His first, at the beginning of his essay, was to see if a parallel could be drawn between the revolution in the West and something similar in the East.[7] His second, dealing with liturgical language, referred to the contemporary Churches, and the efforts to move into local vernaculars in contrast to traditional liturgical languages. Behind the second he notes two principles: (a) a clarification and enlivening of liturgical forms, and (b) a preaching of the faith which matches the spirit of the liturgy.[8] Deeper still, he is echoing a fundamental principle of the Constitution on the Sacred Liturgy, that "texts and rites should be drawn up so that they express more clearly the holy things which they signify" and that the Christian people "should be able to understand them with ease and to take part in them fully, actively, and as befits a community."[9]

As for the first, Jungmann knew that many elements of the Western liturgies had their origin in the East. He notes, for example, the importance of Epiphany, the *Trisagion*, the Kiss of Peace before the consecration and the preference for the litany form of prayer, *Kyrie eleison*. Jungmann discovers the parallel he is looking for when he compares the Byzantine communion prayers with corresponding Greek prayers of the fourth century. Christ, who was once "the Mediator" has become "Christ, our God." He discovers also that the Church, the people of the New Creation, have become instead a people who are sinful and unworthy. In East as in West, the pattern holds: the humanity of Christ was lost sight of, and only his divinity has become important. And the people themselves are shadowed in their own humanity by the majesty of Christ the Divine.

Looking from the contemporary Church, Jungmann's reference to the East is quite narrow. His is looking at the emergence of the Byzantine rite from earlier Greek liturgies. The movement toward the divinization of Christ which Jungmann notes is a small part of the evolution of the rite from the presence of Christ *here within the ritual*, as Cyril of Jerusalem and Theodore of Mopsuestia proclaimed it,

---

[5] Jungmann, 3–8.

[6] Constitution on the Sacred Liturgy, 3.

[7] Jungmann, 9–15.

[8] Jungmann, 98.

[9] Constitution on the Sacred Liturgy, 21.

to the presence of Christ *in his heavenly worship*, as reported by Maximus the Confessor.[10] The Byzantine Church did move in its own way from a bias toward the human Christ to a bias toward the divine Christ, and that movement was indeed in parallel with the Churches of the West.

Jungmann did not take much notice, however, of the full richness of the East. The Nestorian East Syrian Church, for example, emerged as diophysites rather than monophysites from the early Christological controversies. The movement from the human to the divine, if they had one, would not follow the same route. The Alexandrian tradition, to cite another, emerged as monophysites, but with a bias in favor of the divine, not the human. Their movement would not follow the same path either. This is important when we look to the challenge Jungmann might offer to the contemporary East. The Byzantine tradition has done very little by way of liturgical reform. Other Churches of the East have been far more successful in heeding Jungmann's challenge.

As for the second, when Jungmann reflects on liturgical language, he turns once again to the East. He recognizes that the language of the liturgy is one of the things people discuss when changes in liturgy are considered, and he cites Patriarch Balsamon (ca. 1190) that those who do not understand Greek are to celebrate the liturgy in their own language.[11] His effort is to show how the liturgy is and should always be the action of the living Church, and language is a part of it. But he does note, however, how even in the East once local languages became "liturgical languages," and remained so even when they were no longer living languages of the people.

But we return to the fact that Jungmann's interest is in the liturgy of Rome and his hope, offered before him by Anton Baumstark,[12] is that the Roman rite would finally embrace the vernacular languages of the day. Language is a first issue of liturgical inculturation. But it is not the most important one. Jungmann and Baumstark were both concerned to get issues of the vernacular "out of the way," so that the more important issues of liturgical reform could be faced. Jungmann names the final challenge: "how to make palatable to modern man the religious modes of thought and manners of speech which were crystallized 1500 years ago."[13]

As mentioned above, Jungmann gave two directions for the restoration and reform of liturgy. The first is the clarification and the enlivening of liturgical forms. Ancient texts and symbols are not always useful to engage people of another time and place. How the liturgy adjusts itself to new people and a new time is one important task. The second involves a match between the preaching of the faith and

---

[10] The excellent study by *The Byzantine Liturgy,* trans. M. O'Connell (New York: Pueblo, 1986; orig. *Die byzantinische Liturgie*, Trier, 1980) by Hans-Joachim Schultz fully supports Jungmann's position on this point.

[11] Jungmann, 97.

[12] Baumstark said in a 1927 conversation: "I shall not see the day when the liturgical movement reaches its goal." Noted in Jungmann, 98.

[13] Jungmann, 98.

the liturgy itself. This is even more important because liturgy has, we have discovered once again, its own way of thinking and being. It is not something to which one brings one's own pious thoughts and imposes them upon the liturgy. As Aidan Kavanagh has clearly pointed out, liturgy makes sense, formulates its own statements of faith and seeks to educate and form the people into its own spiritual ways.[14] But as Jungmann speaks, he is concerned with the liturgy of the West. He consults the East, but has little to say himself to challenge the East. The East serves as a useful parallel to make several points. But it is not clear that the principles he articulates are directed to the East whose liturgies have their own history, variety and forms of evolution.

The Constitution on the Sacred Liturgy

When Vatican II issued *Sacrosanctum Concilium* at the end of 1963, a greater connection between the liturgy of the West and the liturgies of the East was articulated. The primary aim of the Constitution already noted was reform and renewal of the liturgy in the West. However, from its very beginning, the Constitution addressed the liturgies of the East when it spoke on the level of principle and norm. "Among these principles and norms there are some which can and should be applied both to the Roman rite and also to all the other rites."[15] There are some elements of the decree that concern the liturgy itself, regardless of which ritual form is enacted to celebrate it. Though the Constitution makes this reference to the East only in passing, there is much in the Constitution that does and can apply to the Churches of the East as well.

For example, when the Constitution addresses the full and active participation of the faithful as the aim to be considered above all else, it speaks to the Chaldeans and the Maronites, the Copts and Ethiopians, the Armenians and Byzantines equally as much as to the Latin West. When it speaks of assuring that liturgical symbols identify clearly the truth that the liturgy celebrates and enacts, it names the symbols of the East as well as those of the West. When it speaks of the communal nature of the liturgy, or the variety of ministers required to carry it out, or the organization of the service according to major and minor parts or the adaptation of the liturgy to new cultures, East and West are equally challenged.

The Constitution tells how distortions entered the liturgy and how it is important that these distortions be removed. One of the primary distortions that entered so many Eastern Church liturgies was the imposition of odd elements from the Latin Church. Vestments may serve as but one example, as many Eastern Churches united to Rome adapted Roman vestments in place of their own. As the Latin Church called attention to distortions within itself, many Eastern Churches have

[14] See Aidan Kavanagh, *On Liturgical Theology* (New York: Pueblo, 1984) 74.
[15] Constitution on the Sacred Liturgy, no. 3.

seen no reason to hold on to things Latin, except where it has positively enhanced the spirit of the Eastern liturgy itself.

The Constitution also noted other elements of the tradition that were obscured, such as rendering public prayers silent when they should be recited or sung, or the replacement of primary symbols by secondary symbols. As the Roman Church readjusted its own liturgy in this regard, a similar task presents itself to the liturgies of the East. This is what Jungmann called a clarification and enlivening of liturgical forms.

When the Constitution speaks of the liturgy as intending to "sanctify men and women, to build up the body of Christ, and finally to give worship to God,"[16] it makes no difference if the liturgy be named the Mass, the Divine Liturgy, the Offering of the Mysteries or the Holy Sacrifice. How the liturgy accomplishes its intent is beyond East and West. It is true that Eastern symbols have their own traditions of theology and spirituality, and these must be followed. But if liturgical symbols are intended to "nourish, strengthen and express"[17] faith, Eastern symbols are equally important to consider, and the ability to preach and enact those symbols well is required of the East as well as the West. The symbols of liturgy must speak clearly what they mean. For East as well as West, people must learn again the ways of entering the liturgy as the liturgy itself presents itself.

Liturgies of the East

The simple phrase of Jungmann names the desire of the whole Church to urge its liturgical reform and renewal in the right direction: *liturgy must become pastoral.*[18] Liturgy, in any rite, remains the *Ecclesia orans*, the human Church which gathers in union with Christ to offer his obedient worship to the Father. There are many ways in which Christ can be seen. He may be the Incarnate Christ or the Risen Christ, the Christ of history or the eschatological Christ, the Christ who is present to us here or the Christ who takes us to his presence in God's kingdom. But however Christ is dominantly understood, he is nonetheless the one who gathers us into his own prayer and worship.

It is the whole Church that is gathered, and what God has done for the Church is most important. No imagery of Christ that distorts Christ's own gathering of the people into his own worship of God will be adequate to the called for liturgical renewal. The pastoral nature of liturgy demands that Christ himself be our mediating priest. He is not the recipient of our worship, but the one who makes us able to worship. He is humanly divine and divinely human, and all rituals of the Church that is gathered by Christ must present him, however else they imagine him, as humanly divine and divinely human.

[16] Ibid, 59.
[17] Ibid.
[18] Jungmann, 98.

There is no doubt that Jungmann's challenge is directed as much to the East as to the West. Eastern Churches need to examine how they imagine Christ and how Christ presents himself within the various ritual forms. The Churches of the East are different among themselves and each has its own spirit to preserve for the Church. But the liturgical task which Jungmann announced applies to the East as well.

But how shall this be done? Liturgical reform in the East varies from church to church, as it does from one locality to another. Some control must be put on the search. I would like to offer here some observations of renewal within the United States. And I would speak only of three Eastern Churches where some efforts have been noteworthy. I am most familiar with the Maronite Church in which I have been presbyter for almost twenty years. I can address the challenge somewhat for the Chaldeans and the Byzantines. For the rest, only a few remarks are possible.

The Maronite Church

Jungmann makes little reference to the Maronite Church, but in fact the Maronite Church is more advanced in liturgical reform than any other Eastern Church. The Liturgical Commission of the Maronite Church has already reformed the liturgy by eliminating most of the Latinizing influences imposed upon it, and restoring a liturgical form that is both Maronite and West Syrian in its shape. The work of this commission continues, and the evolution of the liturgical forms continue as well.

As you would expect, the *Service of the Holy Mysteries* is composed of the liturgy of the Word and the liturgy of the Eucharist. In outward form its structure is identical with the liturgy of Rome. The spirit of the liturgy, however, is quite different. The prayers of the Roman liturgy most frequently end: ". . . we ask this through Christ our Lord." In the Maronite liturgy the prayer ending is more eschatological: ". . . and then we will give you glory and thanks."

The Liturgy of the Word begins with the great *Doxology*, an opening prayer, a greeting of peace and the hymn of the Angels. Whether these are sung or recited, there is supposed to be some interaction with the assembly. The Prayer of Incense and Forgiveness, a special element of the Maronite Church, follows, chanted by the priest and responded to by the assembly. This prayer of forgiveness includes a hymn, the Qolo, chanted or recited by everyone. The *Trisagion* follows, with the celebrant intoning and the congregation responding, and this leads to the Psalm before the readings which is also sung by congregation and celebrant. The proclamation of the Word has two or three readings, followed by the homily and the recitation of the Creed.

The Liturgy of the Eucharist begins with the Pre-anaphora. This includes an *Access to the Altar*, the transfer of the offerings while the congregation sings, prayers of acceptance and the use of incense over the gifts and the congregation. The *Rite of Peace* comes next, at which time the peace goes from the altar to the congregation, reminding us that it is Christ's own peace that we share. The Maronite Church employs twelve anaphoras for the Eucharistic Prayer of blessing, each containing the "Holy, Holy," the narrative of institution sung in Syriac, the memorial and invocation of the Spirit, the last several pieces sung in dialogical form between celebrant and assembly. At the conclusion of the Eucharistic prayer, intercessions are prayed by the deacon, to which all answer, "Lord, have mercy."

The Communion Rite begins with a *Blessing*. Then a ritual movement between the bread, the cup and the celebrant's words, linking both the Body and Blood together and placing what is happening within the mystery of the Trinity. During this time the people may sing, leading to the Lord's Prayer. Here too there is constant exchange between celebrant and assembly, more so than similar parts of the Roman liturgy. There is then a brief Penitential prayer and the invitation to communion where the Body and Blood are offered by way of intinction. A prayer of thanksgiving, a final blessing and the dismissal close the service.

How well is this reformed liturgy a clarification and enlivening? Since the Maronite liturgy had become very Latinized, its first attempt at reform was restoration of its West Syrian roots. Archbishop Zayek, in a first effort of renewal of the Maronite liturgy, noted in the introduction: "The Latins, in their liturgical renewal, have eliminated some of their more recently acquired customs and have returned to their more ancient liturgical practices. . . . By the same token, the Maronites can not continue to use these outdated practices."[19]

Beyond that, however, was a deeper need. The Maronite people had their origins in persecution when they fled to the mountains of Lebanon. This was a people who yearned for the day when Christ would set them free. Maronite spirituality is very eschatological, and while it recognizes that the freedom of Christ will come, it must come in hardship and trial. This is the spirit of the West Syrian liturgy they have restored.

But how well is this spirit preached, and how does it take hold of the people and their prayer? Here Jungmann's comment about the conservative nature of liturgy applies to the people as well. Preaching can take the liturgy seriously and speak of its depth. But what do the people hear? This remains the hard task for any liturgical reform, to expect new ways of speaking to become new ways of listening as well. People are still passive unless invited to participate. They are as reluctant to move with the West Syrian text as many Latins are to move with the new vernacular texts. But the experience is at least encouraging.

In the United States, the Liturgy is celebrated in English and Syriac, English and Arabic and Syriac, and occasionally in Arabic and Syriac, depending on the assembly that is gathered. The arrangement of the liturgy is to hold the liturgy of the Word at the *bema*, separate from the altar, which allows the later *access to the altar* to make sense. The Liturgy is not as horizontal as the current Latin rite, but combines instead a mixture of the mysterious and the ordinary. It is hard to celebrate this liturgy in private; it demands interaction by the faithful. And while it

[19] *The Divine Liturgy according to the Maronite Antiochian Rite* (Detroit, 1969) iii.

may not always draw the assembly into the prayers it presents, the fact that their name is given as agents for these prayers is important. The text itself makes it clear that a people must be present. The principle that the full and active participation of the faithful be considered above all else is clear in text, and usually in fact.

The various symbols in the Maronite text are also reasonably clear. Movements from the altar to the assembly in the forms of blessing and peace clearly say that Christ is its source, not we ourselves. The gesture is to place one hand on the altar and the other toward the assembly, or to greet the gifts on the altar and then bring this greeting to the assembly. In addition, blessings that go to the corners of the earth, east to west, north to south, are clear in what they mean and in the way they are presented. As for the ministries involved in the liturgy, concelebration is common, a deacon may assist the celebrant, there may be a sub-deacon, some altar persons, and always a lay reader for all readings but the Gospel. The full Church is involved in the celebration.

There has always been a close link between the Roman Church and the Maronite Church. It is not surprising that, in addition to the removal of Latinisms from its liturgy, the Maronite Church followed with its own sense of clarification and restructuring and has done so in its own Eastern style.

Because my focus has been on the renewal of the Maronite liturgy in the United States, this treatment of a response to Jungmann's challenge remains quite limited. In addition to Maronites, there are other Churches rooted in the West Syrian tradition, such as Churches in India and Churches in Syria which have also engaged a reform and renewal of their liturgy. In this country, the Maronite is the most familiar.

Chaldean or East Syrian

My experience of the Chaldean Church is considerably less than my experience of the Maronite Church. I have examined several different texts and discussed ways in which renewal is happening, but only as an outsider.[20] A former student of mine, Fr. Stephen Bonian, S.J., did experiment with the liturgy in the efforts to reform, but reform itself remains quite slight.

The early Catholic texts show the same kind of Latinisms as did the Maronite texts, but there has been some movement to restore its own primitive East Syrian tradition. In the United States there is a Chaldean diocese with headquarters in Detroit. There seems to be some evolution coming from that arena to continue forms of restoration and renewal. To illustrate what might be possible, I will use the unofficial text prepared by Father Bonian who celebrated this liturgy at Boston College a while back.

---

[20] An early translation by Sr. Mary Loyola Hayde dates from 1939; a more recent version by Solomon Sara, Georgetown University; an attempted renewal text by Fr. Stephen Bonian, S.J., a Chaldean priest who is currently an administrator of a Maronite parish in Oklahoma.

The liturgy of the Word begins with what was once an *Office of Psalms*. A *Doxology* and the Lord's prayer open the service, with a greeting of peace and seasonal opening prayer. As the assembly sits, incense is prepared: ". . . the sweet fragrance of your tender love envelopes us. . . ." A hymn, the traditional *Lakhoumara*, or Praise to Christ, is sung by the assembly and cantor. The *Trisagion* follows chanted by the assembly with interspersions by the cantor. The celebrant then prays: ". . . you find pleasure in those who do your will; turn to us and forgive us . . . ." A reading, prayer of incense for the Gospel and the Gospel itself follow. Then a homily and Creed.

The Liturgy of the Eucharist begins with the Pre-anaphora, a greeting of peace and the uncovering and incensing of the gifts. The Anaphora is that of Addai and Mari with an institution narrative set in what Catholics see to be its proper place.[21] The intercessions and epiclesis follow. An interesting symbol in the Chaldean liturgy is to place a veil on the gifts as they are presented at the altar to signal Christ being placed in the tomb. As the gifts are later consecrated, the removal of the veil signifies the resurrection. The Lord's Prayer is prayed once again, and the celebrant then invites people to Communion. After Communion, a brief thanksgiving follows as does the dismissal blessing.

Though the liturgy outlined above is an experimental restoration and not the official text, it represents a direction that a reform of the Chaldean liturgy might follow. Three elements identify the Chaldean and other East Syrian liturgies. The first is a strong emphasis on the glory of God, beginning with the Lord's Prayer, the *Lakhoumara* and the *Trisagion*. God's glory and God's deeds are paramount. Secondly, it is heavily christocentric in its prayer. Thirdly, it is even more eschatological than the West Syrian tradition. God's kingdom has already arrived. The movement of the text represents this kind of restoration.

I am less sure of how the Gospel or liturgical symbols are preached. One needs more time than a brief experience to determine that. I do not know how the liturgy itself is brought to the spirituality of the faithful. The East Syrian tradition is dominated by a diophysite christology that allows the fully human and fully divine to interact in Christ with no sharing of one with the other. It also suggests that the ritual can serve as an unfolding of God's own victory. There is much that can touch the human imagination here, but I do not know how successful it is as currently presented.

The Liturgy seems to require at least a cantor along with the celebrant and assembly. Apart from these, no other ministers are listed in the text. There seems to be no place for a deacon or sub-deacon, and this is true even in more formal texts. The interchange between celebrant and assembly is less than that of the Maronite Church, but there is promise for full and active participation here as well. It is equally difficult to celebrate this liturgy with no assembly present.

---

[21] Most likely there was no narrative of institution until much later, but Catholics insist it should be there.

The Byzantine Churches

My experience with the Byzantine Church goes back to before the Vatican II Council. My first fascination was the language itself, for the Divine Liturgies in which I took part were frequently celebrated in English. At the time this stood in contrast to the Roman Church where Latin retained its hold. The primary chapel I attended was the Russian Center at Fordham University, which is now located at Scranton University as the Center for Eastern Christian Studies. There was a choir for most of the singing, but the Litany form, which dominated the ritual, was sung by everyone. Even before my entrance into the Society of Jesus, I had participated in the Divine Liturgy in English, Greek and Slavonic.

By the time of the council, and the Constitution on the Sacred Liturgy, I had lost contact with the Byzantine Churches, and spent most of my time working on the reformed Latin rite. At a later point I returned to the Byzantine liturgy, only to discover how alien that once familiar rite had become. The major difference was the Constitution itself, and the way I had come to see the liturgy of the Church. The Byzantine liturgy still had its Litany form, and the assembly still sang with gusto. There was still full and active participation by the faithful. But the form itself had become problematic. There seemed to be not one liturgy going on, but two. I began to realize that the Litany form, conducted by the deacon and the assembly, had very little reference to what the celebrant was in fact doing. If there was to be a restoration, the liturgy of the celebrant needed to come to the front.

Much of the Byzantine rite as currently enacted does indeed enact a particular theology, but not necessarily a liturgical theology. Hans Joachim-Shultz[22] outlines in dramatic fashion just how far this rite had evolved. Where the early rites stressed how the victory was enacted within the ritual itself, the Byzantine ritual overlays that dimension with a second layer of meaning. The ritual is now called upon to raise the assembly into the heavenly worship of Jesus Christ. What the Roman ritual had accomplished in the private arena of people's prayer, the Byzantine accomplished within the ritual itself. It became a celebration of the cosmic Church giving worship to the cosmic Christ.

A first look at the Byzantine ritual must be that which the ordinary person experiences, namely that between the deacon and assembly, presided over by the bishop or priest. The celebrant does indeed evoke some response from the assembly, but the real leader of prayer is the deacon. In the Byzantine liturgy, the deacon has two roles. He leads the congregation in litany forms of prayer and he serves helping the priest. He moves from the assembly to behind the iconostasis, and then back to the assembly to tell the assembly what the priest has been doing. Though a choir usually sings most of the texts, I will assume that the litany belongs to the assembly.

The Liturgy of the Word begins after the preparation of the gifts and the incensing of the Church with the blessing of the celebrant and the litany of peace

---

[22] Schultz, *The Byzantine Liturgy*. Chapters leading to Maximus the Confessor should be noted.

conducted by the deacon. The celebrant sings only the conclusion, as he does for all litany forms. Two other smaller litanies follow. Between the litanies three antiphons are sung as well as the *Hymn of the Incarnation*. The Little Entrance, which is now the procession of the Gospel book, is carried out by the celebrant and deacon while the choir sings prayers for the day. The *Trisagion* follows, and leads into the service of the Word. The epistle, the gospel and homily take place (the homily also can take place at the very end of the service). Another litany, the *Insistent Litany*, with deacon and assembly follows. A second litany to dismiss the catechumens leads to a third litany, that of the faithful.

The Liturgy of the Eucharist begins with the Great Entrance, which is the presentation of the gifts to the altar. The choir or assembly sing the *Cherubic Hymn*, during which the celebrant and deacon offer prayers for the sacrifice. Once the bread and wine are offered, the deacon returns to the assembly to offer the litany of supplication, "for the gifts that have been offered." There is the Kiss of Peace, the Creed and the anaphora, which is said in silence. The "Holy, Holy," and some extrinsic prayers are sung by the choir or assembly. Again the deacon comes forth to lead a second litany, "for the gifts that have been offered and consecrated." The Lord's Prayer and the invitation to communion follow. A special prayer by the assembly is prayed before communion, which combines praise of the Christ who is present and a confession of sins by the people.

After communion, the deacon leads another litany, "having received the divine, holy, precious, immortal, heavenly, life-giving and awe-inspiring mysteries of Christ." This is the very shift that Jungmann wrote of in his essay. How distant Christ has become. At the very end, the celebrant leads the concluding blessings.

If the deacon and the deacon's litany form are set aside, the structure of the liturgy becomes quite different. The celebrant prays many prayers, most to conclude the litanies, some to attend other liturgical pieces, such as the *Trisagion*. He then takes his seat for the proclamation of the Word. The celebrant gives blessing during the Word, but little else. Prayers follow for the Insistent Litany, the litany of the catechumens and the Prayers for the faithful.

In addition to praying the prayer of the Cherubic Hymn, while the choir sings the same, a rather lengthy prayer accompanies it as well. As the gifts are placed on the altar, they become Christ placed in the tomb, though this is less clear than in the Chaldean rite. Later, after the consecration, they also become Christ risen, but this too is somewhat obscure. A prayer for the litany of supplication follows, leading to the Kiss of Peace and Eucharistic Prayer. If the last is said out loud, it follows the classic West Syrian format. The Lord's Prayer and other prayers of blessing introduce communion: "Holy Things to the Holy."

One thing that dominates the actual Divine Liturgy is the substitution of secondary symbols for the primary. The Litany form hides much of what the celebrant is doing, and though it presents a contemplative format for the liturgy, the actual structure of the service is kept from view. In fact, even when the Eucharistic food is not received, there is blessed bread at the end for people to take home. One comment has been made that the liturgy has become too beautiful, and too caught up taking the assembly to the heavenly liturgy that the ordinary workings of the Eucharistic food are silenced. The human Christ has yielded to the Divine. As a matter of fact, the Orthodox really control this liturgical form, and they are quite reluctant to change it.

A Catholic restoration did take place in New Skete, New York, by a community who attempted to restore a primitive Byzantine liturgy.[23] The New Skete liturgy was instructive. It removed much of the diaconal litany form, and brought the celebrant and his liturgy much closer to the people. It began with either the Beatitudes or Psalm 103 (102) as the gifts were being prepared. The celebrant prayed the blessing, the choir sang the Hymn of the Incarnation. The Gospel book was then set on the throne as the people sang: "Come let us worship." The prayers for the day were sung, the priest prayed an opening prayer and the people sang the *Trisagion*. In the New Skete liturgy this led to the proclamation of the Word. The alleluia and a sung prayer of the priest led to the gospel—read by the celebrant itself. The great litany followed, with the conclusion sung by the celebrant.

The Great Entrance was a combination of movement by the ministers and song by the choir. Once the gifts are placed on the altar, the celebrant intones the Creed, and then the liturgy moved immediately to the Eucharistic Prayer. The Prayer of Blessing was said aloud, while the people responded accordingly. The Lord's Prayer, breaking of the bread and communion followed. After communion, a hymn and prayer of thanksgiving led to the blessing and dismissal.

As I read again the New Skete texts, and listen to the liturgy they represent, I do not find it as successful as once I did. It does restore the priest's liturgy to the people, but retains the choir for most of its singing. In fact the whole liturgy continues to be sung, with no respect for other modes of communication. The New Skete restoration was a first attempt, but not much more. Yet it did try to achieve some aspects of the Constitution on the Sacred Liturgy and did manage to present some aspects of the Byzantine spirit as presented through what it thought to be an earlier form of the liturgy itself. It was a movement backward, and that was what made it both good and bad. In the end, however, the community embraced the Orthodox Church, and with it the traditional liturgical form. Any advance in becoming pastoral was lost.

Some Concluding Remarks

There are, of course, many other Eastern Churches in the United States, but these show an even less clear response to the call of the Council and the challenge

---

[23] This Franciscan community adapted the Eastern traditions, and in particular the Byzantine rite, and made serious efforts to reform the rite. At a later time, it joined the Orthodox Church, and thus embraced the traditional Divine Liturgy.

of Josef Jungmann. The Armenian Church as I experience it has moved to restore its primitive beauty, but it retains its other-worldly accent to the Divine Christ. It presents a beautiful Armenian concert, and an awesome presentation of Christ's sacrifice, but it is far removed from the Lord's Supper and the simplicity of the eucharistic meal. The Ethiopians are doing some work to reform the liturgy, but it seems to be haphazard rather than organized. The same is true of their Mother Church, the Coptic Church.

As I end this brief review, and note some efforts of the various Eastern Churches to restore a "pastoral liturgy," I return to my opening remark, that the Constitution on the Sacred Liturgy should apply to the East as to the West. Josef Jungmann's challenge should apply to the East as to the West. But Jungmann himself has noted that liturgy remains a conservative venture. Even where it knows it must change, it is reluctant to do so. It is clear that any reform must be true to each Church's own traditions. The Eastern Churches need to touch again the deep spirit that their own traditions invite them to. In some parts of the East some achievements have been accomplished. But throughout the East, much more needs to be done.

11. Feminist Perspectives

"The 'We' of the Liturgy": Liturgical Reform, Pastoral Liturgy and the Feminist Liturgical Movement

Marjorie Procter-Smith

There can be no question of the fact that the work of Josef Jungmann has exercised vast influence on the course of liturgical study and liturgical reform and development over the past decades. But to what extent can his work be understood as a contributing factor in the development of feminist liturgical practice and theology? And to what extent have issues raised by the feminist liturgical movement challenged and gone beyond the insights of Jungmann and others influential in the more male- and clergy-dominated liturgical movement? And finally, what further questions are raised and conclusions drawn by identifying common elements in the work of Jungmann and the feminist liturgical movement?

At first glance, it would seem that there is nothing feminist about the work of a German liturgiologist. Certainly Jungmann never directly addressed the questions that have most closely defined the feminist liturgical movement: questions of women's access to ordination and to other forms of liturgical and ecclesial leadership and authority; questions of male-dominated language and images about people and God; questions about hierarchical models of liturgical and ecclesial leadership. On the other hand, it is possible to see the seeds of ideas that are later taken up and acted on in the feminist liturgical movement in some of Jungmann's work, particularly in his essay "The Defeat of Teutonic Arianism and the Revolution in Religious Culture in the Early Middle Ages."[1]

As the title suggests, this essay is primarily concerned with the interplay between religious practice and culture that produced a significant shift in piety. It is not until the final ten or so pages of this vast, one-hundred-page article that he addresses the implications of his argument for contemporary issues, and it is in this

---

[1] Included in *Pastoral Liturgy* (New York: Herder and Herder, 1962) 1–101.

final section, called "Conservation and Change in the Liturgy," that he raises issues
that are of interest from a feminist perspective.

Having demonstrated how far the liturgical practice of the Roman Catholic
Church had come from its earlier spirit, Jungmann turns in this final section to
questions of the balance and tension between liturgical change and liturgical
preservation. He notes that at the beginning of the twentieth century, the standard
view of the Roman liturgy was that of an aging but noble building, or as a "precious vessel with even more precious contents" that must be preserved.[2] This view
Jungmann characterizes, with some criticism, as "liturgical antiquarianism." This
attitude that viewed the Roman rite as an immutable, divine artifact, as "inviolable
and unchangeable as the Word of God itself," led to a sense that the liturgy was a
great showpiece, an antiquarian relic that was noble and beautiful, perhaps, but
quite set apart from the life and faith of ordinary believers. Compounding this
problem of the gulf between the liturgy of the Roman rite and the people was the
clericalization of the liturgy. Although this was a process that began centuries before in the Western Church, by the end of the nineteenth century the idea that the
liturgy was the work of the clergy certainly had become the common assumption
of clergy and laity alike. Indeed, the clericalization of the liturgy in the Roman rite
can be paralleled with the professionalization of Protestant liturgies during the
nineteenth and early twentieth centuries, with the addition of trained, vested, and
sometimes paid choirs and musicians who were then expected to perform for a
passive laity.

Although Jungmann's sympathy for the rather romanticized view of the
Roman rite of the Western Church as enshrining a fixed and unchanging content
called "tradition" is clear in this essay, he also acknowledges that the history of the
Western rite, especially up until the Council of Trent, is a history of change and
adaptation to local custom and need.[3] Therefore he notes with satisfaction that
after Trent's artificial freezing of all liturgical change and development that major
jolts in liturgical practice, such as those begun by Pope Pius X, were needed in
order to, as it were, jump-start the natural process of liturgical growth. Fundamentally, he argued, this kind of sudden and unsubtle liturgical change was necessary
for two reasons, reasons that form the foundation of Jungmann's liturgical thought:
the urge to bring current practice into line with a new understanding of the ancient
Christian world, and the need to offer people a liturgical experience that is meaningful and genuinely communal.[4]

Although Jungmann confines his remarks to the practices and reforms of the
Roman Catholic Church, his observations regarding the alienation and perplexity
of the laity in regards to the faith can be applied with equal accuracy to Protestant
laity of the same period. Accordingly, the reforms Jungmann describes and antici-

[2] Ibid., 90.
[3] Ibid., 91–92.
[4] Ibid., 92–93.

pates in the Roman community found resonance in Protestant communities as well. The twin principles of recovery of ancient practices and the creation of communal, participatory worship found wide acceptance within mainline Protestant communities. The recovery of ancient practices intrigued and attracted Protestant groups that had long prided themselves on their supposed faithfulness to the practices of the early Church. And churches that claimed a fundamental belief in the "priesthood of all believers" had to admit that common practice had created a significant rift between professional worship leaders and a passive laity.

Thus it happened that considerable groundwork had already been laid for the rising liturgical consciousness of women as well as other specific groups within the churches, both Catholic and Protestant. What Jungmann describes as "the 'we' of liturgy" began to find expression not only in the feminist liturgical movement, but also in the calls from various ethnic communities for a liturgical recognition of indigenous culture of music, dance, language, and symbolism.

It is also worth noting that Jungmann was perhaps prescient in another sense, when he remarks that the liturgical changes he describes already having taken place at the time of the writing of his article had not been received with pleasure by everyone.[5] Resistance to liturgical change would appear to be as inevitable as the fact of liturgical change itself. Resistance to incorporation of feminist and other concerns has been a factor in the past and continues into the present in many places.

Finally, Jungmann concludes his essay with a plea for pastorally sensitive liturgy, by which he means liturgy that offers "the support of a joyful awareness of Faith and of a Christian life in the harsh everyday world."[6] Here his notion of the "we" of the liturgy makes itself felt in his desire for greater clarity: in the form of the Mass, in the use of the vernacular, in the liturgical year, in preaching. The goal of this greater clarity is a liturgy that invites and encourages the congregation to understand the liturgy as an expression of their faith and to make that faith meaningful for everyday life.[7]

It is a measure of the success of Jungmann's ideas of liturgical reform, perhaps, that a contemporary reading of this essay makes his proposals seem not only common-sense but also to a great degree rather conservative. The broad acceptance of the basic principles of "pastoral liturgy" not only in the Roman Catholic setting Jungmann envisioned but also among mainline Protestant churches has had a dramatic effect on contemporary worship practices, and laid the groundwork for the growth of the feminist liturgical movement. As we have seen, some of Jungmann's most basic principles, particularly that of the participation of the whole ecclesia engaged in its worship, are consonant with feminist liturgical principles. This is not to argue that Jungmann anticipated or even would have approved of the feminist liturgical movement, nor is it to suggest that the feminist liturgical movement

[5] Ibid., 94.
[6] Ibid., 98–99.
[7] Ibid., 101.

was a result of the liturgical movement as proposed by Jungmann. Rather, it can be argued that the basic principles of the liturgical movement opened a door, so to speak, that enabled the questions raised by the feminist liturgical movement to enter the larger discussion.

Certainly, other forces outside the churches were also contributing to the birth of this movement, particularly in North America, where the civil rights movement, the anti-Vietnam War movement, the black power movement and the Chicano movement converged with the women's movement. Questions raised by the "second wave" of the feminist movement in the United States,[8] regarding sex roles, women and work, sexuality, and access to social, financial, and political power resonated throughout existing institutions, including those two bastions of conservatism, the academy and the Church. As women began to find voice and power in the workplace, in professions previously closed to them, and in exercising political power, they were less inclined to accept traditional church teachings regarding the silencing and marginalizing of women in traditional roles. In particular, women in the Church began to question the absence of women from leadership in the churches, especially liturgical leadership. In many ways the churches were in a position to hear these questions to the extent that they had already heard and accepted the shifts in perspective introduced by the liturgical movement. The liturgical movement's emphasis on liturgy as the people's work, the power and responsibility of the laity (which in mainline denominations still includes most women and is made up mostly of women), and collaborative styles of leadership were principles that made it difficult, at least, for churches to continue to insist on the silence and submission of women. The liturgical movement's commitment to creating informed laity willing and even eager to participate in the Church's worship with understanding made it hard, if not impossible, for church leaders to refuse to hear urgent questions from women regarding their participation in their faith and in their churches' worship.

The face of the feminist liturgical movement has changed over the past twenty-five or so years, as new groups find voice and raise questions that contribute to a continually expanding definition of feminism and to a continually self-reforming movement. However, the basic questions and fundamental issues have been identified and continue to occupy the attention of those working in this movement. These principles can be summarized here.[9]

---

[8] The "first wave" of the feminist movement in the US refers to the ninteteenth-century movement for women's suffrage, which also critiqued contemporary religious assumptions and practices. See Elizabeth Cady Stanton, *The Women's Bible*, originally published in 1895.

[9] For further discussion of these issues, see Mary Collins, "Feminist Liturgical Principles," in Marjorie Procter-Smith and Janet Walton, eds., *Women at Worship: Interpretations of North American Diversity* (Louisville: Westminster/John Knox Press, 1993); Marjorie Procter-Smith, "The Marks of Feminist Liturgy," *Proceedings of the North American Academy of Liturgy* 1992; Lesley Northup, "Claiming Horizontal Religious Space: Women's Religious Rituals," *Studia Liturgica* 25 (1995).

First, the desire for and need for feminist liturgy arises out of a sense of alienation from more traditional, male-centered forms of worship. We have noted how a concern for the alienated and uninvolved lay worshipper was an important issue for Jungmann's program of reform. Similarly, as women have come to question their oppression and subjugation, they too have experienced a lack within familiar forms of worship. But here the impulse arises not from above, from the educated or clerical elite who desire to bring the passive and uninterested laity into greater understanding and participation. It arises instead from the alienated themselves, who, perhaps emboldened in some cases by the liturgical movement's rhetoric regarding full participation of the laity, speak up for themselves and express their spiritual needs.

Initially, these needs were expressed in terms of two central issues: access to leadership, and language use. First, women desired to see other women in roles of leadership in the Church and in liturgy, even when they did not want to be leaders themselves. The notion that women were unsuitable for liturgical leadership flew in the face of the experience of many women who were increasingly taking prominent leadership roles in other public arenas, such as law, politics, and similar fields formerly closed to women. Not only could many women (and men) see no reason why women shouldn't be allowed to exercise liturgical leadership, they could see strong reasons why women should exercise such leadership. The presence of women as liturgical leaders signaled, among other things, an acceptance of the authority and God-given gifts of women, and a potent recognition of women's fundamental equality with men. Second, women desired to hear women specifically included and named in the public language of church worship. Language that implied that men and men's experiences and relationships were normative for all human beings and an adequate model for God was not acceptable. Inevitably, the question of language changes, particularly in Scripture and liturgical texts, raised substantial theological questions that continue to occupy the Church. Ironically, Jungmann comments that the translation of the Roman Catholic liturgy into the vernacular will inevitably raise deeper questions regarding the appropriate and helpful interpretation of ancient religious ideas for "modern man."[10] It is this sort of deeper question that is raised by the feminist liturgical movement, first in connection with the simple desire to make use of language that explicitly or implicitly includes women, then, inevitably with the more substantive questions of the meaning of traditional religious ideas for women.

Similarly, the desire to see women in positions of liturgical and other religious leadership positions has led to deeper questions about the nature of leadership and authority and the exploration of alternatives to the traditional hierarchical and autocratic models in place in churches. And likewise the liturgical movement has concerned itself with restoring a model of priesthood and liturgical leadership

---

[10] Jungmann, 98.

that arises from and operates within the midst of the congregation rather than stands apart from and over the community.

However, in spite of the rhetorical statements from many churches and denominations regarding full participation of the laity, the express inclusion of women and women's concerns in the liturgical reforms of the recent past have often met with resistance. Jungmann acknowledges the inevitability of this kind of resistance, noting that even the (to us) very modest liturgical changes that were beginning to be introduced into the Roman Catholic liturgy felt to many observers "as though an ax were being laid to a thousand year old oak."[11] Churches and church leaders have at times responded in similar ways to feminist proposals for liturgical change in the forms of women as liturgical leaders and changes in language to make the presence and participation of women more visible and audible. Defensive responses by male church leaders have ranged from citation of Scripture texts to reference to traditional practice and precedent, to arguments based on supposed differences between men and women.

Clearly the objective of the feminist liturgical movement has been to make real the principle of liturgy as the work of the whole people of God. However, this resistance to women's questions and refusal to hear women's claims on the church and its forms of worship has led many women to separate themselves from existing religious institutions to some degree or another. The feminist liturgical movement has always placed its first priority on meeting the spiritual and liturgical needs and desires of women. Where church bodies and leaders have responded with resistance, groups of women have formed on the periphery or even entirely outside the bounds of institutional churches. The withdrawal of women from full support of mainline churches in North America has been widely noted and researched.[12] This withdrawal takes many forms, ranging from the participation in feminist liturgy groups as a supplement to ongoing participation in one's local church to full formal rejection of existing male-dominated religious institutions in favor of feminist or woman-centered religious identity that may or may not be Christian. It is interesting that the concern of mainline North American churches over membership loss has not given any attention to this phenomenon, but rather has taken a reverse position of attempting to resolve the decline in membership by reiterating or in some cases attempting to return to conservative or even fundamentalist positions, especially regarding women's roles.

Away from the disapproval of institutional church structures, women have begun to create liturgical forms and patterns according to principles that are found

---

[11] Ibid., 94.

[12] For early evidence of this phenomenon, see Rosemary Radford Ruether, *Women-Church: Theology and Practice of Feminist Liturgical Communities* (San Francisco: Harper and Row, 1985). For recent research on the strained relationship between women and mainline Christianity in North America, see Adair T. Lummis, Alison Stokes, and Miriam Therese Winter, *Defecting in Place: Women Claiming Responsibility for Their Own Spiritual Lives* (New York: Crossroad, 1995).

to affirm and empower the struggle of women for liberation. Although actual feminist liturgical events vary widely, certain common elements can usually be found in them, as guiding principles of ritual construction. The most basic and common characteristics cluster around issues of leadership and power. A strong commitment to shared power leads to practices such as shared or rotating leadership and communal participation not only in the liturgical event but also in its planning and preparation. This commitment to shared power and communal leadership leads also to a welcoming of diversity and recognition of particularity of experience within any group. There is resistance to the tendency to universalize from one's own experience, and a desire to create a community that is not only tolerant of difference but celebrates it. Celebration of diversity is easier to celebrate in the abstract than to accomplish, however, and many feminist liturgy groups tend to be racially and ethnically homogeneous. Obviously, feminist liturgies tend to be critical of traditional sources of authority, regarding texts, practices, and indeed the very idea of a monolithic tradition with suspicion. The authority of a text, practice, model of leadership, or doctrine rests not on its claim to be traditional (after all, the silencing of women is also traditional), but on its ability to offer liberation to women. In other words, any liturgical act, event, or symbol is evaluated on the basis of its moral authority. The ability of a given liturgical event to express a prophetic vision of the world and the reign of God that includes the freedom and well-being of women is valued above traditionalism.

A second cluster of feminist liturgical principles focus on communal issues. Women—women' lives, interests, questions, struggles, and hopes—are central to feminist liturgies, rather than peripheral or absent as in traditional liturgies. For example, this focus has generated rituals that have no counterpart in traditional Christian liturgical practice, such as healing services for rape victims, or menopause celebrations. Furthermore, relationships and interconnections between and among women are valued and sacralized, in contrast to traditional Christian liturgies' valorizing of relationships between men. Liturgies commemorating the bonds between mothers and daughters, among sisters, and with female ancestors are common in feminist liturgical practice. This sense of interconnection among women is often broadened to include men and the natural world, expressing a nonhierarchical web-like relationship of mutual interdependence. Feminist liturgies often make use of natural symbols: the seasonal cycles (sometimes linked with women's cycles) and use of natural settings or, when necessary, adaptation of indoor settings with plants, stones, seashells, and the like, to represent an outdoor environment and thus convey a sense of interconnection with the natural world. In a similar vein, hierarchical language for God is eschewed in favor of images that emphasize interconnection and mutuality. God is rarely imaged as a ruler but more often as a parent, friend, or in nonanthropological but immanent terms.

This emphasis on interconnection with the natural, physical world leads also to a positive evaluation of the human body, especially the female body. Where traditional Christianity has often regarded the body as dangerous and the female body as especially so, feminist liturgies prefer to see the female body as representing the image of God, and the physical functions of the female body (traditionally regarded in Christian teaching as polluted and polluting) as sacred. In particular, women's bodily life-cycles, from first menstruation to menopause, are often celebrated and commemorated ritually in feminist liturgical groups, as a counterpoint to the Church's historic distaste for such events in women's lives.

Finally, the feminist suspicion of tradition and texts combined with a commitment to ever-expanding ideas of diversity leads feminist liturgical planners to value creativity and experimentalism over the creation of fixed texts and practices. It is commonplace for feminist liturgies to be created by a particular group of people for a particular group and event or occasion, with no expectation that the liturgical event will ever be repeated. Indeed, the unrepeatability of feminist liturgies is held as a value that not only honors the specificity of any liturgical gathering and event, but also guards against the creation of a new orthodoxy. Feminist liturgical groups value self-criticism and ongoing reform, in the belief that diversity and authenticity are thus best served. At the same time, as the examples cited above suggest, certain practices and assumptions are found commonly among feminist liturgy groups.

Clearly these practices are evolving in reaction against a long history of liturgical erasure, distortion, and suppression of women's stories and participation in Christian worship, as well as in response to more recent rejections. The liturgical movement may have opened a door that admitted the kind of questions feminists were raising about Christian practice in general and worship in particular. But its contributions to the renewal of worship have not been sufficient to create an environment that welcomes feminist questions. In addition to the more general resistance to inclusion of women's questions in the concerns of the liturgical movement, there are also aspects of the liturgical movement that not only distinguished it from the feminist liturgical movement but acted counter to some feminist concerns. Jungmann, and many other leaders of the liturgical movement, saw the goal of the movement as a recovery of ancient patterns and understandings of Christian liturgy. To be sure, Jungmann in particular was concerned that this recovery be more than mere antiquarianism, that it be truly and deeply a renewal of the spiritual and liturgical life of the whole Church.

Nevertheless, the liturgical movement's commitment to the recovery of early Christian patterns of worship has given those who resist the inclusion of women's voices and concerns in the process of renewal a resource for that resistance. Although recent feminist research into roles of women in the early centuries of Christianity has deepened and added nuance to our understanding of the character of the early Christian worship, these data are often rejected or ignored in favor of a more monolithic image of the early church that recognizes only male leadership.[13] Simi-

---

[13] For examples of feminist reconstruction of early Christian history, see Elizabeth Schüssler Fiorenza, *In Memory of Her: A Feminist Theological Reconstruction of Christian Origins* (New

larly, the argument for lack of precedence (which, ironically enough, is the sort of antiquarianism Jungmann objected to, based as it is on a notion of an unchanging Church) is also often cited to prevent the raising of questions arising from women's contemporary experience. Questions of the use of female language for God, for example, or alternative interpretations of the death of Jesus must not be allowed, this argument goes, since they are questions that have not been asked before. Thus an imaginary and rather romanticized notion of the past is allowed to function as a check on new questions, issues, and voices.

The feminist liturgical movement has a more ambivalent attitude toward practices of the past. The origins of the feminist liturgical movement lie in the feminist movement in North America, with its emphasis not on recovery of the past but on empowerment in the present for the future. Indeed, the contemporary feminist movement harbors some suspicion of the past, or at least of attempts to reclaim the past, since the past is understood as a time of loss and repression for women. Nevertheless, to some extent the feminist liturgical movement has looked to the past to know what we have lost, what stories and memories of our foremothers have been forgotten, distorted, or denied. The purpose of such remembering, however, is not an attempt to restore past practices that led to such loss and distortion, but to enable women to name their experience and to claim their voices, in order to prevent loss and distortion of our stories in the future.

Another significant aspect of the liturgical movement is mentioned by Jungmann almost in passing at the conclusion of his essay when he urges the appropriate use of Scripture and a renewal of vital preaching as essential to the process of renewal. Certainly as the liturgical movement was taken up by Protestants the importance of biblical norms received more emphasis. By contrast, the feminist liturgical movement has regarded biblical texts with considerable suspicion, seeing them as a source for women's oppression and silencing as well as a potential source of liberation. Similarly, preaching does not have an important place in the feminist liturgical movement because of the authoritarian model that has prevailed historically, and because the pulpit has been not only a place forbidden to women but also another source of the silencing of women.

What conclusions can we draw about the relationship between the liturgical movement as envisioned by Joseph Jungmann and the contemporary feminist liturgical movement? It would be misleading to suggest that the liturgical movement was the original soil in which the feminist liturgical movement grew until it found itself alienated by resistance to change in the church. The two movements find their origins in radically different places, the one coming from the historical and

---

York: Crossroad, 1983); Karen Jo Torjesen, *When Women Were Priests: Women Leaders in the Early Church and the Scandal of Their Subordination in the Rise of Christianity* (San Francisco: Harper, 1993); Antoinette Wire, *Corinthian Women Prophets: A Reconstruction Through Paul's Rhetoric* (Minneapolis: Fortress Press, 1990).

archeological study of early Christianity, the other from contemporary social movements and the rising educational and professional status of women in twentieth-century North America. Moreover, they have radically different priorities, the one focused on historical and theological norms above all, the other focused on the spiritual and liturgical needs of living women. It would be more accurate to see the two movements as proceeding on paths that are sometimes parallel, sometimes intersecting, sometimes moving apart. The historical point of Jungmann's essay, after all, is to draw attention to the complex relationship between culture and faith, between liturgical change and liturgical preservation, and to attempt, finally, to draw the two together. It may be that where these two liturgical movement most diverge is over the question of whether preservation of historical faith or response to the demand of daily reality is to be the dominant norm.

However, there is an important way in which both movements share a basic foundational premise. That premise is the one that Jungmann made most forcefully in his life's work in liturgical reform: the ideal of pastoral liturgy. If the liturgical movement's interest in the full participation of the laity and Jungmann's commitment to liturgy that has meaning for the daily life of worshippers has ever been taken seriously and at face value, it has been in the feminist liturgical movement. It can only be regarded as a failure of the liturgical movement as a movement to engage the full participation of all worshippers that the issues being raised again and again by feminist liturgical scholars have been relegated to the margins of liturgical reforms. Or to put the point more hopefully, the feminist liturgical questions remain part of the unfinished agenda of the liturgical movement. The "we" of the liturgy, to borrow Jungmann's expression, must be understood to include women, and the voices of women must not be ignored or dismissed as trivial or heretical.

The hope that this issue can remain on the agenda for the liturgical movement, perhaps, lies in a comment that Jungmann makes in his essay regarding resistance to liturgical change. Noting that "it was not the worst of people" who found early modest liturgical change hard to take, he remarks that the very idea of liturgical change seemed to many to be first destructive rather than renewing: the falling of ancient walls, the laying of an ax to the root of a venerable tree.[14] In fact, many of the proposals and practices of the feminist liturgical movement strike some contemporary observers the same way, and they too are not "the worst of people." It may come to pass that as we now look back on the beginnings of the liturgical movement, and marvel that the celebration of the liturgy in the vernacular with the priest facing the people across the table provoked such strong resistance, some time in the future our heirs will look back on the beginnings of the feminist liturgical movement and marvel that such modest proposals evoked such strong objections. I can do no better in closing than to add my voice, and voices of women of faith, to Jungmann's in the final lines of his essay:

[14] Jungmann, 94.

We must reach a situation where the *ecclesia orans* is no longer a mere ideal of liturgical books, partially realized by the celebrating clergy. It is the whole believing people who make up the *Ecclesia* which approaches God in prayer through the liturgy.[15]

[15] Ibid., 101.

IV. PRESENT AND FUTURE IMPLICATIONS

12. Liturgical Theology

Ritual as Reading

Nathan D. Mitchell

Introduction

The implications of the body of Josef Jungmann's work on liturgical history and theology had a profound impact on liturgical studies for several decades of the twentieth century. The focus of his work is crystallized in many ways in his important essay "The Defeat of Teutonic Arianism and the Revolution in Religious Culture in the Early Middle Ages,"[1] especially in its examination of cultural influences on liturgical structures and theology. On the twenty-fifth anniversary of his death, therefore, it seems appropriate to examine some insights and implications of contemporary liturgical theology on the eve of the twenty-first century.

The Triumph of the Secondary

In his provocative study *Real Presences*, Professor George Steiner speaks eloquently of the "arts of negation" that lead many of today's writers to emphasize "emptiness" in their theories of meaning and to affirm "absence" in their theories of language and literature.[2] Yeats's prescient "the center cannot hold" is explained by the disappearance of any "fixed core" of meaning in language. As Gertrude Stein might have said, there is no longer any "there" there. We thus live, Steiner suggests, in a time of "'epilogue' . . . within the logic of the 'afterword.'"[3]

> In recent art and thought, it is not a forgetting which is instrumental, but a negative theism, a peculiarly vivid sense of God's absence or . . . recession. The "other" has withdrawn from the incarnate, leaving either uncertain secular spoors or an emptiness which echoes still with the vibrance of departure. Our aesthetic forms explore the void, the bland freedom which come of the retraction (*Deus absconditus*) of the messianic and divine.[4]

---

[1] In Josef Jungmann, *Pastoral Liturgy* (New York: Herder & Herder, 1962) 1–101; revised and updated from the 1947 version published in the *Zeitschrift für katholische Theologie*.

[2] George Steiner, *Real Presences* (Chicago: The University of Chicago Press, 1989).

[3] Ibid., 228.

[4] Ibid., 229.

We have reached this epilogical impasse, Steiner argues, because the ancient covenant between word and world—which affirms that "any coherent account of the
capacity of human speech to communicate meaning and feeling is underwritten by
the assumption of God's presence"[5]—has been broken. Time was when Western
thinkers agreed that the relation between "sign" and "signified" was real; that
every work of art was essentially an *opus metaphysicum*; that the "meaning" of
history was the history of its meanings. Such assumptions can no longer be made.
Western thought and art today is characterized, Steiner claims, by "the dominance
of the secondary and the parasitic."[6]

   In short, *secondary discourse* (commentary, "interpretation") has replaced
immediacy in both art and literature. Steiner contends that this ominous replacement was bound to result once critics abandoned the (earlier and more traditional)
view that "the best readings of art are *art*."[7] Music provides an apt illustration. Taking Claude Lévi-Strauss's cue that "the invention of melody is the supreme mystery of man," Steiner writes:

> The truths, the necessities of ordered feeling in the musical experience are not irra-
> tional; but *they are irreducible to reason or pragmatic reckoning*. This irreducibility
> is the spring of my argument. It may well be that man is man, and that man 'borders
> on' limitations of a peculiar and open 'otherness,' because he can produce and be pos-
> sessed by music.[8]

Thus, when someone asked Robert Schumann to "explain" a difficult étude, the
composer simply sat down at the piano and played it through a second time. This
suggests that "the criticism of music truly answerable to its object is to be found
within music itself. The construct of theme and variation, of quotation and *reprise*, is
organic to music, particularly in the West. Criticism is, literally, instrumental in the
ear of the composer."[9] In sum, the musical structure "is itself interpretation and composition is criticism."[10] The same can be said, Steiner argues, for the arts of painting,
sculpture and literature. This is why we often find great artists "quoting" one another's work—as Bach does in the *Credo* of his *Mass in B minor*, where chant tunes
by anonymous medieval composers form the spine and marrow out of which elabo-
rately inventive Baroque "fantasies" are spun. This does not mean that Bach's originality—or that of his medieval predecessors—is in any way diminished. On the
contrary, each musical utterance enriches the other. The point, of course, is that Bach
"commented" on musical art by creating musical art of his own–not by producing an
analytic essay or the syllabus for a "music appreciation" course.

[5] Ibid., 3.
[6] Ibid., 7.
[7] Ibid., 17; emphasis added.
[8] Ibid., 19; emphasis added.
[9] Ibid., 20; emphasis added.
[10] Ibid., 21.

Today, however, art is often annexed by criticism, by secondary discourse. "Commentaries on Ezra Pound, on Samuel Beckett, are pouring off the conveyor belt. A mandarin madness of secondary discourse infects thought and sensibility," Steiner complains.[11] Ours is an age of journalism, of spin doctors, of parasitic literary studies "which are the power-house of secondary discourse."[12] Even the notion of "research" has been debased:

> [T]he bulk of doctoral and post-doctoral 'research' into literature, and the publications which it spawns, are nothing more than a grey morass.
>
> The dilution, the trivialization of the concept of research in the humanities, and the regimen of the parasitic which it sustains in our culture, has two causes. The first is the professionalization of the academic pursuit and appropriation of the liberal arts. . . .
>
> The second motive is that of the humanistic imitation of the scientific. In their scale of bureaucratic formalization, of funding, in their eager pretense to theoretical rigour and cumulative discovery, the humanities in our universities . . . strive obsessively to rival the high good fortunes of the exact and the applied sciences. This striving, and the mendacious notion of research which it entails, are themselves founded in the positivism and 'scientism' of the nineteenth century.[13]

In brief, experience has been exchanged for explanation; art has been annexed by artifice, by pseudo-scientific (and largely unreadable) expositions of great writers (composers, sculptors, painters) and their works.[14] Endless commentary and specious exegesis have created a "Byzantine dominion of secondary and parasitic discourse over immediacy, of the critical over the creative."[15] One needs only to read a current issue of *Dissertation Abstracts* to confirm the point. "Our talk is about talk."[16] Steiner concludes that

> we crave remission from direct encounter with the "real presence" or the "real absence of that presence," the two phenomenologies being rigorously inseparable, which an answerable experience of the aesthetic must enforce on us. We seek the immunities of indirection. In the agency of the critic, reviewer or mandarin commentator, we welcome those who can domesticate, who can secularize the mystery and summons of creation.[17]

One need not subscribe entirely to Steiner's condemnation of deconstructionist "pseudo-criticism" in order to concede many of his conclusions. At the core of his counter-proposal—that human language, feeling, and aesthetic meaning infer the

---

[11]   Ibid., 26.

[12]   Ibid., 34.

[13]   Ibid., 35–36.

[14]   Steiner blames the deconstructionists for much of this mischief. See ibid., 53–134, especially 94–134.

[15]   Steiner, *Real Presences*, 38.

[16]   Ibid., 40. Steiner notes that not all commentary is specious, secondary or parasitic. In the tradition of Talmudic exegesis, for example, "commentary underwrites . . . the continued authority and survival of the primary discourse. It liberates the life of meaning from that of historical-geographical contingency. In dispersion, the text is homeland" (ibid., 40).

[17]   Ibid., 39.

"necessary possibility" of God's real presence—lies the notion of *answerability* in art. That notion is intimately linked to Steiner's understanding of the tasks of hermeneutics. "I shall try to elucidate hermeneutics," he writes, "as defining the enactment of answerable understanding, of active apprehension."[18]

> An interpreter is a decipherer and communicator of meanings. He is a translator between languages, between cultures and between performative conventions. He is, in essence, an executant, one who "acts out" the material before him so as to give it intelligible life.[19]

A cellist plays one of J. S. Bach's unaccompanied suites. A dancer performs Martha Graham's "Rodeo" (using Aaron Copland's score). In each case hermeneutics—interpretation—is "understanding in action; it is the immediacy of translation."[20] Hermeneutics is thus direct critical engagement in the art itself, "an act of penetrative response which makes sense sensible."[21] "It is when we experience and compare different interpretations, *that is to say performances*, of the same ballet, symphony or quartet, that we enter the life of comprehension," Steiner insists.[22]

And this brings one back to the idea of *answerability* as the key to a hermeneutics of performance. A performer's interpretation constitutes a *moral act*, one that can never be ethically neutral.

> Unlike the reviewer, the literary critic, the academic vivisector and judge, the executant invests his own being in the process of interpreation. His readings, his enactments of chosen meanings and values, are not those of external survey. They are a commitment at risk, a response which is, in the root sense, responsible. . . .
>
> Interpretative response under pressure of enactment I . . . call *answerability*. The authentic experience of understanding, when we are spoken to by another human being or by a poem, is one of responding responsibility. We are answerable to the text, to the work of art, to the musical offering, in a very specific sense, at once moral, spiritual and psychological.[23]

In short, if history is hermeneutics, hermeneutics is live performance—"action and immediacy."[24] "Interpretation," Steiner notes, "is, to the largest possible degree, *lived*."[25] It is inevitably ethical and *embodied* as well. "The meanings of poetry and the music of those meanings, which we call metrics, are also of the human body. The echoes of sensibility which they elicit are visceral and tactile."[26] And so, the full hermeneutical response is not only critically "answerable," but also ethical, embodied and inward:

[18] Ibid., 7.
[19] Ibid.
[20] Ibid., 8.
[21] Ibid.
[22] Ibid.; emphasis added.
[23] Ibid.
[24] Ibid., 9.
[25] Ibid.; emphasis added.
[26] Ibid.

In reference to language and the musical score, enacted interpretation can also be inward. The private reader or listener can become an executant of felt meaning when he learns the poem or the musical passage by heart. To learn by heart is to afford the text or music an indwelling clarity and life-force. Ben Jonson's term, "ingestion," is precisely right. What we know by heart becomes an agency in our consciousness, a "pace-maker" in the growth and vital complication of our identity. . . . Accurate recollection and resort in remembrance not only deepen our grasp of the work: they generate a shaping reciprocity between ourselves and that which the heart knows. . . . [R]emembrance becomes recognition and discovery (to re-cognize is to know anew).[27]

In sum, hermeneutics is live, critical, embodied, performative, answerable *action*. It demands the risk of an ethical investment that is shared by "performer" and "audience" (= co-performer) alike. Every work of art confronts us, moreover, with an irreducible "otherness" that refuses to be "explained" (still less, explained *away*). As Steiner concludes:

We readers, listeners, viewers, experience the aesthetic, answer to the testing freedom of its ingress into our being, by coming to recognize within its formalities the lineaments of creation itself. Responding to the poem, to the piece of music, to the painting, we re-enact, within the limits of our own lesser creativity, the two defining motions of our existential presence in the world: that of the coming into being where nothing was, where nothing could have continued to be, and that of the enormity of death. . . . It is the aesthetic which, past any other mode accessible to us, is the felt configuration of a negation (however partial . . .) of mortality.[28]

When we imagine fictive worlds, persons and plots within ourselves; when we make "audition resonant to the music via an inner complementarity, at once conceptual and bodily"; when we absorb a painting's light so that it becomes our own eye looking, we "remake the making." Such a hermeneutics of performance is, however, never exhaustive. Not only is "meaning" in a work of art irreducible; it also bears an inexhaustible plenitude, a "surplus" that survives even the most diligent scrutiny. Thus the "final paradox which defines our humanity prevails: there is always, there always will be, a sense in which we do not know what it is we are experiencing and talking about when we experience and talk about that which is. There is a sense in which no human discourse, however analytic, can make final sense of sense itself."[29]

Toward a New Definition of Liturgical Theology

Steiner's critique of the "secondary" and his proposal for a hermeneutics of performance offer a useful framework within which to discuss what is meant by the phrase, "liturgical theology." As David Fagerberg has noted, "Not any and all theological discourse about worship should receive the appellation 'liturgical

---

[27] Ibid., 9–10.
[28] Ibid., 209–10.
[29] Ibid., 215.

theology.'"[30] Many so-called "theologies" of *worship* are in fact a species of *theologia secunda*—second-order theological reflection abstracted from specific instances of experience. "Worship" is studied as an abstract phenomenon common to many cultures and capable of being analyzed by methods based on measurement, observation and statistics. Fagerberg has described this method well: "its service is to analyze, categorize, unpack, and impose schemata to aid understanding. . . . The concern of theology of worship is worship."[31]

In such a scheme, *worship* signifies "a fundamental reality, manifesting the right relationship between God and human beings,"[32] the comprehensive means "by which the Spirit continues [the community's] fellowship and conformity with Christ."[33] In sum, worship is a global reality stretching well beyond the rituals of liturgy to include "the whole of Christian life in service and self-surrender to the needs of the world."[34] In a theology of worship, the liturgical rites themselves are rather insignificant. Instead, the focus is upon how, through God's initiative, human persons are empowered to respond "to the divine action in Jesus of Nazareth."[35]

In addition to theologies *of* worship, it is necessary, Fagerberg argues, to consider "theologies *from* worship." A theology from worship "wants doctrine to be expressed in liturgical form [and] . . . wants worship to be rooted in doctrine."[36] In other words, theology and liturgy are "mutually transitive."[37] Proponents of this method seek to show how "the worship of the Church has influenced doctrine and the doctrine of the Church has influenced worship."[38] Summarizing Geoffrey Wainwright's position, Fagerberg observes that in the "theology from worship" model, worship becomes "the doxological experience from which dogma itself takes its origin." Theology itself becomes "doxological."

> Not only would theology think about worship, it would come from worship. Not only would theology include worship on its menu of thought projects, but theology would become worshipful. . . . The current would flow both ways. The law of prayer would shape, color and stimulate the laws by which we formulate our belief. The law

[30] David W. Fagerberg, *What Is Liturgical Theology? A Study in Methodology* (Collegeville: The Liturgical Press, 1992) 66.

[31] Ibid., 67.

[32] Ibid., 78.

[33] Ibid., 62.

[34] Ibid., 63. Fagerberg discusses at length two examples of such theologies *of* worship: those of Regin Prenter (*Creation and Redemption*) and Vilmos Vajta (*Luther on Worship*). See *What is Liturgical Theology?*, 23–75.

[35] Fagerberg, 12.

[36] Ibid., 12.

[37] Ibid., 75.

[38] Ibid., 12. Fagerberg discusses in detail two examples of theology from worship: those of Peter Brunner (*Worship in the Name of Jesus*) and Geoffrey Wainwright (*Doxology*). See *What is Liturgical Theology?*, 76–142.

of belief would architectonically propose to the worshipping community any correc-
tions or improvements judged necessary, thereby preserving the law of prayer.[39]

But neither theology *of* worship nor theology *from* worship qualifies for what
Fagerberg (and others like Alexander Schmemann and Aidan Kavanagh) would call
"liturgical theology." The primary concern of liturgical theology is not "worship"
considered abstractly or globally, but rather, "liturgical rite as an instantiation of the
Church's *lex orandi*."[40] As Robert Taft has written, because liturgies are historical
actions, they "can only be understood in motion, just as the only way to understand
a top is to spin it."[41]

The fact that *liturgy* is something "in motion" is seminal for developing liturgical theology. "When leitourgia is taken as rite," comments David Fagerberg,

> *it can be called theological because it is faith in motion.* It does not merely serve as
> the raw data for theology or the existential expression of theological dictums, for the
> very reason . . . that liturgical rite is transaction in the mystery which issues in *the-
> ologia prima* which serves as the base for secondary theology. Leitourgia is not a way
> of saying something, it is a way of becoming something. It is not a way of saying the-
> ology, it is how believers become Church. And because it is the Church which theol-
> ogizes, *lex ordandi* establishes *lex credendi*.[42]

Liturgical theology, in other words, is neither secondary discourse nor "didactic interposition."[43] "For what emerges most directly from an assembly's liturgical act," as Aidan Kavanagh has argued, "is not a new species of theology among
others. It is *theologia* itself."[44] That is precisely why Alexander Schmemann insisted that liturgy is neither an *auctoritas* (in the Western scholastic sense) nor a
locus theologicus, but rather "the ontological condition of theology":[45]

> [T]he liturgical tradition of the Church is fundamentally antinomical in its nature. It
> is a cult which eternally transcends itself, because it is the cult of a community which
> eternally realizes itself, as the Body of Christ, as the Church of the Holy Spirit, as . . .
> the new *aeon* of the Kingdom. It is a tradition of forms and structures, but those
> forms and structures are no longer those of a "cult," but those of the Church itself, of
> its life "in Christ." . . . The formula *lex orandi est lex credendi* means nothing else
> than that theology is *possible* only within the Church, i.e., as a fruit of this new life in
> Christ, granted in the sacramental *leitourgia*, as a witness to the eschatological ful-
> ness of the Church, as, in other terms, a participation in this *leitourgia*.[46]

---

[39] Fagerberg, 132.

[40] Ibid., 67.

[41] Robert Taft, "The Structural Analysis of Liturgical Units: An Essay in Methodology," *Worship* 52 (1978) 317.

[42] Fagerberg, 75.

[43] Steiner, 21.

[44] Aidan Kavanagh, *On Liturgical Theology* (New York: Pueblo Publishing Company, 1984) 75.

[45] Alexander Schmemann, "Theology and Liturgical Tradition," in Massey Shepherd, ed., *Worship in Scripture and Tradition* (New York: Oxford University Press, 1963) 175.

[46] Ibid.

When is a cult not a cult? When it is *liturgy*—or rather, when it is *rite*, when it is "actual participation" in *leitourgia*. Thus Robert Taft's image of the top, "understood" only when it is in spinning. Thus David Fagerberg's view that *leitourgia* is "faith in *motion*." Thus Aidan Kavanagh's insistence, in his classic *On Liturgical Theology*, that among Christians a liturgical act is always and inevitably a *rite*:

> Rite involves creeds and prayers and worship, but it is not any one of these things, nor all of these things together, and it orchestrates more than these things. Rite can be called a whole style of Christian living found in the myriad particularities of worship, of laws called "canonical," of ascetical and monastic structures, of evangelical and catechetical endeavors, and in particular ways of doing secondary theological reflection. A liturgical act concretizes all these and in doing so makes them accessible to the community assembled in a given time and place before the living God for the life of the world. Rite in this Christian sense is generated and sustained in this regular meeting of faithful people in whose presence and through whose deeds the vertiginous Source of the cosmos itself is pleased to settle down freely and abide as among friends. A liturgy of Christians is thus nothing less than the way a redeemed world is, so to speak, done. *The liturgical act of rite and the assembly which does it are coterminous, one thing: the incorporation under grace of Christ dying and rising still, restoring the communion all things and persons have been gifted with in Spirit and in truth.*[47]

Here there is no room for the parasitical or the secondary. If "the best readings of art are art" (Steiner), then the best readings of rite are rite. Liturgical theology locates itself within "the structure of a liturgical rite"—as it "actually happens in liturgies and not on paper."[48] Works "about" liturgical theology (even works as wise and worthy as those by Schmemann and Kavanagh) are not *das Ding an sich*. Rather, such a theology must be located *within the ritualizing assembly itself*, within a community "caught in the act" of becoming church, of "doing" a redeemed world.

Liturgical theology is possible only if we understand that "Men and women were created for Eucharistic life. We are homo *adorans*. The Eucharist is humanity fully alive."[49] Such a view has, of course, cosmological implications. It suggests that liturgy enacts what humanity and cosmos were meant to be. For what has been redeemed in Christ (and so may be celebrated liturgically) is "not fundamentally the Church . . . but the World itself."[50] Otherwise Christian "cult" (cult that is *not* cult) collapses "into self-aggrandizing solipsism."[51] Christian liturgy never exists to feather its own nest. And thus, the "worshipping assembly never comes away from [leitourgia] . . . unchanged":[52]

> Theology on this primordial level is . . . a sustained dialectic. Its *thesis* is the assembly as it enters into the liturgical act; its *antithesis* is the assembly's changed condi-

---

[47] Kavanagh, 100–1; emphasis added.
[48] Fagerberg, 12.
[49] Ibid., 226.
[50] Kavanagh, 43.
[51] Ibid., 44.
[52] Ibid., 76.

tion as it comes away from its liturgical encounter with the living God in Word and sacrament; its *synthesis* is the assembly's adjustment in faith and works to that encounter. The adjustment comprises whole sets of acts both great and small, conscious and unconscious, all of which [constitute] . . . the content and significance of the assembly's address to reality itself–both inside and outside church, on the first day and throughout all other days of the week as well.[53]

The celebrating assembly is, therefore, not the object but the *subject* of the liturgical action—a subject that simultaneously acts and is acted upon. The "condition of possibility" for doing liturgical theology is thus *rite as embodied in an assembly's acts of cult and care*. Note that "care" ("pastoral care" of the least and littlest) is an essential component of "cult." For as Marianne Sawicki has argued, these constitute the "two possible modes of Jesus' availability; . . . [they] mutually support each other and are secured in each other."[54] Thus, if David Fagerberg is correct to argue that liturgy is faith in motion; if Aidan Kavanagh is correct to say that for Christians *rite* is "the way a *redeemed world* is done;" if Marianne Sawicki is correct to insist that *care* is essential to Christian cult, then we must say that liturgical theology allows no member of this "trinity"—cosmos, cult, care—to be set in motion unless *all* are set in motion.

This is the case precisely because Easter and *eschaton* are themselves realities that, in this world, can be "read" only by *rite*—i.e., they can be apprehended (recall Steiner's definition of hermeneutics as the *immediacy of active apprehension*) only in and as the assembly's liturgical action. Easter subverts and disrupts *time* (by refusing to let the Dead belong to the past); so too, liturgy subverts and deconstructs *Easter* (by refusing to let it become an event confined to the past). Or to put it in positive terms, both Easter and liturgy transcend the structures (temporal, spatial) that limit and bind human availability. Liturgy (what Alexander Schmemann defined as the *eschaton*—the holy, the sacred, "otherness"—expressed and manifested as "cult") becomes our essential means of crossing the eschatological frontier. As Sawicki writes, "Sacramental liturgy is the means of assimilating to Jesus many persons, communities, and even material elements that, according to our accustomed narrative time line, could not possibly have supported any such connection. Resurrection, then, is 'about' the availability of Jesus as Risen Lord in the activities of caring for the poor and celebrating the liturgy.[55]

In short, Easter ruptures "human temporal existence from the inside out."[56] Sawicki summarizes this point succinctly:

Ordinarily death itself does not destroy human being; rather, death organizes it. Human being is unique, as Heidegger saw, in that it is a "being toward death." Belief

---

[53] Ibid.

[54] Marianne Sawicki, *Seeing the Lord: Resurrection and Early Christian Practices* (Minneapolis: Fortress, 1994) 334.

[55] Ibid., 335.

[56] Ibid.

in resurrection is a belief about time, that is, about the structures of human availability as they are conditioned by our experience of time. Death has meant becoming part of the past, and access to the past cannot be had on the same terms as access to the present. Beyond violating the laws of biology, therefore, resurrection violates the laws of phenomenology. It disobeys the laws of access to the past, to what is. This disobedience is not merely epistemological or psychological, but metaphysical, given that the being of people is really transformed by the way their bodies are written. Resurrection deconstructs the narrative structure by which we grasp the past.[57]

We can now understand how daring Aidan Kavanagh's definition of rite ("the way, so to speak, a redeemed world is done") really is. It suggests that liturgical theology is not primarily the province of professionals. On the contrary, such a theology's principal subject (agent, executant) is the assembly itself as it *does* the liturgical act.

I propose, therefore, that *liturgical theology can be written and read only in and as the assembly's ritual performance.* To borrow George Steiner's language, liturgical theology may be defined as "the critical enactment of answerable understanding, of active apprehension."[58] Liturgical theology is rite reading rite—and it has similarly serious *ethical* conditions and consequences.[59] In liturgical theology, the hermeneutic is in the performance—in the assembly's action.

Ritual as Reading

I am proposing here that we think of *ritual* as a way of "reading" reality—and that we think of *liturgical competence* as an *acquired*, not an infused, skill. In other words, I suggest we think of ritual as a species of *lectio divina*, of holy reading.[60] When the assembly "does" the liturgical act, it engages in ritual reading. This has implications for both *what* is done ("rite") and *how* it is done ("reading"). To explore some of these implications will be the purpose of this third section of my essay.

For most of us today, the "page" has become an electronic reality. As Ivan Illich notes, "The book has now ceased to be the root-metaphor of the age; the screen has taken its place."[61] This revolution has enormous implications not only for our perception of "pages" (now visually imagined as "homepage" or "web page"), but also for our understanding of reading. Augustine expressed amazement that

---

[57] Ibid.

[58] See above, the first section of this essay, for a discussion of Steiner's views about "answerability" as an essential element of critical hermeneutics.

[59] See above, the first section of this essay, for a discussion of the "ethics of (hermeneutical) performance" in light of George Steiner's reassertion of the primary over the secondary and parasitic.

[60] As I shall indicate below, "reading" must be understood not as a solitary function of mind and memory but as a collegial action that is simultaneously cognitive and kinetic, spiritual and sensate. The idea of *lectio divina* is of course familiar from the sixth-century *Rule of Benedict*.

[61] Ivan Illich, *In the Vineyard of the Text: A Commentary to Hugh's* Didascalicon (Chicago: University of Chicago Press, 1993) 3.

Ambrose could "read" with his eyes only; in the twelfth century, pages were optically reorganized to accommodate scholastic *disputatio*; in the fifteenth and sixteenth centuries, movable type replaced the human hand's movement of paint and
pen across parchment; and in our own epoch, electronic pages have become interactive in ways scarcely imagined a short time ago. All this has revolutionized not
only the technologies of alphabet and writing, but the act of reading as well. What
was for centuries in the West understood as "bookish reading" (an activity linked
to scholars in academic settings) has receded. Indeed, bookish reading, Ivan Illich
notes,

> can now clearly be recognized as an epochal phenomenon and not as a logically neces-
> sary step in the progress toward the rational use of the alphabet; as one mode of inter-
> action with the written page among several; as a particular vocation among many, to be
> cultivated by some, leaving other modes to others. The coexistence of distinct styles of
> reading would be nothing new. . . . With George Steiner I dream that outside the edu-
> cational system which has assumed entirely different functions there might be some-
> thing like *houses of reading*, not unlike the Jewish *shul*, the Islamic *medersa*, or the
> monastery, where the few who discover their passion for a life centered on reading
> would find the necessary guidance, silence, and complicity of disciplined companion-
> ship needed for . . . celebrating the book. In order that a new asceticism of reading
> may come to flower, we must first recognize that the bookish "classical" reading of the
> last 450 years is only one among several ways of using alphabetic techniques.[62]

We live, then, in an era of competing "schools" of reading—or more ironically, in an
era where *many modes of reading coexist simultaneously*. In this essay, my concern
is for that kind of skilled reading known as "ritual." When I say "skilled" I do not
mean "elitist." In the Christian community, ritual competence (a species of "reading"
competence) has been radically democratized. It is a skill belonging to the whole assembly and not limited to the few (priests, presiders, hierarchs, experts). In the pages
that follow, I shall attempt to describe what kind of "ritual reading" Christians do and
how it may help shape an understanding of liturgical theology.

1. Page as Performance Piece

During the first several centuries of Christian reading, the page was basically
a performance piece, "a *score* for pious mumblers," meant to be *mouthed*, to be
read aloud, its meanings *tasted* by bodily action.[63] Such pious "mumbling"—
which became institutionalized in performance practices such as the "*ritual recitative*" (the chanting of texts at eucharist and Hours) and the monastic "*lectio
divina*"—presumed that reading is emphatically *not* a retreat to "a world *within*"
(as we often think of it today). On the contrary, reading meant entering "the world
outside," full bore, full body. Reading was not mere mental activity aroused by the

---

[62] Ibid.
[63] Ibid., 2.

eye moving across a page; rather, it was loud motor activity, a fact of flesh and saliva, an unavoidably social and communal enterprise. As Ivan Illich observes:

> In a tradition of one and a half millennia, the sounding pages are echoed by the reso-
> nance of the moving lips and tongue. The reader's ears pay attention, and strain to
> catch what the reader's mouth gives forth. In this manner the sequence of letters
> translates directly into body movements and patterns nerve impulses. The lines are a
> sound track picked up by the mouth and voiced by the reader for his own ear. By
> reading, the page is literally embodied, incorporated.[64]

For us today, pages are either characters moving across a monitor or "plates that ink the mind"; meanwhile, the mind itself is "a screen onto which the page is projected and from which, at a flip, it can fade."[65] But for Christians throughout much of the first millennium, reading was a carnal act of almost embarrassing intensity. Readers understood a page's lettered lines

> by *moving to their beat*, remember[ed] them by *recapturing their rhythm*, and
> [thought] of them in terms of *putting them into [their mouths] and chewing*. No won-
> der that pre-university monasteries are described to us in various sources as the
> dwelling places of mumblers and munchers.[66]

Where the page is a mumbler's "score" to be performed, reading becomes a ritual act whose meanings flow from words *as they move through the body, feel* on the tongue, *mean* in the mouth. Reading is rhapsodic.[67] When "performed" as ritual recitative or *lectio divina*, the texts of Bible and liturgy become part of the performer's biography and physiology. That is why the physical discipline of reading became so pivotal in Western monastic sources like the *Rule of Benedict*. The roots of this tradition are Middle Eastern. Thus, in both "ritual recitative" and monastic *lectio*,

> the book was swallowed and digested through the careful attention paid to the psy-
> chomotor nerve impulses which accompany the sentences being learned. Even today,
> pupils in Koranic and Jewish schools sit on the floor with the book open on their knees.
> Each one chants his lines in a singsong, often a dozen pupils simultaneously, each a dif-
> ferent line. While they read, their bodies sway from the hips up or their trunks gently
> rock back and forth. The swinging and the recitation continue as if the student is in a
> trance, even when he closes his eyes or looks down the aisle of the mosque. The body
> movements re-evoke those of the speech organs that have been associated with them. *In
> a ritual manner these students use their whole bodies to embody the lines.*[68]

Thus, where reading is practiced as ritual recitative or *lectio*, memory is actually *re-membered movement*. The research of Marcel Jousse (a Jesuit anthropologist who

---

[64] Ibid., 54.

[65] Ibid.

[66] Ibid., emphasis added.

[67] Recall that the English words "rhapsode" and "rhapsody" are taken from the Greek roots *raptein* (to stitch together) and *ōidē* (song).

[68] Ivan Illich, *In the Vineyard of the Text*, 60; emphasis added.

worked in Beirut and studied the way Semitic cultures embody sayings) demonstrates the crucial connection between movement and memory.[69] Jousse was able to demonstrate that for many people remembrance is triggered by a well-established sequence of muscular patterns to which the utterances are tied. In short, there is a vital linkage between *utterance* and *gesture*. This is the case for children who are rocked while their mothers sing cradle songs, for reapers who swing their scythes to the rhythm of a harvest song, for rabbis whose bodies sway rhythmically as they mumble psalms and prayers, for Christian monks practicing *lectio*. Variation exists from one culture to another, almost everywhere one encounters some form of

> bilateral, dissymmetric complentarity by which sayings are graven right and left, forward and backward into trunk and limbs, rather than just into the ear and eye. Monastic existence can be viewed as a carefully patterned framework for the practice of such techniques.[70]

Thus reading (understood as ritual, as physical discipline, as *lectio*) is not only incarnate, it is always and inevitably *gestural*. Thinking, cognition and comprehension are not merely "mental processes," they are *embodied performance*. Thinking emanates not solely from the brain's neocortical layer; it also flows from the skin. We quite literally remember with our *bodies*. When such remembering is linked to reading, one sees how radically social, inclusive and egalitarian the phenomena of "ritual recitative" and *lectio* are. Reading is a vocal act that inevitably creates a *public* ambiance, an auditory social space. That is why the *Rule of Benedict* cautioned readers not to disturb others who might be resting, praying or working.[71] Because it is vocal *performance*, reading is a preeminently social activity that effectively democratizes the ritual environment within which it takes place. *All* who are immersed in the "auditory milieu" become *equals* before its sound. Again, that is why monks understood *lectio* as an essentially liturgical act, performed *coram* (in the face of) others—God, angels, or anyone within earshot. The page was not merely a cue card, an archival resource, or a "system" for the storage and retrieval of information; it was a performance piece, a "score for mumblers." The primary organs for "reading" and "remembering" the page were the mouth, the tongue, the skin.

2. A Revolution in Reading

About 850 years ago, however, a series of graphic innovations in the West resulted in the appearance of pages that were no longer "performance pieces," but *texts* optically reorganized for logical thinkers.[72] As a consequence, the very nature of reading changed dramatically during the latter half of the twelfth century. The

---

[69] See *Le Style Oral: Rythmique et Mnémotechnique* (Paris: Foundation Marcel Jousse / Le Centurion, 1981).

[70] Illich, 61.

[71] See *Rule of Benedict*.

[72] Ivan Illich dates the beginning of this revolutionary transition to about the year 1150.

written page ceased to be a "score" intended for vocal performance. Reading *aloud* receded, to be replaced by reading *with the eyes only*. "*Legere*," "to read," became an individualistic activity, silent intercourse between the isolated self and the page.

Ironically, while monasticism is sometimes accused of turning Christianity from an outward-looking religion to an inward-looking one, the tradition of monastic *lectio* actually maintained the older tradition of reading as a *public, social* activity—an embodied "stepping out into the world." It was the graphic innovations introduced by the early scholastics that transformed the page from score to text, from act to archive, from "outward" to "inward." For the schoolmen, the page was no longer a body, a field, a painting, a vineyard, but precisely a *text*, a sequential series of *visual markers* that "told" the reader's *mind* and *eyes*

a. *how to construct an argument* by marshalling facts in proper sequence–*prima, secunda, tertia*, etc.;

b. *how to anticipate an opponent's objections* (the word "*obicitur*" marked the precise point on the page where an adversary's views were lined up for easy demolition);

c. *how to use authoritative sources ("auctoritates") to combat objections* (the place again marked by a textual formula such as "*Sed contra, sicut Augustinus dicit . . .*"); and finally,

d. how to summarize one's own argument (through a formula like "*Respondeo dicendum est . . .*).

Note well: the page's markers (textual formulas—*prima, secunda*; *obicitur*; *sed contra*; *respondeo dicendum est*) are not merely the verbal and cognitive components of a scholastic argument; they are also its *visual expression*.

The rise of *this* kind of reading—where rapt attention to a text's logically structured argument replaces the rhapsodic strategies of *lectio divina* or ritual recitative—made possible the emergence of a new class of readers and scholars. These scholars were clerical professionals who could—and would—come to dominate literacy. The old monastic *democracy* of reading (which assumed that "the book of creation comprises *both* sides of the cloister wall" and that "the arts of this world *and* Scripture *both* tell of God's work")[73] was replaced by a "scribal monopoly." These scribal "experts" ("clerics"—the word was increasingly restricted to the ranks of ordained *men*) defined themselves as "the literate, as opposed to those who are only hearers of the written word, simple lay people."[74] Thus, a new duality supplanted the older, democratic ideal of reading (*lectio divina*) as a radically egalitarian act that unites *all* speakers and hearers in a single acoustic "space." W. H. Auden once remarked that Western poetry is dominated by two opposing views: one sees the poem as idiomatic, choral, civic, the property of a *people*; the other sees the poem as vatic revelation, the work of a seer—private,

---

[73] Illich, 82.
[74] Ibid., 84.

hermetic, sealed. Monastic *lectio* perceived reading as choral, civic, communal; scholastic *disputatio* understood it as vatic, oracular and private.

Thus, the innovative graphics and optical rearrangements that made "scholastic" *pages* possible promoted not only the privatization of reading, but also its patriarchalization in the medieval West. Reading came to be culturally defined as "androcentric activity, a competence reserved to the clergy and those taught by them."[75] As a result, the Western model for universal literacy became *not* the rhapsodic score, *not* the inclusive *lectio divina*, *not* the ritual recitative, but rather the technical, professional skills of scholastic clerks. The resulting apartheid was not only *cognitive* (the habit of putting *thought* above *action*) but *gendered*. Because women were excluded from the clerisy, they were *ipso facto* excluded from the "professions" of reading, teaching and learning. At the same time, the life of lay *men* was often assimilated to that of the scribal monopoly. The *vita clericorum* became *the* "model to which lay men had to aspire, and by which they were inevitably degraded into the 'illiterate,' to be instructed and controlled by their betters."[76] In short, *reading* became an efficient, restrictive, pliable tool for cultural control and social segregation.

Thus, by the end of the twelfth century, Ivan Illich notes:

> [T]he *book* takes on a symbolism which it retained until our time. It becomes the symbol for an unprecedented kind of object, visible but intangible, which I shall call the *bookish text*. In the long social history of the alphabet, the impact of this development can be compared with only two other events: the introduction of full phonetic script, which occurred around 400 B.C., making Greek a language upon which the speaker could reflect, and the diffusion of printing in the fifteenth century, which made the *text* into a powerful mold for a new literary and scientific worldview.[77]

In Illich's opinion, this twelfth-century innovation was far more fundamental and revolutionary than the invention of movable type and mechanical printing techniques (around the year 1460). It established *texts* as the privileged means for both organizing logical thought and regulating social structure. A new relationship between text and mind was established, one that would be essential for the *print* culture that finally did arise in the fifteenth century.

> The text could now be seen *as something distinct from the book*. It was an object that could be visualized even with closed eyes. . . . The page lost the quality of soil in which words are rooted. The new text was a figment on the face of the book that lifted off into autonomous existence. This new bookish text did have material existence, but it was not the existence of ordinary things: it was literally neither here nor there. Only its shadow appeared on the page of this or that concrete book. As a result, the book was no longer the window onto nature or God; it was no longer the transparent

---

[75] Ibid., 85.
[76] Ibid., 86.
[77] Ibid., 115.

optical device through which the reader gains access to creatures or the transcendent. . . . Out of the symbol for cosmic reality [the book] had arisen *a symbol for thought*. The *text*, rather than the book, became the object in which thought is gathered and mirrored.[78]

Inexorably, the bookish text was *objectified* as a visual icon of logical thought and *detached* from its physical source (the book). By the thirteenth century, the scholastic text "floated" above the palpable page. The text (the scholastic argument optically and logically organized in "articles") was "on its way to becoming a kind of vessel that ferries meaningful signs through the space separating the copy from the original; it drops anchor here or there."[79]

3. Consequences for Liturgical Theology

All this had far-reaching consequences for reading and for liturgical theology. The remote roots of what George Steiner calls "the dominance of the secondary" can be traced back to the revolution in reading that began in the second half of the twelfth century. This revolution contributed mightily in the West to a mutation of idioms: "liturgy" became "worship;" "rite" became "rituals;" "liturgical theology" became derivative exegesis and parasitic commentary. Our relation to what is and to what is real was ineluctably altered. The liturgy of Christians (rite, cult and care) and the liturgy of the world (*natura*, including homo sapiens) ceased being "scores to be performed" and became *objects to be contemplated and described*. Rite no longer read rite. "Exegesis and hermeneutics become operations on the *text*, rather than on the world."[80]

Whether liturgical theology is possible in such a climate depends, I think, on whether we define ritual as "a *symbol system* whose aim is to produce *meanings*" or as "a *technology* whose use *transforms the assembly that enacts and embodies it.*" My option is for the latter. But since it may seem strange to define ritual as a "technology," I owe the reader an explanation.[81] The definition is derived, in part, from the work of Michel Foucault. Foucault's project was, in his own words, "to sketch out a history of the different ways in our culture that humans develop knowledge about themselves: economics, biology, psychiatry, medicine, penology."[82] He wished not simply to accept this knowledge at face value, but to look at the sciences just mentioned as "'truth games' related to specific techniques that human beings use to understand themselves."[83]

---

[78]   Ibid., 119; emphasis added.

[79]   Ibid., 118.

[80]   Ibid., 117.

[81]   Some of what follows here appears—in a different form—in my monograph, *Liturgy and the Social Sciences* (Collegeville: The Liturgical Press, 1999).

[82]   *Technologies of the Self: A Seminar with Michel Foucault*, ed. Luther H. Martin, Huck Gutman, and Patrick H. Hutton (Amherst: The University of Massachusetts Press, 1988) 17–18.

[83]   Ibid., 18.

These techniques (technologies) fall into four fundamental categories: (1) *technologies of production*, "which permit us to produce, transform, or manipulate things"; (2) *technologies of sign systems*, "which permit us to use signs, meanings, symbols, or signification"; (3) *technologies of power*, "which determine the conduct of individuals and submit them to certain ends or domination, an objectivizing of the subject"; and finally, (4) *technologies of the self*, "which permit individuals to effect by their own means or with the help of others a certain number of operations on their own bodies and souls, thoughts, conduct, and way of being, so as to transform themselves in order to attain a certain state of happiness, purity, wisdom, perfection, or immortality."[84]

To speak about a "technology of the self" is thus to discuss "the history of how an individual acts upon himself," along with the interactions between self and others as these are driven by strategies of symbol, production or power.[85] Note that this "technology of the self" is not an autistic, idiosyncratic or isolated process. Indeed, the phrase is closely connected to what early Christian writers called *cura animae*, "care of the soul (self)."[86] This *cura* is deployed and exercised chiefly through the practices of asceticism (discipline, control, penance, prayer, purification, etc.). But if self-care is personal, it is also, for Christians, inherently and decisively *social*. It comes as no surprise, therefore, that the ascetic practices of *cura animae* inevitably involve ritual. Thus, technologies of the self include both the "rites" practiced by individuals and the "ritual construction" of the whole *social* order.[87] The reason is that Foucault sees the human body not simply as a private possession but as "a political field."[88] As Catherine Bell describes it:

> For Foucault, the body is "the place where the most minute and local social practices are linked up with the large scale organization of power." The body is a political field: "Power relations have an immediate hold upon it; they invest it, mark it, train it, torture it, force it to carry out tasks, to perform ceremonies, to emit signs." The body is the most basic and fundamental level of power relations, the "microphysics" of the micropolitics of power. Ritualization, Foucault appears to imply, is a central way that power operates; it constitutes a political technology of the body.[89]

From this perspective, then, ritual is a way of inscribing the body personal, the body politic—and their complex, inevitable interactions. Foucault's work (and that

[84] Ibid. Foucault notes that these technologies rarely function separately. Each of them, moreover, "implies certain modes of training and modification of individuals, not only in the obvious sense of acquiring certain skills but also in the sense of acquiring certain attitudes."

[85] Ibid., 19.

[86] See the examples Foucault cites from writers like Gregory of Nyssa; ibid., 20–22.

[87] See Catherine Bell, *Ritual Theory, Ritual Practice* (New York: Oxford University Press, 1992) 97–98. Note her critique of Foucault, 98. Even though Foucault "consistently chooses the nomenclature of 'ritual' to evoke the mechanisms and dynamics of power," he is not "concerned to analyze ritual per se or even to generate a description of ritual as an autonomous phenomenon" (ibid., 201).

[88] Ibid., 201.

[89] Ibid., 202.

of feminist thinkers like Julia Kristeva) has helped us form a new image of the body. No longer is the body a stepchild, "the mere physical instrument of the mind; it now denotes a more complex and irreducible phenomenon, namely, *the social person*."[90] This new image is inescapably linked to ritual.

> For Foucault, the "body" emerged in the late seventeenth century as the arena in which more local social practices were linked to the larger scale organization of power. With examples that range from marking the body with torture to confessional routines and the control of space, Foucault has suggested how "rituals of power" work to forge a specific political "technology" of the body. As *the* medium of the play of power, he argued, the body came to be linked to a new political rationality specifically rooted in the technologies of "bio-power." This historical emergence of the body as a focus, moreover, would constitute a new level of analysis located between biology and the institutional vehicles of force, and giving rise to the human sciences themselves.[91]

This modern reappropriation of the body—its new image as an arena for the ritual negotiation of power and politics—is one of the things that made research in the modern human sciences (e.g., anthropology, sociology) possible.

I suggest, therefore, that *rite* be understood both comprehensively (as Aidan Kavanagh does in the passage from *On Liturgical Theology* cited earlier in this essay) and "technologically" (as Foucault does). The final intentionality of rite is not "to produce meanings" but to produce a ritually inscribed body (both personal and corporate) that knows how, liturgically, to "do" a redeemed world. What is meant by this can be clarified by reference to rite as understood in a classic Christian source, the *Rule of Benedict* (RB). In RB, "rite" was not yet recognized as a separate, specialized category of human behavior (the way modern liturgists and anthropologists like to think of it).[92] Monastic liturgy and ritual were not yet seen, in the early sixth century, as formal activities that are inherently "symbolic, structured, canonical, invariable, non-technical, traditional, and repetitive" in nature. Indeed, RB thought of the monks' three principal daily occupations—chanting the Divine Office (*opus Dei*), manual labor, and "holy reading" (*lectio divina*)—as *the same kinds of activity* requiring roughly *the same amount* of time. [93] Nor is *opus Dei* spo-

---

[90] Ibid., 96.

[91] Ibid., 97.

[92] The modern anthropologist Talal Asad would not quite agree with the opinion of scholars like Catherine Bell who see ritual fundamentally as "a way of acting that distinguishes itself from other ways of acting." He writes, "it does not seem to me to make good sense to say that ritual behavior stands universally in opposition to behavior that is ordinary or pragmatic, any more than religion stands in contrast to reason or to (social) science." See his essay "On Discipline and Humility in Medieval Christian Monasticism," in *Genealogies of Religion* (Baltimore: Johns Hopkins University Press, 1993) 167. Asad is also critical of Clifford Geertz's view of religion and ritual. See "Anthropological Conceptions of Religion: Reflections on Geertz," *Man* (NS) 18 (1983) 237–59.

[93] See the *Rule of Benedict*, chapters 47 and 48.

ken of as though it were *symbolic* action (as opposed, say, to manual labor and *lectio*). Writing about the idea of monastic "rite" in the *Rule*, Talal Asad observes:

> The liturgy is not a species of enacted symbolism to be classified separately from activities defined as technical but is *a practice among others essential to the acquisition of Christian virtues*. In other words, the liturgy can be isolated only conceptually, for pedagogic reasons, not in practice, from the [rest of the] monastic program.
>
> . . . In the *Rule* all prescribed practices, whether they had to do with the proper ways of eating, sleeping, working, and praying or with proper moral disposition and spiritual aptitudes, are aimed at developing virtues that are put "to the service of God."[94]

The virtues of a nun or monk were thus formed by cultivating the ability to behave, bodily, in certain ways (humbly, obediently, compassionately)—*no matter what the particular activity might be*. This is clear from RB's description of the "twelfth step of humility":

> The twelfth step of humility is that a monk always manifests humility in his bearing no less than in his heart, so that it is evident at the Work of God [the Divine Office], in the oratory, the monastery, or the garden, on a journey or in the field, or anywhere else. Whether he sits, walks or stands, his head must be bowed and his eyes cast down. . . .[95]

In RB, ritual is thus perceived as *bodily inscription*, as embodied technology and "practice," as rehearsal or routine. It is a way of acting equally applicable to work in the garden, to a business trip outside the monastic enclosure, or to chanting psalms in the oratory. Obviously, such an understanding of rite has nothing to do with ceremonical grandeur, solemnity or "canonicity." It aims, rather, "at the *apt performance* of what is prescribed, something that depends on intellectual and practical disciplines *but does not itself require decoding*. In other words, apt performance involves *not* symbols to be interpreted but *abilities to be acquired* according to rules that are sanctioned by those in authority: it presupposes no obscure meanings, but rather the formation of physical and linguistic skills."[96] In RB, rite means "thinking' with the skin, "speaking" with the whole human sensorium. Rite's role is to teach the *body* how to develop *spiritual virtues* by *material* means. *Ritual* competence is thus *bodily* competence, for the body is "an assemblage of *embodied aptitudes*, not . . . a medium of symbolic meanings."[97] Strictly speaking, monastic rituals are cognitively "empty," "meaningless."[98] Their significance is acquired and interpreted *by the body*. Their "meaning" is inscribed on the skin, borne by the blood, carved in the bone.

[94] "Toward a Genealogy of the Concept of Ritual," in *Genealogies of Religion*, 63; emphasis added.

[95] *Rule of Benedict*, chapter 7.62-63. Translation in *RB 1980: The Rule of St. Benedict in Latin and English with Notes*, ed. Timothy Fry, et al. (Collegeville: The Liturgical Press, 1981) 201.

[96] Asad, "The Concept of Ritual," 62; emphasis added.

[97] Ibid., 75; emphasis added.

[98] See Frits Staal, "The Meaninglessness of Ritual," *Numen* 26 (1979) 2–22. "A widespread but erroneous assumption about ritual is that it consists in symbolic activities which refer to something else. It is characteristic of a ritual performance, however, that it is self-contained and self-absorbed. The performers are totally immersed in the proper execution of their complex tasks. Isolated

According to RB, then, rite reads rite. The ability to enter into communion with God and others in the liturgical act is a function of *bodies that have learned how to behave ritually*, of bodies that "practice" virtue in much the same way that a pianist's hands "practice" music and "interpret" it through *performance.*[99] Early Benedictinism saw ritual as a technology of the self that "does" a new human identity (personal, corporate) by "doing" a redeemed world. This new identity is not "bestowed" through a single sacramental stroke; instead, it is gradually gathered through the patient learning of skills inscribed on the body. If ritual "rules" seem to govern virtually every aspect of life in RB (eating, working, walking, sleeping, praying), they are aimed at neither regimentation nor ostentatious display.[100] Rather, ritual structures provide the social means—the "institutional resources"— that make the production of a "virtuous self" *possible.*[101] This "virtuous self" *is* the new identity disclosed—slowly, gradually—through technologies of confession and self-examination, through the myriad "rules and rites" that accompany work (manual labor), through prayer (*opus Dei*) and reading (*lectio divina*).

In sum, "ritual" in RB is a *quality* that characterizes communal behavior,[102] rather than a separate species or category of human action. It is closer, perhaps, to Herbert Fingarette's description of rite (*li*) in Confucian thought:[103]

> Rite brings out forcefully . . . the inherent and ultimate dignity of human intercourse; it brings out also the moral perfection implicit in . . . dealing with others as beings of equal dignity, as free coparticipants in *li*. . . . [T]o act with ceremony [i.e., with *li*] is to be completely open to the other; for ceremony is public, shared, transparent; to act otherwise is to be secret, obscure and devious, or merely tyrannically coercive. It is in this beautiful and dignified, shared and open participation with others who are ultimately like oneself that man realizes himself. Thus perfect community of men . . . becomes an inextricable part, the chief aspect, of Divine worship. . . .
>
> . . . Instead of being diversion of attention from the human realm to another transcendent realm, the overtly holy ceremony is to be seen as the central symbol, both

---

in their sacred enclosure, they concentrate on correctness of act, recitation and chant. Their primary concern, if not obsession, is with rules. There are no symbolic meanings going through their minds when they are engaged in performing ritual."

[99] See Asad, "The Concept of Ritual," 76.

[100] See Staal, "The Meaninglessness of Ritual," 4: "Ritual, then, is primarily activity. It is an activity governed by explicit rules. The important thing is what you do, not what you think, believe or say."

[101] See Talal Asad, "Notes on Body Pain and Truth in Medieval Christian Ritual," in *Geneaologies of Religion*, 83–124.

[102] One might even say that in RB, "ritual" is what renders human behavior (even if practiced individually) communal.

[103] *Confucius: The Secular as Sacred* (New York: Harper & Row, 1972) 16. Fingarette is commenting on the Chinese notion of *li* (usually translated "holy rite" or "sacred ceremony"). He argues that ultimately this notion refers not to any "ritualism" but to the idea that we engage in the art of becoming human by learning the ritual repertoire of the human community, i.e., by dealing with all others as "beings of equal dignity."

expressive of and participating in the holy as a dimension of all truly human existence.[104]

Such is also the basic attitude toward ritual in RB. Rite is not the formalized presentation of "condensed corporate symbols" that encode "canonical meanings" and guarantee "social cohesion." Rather, rite is a technological means of acquiring a "new self"—an identity defined by *solidarity* with all others as "beings of equal dignity" and by *participation* in a life that "in its entirety finally appears as one, vast, spontaneous and holy Rite."[105] RB understood that only *rite* can read rite, that liturgical theology *is* ritual performance. That is why–to the dismay of many modern readers—RB contains precious little in the way of glowing chapters on the "meaning" of prayer or the "spirituality" of the liturgy or the profound cultic character of *Opus Dei*. It is also why RB could claim the monastery's *tools* (hoes, rakes, shovels, hammers, pens, knives, etc.) must be handled as if they were *uasa sacrata altaris*.[106]

Note, in conclusion, that liturgical theology is *neither* a theology "of" / "from" worship *nor* ritual understood as a symbol system geared to the production of meanings. Rather, the "rite" that both *reads* and *is read* by liturgical theology emerges from bodily inscription, from what Michel Foucault called a "technology of the self," from the assembly's performative hermeneutic (described by George Steiner as "art reading art," as the enactment of answerable understanding, active apprehension). To liturgical theology of this kind, Aidan Kavanagh pointed the way when he wrote of the difference between "liturgy" and "worship."

> What emerged from this period of immense stress [Renaissance, Reformation] was a rather novel form of endeavor known as "worship" rather than "liturgy" in its previously understood sense. The result was that western Christianity as a whole . . . embarked upon a hitherto unknown way of dealing with the Word of God in its written, incarnate, and ecclesial manifestations. This way was, due to the nature of the new "worship," increasingly shorn of the witness of rite as I have tried to describe it. The place vacated by rite was gradually taken over by the witness of *texts* of various sorts, texts which were designed, approved, and authentically interpreted no longer by the sustained liturgical *gestes* of the faithful assembly itself but by the growing body of precise, didactic, and normative theological formulations emanating from academic, bureaucratic, and other ecclesiastical bodies and enforced by law. Secondary theological influence increased greatly, primary theology receded. The *orthodoxia* of rite, anchored in the assembly's liturgical act, dissolved to be reassembled as an orthodoxy of concepts, propositions, and approved insights.[107]

At the heart of liturgical theology lies the assembly and its action—messy, smudged and flawed, perhaps, but real as life itself. That is the *orthodoxia* that *prima theologia* aims to unfold.

[104] Ibid., 16–17.
[105] Ibid., 17.
[106] RB 31.10.
[107] Kavanagh, *On Liturgical Theology*, 117–18; emphasis added.

13. Liturgy and Ethics

Pastoral Liturgy and Character Ethics:
As We Worship So We Shall Be

Don E. Saliers

An unmistakable trajectory in Josef Jungmann's emerging view of Christian liturgy points toward moral and ethical implications of the worshiping assembly's liturgical action. To be sure, he was not a liturgical reformer, but his theological critique of liturgical tradition provides a basis for developing some of those implications. While he does not cite Virgil Michel's well-known words, he might well have done so: ". . . The liturgy is the indispensable basis of Christian and social regeneration."[1] Both Jungmann and Michel recognized, though in different modalities, what the New Testament witnesses: worshiping God in the name of Jesus Christ requires a way of life. To say one loves God while despising the neighbor is at once a contradiction and a lie. Justin Martyr's early third-century *Apology* states the intrinsic connection between participation in the Eucharist and caring for the orphan, the widow and all in need. This, in turn, echoes St. Paul's critique of certain persons in the Corinthian community whose neglect of the hungry he regarded as a violation of the Eucharist. This is clearly an ethical critique of cultic substance.[2]

I propose to make explicit what seems strongly implicit in Jungmann's conception of pastoral liturgy, and to reflect on some salient features of the interrelatedness of liturgy and ethics that follow from that conception. His synoptic view of the ebb and flow of the Arian controversy with its massive doctrinal consequences, and of the devolution of liturgical participation in recent centuries, creates a powerful matrix for his pastoral / liturgical proposals. Thus when he claims that liturgy "must become pastoral," I discern a point of departure for recovering the intrinsic connection between liturgy and the Christian life, hence between liturgy and ethics for our context.

---

[1] Virgil Michel, O.S.B., "Liturgy as the Basis of Social Regeneration," *Orate Fratres* (1934–1935).

[2] He recognizes this point elsewhere. See Josef A. Jungmann, S.J., *The Early Liturgy,* trans. Francis A. Brunner, C.SS.R. (Notre Dame, Ind.: University or Notre Dame Press, 1959) 34.

Jungmann did not make an explicit proposal for specific ethical consequences flowing from the liturgy, as did Virgil Michel. But one can detect an impulse to raise the questions. Our idiom is much more direct. We now ask: How are social justice commitments reflected in liturgical celebrations? And, conversely: How does Christian liturgy shape the communal and individual capacity for responsible ethical judgements and moral action in the service of God and neighbor? But I think there is a basis in Jungmann for these questions. For example, he insists on bringing forward the inner meaning of the eucharistic celebration at every turn. Thus he contends that in the Baroque period an exclusive focus on Real Presence obscured the communal interchange between celebrant and people, diminishing the Word in readings, prayer, songs of praise and thanksgiving. "The measure in which the sacramental Presence becomes central, is also the measure in which truly sacramental thinking fades out."[3] His eye is on how the eucharistic liturgy *ought* to nourish the whole life of faith. It is this "ought," this normative vision of the shaping power of the liturgical assembly that catches one's attention. Precisely the gap between the "ought" of normative ideal and the "is" of actual practices constitutes a perennial tension for thinking about relations between Christian liturgy and ethics.

Running through Jungmann's essay and his larger writings is a strong appreciation for the continuity and conserving nature of liturgical tradition, especially for the artistic dimensions of the awe-inspiring periods of faithful practice. He stoutly resists, however, a liturgical "antiquarianism" which longs to recover the aesthetic feel without the real connection with the inner meaning of Christian liturgy "in spirit and in truth." The rich liturgical aesthetic of the Baroque, for which some still yearn, does not seem to be complemented by attention to questions of moral formation. It is not that piety or moral formation was simply missing in late Medieval or the Baroque periods, for the exercise of private devotions, the books of prayer and hymns were all part of pious practice. Such devotional practices undoubtedly form the faithful in certain interior dispositions and attitudes. The issue for Jungmann is whether the liturgical action of the whole assembly could be said to be formative of the "full grasp of the Faith."[4] This, I propose, would have to include the formation of moral character within a framework of social/ethical holiness. His concern was with the bifurcation, or "parallelism" of devotional and liturgical worlds. The domain of the "liturgical" and of the "devotional" were tightly defined and so practiced; the sacramental transaction and the cultivation of moral dispositions were thus external to one another.

---

[3] Josef A. Jungmann, S.J., "The Defeat of Teutonic Arianism and the Revolution in Religious Culture in the Early Middle Ages," *Pastoral Liturgy* (New York: Herder and Herder, 1962) 88.

[4] This phrase, "full grasp of Faith" appears several times toward the end of his essay. My argument contends that this must include more than intellectual understanding of doctrine. To be "full," by which I think he meant "mature" as well as "adequate," the grasp of Faith in and through liturgical participation includes appropriate dispositions and intentions to act morally and ethically congruent with the mystery of the self-giving of Christ.

The normative view that emerges at the end of Jungmann's historical survey is stated succinctly: ". . . liturgy which represents essential prayer which the Church offers to God in unity with her Lord."[5] Thus liturgy is to be open to the *people* who assemble and to their lives as offered in union with Christ. His aim is that the public worship of God "become both an invitation and a help to real adoration 'in Spirit and in truth': it must become the support of a joyful awareness of Faith and of a Christian life in the harsh everyday world."[6] When Jungmann proposes that liturgy become *pastoral,* he opens the possibility of reconfiguring relationships between liturgical participation and the way Christians are to envision the good and thus live faithfully in the turmoil and challenges of everyday life. In short, he appears prepared to rethink relations between liturgy and ethics in the "harsh everyday world" of our present historical and cultural contexts—perhaps in ways he did not himself envision, but certainly in ways congruent with central themes promulgated by the Second Vatican Council.

The Anglican Dean William Inge is reported to have observed that the Church which marries the spirit of the age will become a widow in the next generation. Questions about the perennial and the passing in Christian life and theology are nothing new, they are present from the first self-reflection of Christian thought. Josef Jungmann's challenge to discern what is essential from what is "passing fashion" sounds now at a time when, at least in North American cultural ethos, the need for such discernment is forced upon us. From the beginning, Christian worship of God in the name of Jesus Christ fuses together the cultic and the ethical, the material and the spiritual, the sacramental and the humanly responsible dimensions of faith. Therefore it is an essential feature of Christian liturgy that it form human beings in the specific identity as the Body of Christ and in the character befitting love of God and neighbor. Any pastoral inquiry into the nature of liturgical practice will inevitably uncover questions of spirituality and hence, questions of the identity and relevance of formation in those qualities which characterize the Christian life. Any consideration of the gifts and graces of faith named as "fruits of the Spirit" are necessarily ethical. That is, kindness, forbearance, courage, and compassion are shown in social relatedness to neighbor as well as to "enemy."

There are, of course, many ways to frame relationships between the worship of God and Christian ethics. Rather than address questions of obligation or how liturgy contains particular ethical principles, I will focus on "character ethics."[7] This is in part because liturgy that becomes ethically didactic actually easily loses

---

[5] Jungmann, op. cit., 93.

[6] Ibid., 98–99.

[7] The term "character ethics" emerges in contrast to "ethics of obligation" which focuses upon rules, commands and ethical principles and the casuistry surrounding them. Recent literature also contrasts "character ethics" from "deontological" ethics. The writings of Stanley Hauerwas have brought "character ethics" into particular prominence. See for example, his *Character and the Christian Life: A Study in Theological Ethics* (San Antonio: Trinity University Press, 1975).

its character as praise and worship of God. Yet, as I shall argue, there are indelible moral and ethical teachings in the lections, hymns, and preaching dimensions of authentic Christian liturgy. To praise and thank God, to attend to the Word and to enact the Paschal mystery cannot be *reduced* to ethics while nevertheless forming Christian identity and character. More positively, our attention focuses on liturgy and the ethics of character because this is the most illuminating way of including what the tradition calls the fruits of the Spirit, and the deep pattern of religious affections which constitute faithful Christian life. In what follows, I propose four theses: (1) Relations between liturgy and ethics are most adequately formulated by specifying how certain affections and virtues are formed and expressed in communal prayer and ritual action.[8] (2) Liturgical practices operate at many different levels in human spiritual formation to shape the conditions for moral imagination. (3) Eucharistic participation is the richest available context for the formation of compassion, justice and hope—required for service of God and neighbor. (4) Christian ethics are marked by an unmistakable eschatological framework that is essential to authentic Christian liturgy. While not exhaustive, such theses provide one way to unfold what is congruent with Jungmann's notion of the "full grasp of Faith" mediated through liturgical participation.

Affections and Virtues Formed in Communal Prayer and Ritual Action

How are questions of Christian ethics framed in the context of liturgical action? Certainly in the general sense we can agree that liturgical practices bear upon ethical and moral discourse precisely because any substantive ethical discernment and subsequent action is more than "ethical." That is, to act with human maturity amidst the struggle to live in accordance with what is good involves more than following ethical rules. The very following or "applying" principles is not another rule, but a complex practice requiring such matters as appropriate desire, motivating affections, and consistency of intention-action patterns in our lives. In short, to become ethical is to take on a rich affectional regard for the world. By "affection" I mean something constitutive of human personhood. The deepest aspects of our being human are clarified by discovering what we hope for, love and cherish most deeply, what our fears are, and what we would be willing to die for. In short, we know more about ourselves when we know one another's (and our own) deep affections. These are not the same as passing feelings or moods. Deep affections constitute a pattern of being attuned to our social and personal worlds—and thus can describe the human heart in the biblical sense of that expression. Furthermore, deep affections are themselves social forces, and also characterize communities of discourse and practice.

---

[8] This was first proposed in my essay, "Liturgy and Ethics: Some New Beginnings," *Journal of Religious Ethics*, vol. 7, no. 2 (Fall 1979), and reiterated in chapter 13 of *Worship As Theology: Foretaste of Glory Divine* (Nashville: Abingdon Press, 1994).

Among the conditions that nurture and sustain our moral awareness are communal ritual actions. Moral awareness requires a community that gathers to tell its founding memories, to rehearse its fundamental attitudes, and to symbolically enact over time the root images and narratives by which it lives and understands how to become human, and to live worthily. Christian liturgical action does these things in the name of Jesus, remembering the whole revelatory pattern of divine creation, covenant, redemption and promised Kingdom. Thus the affections and virtues relevant to our concern here are those rooted and grounded in Christ. The moral life of Christians is the embodiment, over time, of those virtues and affections which characterize what St. Paul and the tradition have called "life in Christ."

When the Constitution on the Sacred Liturgy speaks of liturgy as the "source and summit" of the Christian life, it claims the unity of worship and ethics, for how we acknowledge God in worship and how we live have the single source in Christ. They have a single teleology in the gracious promises of God's Rule and Reign. One way to grasp this truth claim is to consider how human beings receive and practice the way of life this entails. So gratitude to God, hope in the saving work of Christ, love of God and neighbor, a passion for justice and mercy congruent with God's promises, along with the capacity to repent of sin and failure to so live—all these are part of the actual practice that begins and ends in faithful liturgy. But the living of such a distinctive pattern of life in the world of social forces requires a place where the stories, the teachings and the mystery are continually represented. That place is the liturgical assembly.

We might speak of the qualities of existence formed by faithful liturgy as "liturgical spirituality" or, in Louis Bouyer's classical terms "liturgical piety."[9] Jungmann certainly recognized this in his turn toward "pastoral liturgy." My point is simply that we can no longer speak of a liturgical spirituality or piety *without* also referring to formation of moral dispositions and a vision of the good God wills for the world. The liturgy does not itself do our ethical reasoning for us. In fact there is and ought to be legitimate disagreement among faithful Christians on serious issues. The liturgical assembly is not in the first instance an ethical forum. But in the very act of gathering about the book, the font and the altar, we must attend to the Word and sacraments which invite and empower the Christian assembly to "practice these examples of virtue," as Justin Martyr put it.[10] It is always tempting, especially in our own contentious age to make the purpose of liturgy into an instrument

---

[9] See Bouyer, Louis, *Liturgical Piety*. (Notre Dame, Ind.: University of Notre Dame Press, 1955). I have always been drawn to the pregnancy of his observation, in speaking of a true liturgical movement, that "liturgy will never be lived again so long as it is cultivated as a kind of evasion from actual life, and not as the supernatural leaven by which our whole life must be permeated so as to conform . . . to the life of Christ. . . ," 254.

[10] He uses this phrase in speaking of what preaching does. See Justin Martyr's *Apology*, chapter 67. Cf. *The First Apology of Justin, The Martyr,* trns. Edward R. Hardy in *Early Christian Fathers*; Vol. I in "The Library of Christian Classics," (Philadelphia: The Westminster Press, 1953) 287.

for the moral and ethical transformation of persons and society. This is attractive in a time of great turmoil, but to make this the sole purpose of liturgy would be to subvert how Christians are formed in the affections and virtues we have mentioned. The formation of Christian character requires the fullness of both the glorification of God and the sanctification of all that is human. Praise and thanksgiving fitting to the fullness of God in Christ is the *cantus firmus* of faithful liturgy—always offered in union with Christ. But in this very "offering" is the paradoxical mystery of first receiving and then being inSpirited for service of Christ in the world.

To offer ourselves in union is thus to discover the mystery of receiving grace by the work of the Spirit. Whatever we have to offer has already been conferred. Therefore at the heart of the Christian moral vision and its ethical consequences is gratitude and acknowledgment of God. So when St. Paul admonishes the church at Rome to present themselves "as a living sacrifice, holy and pleasing to God, your spiritual worship,"[11] he is speaking of the whole Body of Christ as a community of gifts. Here again, the inner connectedness of worship and a way of life is startlingly clear.

Such a view of the formation of affections and virtues by faithful Christian liturgy is haunted by a fundamental question which is also posed by many today as an objection. What about the enormous disparity between this normative account and the actualities in the life of our churches? The "ought" of such formation is severely tested by the "is" of church members who still harbor racial hatred, religious and ethnic violence, and who continue to neglect the suffering. Here we must face the fact that there are many other formative powers at work in our lives, some of which are more determinative of our moral dispositions (or lack thereof) and ethical decision-making than is liturgical participation. Without denying the objective character of what faithful liturgical celebrations offer, we must also allow that the "full grasp of Faith" cannot be guaranteed by mere attendance. The vision of God's good for the world and the grace freely offered in the assembly about the book, the font and the table, must also be practiced. To this point we will return.

Multiple Levels of Formation of Moral Imagination in the Liturgy

Part of the answer to the question just posed is found in the multiple ways in which character formation in the graced human affections takes place over time. As in all moral formation, no person is formed instantly. Even in the most dramatic instances of conversion "experience" we find that growing into the fullness of faith takes time and continual participation. Sometimes a person may be converted intellectually to certain teachings or beliefs, but not be changed in terms of basic emotional maturity. Other times persons may have dramatic episodes of emotional experience, but not understand the form of life they are drawn to. Still other examples can be cited in which a person is converted to a strong decision to "will" one's life to

---

[11] Rom 12:1b, *The New American Bible.*

God, but lack both the enduring emotional depth and the understanding what the life of faith entails over time. Jesus' parable of the sower puts the issue graphically.

In addition to these factors in the moral development of human beings, the data of liturgical participation show a complex set of formative practices. Growing into the "full stature" of Christ requires entering the liturgy at various levels of engagement of the affections and virtues. Here I will analyze four interrelated "sub-practices" of liturgical participation: readings, prayers, cycles of time, and sacramental ritual acts. Each of these is required for a "full grasp of the Faith." Attending to these practices is necessary in allowing liturgical experience to shape our moral dispositions, the affections and virtues. The bearing of liturgical participation on Christian character depends, in part, on learning to "practice" listening, praying, and bodily engagement. While participation in the gathered community at worship is central to on-going formation, in our present cultural context catechesis into liturgical symbols and biblical narratives and images is essential.

The "liturgy of the Word" focuses on God's voice and our attentive listening. The use of Psalm 95 is significant in the morning office: "Listen today to God's voice, harden no heart."[12] In the Mass liturgy, following the Entrance Rite, the biblical readings unfold from the prophets and Law, the epistles to the churches and the Gospels. These are to be heard each in their own integrity, but also as the basis for the preaching act in the homily to follow. Psalmody forms a biblical song linking the First Testament to the Second Testament. While not every lection and psalm is directly ethical, a vast range of them contain specific teachings. Each demands knowing the form and the context—prophetic, epistolary, and gospel accounts. Among the reforms of the Second Council, the cycles of readings—now including the prophetic and wisdom teachings which had not been previously in the lectionary—are among the most significant for the formation of moral and ethical consciousness. The recovery of the great social vision of the late prophets and the amplitude of the Bible is clearly present, "lavished," in the words of *Sacrosanctum Concilium,* upon the people of the assembly. The recovery of the amplitude of God's Word read, proclaimed, and sung in the assembly may be considered revolutionary, particularly in light of its shared ecumenical consequences.[13]

My point here is that strong direct ethical teachings concerning justice, mercy, and compassion permeate the Liturgy of the Word, from the classical texts in Isaiah and Micah ("What does the Lord require of you but to do justice, to love mercy, and to walk humbly with your God" 6:8ff.), to the pastoral/moral admonitions and teachings in Pauline and pastoral letters, to the teachings of Christ. Hearing

---

[12] One of the antiphons for use with Psalm 95 from the ICEL Psalter project, found in the ostinato setting by Christopher Willcock, S.J.

[13] Every major Christian denomination has shared in the initial impulse toward a common lectionary, though with some significant variants, since 1969. I think Jungmann would find the adaptation of a three-year cycle of readings among the various churches of the Reformation an encouraging step. Certainly he found this greatly strengthening the Roman Mass Rite.

and reflecting on these dimensions of the Word is crucial to both Christian identity and moral formation. The principle of continuous reading from the epistles also brings the worshiping assembly into "hearing" the pastoral life of the early Christian communities. This provides a realistic picture of ethical tensions and directives permeating the struggle to be faithful. In hearing readings from the Corinthian letters, for example, we encounter the patterning of the virtues in particular human contexts—all grounded in a conception of what it means to be the Body of Christ in the social/political world of human forces.

All the readings are "heard" in light of the voice of Christ speaking in the prophets, the psalms, and especially in the Gospels. The parables, with their imaginative shock through images such as the woman searching for the coin, the laborers in the vineyard, and the wedding banquet—all work in counterpoint to direct teachings. The portrayal of life with God and neighbor is indelibly social, providing the attentive hearer with images of how to live. In this sense the liturgy can be said to "teach ethics." But all ethical teachings are found in the matrix of the narrative of the person and work of Christ, especially in his actions and in his suffering, death, and resurrection. The heart of this lavishing of Scripture on the people is found in the breadth of exposure to each of the Gospels in turn, now read in a more comprehensive fashion over the liturgical cycles of time. The ethical teachings are to be heard and learned and practiced as intrinsic to the mystery of faith made palpable in the sacramental actions at the table, the font, and in all the passages of life.

Equally important in the liturgical life of the assembly are the restored intercessions as "prayers of the faithful." Liturgical participation thus requires learning to "pray with" Christ's on-going intercession, and to be attentive to the Holy Spirit's "sighing in us and through us" when we do not know how to pray for ourselves as we ought. In this sense the linkages between liturgical participation and ethics of character is found in the inner connection between learning to pray and becoming a person (and a community) "in Christ."

Drawing on previous work, let me sketch four aspects of intercessory prayer in liturgy that are part of character formation.[14] In praying with and for others we discover a sense of solidarity with all in need. The "prayers of the faithful" are literally a school for compassion. In identifying the suffering of the world and learning to lift it continually to God through Christ, we deepen a fundamental capacity manifest in Christian ethical action. Secondly, praying for others brings us to awareness of our own vulnerability—our mortality and the malleability of our own wills. This creates, in mature communities, a humility born of human solidarity as the Body of Christ praying for the world. Thirdly, a moral intentionality is gained in addressing the world to God. We learn to bring our own life experience and the struggles with ambiguity and ambivalence to the act of praying with Christ. Presumptive prayer

---

[14] See especially "Liturgy and Ethics: Some New Beginnings" recently reprinted in *Liturgy and the Moral Self: Humanity at Full Stretch Before God*, ed. E. Byron Anderson and Bruce T. Morrill, S.J. (Collegeville: The Liturgical Press, 1998) 27–32.

must, over time, give way to the human reality we must live, if we are to be truthful in such prayer. Finally, intercessions conjoin with the various modalities of prayer which run from the opening *Kyrie*, through the collects, into the eucharistic prayer itself, thus bringing to awareness to need for the ministries of the Body of Christ to be intentional. To pray the prayers of the faithful with integrity over time is to be included in the social vision and work of the Rule and Reign of God: becoming "doers and not hearers only" of the Word. Because each of these sub-practices, and others we could also name, operate on us at many different levels, living through time is required to be continually formed and re-formed into Christ.

Because Christians must continue to live out faith in the world of moral ambiguity and in the field of forces which pull us away from liturgical formation, conversion never ends. If this is so, our moral and ethical formation never ends. Here is the intrinsic connection between sanctification and our participation in the new creation of God—a reality at once social/ethical and eschatological.

Eucharistic Formation in Compassion, Justice and Hope

Participation in attending to God's Word and the prayers of cycles of feasts and seasons, as well as through all the seasons of our lives, culminates in participating in the eucharistic action of Christ. This is clearly evident throughout Jungmann's work, and especially evident in the direction his essay moves. The interpenetration of Word and sacramental action in the Eucharist is thus required for a "full grasp of Faith" which animates Christian ethical action in the world. Christian conversion points toward participation in the Messianic banquet that continually offers the grace of Christ to a lacerated, self-destructive world. Yet comprehending what the Eucharist gives and asks humankind takes continual practice over time. No one dares presume to claim the fullness of this mystery in language, much less claim to have made it fully manifest in all its spiritual and ethical dimensions. Yet it is the most radical meal, the most revolutionary symbolic action in which human beings can partake.

What makes eucharistic participation so crucial to the formation of virtues and affections which characterize the life of faith? Because it is the very body memory of Christ and the true pattern of what our lives are to become. To enter the eucharistic prayer is to pray our identity in the whole sweep of God's creating, redeeming and consummating intention for the cosmos. Here we find again and again the whole *exitus and reditus* of God pronounced as praise and thanksgiving. This orients us to our created origin and destiny and reason for being. But the prayer is conjoined to the action of Christ, and we are to receive him bodily under the form of a meal. As Christ takes the bread and cup, so do we; as he blesses God for all things, so do we; as he gives himself for us, so we are to give ourselves for others—blessed, broken, in solidarity with his unfathomable self-giving for the redeeming and sanctifying of all that is creaturely. As Christ sent the Apostles and all who have served and witnessed to him, so we are sent at the conclusion of the Eucharist, to live as we have prayed.

It is one thing to hear the ethical teachings of Jesus, whether directly or in the imaginative form of the parables. It is another to participate bodily in ritual actions which rehearse how we are to regard and to relate to one another in everyday life. The physical gestures and movements of eucharistic participation give us the pattern of relationship which defines love of God and neighbor. There conjoined are mutuality of respect, equality before the gracious self-giving of Christ, and accountability to faithful participation. Each new generation may discover fresh dimensions of the justice entailed by sharing the meal. Thus in our own time, so filled with awareness of hunger, homelessness and suffering, is it any wonder that we connect eucharistic bread with our being "bread for others." Thus, for example, in one recent Eucharistic Prayer we hear in the epiclesis: "Let these be for us the body and blood of Christ that we may be his Body in the world redeemed by his blood."[15] Thus receiving the Bread of Life entails that we ourselves will be bread for others.

Participation in the ritual actions of the eucharistic celebration, whether simple or elaborate, requires more than physical presence; it means participation in the Word, the song, the prayer and the meal as a living ecclesial community. This cannot be done unless we bring our lives to the Word and to the Paschal Mystery. This in turn invites participation in the very life of God poured out for the sake of the world. "Opening up the ethical levels of meaning in the shared meal in the name of one who creates and redeems a world from itself transforms not simply the interior life of feeling and desire, but the social relationships that make us human in the sight of God."[16]

Christian Ethics are Marked by Eschatological Vision

The relationship between Christian liturgical practice, ethical theory and Christian moral character moves well beyond Jungmann's turn to "pastoral liturgy." The issues are also well beyond the scope of these reflections. Yet there remains one salient feature of Christian liturgy that Jungmann did not develop—a feature that is central to more recent liturgical theology. All Christian liturgy is eschatological. By this I mean that every act of prayer calls upon the God who has promised, and who is steadfastly faithful to those promises to redeem all creation. Every liturgical act is open to the future of God. This is especially true of the eucharist which remembers by thankful recital, and proceeds to invoke the Spirit to make real the redemptive power of Christ's offering, then concludes by anticipating what is yet to be in fullness. This is especially signified with the eschatological prayer of Christ following the great Amen, before the breaking of the bread. For

[15] *The United Methodist Hymnal*, (Nashville: The United Methodist Publishing House, 1989) and in the *Book of Worship* (1992) in the Eucharistic Prayer.
[16] Don E. Saliers, "Afterword: Liturgy and Ethics Revisited," in Anderson and Morrill, op. cit., 224.

there we join him in pleading that God's Kingdom may yet come. This renders the eucharistic meal itself a "foretaste" of the promised Messianic consummation.

The images by which the Messianic banquet yet to come are unmistakably social: Jerusalem, the city coming down from heaven, a feast on the mountain to which all nations shall come, a time and place in which death will be no more, and a river for the healing of the nations. Such social images carry enormous ethical implications. They must not be reduced to mere apocalyptic projections. Here we begin to grasp the interconnection between Christ's parables of the Kingdom and the eucharist as eschatological meal. Likewise, baptism is equally proleptic—whether as infants or adults. For "dying and rising" with Christ cannot be fully grasped until the whole of life is comprehended. Baptism is the initiatory sign of the eschatological promise. Through all of life it is a *cantus firmus* of God's gracious promise of eternal life in Christ.

Ingredient in the levels of participation in liturgical assembly about the waters of baptism, the oils of healing, the Word of prophesy and the kenotic glory of the banquet, is a vision of the good. This vision of God's final teleology for all of creation in Christ marks a distinctive element in Christian ethics. At one and the same time this relativizes all lesser human good, yet supplies the moral imagination with root images to sustain intention and action amidst the ambiguities of human existence. Christian liturgy continually orbits around the eschatological promises, devoting specific feasts and seasons to it. The liturgical year itself begins in the eschatological tensions between the "already" of Christ and the "not yet" of the Kingdom. Only because Christ has come in the flesh in human history can the Church cry out the ancient Advent cry: "Come, O Come Emmanuel" on behalf of the world.

There have been long periods in which this eschatological dimension of Christian liturgy was obscured, collapsed into apocalyptic final judgement, or turned into pious personal hope for heaven. But we can no longer grasp of "fullness of Faith"—so close to Jungmann's hope for the future of Christian liturgy—without a thoroughly eschatological understanding of what it is we do in praying, singing, and celebrating Word and sacrament over time. Liturgical participation does not remove the responsibility of struggling with the moral and ethical dilemmas of our age. The liturgy is not an ethical forum. How liturgical life leads to specific ethical decisions requires specific attention to contexts. As Gordon Lathrop has observed, a liturgical orientation already "gives points of reference and directions of significance . . . shared by the resultant course of ethics: that this is God's world, not ours; that we are fellow creatures, along with many others; that the care for the earth and the use of what we need in the world are given to us all in common; that our creatureliness and our insertion in the community of creatures indicate limits on our existence; that none of the boundaries we draw between ourselves are ultimate; that all the boundaries must be judged before God."[17]

---

[17] Lathrop, Gordon, "'O Taste and See': The Geography of Liturgical Ethics" in Anderson and Morrill, op. cit., 49.

We have now begun to retrieve an essential insight: *every* liturgical assembly in the name of Jesus is itself an eschatological act in the world, a manifestation of the faithfulness of the triune God of heaven and earth. Every act of justice, each act of compassion, every faithful attempt at moral discernment in the midst of rival claims, can reflect the hope of the world in Christ. Christian liturgy, even in an age of distraction, violence, and demonic powers, is yet able to grace human life to grasp in faith, and to strive for the good "in Spirit and in truth." As Jungmann would be first to say, liturgical life must continually be informed by pastorally-oriented catechesis and mystagogy. Liturgical piety and ethical engagement reflect two sides of the same saving mystery of God in Christ, made present by the life of the Spirit in the Church.

14. Spirituality

Building a House for the Church

Michael Downey

Josef A. Jungmann's *Pastoral Liturgy* [1] is a collection of historical studies as well as articles from periodicals with a purely practical purpose. "The Defeat of Teutonic Arianism and the Revolution in the Religious Culture in the Early Middle Ages,"[2] the focal essay around which the essays in the present collection are gathered, falls into the first category. The distinction made by Jungmann himself should not be drawn too sharply, however, since both types of essay are to serve the "current liturgical renewal on a foundation of well-founded Christian tradition."[3] Jungmann makes it clear that what is dug out of historical sources through painstaking research should bear upon the details of the practical life of the Church.[4] In Jungmann's spirit, and in accord with the purpose of this commemorative volume, I hope to offer a small contribution to the current liturgical renewal, providing some insight into liturgy precisely as pastoral.

My focus here is on spirituality, specifically Christian spirituality. In what follows, I shall be looking at the spirituality of a particular community as expressed in its efforts to build a church at once in keeping with its own well-founded monastic tradition, as well as being appropriate to the liturgical reform rooted in the renewed christology and ecclesiology articulated in the documents of the Second Vatican Council. My aim is not to spell out a liturgical spirituality, or a spirituality of pastoral liturgy. Rather my hope is that the probings which follow will help clarify the nature of Christian spirituality, and identify a framework for understanding the distinctive features of a particular Christian spirituality.

Christian Spirituality

The term "Christian spirituality" conveys a vexatious multiplicity of meanings.[5] Amidst this wide range of usage, contemporary studies usually distinguish

---

[1] Josef A. Jungmann, *Pastoral Liturgy* (New York: Herder and Herder, 1962).

[2] *Pastoral Liturgy*, 1–101.

[3] *Pastoral Liturgy*, preface.

[4] *Pastoral Liturgy*, preface.

[5] For a sample of the various uses of the term see Lawrence S. Cunningham and Keith J. Egan, *Christian Spirituality: Themes from the Tradition* (Mahwah, N.J.: Paulist Press, 1996) 22–28, Appendix to chapter 1: "Some Definitions/Descriptions of Christian Spirituality."

four interrelated levels of meaning of the term "spirituality": (1) a fundamental dimension of human being; (2) the full range of human experience as it is brought to bear on the quest for personal integration; (3) the expression of insights about that experience, i.e., the formulation of a teaching about the lived reality, often under the influence of some outstanding spiritual person; (4) a disciplined study of spiritual experience, or of the experience of the spiritual life.[6]

For the student of Christian spirituality, it is intriguing that Jungmann's essay on the defeat of Teutonic Arianism opens with a discussion of Pierre Pourat's four volume history of the spiritual life.[7] Pourat's "Christian spirituality" is a "disciplined study" (as in 4 above), an instructive guide through changes in spiritual history which have had effects far beyond what is often thought of as "the spiritual life." Jungmann recognizes Pourat's achievement, but indicates that the study is perhaps most instructive in what it does not include. Pourat's first volume concludes, for the West, with the death of Gregory the Great; the second volume, after a cursory glance at Cluny, begins with Bernard of Clairvaux. Pourat omits the period between the close of the Patristic age to the dawn of Scholasticism in his telling of the history of Christian spirituality in the West.

In view of the four interrelated levels of meaning introduced above, Pourat's omission amounts to conducting a "disciplined study" in a way that leaves out of the loop the experience of life in Christ throughout the course of half a millennium. This is problematic for Jungmann since "no period has ever seen a greater revolution in religious thought and institutions than that which took place in the five centuries between the close of the patristic age and the dawn of scholasticism." During this period there were "certain shifts of accent and changes of viewpoint having consequences so wide that they have left their mark on all subsequent ages right down to our own times."[8]

Aside from his gentle critique of Pourat's work, Jungmann does not have much to say about spirituality in any explicit sense of the term. Or, it may well be that spirituality is Jungmann's governing concern throughout. He writes: "Our theme concerns changes which have taken place *somewhere behind the world of sensible appearances*, but which are revealed both in cultural and artistic forms" (emphasis mine).[9] My contention is that in using the phrase "somewhere behind the world of sensible appearances" what Jungmann has in mind is the human spirit. Further, I suggest that he is referring to the region of the human spirit in tensive interaction with the Spirit of God, Spirit of Christ. Today this tensive interaction is spoken of more commonly as "spirituality."

---

[6] For a fuller treatment see Michael Downey, *Understanding Christian Spirituality* (Mahwah, N.J.: Paulist Press, 1997) chapter 2: "What is Christian Spirituality?"

[7] Pierre Pourat, *La spiritualité chrétienne*, 4 volumes. Many editions have appeared since 1918. Jungmann's references are to volumes 1 and 2 of 1926 and 1927 respectively.

[8] *Pastoral Liturgy*, 1.

[9] *Pastoral Liturgy*, 2.

If my reading of Jungmann is correct, then his understanding of spirituality is much richer and more supple than understandings of "spirituality" that prevailed during his formative years. Such understandings tended to equate spirituality with prayer, disciplines of meditation, the cultivation of "the interior life," the rigorous pursuit of the life of perfection, grooming "the spiritual life" as if it were *a* dimension of the Christian life. Because for Jungmann, what goes on "somewhere behind the world of sensible appearances" is "revealed," or expressed, in "cultural and artistic forms"—in the socio-symbolic order through which human beings receive and shape meaning and identity. His view of spirituality is inclusive of the wider network of means by which human beings perceive and pursue meaning, purpose, and value.

As I understand it, Christian spirituality is not *one* dimension of the Christian life; it *is* the Christian life in its entirety: Being conformed to the person of Christ, brought into communion with God and others through the presence and power of the Spirit of God, Spirit of Christ. But, following Jungmann, the tensive interaction between the human spirit and the Spirit of God is revealed or expressed in "forms," that is in words, events, gestures, actions, objects, and so on. And it is by investigating these that there is insight to be gained regarding the "shifts of accent and changes of viewpoint" occurring "somewhere behind the world of sensible appearances."

Identifying a Field of Investigation
for Understanding Christian Spirituality[10]

I have identified seven focal points of investigation for coming to a clearer understanding of the distinctive features of a Christian spirituality. Whether as lived experience or disciplined study, the concern of Christian spirituality is with the human experience of the Christian spiritual life. In other words, Christian spirituality is concerned with the relationship between the Spirit of God, Spirit of Christ, and the human spirit, in a way that attends to both realities in dynamic interaction. The Spirit of God, Spirit of Christ is present and active in human persons:

1) within a culture;
2) in relation to a tradition;
3) in light of contemporary events, hopes, sufferings and promises;
4) in remembrance of Jesus Christ;
5) in efforts to combine elements of action and contemplation;
6) with respect to charism and community;
7) as expressed and authenticated in praxis.

This framework can be used by those who are studying spirituality in a disciplined way, as well as by those who are simply attempting to come to a deeper understanding of spirituality, their own or others', past or present.

[10] See Michael Downey, *Understanding Christian Spirituality*, 120–22. This framework was developed further in a paper delivered at the annual meeting of the American Academy of Religion in San Francisco, November 1997.

It is important to note here that the study of Christian spirituality is not concerned simply with the examination of written texts. One of the great riches of Christian spirituality is the range of genres in which the experience of the Christian spiritual life is expressed. Considering only written texts leaves so much out of the loop. One of the advantages of the sevenfold framework introduced above is that it can be used in examining a scriptural or theological text, a legend of a saint or a painting of her with eyes turned heavenward, a type of religious vesture or sacred music, a kind of church architecture or sculpture, stained glass windows in a cathedral, dance, or the enactment of a rite. It is useful to consider the object of study in view of these seven focal points. One might ask: What is the *culture* within which this depiction of the Last Judgment was painted? When considering a treatise on virtue, one might ask: What are the religious and theological *traditions* reflected, adhered to, departed from in this text? What are/were the significant *events, hopes, sufferings, and promises of the age* in which this score of music was composed? How does it reflect, nuance or critique them? How is the *memory of Christ* expressed, or what is the dominant image of Christ being expressed, in this bronze? What is the view of the relationship between *contemplation and action* expressed in this stained glass depiction of Mary with book-in-hand? Or with Jesus in her arms? Or with hands folded in prayer? What is the understanding of *charism and community* expressed in the uniform attire of women religious prior to the Second Vatican Council? And what understandings of charism and community are expressed in the very different attire of women religious today? And finally, what is the form of *praxis* appropriate to the presence and action of the Spirit discerned in these foci? These are the sorts of questions that might be raised. In the answers to these questions lie the distinctive contours of a particular Christian spirituality.

In this essay, attention is given to the architectural design of a church as expressive of a distinctive Christian spirituality. Following Jungmann's lead, I will look to a specific "artistic form," the Mepkin Abbey Church near Charleston, South Carolina, which "reveals" or expresses "changes which have taken place somewhere behind the world of sensible appearances," i.e., the spirituality of the monastic community of Mepkin Abbey. This I shall do in light of the sevenfold framework introduced above, attending first to the culture, traditions, and events that have shaped the spirituality of the monks at Mepkin.

Planting in the Deep South[11]

"Mepkin" is most likely an Indian word. According to local conjecture, it is probably the contraction of a word or words of the Native-American peoples who once inhabited the "Low Country" of South Carolina. "Mepkin" might well mean

---

[11] Sources for this account are found in the Archives of the Abbey of Our Lady of Mepkin, Moncks Corner, South Carolina.

"lovely" or "serene." The origins of this captivating three-thousand acre Cooper River plantation can be traced back over three hundred years. In 1681 Mepkin Plantation was established. From colonial times until the early 1900s, rice was grown on approximately six hundred acres called "Mepkin." The land was ac-quired in 1762, before the American Revolution, by the patriot Henry Laurens, a noted South Carolina statesman. After the death of Henry Laurens in 1792, Mep-kin remained in the hands of the Laurens family until 1851. For a considerable time it was abandoned as a plantation and residence. It changed owners repeatedly until 1936, when the large old plantation was purchased by Henry R. Luce, the philanthropist and publisher, most notably publisher of *Time* and *Life* magazines, and his wife, Clare Boothe Luce, a convert to Catholicism who was received into the Church by the celebrated Fulton Sheen in 1947. It is with the Luces that we find the beginnings of the story of the monks at Mepkin. Who are they? How and why did they come to this serene and lovely land of Mepkin?

The monastic community at Mepkin stands within a tradition that is centuries old. The monks at Mepkin are commonly called Trappists. The correct name of the Order to which they belong is the Order of Cistercians of the Strict (or Stricter) Observance. Hence, they are more properly called Cistercians. Their Order goes back to the reform of monastic life at Cîteaux in 1098. The name "Trappist" comes from the Abbey of La Trappe in Normandie, France, where Armand-Jean de Rancé (d. 1700) reestablished a pristine, quite austere form of Cistercian life after it had become moribund and insipid in its expression of the monastic spirit. Exiled dur-ing the French Revolution, monks from La Trappe went first to Switzerland, then to England. Returning to France in less hostile times, they revivified monastic life once again in abbeys throughout the country. One of these was the Abbey of Melleray, reestablished in 1817. The Abbey of Gethsemani in Kentucky was founded in 1848 as a "daughter house" of Melleray, and is the first enduring foun-dation in the United States springing from de Rancé's reform. Mepkin's roots lie in the Trappist Cistercian monastery at Gethsemani.

How did Mepkin, planted in the Low Country of the deep American South become home to a Roman Catholic community of monks with roots long, deep, and strong in France? In 1949, Emmett Michael Walsh, the Roman Catholic Bishop of Charleston, received Mepkin as a gift from Henry R. and Clare Boothe Luce with the understanding that the property would be given to a religious com-munity. At the urging of Mrs. Luce, Bishop Walsh offered over three-thousand acres, a major portion of the property, to the monks of the Abbey of Our Lady of Gethsemani in Kentucky for the purpose of founding a new monastery. The Geth-semani of post-World War II America was overflowing with new recruits, and ready to found a new "daughter house" through the Luce's generous gift of land.

What did the first wave of founders come upon when they arrived on 14 No-vember 1949, after the long and grueling journey from Gethsemani in Kentucky to the new foundation in South Carolina? There was a gardener's house at the entrance to the estate, a modern two-story edifice, several guest cottages and other sorts of accommodation used for seasonal occupancy by Mepkin's previous owners. There was not much more. Now, as then, a good deal of the property is timberland, nestled in the heart of the deeply Protestant South. Even today, the one diocese of Charleston covers the entire state of South Carolina.

The foundation of Mepkin did not take place all at once. Indeed it might be more accurate to speak of three waves of founders, most of whom were Polish-Americans from the "rust belt," especially "big shoulder" cities like Chicago and Cleveland. Several were veterans of the Second World War. But even with such sturdy stock, Mepkin was not an immediate success. Economic strains and the severity of the summer climate posed real challenges to the nascent foundation. Several of the original group of twenty nine left the community, no doubt because of rugged living conditions and the intense summer heat. The monastery's future was at times very uncertain in the early days. Thus Gethsemani sent a group of seven monks to offer assistance and bolster the strength of the fledgling monastic community. At the time, they were referred to as "the Seven Gifts of the Holy Spirit." In 1955 a third wave arrived to offer further assistance to the young community.

Under its first two abbots, Dom Anthony Chassagne and Dom Aidan Christian Carr, the monastic community at Mepkin remained small, tucked away and largely unknown amidst their mostly African-American, Protestant neighbors. Mepkin's virtual anonymity was very much in keeping with the Trappist spirit of hiddenness and obscurity. The monks constituted a quiet presence and, in many ways, were an unremarkable community, especially in contrast to larger monasteries like Gethsemani in the "American Holy Land" of Kentucky, or Saint Joseph's Abbey in Spencer, Massachusetts, located in regions with a higher Roman Catholic population. Indeed, Gethsemani's most celebrated son, Thomas Merton, wrote of Mepkin:

> Gethsemani made a foundation in 1949 in South Carolina, on a large old plantation donated by Henry R. Luce and Clare Boothe Luce. Mepkin is one of the quietest and most beautiful monasteries of the Order. Still small and practically unknown, it moves peacefully along the way of a Cistercian foundation that is not in too big a hurry to become enormous.[12]

Preceding and just following the Second Vatican Council, monastic life at Mepkin was similar to that in other monasteries of the Order of Cistercians of the Strict Observance. The Trappist discipline entailed strict adherence to the ideals of simplicity, solitude, poverty, communal prayer, worship, and especially manual work and personal austerity. Silence was a hallmark of Trappist life, and most communication among the monks took place by means of a sign language. Verbal communication was the exception. The discipline of enclosure was strictly enforced, illustrative of a strong separation between the monastic life and life "in the world." Indeed so much of the monastic regime served as a stark reminder that those in the

[12] Thomas Merton, *The Silent Life* (New York: Farrar, Straus & Cudahy, 1957) 124–25.

monastery had "fled the world" to embrace a life of self-sacrifice and penance. On the face of it, Trappist life seemed quite severe, and their Order was often considered (quite incorrectly) to be the strictest form of religious life in the Church. This impression still lingers among some.

Whereas the first two abbots of Mepkin were formed in an approach to religious life thus described, and received their theological training prior to the Second Vatican Council, the third abbot of Mepkin was educated during the Second Vatican Council and entered Gethsemani in 1972 while the spirit of the council was in full flower. Francis Kline, monk of Gethsemani, was elected Abbot of Mepkin in 1990. He brings to the office of abbot a rich formation in monastic sources and the Cistercian patrimony, both of which were neglected or not well integrated in the theological and spiritual formation within Trappist monasteries prior to Vatican II. Kline also brings a deep love of the arts—music, fine art, architecture, literature—preserved through the monastic tradition as well as through other traditions of Western culture. Perhaps what is most distinctive in his abbatial leadership is a profound appreciation for the renewed vision of the church articulated in the documents of the Second Vatican Council.[13] Under his guidance, the monks at Mepkin have grown in their awareness of themselves as a community related to the larger Church around them. This stands in marked contrast to earlier monastic self-understandings in which, if not in theory then certainly in practice, the monastery was thought to be a self-sufficient ecclesial reality removed from and unmoved by the exigencies and demands of the Church and of the world. Monks "left" the world and, removed from the duties of the apostolate and the pastoral ministry, left the gifts and the tasks of churchly life in the hands of others. But Francis Kline has cultivated a monastic self-understanding in which the brothers at Mepkin form a praying community within the Church universal. Rather than being removed from the Church, the monks at Mepkin are ineluctably in the midst of the joys and the sorrows of all the People of God, at the heart of the Church's mission to live and proclaim the gospel of Jesus Christ.

Building a House for the Church at Mepkin

The construction of the new Mepkin Abbey Church is among the most significant developments in Mepkin's fifty-year history. In 1989, prior to the election of Francis Kline as third abbot of Mepkin, the monastic community began discussions concerning the renovation of its original church, an unremarkable structure in every way. Originally intended to serve as a refectory, it was decided instead that the refectory building would serve as a temporary church until such time that a permanent one could be built. In accord with the earlier Trappist discipline, visitors to the refectory-become-church were relegated to the back of the church, separated by architectural design from the monastic community at prayer and worship.

---

[13] See Francis Kline, *Lovers of the Place: Monasticism Loose in the Church* (Collegeville: The Liturgical Press, 1997).

Illustration A

In many monasteries, visitors were separated from monks by a wall from floor to ceiling, so that the monks could be neither seen nor heard clearly. Nor could the liturgy! It is intriguing to note that even today the separation-by-design of visitors and retreatants from the monastic community at prayer and worship continues in some Cistercian monasteries.

In January 1991, now under Kline's abbatial leadership, the community took up with greater vigor their discussions regarding the renovation of the original church. They chose Frank Kacmarcik for the liturgical design of the project, with Theodore Butler as architect. After lengthy consultation it was decided to change direction and proceed with the building of an entirely new structure.

The Mepkin Abbey Church is the first in importance of the many buildings that make up the monastery, the centerpiece of the whole monastic complex. The building is "a house for the church of Mepkin" which has a distinctive personality, and is a unique expression of Mepkin's style of liturgy and monastic hospitality. It expresses the identity of the monastic community and its vision for the future. The monks form an *ecclesiola*, a little church, which finds its place within the *ecclesia*, the wider church, the Church universal. Monks are part of the Church, the People of God, and called along with them to full, conscious, and active participation in

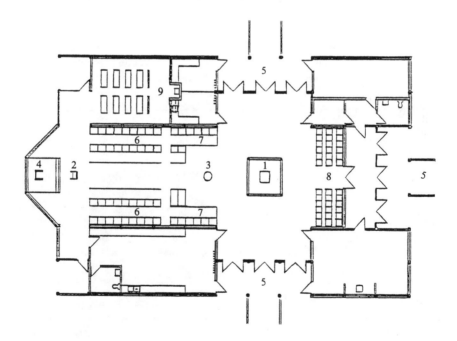

Illustration B

liturgy, especially the Eucharist, which is the source and summit of Christian life.[14] The form of the church follows its function (numbers in brackets refer to the floor plan in illustration B): the centrality of the altar [1]; the placement of ambo [2] and font [3]; the relation of choir stalls [6] to altar [1]; the relation of retreatants and guests [7] to the monastic community [6]; the location of casual visitors [8]; the creation of a smaller more intimate space for reservation of the Blessed Sacrament and private prayer [9]; the very location of the church at the center of the monastic complex, all bespeak a profound theology of monastic, ecclesial, Christian life. When considered alongside the original church at Mepkin, it is altogether clear that there have been "changes . . . behind the world of sensible appearances," revealed in the "artistic form" of the Mepkin Abbey Church.

The design of the church at Mepkin is considerably different from other Trappist Cistercian churches both in the United States and abroad, many of which still separate the monastic community from visitors and retreatants by architectural design. Without prejudice to the complexity of the issue, it may be that the hospitality characteristic of the culture of the Old South has been embodied in a very distinctive fashion as the monks of Mepkin have attempted to give expression to the ancient monastic discipline of hospitality in their own cultural milieu.[15]

At Mepkin, entrances [5] to the church converge on the altar, which is reverenced with a profound bow on entry and upon departure from the church. There is no central image of Christ in the church. It is, rather, the act of assembling for prayer and the assembled while praying, especially at the Eucharist, which is the central Christological image. It is in the gathering for prayer and worship—monks, retreatants, guests, and visitors—that the Body of Christ is brought to form. The design of the church expresses the recognition that there must be room enough for the many parts of the Body to stand forth in prayer. But this is done in such a way that it is altogether clear that the core, the heart, of the community is the monastic brotherhood at prayer, bound by vows for the purpose of living the contemplative life, understood in more traditional terms.

All the baptized are welcome to the celebration of the Liturgy of the Hours and worship. The relation of retreatants and guests to monks, together with the placement of visitors, is expressive of a distinct understanding of the interplay of charisms in service of the community. The location of the chair [4] is itself indicative of the importance of the charism of leadership and authority in the church, and particularly in the monastery in which the abbot is understood to hold the place of Christ.[16] All present in the church are arranged so that the dialogical and relational

---

[14] The oft-cited phrase, selected as the title for this commemorative volume, is from the Second Vatican Council's Constitution on the Sacred Liturgy, *Sacrosanctum Concilium*, no. 10.

[15] The importance of monastic hospitality is expressed in the exhortation in chapter 53 of the Rule: "Let all guests be received as Christ." See *The Rule of Saint Benedict: in Latin and English with Notes (RB* 80). Timothy Fry, ed. (Collegeville: The Liturgical Press, 1981).

[16] See *The Rule of Saint Benedict*, chapter 2.

Illustration C

character of Christian prayer, psalmody, and worship can be brought to fullness of expression.

The church combines enduring forms with the liturgical vision of the community in a way that evokes a particular aesthetic or ethos of the monastic tradition. The building is almost barn-like in its utter simplicity. It is a place with space. It is light and airy.[17] In part this is because of the many clear windows in the church's clerestory, as well as the church's many clear glass doors [5], a rarity in a monastic church. The church seems to open out to its surroundings, bespeaking a specific understanding of the relation between church and world. It also communicates a unified vision of contemplation and action. Such a view does not allow for relegating prayer and contemplation to an "enclosed monastic community" behind a wall which separates it from "the world" awaiting transformation by the sanctifying activity of clergy, apostolic religious and laity.

The Mepkin Abbey Church invites the recitation and singing of the psalms, the lifting of the mind and heart in doxology, which is itself contemplation in action. In the Cistercian tradition there is an affirmation of the centrality of the heart, the primacy of *affectus*.[18] In this tradition both contemplation and action are understood to be rooted in one and the same source, the human heart. Consequently there is no separation, only a notional distinction, between action and contemplation. Contemplation does not spring from one faculty, and action from another, as if the human person were made up of separate parts. Rather, contemplation and action are coefficients in the human heart's longing for God.

A Place of Word and Light

In the Cistercian tradition, the Word of God is to be worthily proclaimed, sung, heard, celebrated, and appropriated. The Mepkin Abbey Church is a place where there is space for words to be spoken and sung in a way that allows the Word to stand forth beneath and beyond the words.[19] The wooden vault supported by southern yellow pine beams adds height and grace to the building, enhancing its acoustical properties. The Zimmer Organ at Mepkin is in the French Classic style, an instrument which joins digital technology and pipes. It is ideal for a monastic community, whose repertoire may range from very simple music to the complex.

The church invites the enjoyment of contemplative moments, indeed of prolonged contemplative experience, in and through the design of the building itself.

---

[17] On the importance of light in the Christian spiritual and mystical tradition see William Johnston, *Mystical Theology: The Science of Love* (Maryknoll, N.Y.: Orbis Books, 1995) 57 ff.

[18] For a helpful explanation of the heart and *affectus*, see Marie-Dominique Chenu, "Les catégories affectives dans la langue de l'École," in *Le Coeur*, vol. 29 of the series *Études carmélitaines* (n.p.: Desclée de Brouwer and Cie, 1950) 123–28.

[19] For a helpful introduction to the centrality of the Word in monastic spirituality see Michael Casey, *Sacred Reading: The Ancient Art of Lectio Divina* (Ligouri, Mo.: Ligouri, 1996).

Illustration D

Illustration E

This is because the architectural design is itself expressive of a particular under-standing of God.[20] To be plain: how we understand God is how we will build our churches. At Mepkin, the floor plan is profoundly incarnational, allowing room for the Body of Christ in all its members at prayer and worship to be brought to full-ness of form. The elevation is lean, clean, uncluttered, thin. The form is sheer po-etry in light: penetrating light at play with the simple, stark, and spare. In other words, the Mepkin Abbey Church expresses a deeply Cistercian spirit which is at once kataphatic and apophatic. Thin clean lines, shafts of light, the play of sound, invite the eye and the ear of the heart to behold the beauty of God precisely in the recognition of what is missing, in the draw of the human heart beyond what is given in the simplest of forms. This occurs precisely through the design and crea-tion of a space in which we know ourselves to be *in God, in Christ,* precisely by being in the place.

Conclusion

The praxis of building a house for the church at Mepkin may be understood as bringing to "artistic form" the "changes which have taken place behind the world of sensible appearances" in the life of the community of Mepkin. The building it-self expresses a distinctive Christian spirituality, shaped by monastic culture and the culture of the Deep South, by specific Cistercian and Trappist traditions, as well as by particular events which have affected the small and vulnerable commu-nity at Mepkin. The centrality of the altar, the convergence of entrances toward it, as well as the placement of monks, retreatants, guests, and visitors all express the central image of the Body of Christ which comes to full form in the praxis of prayer and worship. In this praxis, the various charisms within the Christian com-munity stand forth, be it the abbot's gift of leadership and authority, or that of the director of religious education on retreat who voices her petition for the well-being of her pastor and the catechumens entrusted to her care. This is a praxis in which action and contemplation spring from a single source, the human heart, awakened by the Word proclaimed, heard, sung, celebrated, appropriated in a place where the radiant heavenly Light fills an earthly dwelling place, a modest jewel, stark and spare, that is the house for the whole church at Mepkin.

The spirituality expressed in the architectural design of the church at Mepkin is one of Place, Word, and Light. This is deeply Cistercian spirituality, in which Word and Light are central, and in which art and architecture allow enough room, space wide and deep enough, for both to stand forth. But a contemporary Cister-cian spirituality must give expression to these in such a way that accounts for local culture, for developments within a living tradition, and for the influence of con-temporary events, hopes, sufferings, and promises. The monks at Mepkin have

---

[20] For a fuller treatment of the spirituality expressed in Cistercian architecture see Terryl N. Kinder, *L'Europe cistercienne* (La Pierre-qui-Vire: Éditions Zodiaque, 1997).

expressed profoundly Cistercian convictions in view of these factors, but in a way that takes with utmost seriousness the renewed ecclesiology and Christology prompted by the Second Vatican Council, specifically the council's recognition of the diversity of charisms, its affirmation of the universal call to holiness, its encouragement of the full, conscious, and active participation of all the baptized in the liturgy, specifically the Eucharist as source and summit of Christian life.

There is no doubt that other architectural designs have been influenced by, and have given expression to, the governing convictions of the renewed ecclesiology of the Second Vatican Council. The singular achievement of the Mepkin Abbey Church is the particular way in which it brings to artistic form the conviction, "behind the world of sensible appearances," that the *sine qua non* of the renewed ecclesiology of the Second Vatican Council is the cultivation of the contemplative dimension of the Christian life. The monks of Mepkin have built a house for the church, a place wherein the People of God find themselves *in Christ* and know themselves to be *in God*. This is a profoundly Cistercian intuition: Not that God is in us, but that we are in God. It is expressed in the painstaking effort to craft a modest jewel, a shimmering space wide, high, and deep. In it there is room enough for the heart to be washed in the ebb and flow of the Word, and for the eye to be lifted by shafts of Light so that it may behold in a crust of bread and a cup of wine the Body of Christ in the Spirit, to the glory of God the Father.

15. Art and Architecture

The Defeat of Visual Aesthetic Arianism

Mark E. Wedig, O.P.

Josef Jungmann's essay "The Defeat of Teutonic Arianism and the Revolution in Religious Culture in the Early Middle Ages," discloses, above all else, a people's participation in a rich spiritual life. In this essay history serves "a higher theological purpose: the discernment of what is an essential possession in religious life. . . ."[1] For Jungmann, despite the barbarisms and apostasies in Western Christianity, a great inner religious value endures, often lodged in the symbolic and imaginative forms of culture. Especially the unfolding themes or patterns of Christian worship, the arts, music, and preaching reveal this inner religious sense. Jungmann emphasizes that these symbolic forms often persist exposing the limits of mere dogmatic expression. Liturgy, art, architecture and the other figurative sources of Western Christianity manifest the faith of the people often when theoretical assertions fail to communicate those truths.

A pivotal aspect of Jungmann's contribution to the recovery of a people's faithful participation in religious life is his recovery of their visual aesthetic participation. Art and architecture remain important theological sources in themselves for deciphering religious life. Image and edifice both safeguard and transform the Christian tradition in ways other symbols do not. Therefore interpreting the role of these visual media is similar to unraveling the meaning of the liturgy and other mystagogical sources. They represent the practical religious fabric of an evolving culture. Jungmann's commitment to appropriating the religious value of Western culture leads him evermore deeply into the resources of the people's visual aesthetics, especially when other forms fail to embody that value.

By focusing on Jungmann's "The Defeat of Teutonic Arianism" and accompanying essays in the volume *Pastoral Liturgy*,[2] I will review his understanding of art and architecture as theological sources. In order to do this, first I will delineate what he means by the practical and pastoral framework of image and edifice. Like

---

[1] J. A. Jungmann, S.J., "The Defeat of Teutonic Arianism and the Revolution in Religious Culture in the Early Middle Ages," in *Pastoral Liturgy* (New York: Herder and Herder, 1962) 2.

[2] J. A. Jungmann, S.J., *Pastoral Liturgy* (New York: Herder and Herder, 1962) hereafter cited as *PL.*

worship and preaching, visual aesthetic activity in Christianity functions primarily as proclamation. Here I will elucidate what Jungmann means by art revealing kerygma. Following this I will demonstrate how he narrates the triumph of Christian kerygma in the art and architecture of the West. For Jungmann, the practical visual aesthetics of Western peoples ultimately safeguards orthodoxy, especially subverting the heresies of the Gothic pieties. Nevertheless art and Christian mystery remain in tension. For Jungmann, Western visual aesthetic concerns obscure Christian kerygma especially because of the independent criteria of the art forms themselves. In relationship to this, I will introduce the ideas of contemporary art historian Hans Belting who, I believe, extends this visual aesthetic thesis of Jungmann by taking into consideration how art and public religion are pitted against each other in the post-Renaissance Western world.

Art and Architecture as Pastoral Practice

Jungmann interprets Christianity primarily through its practices. For him, religious practice protects, maintains, and manifests the Christian faith more than religious theories or doctrines. Practice is the indispensable husk of an inner religious life. As Jungmann puts it: ". . . a tortoise-shell protecting religious life . . . a store-house of religious life. It has arisen out of an intense religious life and experience, as the protective bark grows from the life of the tree."[3] Liturgy, the arts, architecture and preaching make up this practical religious husk and remain a fundamental expression of the people's faith.

In order for liturgical and aesthetic practice to remain authentic, however, it must remain pastoral. Religious practice becomes pastoral when it is conscious. A pastoral liturgy, like a pastoral aesthetics or homiletics is a self-conscious exercise, making what is conventional, habitual, and customary evermore intentional and understood. Pastoral theology determines what makes Christianity conscious, constantly clarifying the practice of faith. For Jungmann, pastoral deliberation gives reasons for a people's participation in worship, art forms and other indispensable modes of Christian life. It is being able to grasp the unique value of religion through its application. A conscious religious practice arouses and keeps alive the treasures of the faith.[4]

Significant here is Jungmann's location of art and architecture in the practical and pastoral dimension of theology. For him visual aesthetic forms should not be detached or abstracted from the fundamental pragmatic environment of Christianity. Image and edifice should not be understood as extraneous from or superfluous to a people's custom and ritual and therefore investigated strictly by themselves.[5] Instead art and architecture, like liturgy, represent the basic texture and fabric of

---

[3] Jungmann, "Christianity—Conscious or Unconscious," *PL*, 325.
[4] Ibid., 332.
[5] Jungmann, "Liturgy and Church Art," *PL*, 357.

Christian culture. They are the bark of the tree, which protects, sustains, and re-generates Christianity. No adequate understanding of the faith can be dislocated from these vital and practical structures and patterns.

In addition, Jungmann's pastoral aesthetics determines what image and edifice mean as religious manifestation. A pastoral aesthetics interprets the developments of art and architecture in terms of the Church's consciousness about its expression. Aesthetic developments can be assessed and judgments can be made in terms of their authentic and inauthentic embodiment of faith in particular episodes of cultural history. Art and architecture can mirror, deflect and even re-orient the religious deposit of faith. For Jungmann, the authenticity and inauthenticity of faithful aesthetics is determined by how art and edifice relate to other forms and patterns of the religious culture. Pastoral aesthetics correlates liturgy with art and architecture and likewise with other figurative sources, disclosing the "changes which have taken place somewhere behind the world of sensible appearances, but which are revealed both in cultural and artistic forms."[6]

Art and Architecture as Proclamation

Church art professes or proclaims the Christian faith. Like liturgy, visual aesthetic activity heralds an essential message. Complementary to but distinct from dogmatic assertion, picture and building announce belief. They extol the mystery of Jesus Christ instead of explaining it. Jungmann likens the people's involvement in art and architecture to their faithful participation in homily, hymn, creed and blessing prayers. Artistic sources protect and exhibit the verity of the Christian message in the act of symbolic, embodied communication. Jungmann explains:

> Church art is a profession of faith, just as public worship itself is profession and procla-mation. Church art proclaims first of all, therefore, those facts which lie at the base of the Christian world-order; thus they are the same as those which are accentuated in the Apostles' Creed, the same as are observed in the feasts of the Church.[7]

Art and architecture preach the faith. They acclaim the news of Jesus Christ in the same way ritual events disclose that mystery.

Moreover, both image and edifice constitute the kerygma of Christian faith. Like the liturgy, visual aesthetic forms mirror, manifest, and unfold the essential Christian mystery. Pictures and buildings herald basic truths of Christian faith, making tangible the continuous phenomenon of Jesus Christ in place and time. They are public ecclesial witness to a message found both in the public ministry of Jesus and in the mystery of his death and resurrection. Art and architecture bequeath that essential proclamation in paint, glass, cloth, wood, stone, brick and mortar. Therefore they are a distinct genre or idiom of that gospel. They invite

---

[6] "The Defeat of Teutonic Arianism," *PL*, 2.
[7] "Liturgy and Church Art," *PL*, 360.

participation in Christian mystery through particular media. In that sense they are a discourse of belief which manifests the meaning of the *kergyma* of Jesus Christ in sheer material construction.

Art and Architecture Share the Proclamation with the Liturgy

As already indicated, Jungmann sees the history of the Church most fundamentally as the history of its practices. The Church is manifest truly where the Gospel is heralded. Liturgy, preaching and art share that practical fare and facilitate the common task of proclaiming the mystery of faith. They make up the symbolic fabric of faith which reveals the Christian kerygma. Therefore the fullness of faith is made apparent in these forms when they cooperate in the common charge of preaching and professing. The degrees of authenticity of proclamation depend on the integration of liturgy, art, architecture and other figurative forms of the tradition. In other words, the kerygma is embodied best in the synthesis of image, edifice, and worship.

The critical dimension of Jungmann's historical work concerns judgments about the authenticity or inauthenticity of religious practices. For him, the mystery of Christianity is defaced or obscured when one practice becomes detached from or unconscious of another. Therefore art and architecture can both adopt or eschew the indispensable deposit of faith. Art and architecture can function cooperatively with that message or obscure it. For example, Jungmann recounts how in the ancient Roman and Byzantine Christian churches, art and liturgy serve as partners or companions in expressing the faith of the people. Especially in the first five centuries of Christianity art facilitates worship in bringing out the fullness of Christian mystery.[8] The close association of liturgy, art, architecture, music, and preaching in the ancient expression facilitates a more complete rendering of the faith.[9]

Nevertheless Jungmann's great attraction to this ancient integrated expression in liturgy and art leads him consequently into epochs where worship and art become disconnected from each other. His preoccupation with the religious life of people in the Middle Ages, reflected so well in "The Defeat of Teutonic Arianism," draws him more deeply into a people's uniquely visual aesthetic participation in Christian mystery often dislocated from official corporate liturgy. Medieval art and architecture bare the piety of the Teutonic peoples who seek redemption through subjective ocular participation in Christian mystery. In this epoch, the people's participation in the Church and its mystery is vicariously vi-

---

[8] Jungmann employs the concept of *mysterium* found in Ildefons Herwegen's *Kirche und Seele, Die Seelenhaltung des Mysterienkultes und ihr Wandel im Mittelalter* (Münster: Aschendorff, 1926) where Herwegen speaks of the unified idiom which represents the fullness of mystery, best exemplified by the ancient Church. Also see: Ildefons Herwegen, *The Art—Principle of the Liturgy* (Collegeville: The Liturgical Press, 1931) and *Liturgy's Inner Beauty* (Collegeville: The Liturgical Press, 1955).

[9] "Liturgy and Church Art," *PL*, 362–63.

sual and disassociated from assembled eucharistic worship. A people's religious spirituality is translated by the strictly visual and subjective pieties of the individual Christian instead of a more synthetic and corporate consciousness.[10]

Jungmann's interest in medieval piety consequently leads him to affirm the social and epistemological autonomy of the image and edifice for expressing practical religion. Art and architecture can mediate the faith independently from liturgy or preaching. Seemingly incongruous to his work as a liturgical theologian, Jungmann identifies the sovereignty of art and architecture over other theological sources, including liturgical texts. Here the people's visual aesthetics is a double-edged sword. Especially in the Latin West art exhibits the Church independent from its official liturgy. In this case corporate visual aesthetic concern becomes "itself liturgy,"[11] embodying the people's religious life. In this sense, art mirrors the corporate spirituality of a culture directly and can even subvert the official prayer of the Church and other canons of faith.

The Defeat of Aesthetic Arianism

Church art and architecture are judged best according to their soteriological significance. As Jungmann puts it: "The great theme of Church art of all time is the history of redemption, especially the more decisive section of this history: the foundation of redemption in the appearance of Christ and His works."[12] At the center of that redemptive mystery lies the divinization of humanity uniquely revealed in Jesus Christ. Like liturgy and preaching, art bares that divine embodiment. Therefore images and edifices, and other symbolic expressions in Western Christian history disclose belief in God's fundamental relationship with the human condition. Jungmann ultimately narrates the people's accord with that mystery in their refusal to settle simply on one aesthetic image, pattern or theme to epitomize that divine embodiment. The communication of Christ's redemptive mystery necessitates a certain aesthetic ambiguity.

Nevertheless the foil to orthodox belief and practice in the West remains the subjective pieties of what Jungmann identifies as "Teutonic Arianism." Such pieties encompass the moralisms and individualisms which obscure participation in the mystery of Christ and which furthermore even denounce belief in God's mediation through Christ altogether. This reticence to believe in that mediation ultimately manifests overly literal, historical and personal interpretations of Christ. Therefore in the history of the Western Church, certain spiritualities eschew participation in Christ's redemptive mystery by breaking-up what Jungmann refers to as the fundamental "Easter motif" of the Christian kerygma.[13]

---

[10] "The Defeat of Teutonic Arianism," *PL*, 6–9.
[11] "Liturgy and Church Art," *PL*, 357.
[12] Ibid., 359.
[13] "The Defeat of Teutonic Arianism," *PL*, 6.

Moral concern for the individual's salvation often overshadows the symbolic fullness of Christ's redemption. Jungmann portrays the visual aesthetic dismantling of Easter as follows: "It has long been realized, however, that medieval art in particular and also modern religious art have only made use of a very small selection from this rich store of material."[14] Western piety tends to eclipse the kerygma by narrowing certain elements of the christological mystery. Therefore the people's visual aesthetics is judged in terms of how well it reflects the entire liturgical calendar; how well it exhibits a more replete revelation of Christ's redemption in the liturgical ordo. In addition, the extent to which the entire liturgical ordo affects church art and architecture, the more authentic it is. For Jungmann, the ancient aesthetics, like the ancient liturgy, holds a wide breath of themes or patterns of the kerygma in tension. Mystery is abundant in art and environment when the Easter motif, the paschal mystery, unfolds.

Yet in the West the affinity for a more private and subjective understanding of grace obstructs the broad array of christological patterns. Church art in the West increasingly becomes compressed into two narrowly defined christological themes. The infancy of Jesus, extended to include the life of Mary, and Christ's passion define the scope of visual aesthetic subjects.[15] These themes become the occasion for individual visual participation. Images about Christ's infancy and passion function as subjective passage to God and Christ. The narratives of art, often focused on the more festive parts of the Church calendar, provoke private and subjective religious responses. The kerygma becomes reflected through the prism of this exclusive and personal piety instead of corporate and ecclesial spirituality.

This propensity for subjective and private spiritualities relates to an epistemological bias in Western art. In other words, Jungmann's theological reflections about art and architecture relate to a larger philosophical critique worth pondering. He recognizes the great technical achievement of Renaissance and Baroque art and architecture in the West, yet he negatively assesses the privatization of artistic achievement. Such critique focuses on certain Western illusions about visual aesthetic progress played out in the mastery of individual artists. For Jungmann, the development of artistic and architectural skill and technique, along with an increased focus on artistic agency, correspond to a Western cultural defeat of authentic public religion. The visual aesthetic sophistication of the Renaissance and Baroque periods on the one hand celebrates the subjective exploitation of image and building, yet at the same time evinces the demise of a corporate sense of mystery. As Jungmann elucidates:

> The Last Supper of Leonardo da Vinci is a marvel of psychological penetration and dramatic form. But no longer has the artist set the mystery itself in the centre, but has taken a subsidiary scene. . . The Gothic winged altars and the Baroque altar super-

---

[14] "Liturgy and Church Art," *PL*, 359.
[15] Ibid., 363–65.

structures are superb creations, in their own way; but the fundamental liturgical idea from which the whole development derived and which was all-controlling in the first century . . . has almost become lost.[16]

He laments the loss of public or corporate transcendence once embodied in much more modest aesthetic achievement.

Jungmann's aesthetic thesis concerns the detachment of art from an objective mystery which is directly linked to corporate participation in symbol. Likewise he is critical of the artist's role in isolating religious themes for the purposes of art itself or the individual's acumen. Such visual aesthetic abstraction can be likened to spiritualities which focus on shards of the tradition for subjective purposes. Even though Western artists in the Renaissance and Baroque periods made great technological advances in their rendering of visual forms, the powerful role of image in communicating the Christian kerygma is dissipated because of the primacy of subjective aesthetic concerns on the part of both the artist and the onlooker.

The Victory of the Kerygma in Modest Visual Forms

Jungmann's critique of Western visual aesthetics, in which he underscores the rupture between artistic values and public Christianity, relates to his understanding and endorsement of aesthetic principles that stem from the modern liturgical and catechetical movements. Even though these aesthetic judgments and practices continue to be debated in the contemporary Western Church and culture, Jungmann's visual philosophy can be situated in terms of a specific genre of modern Catholicism and can be helpful for fathoming the fundamental visual aesthetic principles of recent ecclesial reform.

First of all Jungmann himself was sympathetic to the self-conscious and humble styles associated with a certain group of Swiss and German architects and designers affiliated with the liturgical movement.[17] Even though he refrained from a full endorsement of twentieth century visual aesthetic primitivism, Jungmann clearly defends the austere and streamlined art and architectural forms of modernity in terms of the modesty of new beginnings. For him a bare bones visual aesthetic can be understood in terms of an incipient symbolic return to mystery and public religion. The ultimate victory of the Christian kerygma would be reflected in the defeat of Western culture's dominant reliance on subjective pieties. Therefore the Church inaugurates a self-consciously humble spirituality which subverts the dominance of subjective visual aesthetics and privatized worship in the West. This religious approach eventually gives way to a new corporate value for art and ritual, as Jungmann illustrates:

[16] Ibid., 366.
[17] Karl Moser, Hermann Baur, Fritz Metzer, and Rudolf Schwartz.

> Today in Church architecture no one asks: how do people, living in the great periods of artistic achievement, design a church or an altar? They ask: What is a church? What is an altar? . . . This does not imply the rejection of art in Church. It means, however, that it must fit into the over-all plan of the liturgy and remain firmly rooted in a religious conception, not only in the personal experience of the artist. . . .[18]

The bias for aesthetic subjectivity and privatized spirituality in the Western modern world would be supplanted by self-conscious and modest religious forms. Contemporary art and architecture, like contemporary liturgy would be renewed by simple, pastoral and therefore functional forms. Jungmann claims that the crafting of these forms is the construction of a "conscious" Christianity in which people answer "What is a church? what is an altar, what is a pulpit, what is a candlestick? And thereupon they fashioned a style out of their own perception of what was genuine expression of a true thought, just as the men of olden days had done."[19]

It is reasonable to conclude that Jungmann's visual interpretations follow what contemporary art history has identified as "modernist" criteria for image and edifice. Much has been written about the powerful art movement which emerged in Europe in the early twentieth century declaring a return to a more primitive and self-conscious visual standard.[20] In order to save art from the radical cultural pluralism of late nineteenth-century industrial Europe, avant-gardes advance the values of abstract form and aesthetic genius.[21] An educated elite in North Atlantic cultures become convinced that a new primitive visual aesthetic style would rescue the Western industrialized world from its social downfall. Society could retrieve a universal symbolism through the reductionistic visual forms of sanctioned artistic prophets.[22]

It is left to the "postmodern" debates in contemporary art criticism to determine whether such visual artistic solutions are explained best in terms of explicitly defined cultural limits. However it is clear that contemporary theological scholarship needs to address the explicit visual aesthetic claims which declare those limits. First, because it is possible to relate modernist aesthetics to twentieth-century ecclesial, liturgical, and social movements and their desire to appropriate renewed primitive Christian forms.[23] Like other influential German and French theologians

---

[18] "Liturgy and Church Art," *PL*, 367.

[19] "Christianity—Conscious or Unconscious," *PL*, 333.

[20] For a good overview of modernist theory, see: Charles Harrison and Paul Wood, eds. *Art in Theory 1900–1990: An Anthology of Changing Ideas* (Oxford: Blackwell, 1992).

[21] Donald Kuspit, *The Cult of the Avant-Garde Artist* (New York: Cambridge University Press, 1993) 1–63.

[22] Rosalind E. Krauss, *The Originality of the Avant-Garde and Other Modernist Myths* (Cambridge: MIT Press, 1993) 1–4 and Mark A. Cheetham, *The Rhetoric of Purity: Essentialist Theory and the Advent of Abstract Painting* (New York: Cambridge University Press, 1991).

[23] Franck Debié and Pierre Vérot, *Urbansime et art sacré: une aventure du XXe siècle* (Paris: Criterion, 1991); Paul Rabinow, *French Modern: Norms and Forms of the Social Environment* (Cambridge: MIT Press, 1989); Mark E. Wedig, "The Hermeneutics of Religious Visual Art in *L'Art Sacré*

of this century, Jungmann favors the foundational visual aesthetics of modernist artists and architects. Second, because there is a need to determine the extent to which the explicit visual aesthetic standards advocated by twentieth-century church reform[24] are aligned with the highly critiqued artistic agenda of modernist avant-gardes. In other words, can the retrieval of a more ancient and rudimentary liturgy in the church reforms of this century be linked to the primitivism of aesthetic modernism?[25]

Even though I suggest that Jungmann's ideas can be aligned with the aesthetic criteria of modernism, the primitivist-universalist criteria are not the most compelling and consequential aspect of his aesthetic suppositions. There are questions raised by Jungmann about the failure of artistic subjectivity and the consequent destruction of public religion that remain more important to contemporary discussion about the dissolution of public symbol. In other words Jungmann's critique about the inalterable tension between art and religion in the post-Renaissance culture of the West remains pertinent to theological concern about the loss of public religion. I suggest that there are values raised by Jungmann's thesis about aesthetic subjectivity that warrant review by those particularly interested in both the religious and artistic crisis of contemporary culture.

The Retrieval of the Image and the End of the Era of Art

For Jungmann artistic and architectural forms, like the liturgy itself, are understood best as arising out of a cultural matrix. He follows aesthetic approaches which emerged from German and French art criticism of the 1950s, which questioned the study of art forms in themselves. The fusion of art and ideology, especially in Nazi visual propaganda, led to methods which insisted on identifying the social and political context of all visual forms. For instance Jungmann prefaces his approach to understanding church art by emphasizing that

> . . . in recent decades the history of art has considerably altered its approach to its subject. It is no longer content to point out and describe isolated works, nor yet to classify definite periods according to attitudes of style and form, but now it inquires rather into the intellectual forces behind the appearances, into social, political, philosophical and religious ideas and ideals of which they are the expression.[26]

1945–1954 in the Context of Aesthetic Modernity," (Ph.D. Dissertation: The Catholic University of America, Washington, D.C., 1995) 19–35.

[24] As set up in documents such as *Constitution on the Sacred Liturgy* (1963), para. 122–130 *The General Instruction on the Roman Missal* (1969), paragraphs 253-280 and *Environment and Art in Catholic Worship* (1978).

[25] The US Bishop's Committee on the Liturgy has initiated the writing of a new document which will replace *Environment and Art* (1978). This work in-progress about adequate visual aesthetic norms for the contemporary Church attempts to supplant some of the modernist assumptions of the earlier document.

[26] "Liturgy and Church Art," *PL*, 357.

When image and edifice are understood as integral to the mediation of culture then visual aesthetics cannot develop above or outside of social, political and religious interpretations. This contextual aesthetic approach identifies the problem of how art after the Renaissance and particularly in Modernity became increasingly inter-preted through subjectivity and consequently divorced from popular religious meaning. This can be seen particularly in the separate criteria for aesthetic and religious authority. Corporately sanctioned religious-aesthetic forms are sup-planted by individual and subjective artistic criteria in the modern Western world. Eventually the loss of the popular religious value of the image can be attributed to its being relegated to museum culture and elitist aesthetic purposes.

For Jungmann the recovery of religious mystery and symbolic meaning is linked to the retrieval of a corporate aesthetics in a people's spirituality. The rebirth of religious consciousness in the modern Western world is dependent on a renais-sance of publicly endorsed art and ritual. The failure of a public church art and other corporately sanctioned symbols is related to an epistemological crisis in Western culture. In other words individual and subjective spiritualities eclipse symbolic consciousness. I suggest that there are ways to further this aesthetic the-sis introduced by Jungmann and other modern religious reformers.

Contemporary aesthetic critiques extend the reasons for the divorce between the image and religion in the post-Renaissance and modern Western worlds. A number of art historians identify what they see as the Western academy's dread of the visual and consequent iconoclastic campaigns. Here it is suggested that both the religious and artistic intelligentsia in the West systematically undermine the power of the image. Hans Belting's *Likeness and Presence: A History of the Image Before the Era of Art*[27] stands as the centerpiece of that critique.

Belting's thesis can be understood as the attempt to recover the immanent presence of the divine in the image before the invention of art. For him, both reli-gious and artistic subjectivity tames and even annihilates the visual. With the emergence of the "era of art" in late Medieval and early Renaissance cultures, came the distrust and destruction of the visual and the need to domesticate it. For Belting the theologians and the artists create a cooperative leadership which fos-ters a campaign of image-destruction. The word-fixations of a religious elite and the need to interpret aesthetic perception through the subjectivity of the artist's imagination prevails over the visual resources of Western culture. The theologian and the artist together redirect the mystery of the image to match their perceptions. As a result of this, images lose the ambiguous and therefore mysterious properties they manifest in cultures where they remain the possession of all people.

---

[27] Hans Belting, *Likeness and Presence: A History of the Image Before the Era of Art*, trans. Ed-mund Jephcott (Chicago: University of Chicago Press, 1994). Also a less successful attempt to locate an all pervasive iconoclasm in the West is David Freedberg's *The Power of Images: Studies in the His-tory and Theory of Response* (Chicago: University of Chicago Press, 1989).

In the West, the rise of subjectivity, evidenced by the simultaneous "advance" of aesthetic depth perception and the theologian's power to interpret Christian texts, gives rise to various forms of iconoclasm. Such a framework reflects the move away from the dangerously contradictory world of visual response. Christianity joins up with other forms of "enlightened" culture in eradicating popular visual "texts." Significant visual events of meaning become repressed or extricated from Western cultural memory. The loss of the visual corresponds to the defeat of the sacramental. One can correlate the taming of the visual through the perceptions of individual genius with the instrumental and highly philosophical explanations for sacramental grace by the theologians. The drive toward a more scientific and rational explication for religious phenomena is paralleled by a hatred for the visual.

This thesis extends Jungmann's critique of Western subjectivity and its role in the aesthetic and sacramental mediation of religion. What Jungmann understands to be the subjective misperception of medieval Teutonic pieties is instead the encroachment of Western "enlightened" culture and how it affects the eradication of sacramental religion. The need to subdue and even conquer the visual reflects an ultimate fear of where popular religiosity will take Christianity. The theological drive toward intelligibility and the artistic drive toward precise norms for perception are parallel events which both suppress popular religious response. The fundamentally religious-visual response ironically is downplayed by both aesthetic and theological interpretations. Art and theology destroy both image and religion.

Jungmann's advancement of pastoral theology aims to restore corporate participation in Christian mystery. The defeat of the subjective pieties of Western Christianity would lead to corporately sanctioned art and ritual. For him the problem remains the individualisms and moralisms which mediate Western Christianity and ultimately eclipse the kerygma. I suggest, however, that Jungmann is missing a piece of the puzzle. Jungmann's interest in restoring a more pastoral and therefore conscious Christianity, needs to take into account the fundamental fear of visual sacramentality in Western Christianity. By examining how a rudimentary iconoclasm in the West downplayed popular religious response, more can be said about the role of the visual in mediating that tradition. The true restoration of a pastoral liturgy or a pastoral aesthetics demands a conscious recognition of the repression of visual embodiment in both the aesthetic and theological dimensions of Western Christianity. Belting's ideas therefore complement Jungmann's pastoral aesthetics through the challenge of his radical visual sacramentology. By identifying the iconoclasms which substantiate the Christian understanding of grace, one is released to consider the visual realism which authenticates sacramental participation. Here visuality demands immediacy in ways other symbols do not. The image requires somatic encounter with the divine and therefore the human experience of the sacred is rendered radically particular through visual likeness. The differentiation between subject and object is obscured through ocular response. The gaze demands the uncompromising authority of the one incarnated.

Jungmann's project ultimately calls for a spirituality renewed by lost and forgotten practices which bring the Christian closer to the threshold of mystery. For him mystery is disclosed by the reservoir of the collective religious imagination. The truth of Christ's redemption lies in the shared perspective of ritual, art and other figurative sources. In order to appreciate the more replete rendering of mystery suggested by Jungmann's insights, further exploration into the lost and forgotten visual wellspring of the Christian tradition is needed.

Conclusion

I conclude by suggesting that both Jungmann's and Belting's insights about visual aesthetic culture in the West help fashion new criteria for the advancement of Church art and architecture. Their ideas about the role of image and edifice in mediating a religious tradition can provide certain foundations for developing a pastoral aesthetics for the contemporary Church. A few of those criteria may be considered as follows:

Jungmann's and Belting's identification of a long-standing bias about art and architecture in the post-Rennaissance Christian West can serve as the starting point for aesthetic ministry. How do ecclesial communities address the religious cultural iconoclasms which substantiate Western Christian pieties? Image and edifice suffer from having become the possession of a high culture. Art and architecture become valued distinct from essential social factors and therefore are appropriated by their divorce from the cultural matrix. In other words, they are appreciated for their social autonomy. Incongruous to intended purposes, both building and image become superfluous to the popular social fabric. They decorate the faith instead of determine or manifest it.

Consequently, a pastoral aesthetics attempts to restore the authority of image and building as fundamental resources of the Christian tradition. Reading the tradition visually is essential to Christian pedagogy. With this approach, pictures and edifices can be understood as "texts" in the same way that liturgy and creed can. They herald fundamental Christian truths precisely through their practical facility. When visual resources are understood in terms of their fundamental role in mediating the religious tradition, they are correlated with other integral cultural developments of that tradition.

Therefore a pastoral aesthetics teaches others how to "read" images and buildings. A clearly articulated hermeneutics of visual Christianity demands knowing the languages and histories of images and buildings. A pastoral aesthetics bridges visual religious symbol to evolving culture. It delineates how the faith is mediated uniquely by art and architecture without disassociating visual mediation from other texts. In Western Christian contexts, this especially means identifying and understanding both the implicit and explicit iconoclasms which have affected the evolving visual hermeneutics of Church and culture.

Lastly, a pastoral aesthetics demands knowing how visual texts often substantiate the "underside" of the Christian tradition. It identifies how visual texts mediate the lost, forgotten and feared presence of the Christian God. It reveals how visual objects embody a radical sacramentality. Therefore pastoral aesthetics advocates the liberation of theology and ministry through the power of the gaze.

16. Music

Liturgical Singing: A Case for *Theologia Prima*

John K. Leonard

In "The Defeat of Teutonic Arianism and the Revolution in Religious Culture in the Early Middle Ages"[1] Josef Jungmann presents a broad outline of the "shifts of accent and changes of viewpoint" that took place in western Christianity between the end of the patristic era and the twelfth century, "having consequences so wide that they have left their mark on all subsequent ages right down to our own times." His task was "to illuminate, within the period mentioned, the history of the kerygma against the background of the history of dogma" while focusing primarily on the liturgy and Christian art. He noted further that his "outline" was

> . . . designed to encourage younger men (sic) to undertake more detailed work, the aim of which would be to make the minutiae of historical study serve a higher theological purpose: the discernment of what is an essential possession in religious life, and what the passing fashion of an age.[2]

The present essay, though inspired by Jungmann's challenge, is not yet the specialized study of early medieval music that he perhaps envisioned a liturgical musicologist would do. Instead it is a reflection on liturgical singing which, I suggest, is itself "an essential possession in religious life" and experientially more important for transmitting the faith of the early Church than all the dogmatic deliberations and politically motivated word changes that inevitably affect—sometimes supply—the words that we sing. Liturgical singing, even when it is only heard by participants (though this is not the ideal), engages the assembly in an actual experience of giving "Glory to God: Father *and* Son *and* Holy Spirit" *and simultaneously* "Glory *to* God, *through* Christ, *in* the Spirit. Those who sing God's praise do not have to be able to explain the difference; by *singing* either formula, they actually proclaim/embody as their own the faith of the church who gave them these sacred words to sing. However one articulates the cognitive content of the song, one must actually sing it in order to participate in the cosmic praise of God, the climax of which the church experiences in the Paschal Mystery of Jesus Christ.

[1] Reprinted in *Pastoral Liturgy* (New York: Herder & Herder, 1962) 1–101.
[2] Ibid., 1–2.

This essay on liturgical singing is in two parts: first, a reflection on the experience of Mystery as origin of both *theologia prima* and *theologia secunda* and the relationship between the two using the liturgical singing of the creed as an illustration; second, a reflection on liturgical singing and its embellishments as expressions of *theologia prima* with tropes from the Winchester Troper as an illustration.

I. Experience of Mystery

> "Tell me," said the atheist. "Is there a God—really?" Said the Master, "If you want me to be perfectly honest with you, I will not answer." Later the disciples demanded to know why he had not answered. "Because his question is unanswerable," said the Master. "So you are an atheist?" "Certainly not. The atheist makes the mistake of denying that of which nothing may be said." After pausing to let that sink in, he added, "And the theist makes the mistake of affirming it."[3]

At the root of all religious traditions is the human encounter with That-Of-Which-Nothing-May-Be-Said. The Numinous, the Holy, the Ultimate, the Sacred, the Whole, the All-Encompassing, the Inexhaustible, Being Itself or its Ground, the One, the No-Form, the No-thing, the Ineffable, "God,". . . . None of these are even adequate descriptions but mere attempts to bring into focus what is so pervasive and so near that it often goes unnoticed,[4] "fingers" that point to Mystery. Our awareness of Mystery sometimes bursts upon our consciousness or emerges gradually, almost imperceptibly but every human experience is potentially a trigger of this awareness, a vehicle in and through which we encounter the ever transcendent-yet-immanent God.

> We discover and engage God in the "liturgy of the world," that "terrible and sublime and terrifying liturgy, breathing of death and sacrifice, which God celebrates" through the length and breadth of human history. . . . We thus affirm the sacramental principle that the created world can and does manifest the divine and so enables our relationship with God and in God with each other.[5]

Theologia Prima

The initial response to such an encounter is to fall on one's face in silence; perhaps an inarticulate gasp, "Ah, Ah!" in terror and amazement. If we are wise as the Master in DeMello's *apophthegmaton*, we realize that "nothing may be said."

---

[3] A. DeMello, *One Minute Nonsense* (Chicago: Loyola University Press, 1992) 21.

[4] J. Shea, *Stories of God: An Unauthorized Biography* (Chicago: Thomas More, 1978) 15–16.

[5] *The Milwaukee Symposia for Church Composers: A Ten Year Report.* © Archdiocese of Milwaukee; (published jointly at Washington, D.C.: National Association of Pastoral Musicians and Chicago: Liturgy Training Publications, 1992), n. 11; the internal quotes are from Karl Rahner, "Considerations on the Active Role of the Person in the Sacramental Event," *Theological Investigations XIV: Ecclesiology, Questions in the Church, The Church in the World*, trans. David Bourke (New York: Seabury Press, 1976) 169.

Nevertheless, the experience itself includes, even demands our acknowledgment and so we find ourselves trying to express and embody the experience of Mystery in the open-ended, ambiguous, even incomprehensible language of exclamations: "O my God!" "Have mercy!" "Jesus Christ!" But no litany of exclamations suffices and we find ourselves elaborating these initial exclamations into poems, songs, stories, dances, and ritual repetitions of physical, emotional and imaginative aspects of the encounter itself.[6] Eventually—depending on the power and force of the initial encounter and subsequent experiences encapsulated and conveyed through its multiple expressions—we find ourselves remembering the encounter and realizing it anew in sacred rituals.

In theological jargon, these immediate, passionate, exuberant expressions and their elaborations are categorized as *theologia prima* or "first order" religious language. (And it is in this sense that the liturgy is the church's "first" theology.[7]) In his masterful work, *An Experience Named Spirit*, John Shea describes how, "first order" language comes

> . . . rushing out of the experience, tumbling over itself in the effort to express what has happened. But what has happened has been the immanent touch of a transcendent God. The experience is essentially ineffable. The soul cheerfully admits this; and then continues to bubble forth image after image. What has happened is more than words can say but we cannot stop saying words.[8]

These languages arise in the initial acknowledgement that one has indeed encountered the Holy. Like the languages used to express love and every other transcendent reality, this initial acknowledgment is exaggerated, poetic, and metaphorical. Inexact and imprecise, *theologia prima* is ultimately unconcerned with the literal, rational, "orthodox" meaning attached to words. Instead it seeks not merely to express a "truth" that is more than literally true, but to provide a vehicle for—or at least serve as a catalyst to trigger—an holistic experience of the same transcendent-immanent-and-somehow-incarnate Reality that was first encountered. When the many forms of *theologia prima* find effective expression in liturgy, for example, they work together to "weave a pattern of access" to the transcendent which has previously revealed Self in and through the encounter(s) that gave rise to these languages:[9]

[6] J. Shea, *An Experience Named Spirit*, (Chicago: Thomas More, 1983) 61–68.

[7] Cf. *Sacrosanctum Concilium,* n. 10. Prosper of Acquitaine's maxim, "Legem credendi lex statuat supplicendi" (the rule of prayer establishes the rule of belief), i.e., the way we pray *(theologia prima)* fixes or determines what we must believe *(theologia secunda)* is the classical source for this notion; see Paul DeClerk, "'Lex orandi, lex credendi,' Sens originel et avatars historiques d'un adage équivoques," *Questions Liturgiques* 59 (1978) 193–212 and Geoffrey Wainwright, "VII. Lex Orandi," and "VIII. Lex Credendi" in *Doxology* (New York: Oxford University Press, 1980) 218–83.

[8] Shea, *Experience*, 68.

[9] Cf. Xavier John Seubert, "Weaving a Pattern of Access: The Essence of Ritual," *Worship* 63 (1989) 490–503 and his "Ritual Embodiment: Embellishment or Epiphany?" *Worship* 63 (1989) 402ff.

> While our words and art forms cannot contain or confine God, they can, like the
> world itself, be icons, avenues of approach, numinous presences, ways of touching
> without totally grasping or seizing.[10]

The languages of *theologia prima* are adequate and appropriate insofar as they
continue both to link the community to the originating experience and provide access to Mystery in the present. Having arisen in the initial attempts to express the
inexpressible, they continue to be effective insofar as they remain ambiguous and
inexact, flexible and capable of carrying multiple meanings because the experience
itself defies precision. Their strength lies in the tension created by the juxtaposition
of what is logically opposed or unfathomable.[11] Their proper context is worship
and mystagogia where the constant interplay of all the languages and sensate experiences, the weaving of sound, smell, taste, image, imagination, memory, understanding, in short of the whole physical-emotional-spiritual-intellectual experience
provides the greatest chance that participants will be ushered into the presence of
saving, healing Mystery.

But the human mind is rarely satisfied with the primal expressions of the
soul's exuberance and, seeking a clearer cognitive grasp of what happened, returns
to these initial expressions and explores the meaning of what happened and the relationship with Mystery uncovered therein. The mind is, of course, already at work
as the earliest exclamations are expanded into phrases and elaborated into songs,
poems and stories. Here the mind comes to some "touchstone truths and states
them in a first-order language of its own."[12] Shea notes,

> It is not always easy to distinguish the first-order language of the religious experience
> and the first-order language of cognitive appropriation. Some Biblical candidates
> might be: "God was in Christ reconciling the world to himself" (2 Cor 5:19) or "It is
> precisely in this that God proves his love for us: that while we were still sinners, Christ
> died for us" (Rom 5:8). Expressions like these try to deliver the cognitive content of
> the experience. They might be called the basic beliefs of faith.[13]

These "basic beliefs" are attempts to encapsulate the experience and make it permanently available as 'distilled truth' or affirmations of faith long after the actual
experience ends. But even these "beliefs" are expressed in language that reveals
something more than literal truth. The language of these beliefs is itself doxological, i.e., acknowledgment of what God has done articulated in the first-order language of praise. In the texts cited above by Shea, Paul is not formulating doctrine
much less providing simple factual information. He has distilled from his experi-

---

[10] Bishops' Committee on the Liturgy, *Environment and Art in Catholic Worship,* (Washington, D.C.: NCCB, 1978) n. 2.
[11] See among others, Philip Wheelwright, *Metaphor and Reality* (Bloomington: Indiana University Press, 1962) esp. 45–91; Sallie McFague, *Metaphorical Theology* (Philadelphia: Fortress, 1982).
[12] Shea, *Experience,* 69.
[13] Ibid.

ence of the Risen Christ cognitive insights that can only be expressed as praise. Paul has encountered Mystery and he now lives in wonder! The liturgical use of Paul's letters from the earliest days indicates that they did indeed serve as vehicles for or triggers of the encounter even as they struggled to "deliver the cognitive content" of an early Christian experience of it.

Theologia Secunda

But the mind is not satisfied there. It not only crystallizes religious experience into formulas of belief, it begins to investigate the meaning and validity of these basic beliefs and seeks intelligibility and coherence, identifying their interrelatedness and asking further questions about them. Schillebeeckx demonstrates the process in the following:

> If we should affirm our belief that in Jesus God saves human beings ("first-order assertion"), how then are we to understand Jesus himself, in whom God's definitive saving action has become a reality ("second-order assertion")? One is already a Christian in entertaining the former conviction, even though at the level of "second-order" affirmations a whole range of nicer distinctions and definitions may exist. . . . In a second phase of reflection the quest must be for a fitting answer to the question of how it is possible that whoever is brought in contact with Jesus is confronted with God's definitive saving activity.[14]

Arius of Alexandria tried his hand at "second-order assertions" in an attempt to explain the "basic belief" about "God in Christ;" the debate which ensued raged on for centuries. It is always more difficult and dangerous to articulate in precise and positive terms what the truth is than to say what it is not. The Christological questions that many thought settled by Chalcedon (451) have repercussions in the present. As Karl Rahner has written, it will do no good simply to repeat what has already been said, for "the truth of faith can only be retained by continuous efforts in its regard . . . . one can only possess the past by making the present one's own."[15]

John Shea points out that this kind of reflection, which we may call *theologia secunda*, is fueled by the developments and insights of the human and natural sciences which enter into a kind of dialogue with belief as faith seeks intelligibility and coherence. In a second step, this theology attempts to spell out the moral/behavioral implications of basic beliefs to all areas of human life: What difference does our relationship with God make for our careers, politics, marriages, wealth, prestige, interactions with non-Christians, medical procedures, etc.? Indeed, the God-world relationship permeates and pervades all the relationships and events

---

[14] Edward Schillebeeckx, *Jesus: An Experiment in Christology* (New York: Seabury, 1979) 549.

[15] "On the Theology of the Incarnation," *Theological Investigations*, IV (Baltimore: Helicon, 1966) 105. Rahner launched a reassessment of Chalcedon in the 50s and many theologians have taken up the challenge he began; for an excellent overview see Elizabeth Johnson, *Consider Jesus: Waves of Renewal in Christology* (New York: Crossroad, 1992).

which together weave the fabric of human existence. Finally, theology turns self-critical to explore how religious belief and moral teachings function in the lives of individuals and in the community: Do they continue to disclose the ultimate nature of the divine-human mystery or are they being used as the "opiate of the oppressed" and weapons of control that legitimate oppression? "The question 'Who wins?' tries to keep belief and theology honest and make them true servants of the experience named Spirit."[16]

Prima and Secunda

Especially with regard to the liturgy, *theologia prima* and *theologia secunda* are complementary. The Christian community needs a "second-order," theoretical language that stresses disinterested inquiry and understanding, answering all that can be asked and knowing what can't be answered; evolving and developing methods of inquiry to state the "truths" as objectively as possible. It is important to note that because the Reality remains ineffable, even this language is unavoidably metaphorical. But the community also needs a language which can incite it to respond inter-subjectively and as whole human beings to God's self-offer and to dispose them to God. The liturgy must provide both "primary" and "secondary" theologians (the ordinary folks in the pews and the ivory tower intellectuals) with time and space for the encounter in which they commit themselves entirely to Christ and to God in their lives in community and in the world. Otherwise they will search elsewhere to satisfy their thirst for Mystery and theology will become a human science without real spiritual insight. *Theologia secunda* must in turn critique *theologia prima* to keep it in contact with the living faith of the church, what Robert Taft has called the "genetic vision" of the church at present, lest liturgy become idolatry or a museum piece and Christians are subject to archaism on the one hand or the whims of subjective fancy on the other.[17]

But one would not expect the kind of language used in *theologia secunda* to be very useful in the liturgy even though liturgical and other "primary" texts are necessarily used in theological reflection. The language of *theologia secunda* predominates in formulations of doctrine and dogma but few people have been ushered into life-transforming encounters with God by reading conciliar statements or catechism definitions. At best, they are moved to say "Aha! that's just what I thought" or "That does (doesn't) make sense." or "So that's the official teaching on this topic." But I doubt any have been moved to fall on their faces in silence or to sing and dance a *Te Deum* because they have encountered God in and through the Catechism—even the leather-bound, gold-leafed edition!

---

[16] Shea, *Experience*, 70–76; The self-critical function of theology is to the forefront in Liberation and Feminist Theologies of the last thirty years; see among others Elizabeth Johnson, *She Who Is: The Mystery of God in Feminist Theological Discourse* (New York: Crossroad, 1994) esp. chapter 2.

[17] David N. Power, "Two Experiences of Faith: Worship and Theology," *Concilium* 82 (1973) 95–106.

When it is incorporated directly into the liturgy, *theologia secunda*, as important as it may be, more often than not gets in the way of the holistic sacramental encounter for it tends to force people into the cerebrum and out of the body rather than contributing to an holistic experience. Imagine being an early fourth-century Christian who from childhood has been praying "Glory to the Father through the Son in the Holy Spirit" only to find out that because Arius and his ilk are using this doxology to subordinate the Son—whatever that means—you must now change your prayers to remain orthodox. The same thing happens in many liturgical assemblies where well-meaning but none-too-subtle liturgists delete all the masculine God language in familiar hymns because there *are* heretics in the church who *do* use this language to subordinate women. These kinds of changes—necessary though they may be—"raise consciousness," or touch off negative emotions. When supported by sanctions and anathemas or partisan labeling, they reduce faith to intellectual assent or even worse, political correctness. Participants are prevented from full, active and conscious participation in the liturgy because they are too *self*-conscious about what they are saying.

However, this self-consciousness is not inevitable. If the other languages of the liturgy are healthy and effectively weaving the pattern of access to Mystery, the "objective" and "disinterested" formulations of *theologia secunda* or justice-inspired word changes may be transformed precisely by their context. When their latent metaphorical quality is brought to the fore by their context which is predominantly metaphorical, they may be freed to express and evoke a holistic encounter with Holy Mystery. The Creed provides an example of this process.

The Nicene Creed: Theologia Secunda or Theologia Prima?

The earliest creeds were strings of first-order assertions used precisely in baptismal celebrations wherein the individual and the community encountered the saving, healing presence of God (*theologia prima*). It is well known that the baptismal creeds were used in East and West[18] long before the Councils of Nicea (325), Constantinople (381), and Chalcedon (451) reformulated them with 'second-order assertions' concerning the divine *ousia* and *hypostases* in an attempt to settle the Christological controversies and spell out the orthodox implications of the older professions of faith.[19] However, when the Nicene Creed was inserted into the

---

[18] See for example the creedal formula in three-fold interrogation in the *Apostolic Tradition* attributed to Hippolytus (ca. 215); G. J. Cuming, ed. *Hippolytus: A Text for Students* (Bramcote Notts: Grove, 1976) 19.

[19] On the history and development of the Nicene Creed see B. Capelle, "Le Credo," *Cours et Conferences*, VI (Louvain, 1928) 171–84 and Jungmann, *Mass of the Roman Rite*, vol. I (New York: Benziger, 1951; Reprint Westminster, Md.: Christian Classics, 1986) 461–74; H. J. Carpenter, "*Symbolum* as a Title of the Creed," *Journal of Theological Studies* 44 (1943) 1–11; J. H. Crehan, *Early Christian Baptism and the Creed* (Oxford, 1950); T Camelot, "Les récentes recherches sur le Symbole des Apôtres et leur portée théologique," *Revue des sciences religieuses* 39 (1951) 323–27; J.N.D. Kelly,

Eucharist—in the East and in Spain during the sixth century, in Francia during the eighth, at Rome only in the eleventh century—it no longer functioned simply as a doctrinal formula and litmus test of orthodox faith (though it apparently continued to keep Arians and Semi-Arians from the assembly). In its new location as part of the whole complex of liturgical signs, songs, gestures and images, the Creed was now experienced also as doxology—expressive and evocative of relationship with a trinitarian God. Pseudo-Dionysius (ca. 515) even refers to the creed as *eucaristia*.[20] The inclusion of anti-Arian and anti-Macedonian phrases hammered out at the councils changed the biblical wording of the baptismal creeds into an abstract polemic with even more focus on the eternal divinity of the Logos:

Ex Patre natum ante omnia saecula	Born of the Father before all ages,
Deum de Deo, lumen de lumine	God from God, Light from Light,
Deum verum de Deo vero	True God from True God,
genitum non factum	begotten not made,
consubstantialem Patri	consubstantial with the Father,
per quem omnia facta sunt.	through whom all things were made.

But note, although unavoidably abstract in its use of second-order assertions, the very stringing together of these phrases echoes the Prologue of John's Gospel and, in Jungmann's words, "round(s) out the profession of faith into a tiny hymn."[21]

We do have theological clarity in the text. Those who recited this creed in the first decades of its importation into the liturgy probably did so self-consciously and "from their heads." But in the *performance* of the Creed in very short order we have much more than "cognitive content" expressed. In the West, where it was sung only on Sundays and major feasts the Creed contributed to the experience of festivity. Furthermore, it was to be chanted by the entire assembly[22] and its oldest chant settings were simple recitation tones like that used in the preface. In the eleventh century, when the Eucharistic Prayer was being prayed "silently" and the verses for the entrance, offertory and communion processions had already been abbreviated or eliminated, the comparable prominence and length of the Creed gave it dramatic importance. Not much later, when the assembly's role was taken over completely by trained singers and polyphonic choirs, the musical splendor of the Creed came often to surpass all the other portions of the Mass.

Early Christian Creeds (3rd edition New York: 1981); J. Stevenson's *Creeds, Councils and Controversies: Documents Illustrative of the History of the Church A.D. 337–461* (London: SPCK, 1966) remains a fine source for tracing the relationship of the various creeds that were in use at the various councils.

[20] *De Ecclesiasticis Hierarchia*, III, 3, 7; Jungmann points to the intrinsic relationship between creed and eucharistic prayer in *Mass of the Roman Rite*, I:473–74 and nn. 73–74.

[21] *Mass of the Roman Rite*, I:465.

[22] Jungmann notes witnesses from the ninth to thirteenth centuries for the singing of the creed by all. See *Mass of the Roman Rite*, I:471–73.

Not long after it became part of the Roman Mass, the performance of the Creed included yet another element of *theologia prima*: the communal genuflection at *et incarnatus est*. Of course this brought great attention to these words, now experienced as the center of this central chant of the Mass. Jungmann wrote:

> We therefore fall upon our knees at the words *Et incarnatus est*, in awe of the mystery. Some of the grandest creations of ecclesiastical music have here made the devout offering of their greatest endeavor, in the effort to help us conceive the meaning of that tremendous descent of the Son of God from heaven to bring peace to earth.[23]

Of course, the phrases emphasizing the preexistent divinity of Christ and the Spirit in answer to the heresies were not disregarded or passed over in musical settings. But the musical and gesticular emphasis on *et incarnatus est* transformed the experience of the Creed from a polemical refutation of heresy (*theologia secunda*) into performative praise (*theologia prima*). Certainly those concerned about orthodoxy may have been aware of the "cognitive content" of the faith crystallized in this text but the interplay of text, music and gesture now ushered participants into the very heart of the ineffable mystery: God in Christ reconciling humanity; humanity responding by falling to its knees in wonder and awe. Even if there was undue emphasis on this element, the experience of encounter that it served was alive and well; otherwise no one would have bothered setting it to music or adopting the genuflection at its center.

Such is not the case in the current reform of the liturgy. The Creed is no longer experienced as performative in this rich sense and it is certainly a good thing that composers are spending much more energy on settings for the Eucharistic Prayer and its acclamations. But something else is indicated when week after week the Creed is mumbled through, its rubric calling for a profound bow at *by the power of the Holy Spirit he was born of the Virgin Mary and became man* is universally ignored, and even bishops neglect to kneel at those words on March 25 and December 25.[24] The performance of this text has ceased to link most participants with the originating experience of God in Christ and subsequent manifestations of this same encounter.

For many the patriarchal context and masculine language for God and humanity have made the Creed an obstacle. But the lack of music and gesture have also deprived the text from being experienced as metaphorical praise in traditional language. Either we are too self-conscious or we are numb; if the Presence is experienced through this vehicle at all, it must struggle mightily to do so.[25] The Creed has lost its power to bring us to our knees, not because we are no longer amazed by

---

[23] Ibid., 465–66.

[24] *General Instruction of the Roman Missal*, no. 98: The profession of faith is said by the priest together with the people (see no. 44). At the words *by the power of the Holy Spirit*, etc. all bow; on the solemnities of the Annunciation and Christmas all kneel.

[25] Again, see Xavier Seubert's articles mentioned above in note 4.

the mystery of the incarnation but because the language of the Creed has been divorced from our struggle to recognize and articulate the mystery in contemporary language in our preaching, catechesis, mystagogia, morality, art and music.

II. Singing the Mystery: Music as Theologia Prima

While it is precisely the interplay of the many languages of *theologia prima* that weave the pattern of access, it goes without saying that each one of these has its own way of expressing and evoking the encounter. The Milwaukee Symposia for Church Composers (1982–1992) reflected on music's sacramental power in their *Ten Year Report* and argued that it is rooted in the nature of sound itself:

> Sound itself is our starting point for understanding music and its capacity to serve as a vehicle for God's self-revelation. Sound's temporality, for example, symbolizes a God active in creation and history; its seemingly insubstantial nature symbolizes a God who is both present and hidden; its dynamism symbolizes a God who calls us into dialogue; its ability to unify symbolizes our union with God and others; its evocation of personal presence symbolizes a God whom we perceive as personal. . . . Music is able to elicit wonder without distancing us from God's presence and is able to effect our union with other worshipers and with God in a particular and unparalleled way.[26]

If the liturgical text itself, whether prose or poetry, is an expression of and vehicle for disposing us to the encounter, and music by its very nature is a natural vehicle for the self-revelation of God, it is understandable why combining text with music in singing plays such an important role in liturgy.

> Just as the inflection of human speech shapes the meaning of our words, so can music open up new meanings in sung texts as well as the liturgical unit that is the setting for such texts. Furthermore, the extended duration that musical performance adds to a text . . . can contribute to the heightening and opening up of a text.
> . . . Music has a natural capacity to unite the singer with the song, the singer with those who listen, singers with each other. Christian ritual song joins the assembly with Christ who is the source and content of the song. The song of the assembly is an event of the presence of Christ.[27]

From the earliest days singing enjoyed a privileged place among the languages of *theologia prima*, both inside and outside Christianity.[28] In his sermon on liturgical singing, Niceta of Remesiana (c. 370–414) answers the objection that singing is superfluous by tracing the history of singing in both Testaments, emphasizing especially the psalms. He summarizes this history with the following exhortation:

---

[26] *The Milwaukee Symposia for Church Composers: A Ten Year Report.* © Archdiocese of Milwaukee; (published jointly at Washington, D.C.: National Association of Pastoral Musicians and Chicago: Liturgy Training Publications, 1992) n. 13.

[27] Ibid., nos. 14–16. cf. *Sacrosanctum Concilium*, no. 7.

[28] See especially Johannes Quasten, *Music and Worship in Pagan and Christian Antiquity*, trans. Boniface Ramsey (Washington D.C.: Pastoral Press, 1983) and Edward Foley, "The Cantor in Historical Perspective," *Worship* 56 (1982) 194–213.

These things being so, brothers [and sisters], let us have full confidence in carrying out our ministry of song. Let us believe that we have been given a very great grace by God who has granted to us to sing the marvels of the eternal God in the company of so many and such great saints, prophets and even martyrs. With David we "sing to the Lord for he is good," with Moses, . . . Hanna, . . . Isaiah, . . . Habacuc, . . . Jonah and Jeremiah, . . . the three children in the flames, . . . With Elizabeth [sic] our soul magnifies the Lord.

Can any joy be greater than that of delighting ourselves with psalms and nourishing ourselves with prayer and feeding ourselves with the lessons that are read in between? Like guests at a table enjoying a variety of dishes, our souls feast on the rich banquet of lessons and hymns.[29]

Niceta thus acknowledges not only the delight of singing hymns, psalms and canticles, but recognizes that listening to the lessons which were undoubtedly cantilated, was an integral part of the experience.

As important as the words were, there was a profound appreciation in the Mediterranean world for wordless singing with which cantors and scholas embellished their singing. Augustine comments on the *jubilus*—the long melisma that was added to the final syllable of *Alleluia* and other chants—as follows:

The one who sings a *jubilus* speaks no words for it is a song of joy without words; it is the voice of a heart poured out in joy which tries as far as possible to express the feeling even when it does not understand the meaning. When you rejoice in your exultation, you burst forth from certain words that can hardly be said or understood to a voice of exultation without words; so that it seems you are indeed rejoicing but it seems your joy is so great that it cannot be expressed in words.[30]

No doubt those who sang or heard the 124-note *jubilus* assigned in the Old Roman tradition to the *Alleluia, Pascha nostrum* for Easter Mass and vespers would know what Augustine was talking about. Any one who has sung the *Gloria*-refrain to the

---

[29] "Quae cum ita sint, fratres, iam pleniore fiducia hymnorum ministeriorum fideliter impleamus, ingentem nos credentes a Deo gratiam consecutos quibus concessum est cum tantis ac talibus sanctis, prophetis dico adque martyribus, Dei aeterni cantare miracula. Hinc cum David 'Domino confitemur quoniam bono est,' cum Moysi, . . . Anna, . . . Esaiah, . . . Ambacum, . . . Ionah cum Hieremiam, . . . cum tribus aeque pueris quasi in fornace positi, . . . cum Helizabeth 'Dominum Anima nostra Magnificat.' Quid hac utilitate commodius? quid hac delectatione iucundius? nam et psalmis delectemur, et orationibus rigamur, et interpositis lectionibus pascimur. et vere, sicut boni conviviae ferculorum varietate delectantur, ita nostrae animae multiplici lectione et hymnorum exhibitione saginantur." *De Utilitate Hymnorum*, ed. C.H. Turner, "Niceta of Remesiana II: De Utilitate Hymnorum," *Journal of Theological Studies* 24 (April 1923) 233–52 [239]; Eng. trans. G. G. Walsh, S.J., *Fathers of the Church*, 7 (New York: Fathers of the Church, Inc. 1949) 65–76 [73–74].

[30] Qui jubilat non verba dicit, sed sonus quidam est laetitiae sine verbis: vox est enim animi diffusi laetitia, quantum potest experimentis affectum non sensum comprehendentis. Gaudens homo in exultatione sua ex verbis quibusdam, quae non possunt dici intelligi, erumpit in vocem quandam exultationis sine verbis; ita ut appareat, eum ipsa voce gaudere quidem, sed quasi repletum nimio gaudio, non posset verbis explicare quod gaudet. *Ennaratio in Psalmum 99:4.* Corpus Christianorum Series Latina 39 (Turnhout: Brepols, 1956) 1394; Migne, PL 37, c. 1272.

Christmas carol, "Angels We Have Heard on High," the Great *Alleluia* at the Easter Vigil or even the solemn dismissal of the Easter Octave[31] would probably agree.[32] There is an overwhelming sense of joy expressed and experienced by almost all who know and join in singing these melismas.

Tropes

Some four hundred years after Augustine's commentary, however, the word-less *jubilus* was causing a young monk of St. Gall a bit of difficulty:

> When I was still young, and the *longissimae melodiae*—repeatedly entrusted to memory—escaped my poor head, I began to reason with myself how I could bind them fast. In the meantime it happened that a certain priest from Jumièges . . . came to us bringing his antiphonary in which some verses had been written below the *sequentiae*. . . In imitation of them I began to write *Laudes deo concinat orbis universus*. . . I took these lines to my teacher, Iso, who commended my industry, took pity on my lack of experience, praised what was pleasing and set me on improving what was not, saying "The individual movements of the melody should receive separate syllables." Hearing that I immediately corrected those which fell under *ia*; those under *le* and *lu*, however, I left as too difficult; but later, with practice, I managed it easily—for example in *Dominus in Sina* and *Mater*. . .[33]

Whether or not Notker Balbulus explains here the actual origin of the sequence or *prosa*, this *Proemium* to his *Liber Hymnorum* indicates that the wordless *jubilus* was no longer being experienced by him as joy "so great that it cannot be expressed in words." These *longissimae melodiae* were for him and apparently for others, a burden.[34] Yet their context within the liturgy as celebrated in the aftermath of the Carolingian renaissance of Christian prose and poetry, sparked his own creative genius and gave rise to yet another—this time derivative—form of *theologia prima*.

A trope is a musical and/or textual embellishment of a liturgical chant.[35] Whereas "liturgical chant" in this case refers to a piece from the fixed repertory—

[31] "The Mass is ended, go in Peace, Alleluia, Alleluia; Thanks be to God, Alleluia, Alleluia!" The text with the Gregorian setting is still regularly printed in Catholic hymnals, missalettes, and orders of worship.

[32] For a musical transcription see John [Brooks-]Leonard, *Easter Vespers in Early Medieval Rome: A Critical Edition and Study*, Ph.D. Dissertation (University of Notre Dame, 1988) 40–43.

[33] Notker Balbulus (ca. 840–912), "Preface" in his *Liber Hymnorum*; text in Wolfram von den Steinen, *Notker der Dichter* (Berne, 1948) II (Editionsband), 8–10, 160; another English transl. appears in Richard L. Crocker, *The Medieval Sequence* (Berkeley: University of California Press, 1977) 1–2.

[34] Jungmann postulates that melismatic chant in general and the *jubilus* in particular were "not agreeable to the musical sensibilities of the northern peoples;" *Mass of the Roman Rite* I:436.

[35] J. Handschin, "Trope, Sequence, and Conductus," in A. Hughes, ed. *The New Oxford History Of Music, II: Early Medieval Music upto 1300* (London: Oxford Univ. Press, 1954) 128–74. The editors of the 55-volume *Analecta Hymnica Medii Aevi* included only those tropes in verse, thus omitting a considerable number including many of the oldest and most important pieces in the repertory: ed. C. Blume, G.M. Dreves, H. M. Bannister, 47: *Tropi Graduales. Tropen des Missale im Mittelalter, I.*

from the eighth century onwards propagated in a fairly uniform manner and eventually imposed by imperial or ecclesiastical authority[36]—tropes were entirely optional and their repertory differed considerably from region to region and even from church to church. Some apparently originated as texts set to preexisting melismas as Notker described, but soon the troping of Mass Propers (*Introits, Graduals, Offertories, Communions*) and of the Ordinary (*Kyrie, Gloria, Sanctus, Agnus Dei, Ite/Bendicamus*) included the composition of new texts *and* melodies interpolated right into the received chant itself.

For those who idealize the "noble simplicity" of the Roman Rite, tropes constitute prime examples of the medieval accretions that came to smother the liturgy. For this study, however, tropes provide additional evidence that the religious experience was very much alive and finding ever new forms of poetic and musical expression. In his discussion of the myriad creations that one encounters in the Christian tradition, John Shea notes that "theology" results when the *mind* "answers the experience" of God in Christ mediated through the core myth (Gospels/Bible) and the core ritual (Eucharist/Sacraments). However,

> When the *imagination* answers the experience mediated through the core myth and ritual we move toward a new and contemporary embodiment of the experience [*theologia prima*]. The new embodiment attempts to express what was found in the experience and evoke that in all others who come in contact with the imaginative work [italics and bracketed phrase mine].[37]

For Shea, these imaginative recastings of the core experience are important first because they indicate that the core myth and ritual are triggering an experience that is deep and powerful enough to evoke an imaginative response.

> A Christian culture of poems, plays, music, sculpture, and painting is not merely the take-it or leave-it periphery of the indispensable center of Bible and Liturgy. It is a sign that Bible and Liturgy are vibrant realities.

Tropen zum Ordinarium Missae (Leipzig, 1905) 49, *Tropi Graduales. Tropen des Missale im Mittelalter, II Tropen zum Proprium Missarum* (Leipzig, 1906). A major reediting of the entire trope repertory, the *Corpus Troporum. Studia Latina Stockholmensis* has been underway since 1975 under the direction of G. Björkvall, G. Iversen, and R. Jonsson of Stockholm.

[36] Apart from the Creed the texts of the Ordinary for the Roman Mass (*Kyrie, Gloria, Sanctus, Agnus Dei*) seem to have been fixed by the time of Sergius I (689–701). The Propers (*Introit, Gradual, Tract/Alleluia, Offertorium, Communion*) were pretty well fixed by the mid-7th century, though the six earliest manuscripts date only from the 8th and 9th; R.-J. Hesbert, *Antiphonale Missarum Sextuplex* (Brussels, 1935). It should be noted that the verses for the Alleluias on ordinary Sundays (*In domincis diebus per circulum anni*) were not fixed until much later and appear separately from the other proper chants in most of these manuscripts; see for example the Gradual of St. Gall, (*Codex Sangallensis* 339) *Paléographie Musicale*, 1 (Solesmes, 1889) 126–30 where 26 *alleluias* are listed in the order of the psalter. On the authority of liturgical texts and manuscripts see the important discussion in C. Vogel, *Medieval Liturgy: An Introduction to the Sources*. rev. and transl. W. G. Storey and N. K. Rasmussen (Washington, D.C.: Pastoral Press, 1986) 62–64.

[37] Shea, *Experience*, 66.

Secondly, the artistic creations of a tradition provide fresh access to the founding salvific experience. Since they are inspired by the living relationship to God expressed in the core myth and ritual, they have the possibility of evoking the felt-experience of that relationship.[38]

It is possible to detect in the tropes some of the ways the Christian imagination "answered the experience as mediated" through the fixed chants of the liturgy. From the time of the New Testament, the Christian imagination had already become quite adept at hearing in the psalms the *vox Christi*, the voice of Christ, head and/or members depending on the particular psalm or phrase.[39] The tropes take this tradition a step further by making the Christological/Christian understanding of the psalm quite explicit. In some cases, this is done using creedal and doctrinal language (*theologia secunda*). Some tropes announce the mystery of the day and call the assembly to join in the singing, some weave other biblical passages or phrases from the life of a saint into the chant suggesting connections that might otherwise be missed; still others provide mystagogical commentary on each phrase of the official chant. The fact, however, that tropes were usually written only for the more important festivals of the local community together with the actual melodies that were recorded would have contributed to a profound sense of wonder and delight.

The texts for two introit tropes from the Winchester repertory are printed below. The chant itself, which was sung by the entire schola (in monasteries this could be all those in 'choir'), is printed in bold; the tropes in regular typeface, would have been sung by one or two cantors.

Trope for the Easter Introit: RESURREXI[40]

Psallite, regi magno devicto mortis imperio, eia:
Resurrexi et adhuc tecum sum, Alleluia
Dormivi, pater, exsurgam diliculo, et somnus meus dulcis est mihi:
Posuisti super me manum tuam, Alleluia
Ita, pater, sic placuit ante te, ut moriendo mortis mors fuissem, morsus inferni et vita mundo: **Mirabilis [facta est scientia tua,]**
Qui abscondisti haec sapientibus et revelasti parvulis, **Alleluia, Alleluia.**
En ego, verus sol, occasum meum novi, et super eum solus ascendens :

---

[38]   Ibid., 66–67.

[39]   See the seminal work by Balthasar Fischer, "Le Christ dans les Psaumes" *La Maison-Dieu* 27 (1951) 86–109 = "Christ in the Psalms," *Theology Digest* 1 (1953) 53–57; and Fischer's introduction to *Dich will ich suchen von Tag zu Tag: Meditationen zu den Morgen- und Abend-psalmen des Stunden-buches* (Freiburg: Herder, 1987) 14–23 = "Praying the Psalms in the Light of Christ" *Assembly* 15:3 (March 1989) 434–36. See also J. Leonard, "The Mind of Christ: The Prayers and Psalms of the Easter Season" *Assembly* 14 (March 1988) 396–97; and his editorial introducing Father Fischer's article in *Assembly* 15 (March 1989) 433–40.

[40]   Alejandro E. Planchart, *The Repertory of Tropes at Winchester,* vol. 2, (Princeton: University Press, 1977) 147, 153; W. H. Frere, *The Winchester Troper.* Henry Bradshaw Society, 8 (London, 1894) 176.

Ps. Domine probasti me [et cognovisti me]
(= Psalm 138/139:18, 5, 6 and 1-2)

Sing the psalm with the great king, commander, vanquisher of death, indeed:
I have risen and I am with you, Alleluia
I have slept, Father, and I will arise at dawn, for my rest is sweet to me:
You have placed your hand upon me, Alleluia
Thus, Father, such was your pleasure, that by dying I would become the death of death, the bite of hell and the life of the world:
How wonderful is your knowledge
which was hidden from the wise and revealed to the little ones,
Alleluia Alleluia
Lo! I, the true sun, have known my setting, and alone [my] rising above it.
Ps. **Lord you have searched me and you know me . . . .**

Trope for Christmas Introit, PUER NATUS EST[41]

Ecce adest de quo prophetae cecinerunt dicentes:
Puer [natus est nobis]
Quem Virgo Maria genuit:
et filius datus est nobis
Nomen eius Emmanuel vocabitur:
cuius imperium super humerum eius
et vocabitur nomen eius, magni consilii angelus.
Rex, lumen de lumine, eia, regnat in iustitia, cantate, eia, de virginis fecundia:
[*Ps.*] Cantate Domino [canticum novum: quia mirabilia fecit]
Quod prisco vates cecinerunt tempore sancti, cernitis impletum, psallentes dicite cuncti:
Puer [natus est nobis]
Daviticae stirpis genuit quem Virgo Maria:
et filius datus est nobis
Perdita restaurans et restaurata gubernans:
cuius imperium super humerum eius
et vocabitur nomen eius, magni consilii angelus.
Hodie natus est nobis rex regum, dominus, hodie venit nobis salus mundi, redemptio nostra eia, dicamus omnes:
Gloria Patri [et Filio et Spiritui Sancto; sicut erat in principio, et nunc, et semper et in saecula saeculorum. Amen]
Deus pater filium suum hodie emissit in mundum, de quo gratulanter dicamus cum propheta:
Puer [natus est nobis et filius datus est nobis]
Qui sedebit super thronum David et in aeternum imperabit:
Cuius [imperium super humerum eius]
Ecce veniet deus et homo de domo David sedere in throno:

---

[41] Theses introit tropes are reconstructed with modern notation in Planchart, *The Repertory of Tropes at Winchester*, vol. 1 (Princeton, 1977) 301–05. This Christmas text is printed in W. H. Frere, *The Winchester Troper*, 5.

et vocabitur [nomen eius,]
Eo quod futura annuntiabit:
Magni [consilii angelus].
(= Isaiah 9:6 with Psalm 97/98: 1-2)

Behold, he is here about whom the prophets foretold saying:
A Child is born to us
To whom the Virgin Mary has given birth
And a Son is given to us
His name will be called Emmanuel
Whose government is upon his shoulders.
And his name shall be called the Angel of great Counsel,
King, light from light, indeed, he reigns in justice, yes sing of the fruitfulness of the Virgin:
***Ps.* Sing to the Lord a new song because he has done wonderful things.**
Now that what the holy prophets sang in ancient days is fulfilled,
all together sing the psalm and say: **A Child is born to us** whom the Virgin Mary bore from Davidic stock: **And a Son is given to us**
Restoring the lost and governing the restored: **Whose government is . . . .**
Today is born to us the king of kings, the Lord, today the salvation of the world, our redemption, has come to us; indeed let us all say.
Glory to the Father . . .
Today, God the Father has sent his Son into the world, wherefore giving solemn thanks let us say with the prophet: **A Child . . .**
Who sits on the throne of David and will reign forever: **Whose government . . .**
Behold the God and Man will come from the the house of David to sit on the throne.
And his name shall be called . . .

It is impossible for us to experience what it was like to sing these chants in the ninth or tenth centuries, but the reader can at least observe the method: the composers drew from a variety of biblical, patristic and doctrinal sources and wove these together with the texts assigned to these feasts. In actual performance, the cantor (or cantors) who sang the tropes thus functioned as the mystagogue who does not explain but rather suggests a way of entering ever more deeply into the mystery being celebrated so that those who sing the official psalmic or prophetic text might actually experience the wonder and awe that is inevitable when one encounters Mystery.[42]

---

[42] It occurs to me that The *Sourcebook Series* published by Liturgy Training Publications, Chicago, is not unlike the troping phenomenon in that the editors have gleaned from these same sources as well as from the poets and composers of every age, poetic and reflective texts and commentaries to help contemporary Christians to enter more deeply into the mystery celebrated in *Advent, Christmas, Lent, Triduum, Easter, Baptism, Liturgy, Marriage, Death.* Of course, the modern understanding of the liturgy has required that these mystagogical reflections complement the liturgy from outside rather than be woven into the chants, but their value for unpacking the experience and leading participants more deeply into holistic participation cannot be exaggerated.

The fact that all tropes and almost all sequences[43] were eliminated in the Tridentine reform is a pretty good indication that this early medieval art form, like the *jubilus* before it, had ceased to be an effective vehicle for "evoking the felt-experience" and had become an obstacle and a burden long before Trent.[44] The churches of the Reformation would find in participatory vernacular hymnody a fresh way to enter more fully into the mystery being celebrated. Catholics of the counter reform would experience instead the sumptuous architecture and rich harmonies of the Baroque surrounding and saturating them like incense in a Byzantine monastery as a way of participating in the mystery of Christ. In every case and up to the present, liturgical singing itself is essential to the experience of the faith.

Conclusion

Jungmann's challenge to younger scholars warrants a much more detailed answer and there is much in the chants, hymns, tropes and sequences from the early Middle Ages that would further illuminate the revolution of religious culture he describes. To further the renewal of the liturgy for which Jungmann worked his entire life may still benefit from more historical and theological analysis, but until we relearn the imaginative skills of *theologia prima*, we will continue to allow the cognitive content to block access rather than contribute to weaving the pattern of access to the saving and healing presence of the God whom we seek. In the language of the psalmist, we must "Taste and see" i.e., "taste, smell, feel, hear, look, sing, dance . . . and *then* understand; experience with our whole being and then perhaps unpack, analyze, reflect and discern the cognitive content—but even moreso, be transformed thereby into the Image of the Unseen.

[43] Cf. Jungmann *Mass of the Roman Rite,* I: 436–40. Only the sequences for Easter—*Victimae Paschali,* Pentecost—*Veni Sancte Spiritus,* Corpus Christi—*Lauda Sion,* and Mass for the Dead—*Dies Irae* were retained. *Stabat Mater,* long ascribed to Jacopone de Todi (d. 1306) but possibly written much earlier was assigned as sequence to September 15 only in 1727. In the Missal of Paul VI, only the first three of these have been retained as optional.

[44] Ibid. Already in the fifteenth century many missals, especially in Italy, had ceased to reproduce tropes and sequences.

17. Liturgy and Culture

"Lands Rich in Wine and Oil": Culture and Conversion

Regis A. Duffy, O.F.M.

Classics such as Vergil's *Aenied,* J. S. Bach's *Art of the Fugue,* or Claude Monet's *The Waterlily Pond* share a unique characteristic—they invite a number of readings or interpretations. These varying interpretations in no way diminish the unique quality of the classic but serve to remind us of the inexhaustible richness of such works. While Jungmann's article, "The Defeat of Teutonic Arianism" may not be a classic on that level, it remains a seminal work whose command of sources and methodology, and its many insights provoke our admiration and provide an inspiration and incentive for today's scholars. And Jungmann's work does invite a number of readings as this volume gives witness.

Jungmann's anti-Arian Thesis

In the opening pages of his article, Jungmann contrasts early Christian and early medieval religious culture. Many of us first became familiar with these contrasts through Jungmann's analysis. Relying on the earlier insight of Idelphonse Herwegen, he suggested that the sense of mystery and the corporate nature of liturgy in the early Church had been supplanted by human action and subjective concerns of the early medieval period, concerns typically Germanic.[1] Among the cited liturgical examples of this medieval development are: the priest distanced from the people, the Eucharistic Prayer prayed in silence, the reception of the Eucharist as the exception rather than the rule of participation, the architectural removal of the altar from the congregation, and the handing over of the vessels at ordination.

These liturgical aberrations are eventually traced to the Germanic culture which received the Christian faith within its own world view. Again echoing Her-

---

[1] J. Jungmann, "The Defeat of Teutonic Arianism and the Revolution in Religious Culture in the Early Middle Ages," *Pastoral Liturgy* (New York: Herder & Herder, 1962) 1–101; here, 7. I use the term "Germanic" rather than "Teutonic" in deference to current usage.

wegen's earlier work, Jungmann describes the highly subjective world of these new converts who eventually accept Arianism. The trajectories of that heresy and its liturgical expression counterpoint as they spread from the Spanish church of the Visigoth period through the Scoto-Irish Church to the Carolingian Empire. Jungmann is careful to point out that this direct "recoil from" Arianism of an earlier period has become indirect by the Carolingian period.[2] Ultimately, Jungmann argues, the underlying reason for the contrasts and transformations of liturgical piety from the early Church to the early medieval Church are to be found in this world of Arianism and anti-Arianism.[3]

Jungmann carefully summarizes the key tenets of Arianism and how this heresy is played out in Spain where its liturgy is clearly marked by the Arian controversy in its prefaces and forms of address: "We are struck by the frequency with which God is referred to as the Trinity and where Christ is named where God is meant. This was not the customary language of the early Fathers."[4] These same concerns and their liturgical expression eventually find their way into the Gallican liturgies.

Jungmann then examines the evangelization of the Germanic peoples. Their catechesis notably skirts the mystery of Christ to such an extent that "it seems to be God who was born of a virgin, who has suffered insult and scorn, blows and scourging for us."[5] This Christ-God replaces former gods as the national hero or clan God. Jungmann quotes with approval the verdict of H. Wiedemann: "the Teutons were not converted to Christianity, but to Christ whom they recognized as a stronger deity."[6]

There are several points to be noted in Jungmann's argument. First, Jungmann accepts Herwegen's assessment of the Germanic peoples as caught up in a vortex of becoming rather than in the classical sense of being. Second, liturgy generally reflects orthodox reactions to heresy, in this case, Arianism. Thus, Arianism is the catalyst for these liturgical reactions and changes. Thirdly, the liturgical "paper trail" begins with liturgical reactions to Spanish Visigothic Arianism, then the Scoto-Irish continuation of these reactions that are eventually brought to the

---

[2] Ibid., 16–22; for his remarks on the direct and indirect recoil, see Ibid., 38. For a discussion of the initial Arian evangelization of the Germanic peoples, see M. Wiles, *Archetypal Heresy. Arianism through the Centuries* (Oxford: Clarendon Press, 1996) 40–51; E. A. Thompson, *The Visigoths in the Time of Ulfila* (Oxford: Clarendon Press, 1966); E. A. Thompson, "Christianity and the Northern Barbarians," *The Conflict Between Paganism and Christianity in the Fourth Century*, ed. A. Momigliano (London: Oxford University, 1963) 56–78. Throughout the chapter, when citing the letters of Boniface, I use *The Letters of Saint Boniface*, trans. E. Emerton (New York: Columbia University, 1940).

[3] It is interesting to note that Johannes Quasten had made a similar argument: the eucharistic piety of the fourth century was radically changed as a response to the Arian heresy. Cf. J. Quasten, "*Mysterium Tremendum*. Eucharistische Frömmigkeitsauffassungen des vierten Jahrhunderts," *Vom Christlichen Mysterium. Gesamelte Arbeiten zum Gedächtnis von Odo Casel OSB*, ed. A. Mayer, J. Quasten, B. Neunheuser (Düsseldorf: Patmos, 1951) 66–75. Quasten cites neither Herwegen nor Jungmann.

[4] Jungmann, "The Defeat of Teutonic Arianism," 30–31.

[5] Ibid., 43.

[6] Ibid., 41, n.13.

Continent, to the Carolingian lands and then, to the Germanic peoples. Fourth, Jungmann demonstrates a broad knowledge of the historical and incipient cultural scholarship of his day and uses it to fashion an historical thesis about certain liturgical developments.

Fifty years after the publication of "Teutonic Arianism," the reader might wonder whether Jungmann would change his thesis in any way, given the quantum leaps in historical and cultural methodologies and their results. What we can be sure of is that Jungmann would have made the same creative and wide-ranging use of related disciplines in studying the connection between Teutonic Arianism and liturgical change. It seems appropriate, then, to initiate a dialogue between Jungmann and more recent studies in culture. There are many legitimate theories and definitions of culture.[7] Broadly speaking, I understand culture as providing a lens for understanding created reality that permits us, by means of symbolic language, to communicate to others the values and meanings that derive from that reality.[8]

The first question to be asked, then, concerns the accuracy of Herwegen's and Jungmann's assumptions about the cultural character of the Germanic peoples. David Bullough's caution is worth recalling: "The contrast between the Christian 'Romano-Germanic' kingdoms and pagan Germany beyond the old frontier is very real and it would be foolish to underrate it: but it is equally important not to exaggerate the differences between the two societies."[9] Jungmann's cultural assumptions, then, would seem to be linked to a second question about conversion: From what or to what were these peoples converted? Such a question implies that there is always a sociocultural context to the process of conversion. Each question merits some discussion.

My response, therefore, to the cultural dimensions of Jungmann's article will have two parts. The first section will deal with the currently debated problem of cultural identity and its link with conversion and its liturgical expression. Conversion, however, always takes place within a specific cultural context which it both benefits from and challenges. The second part, therefore, will study how the conversion process was understood and facilitated from the time of Boniface's missionary activities into Carolingian period and some cultural corollaries for assessing the liturgical activity of that same time frame.

---

[7] For summaries of this pluriform situation, see *Cultural Analysis. The Work of Peter L. Berger, Mary Douglas, Michel Foucault and Jürgen Habermas*, ed. R. Wuthnow et al. (London: Routledge & Kegan Paul, 1984); K. Tanner, *Theories of Culture. A New Agenda for Theology* (Minneapolis: Fortress Press, 1997).

[8] R. Duffy, *An American Emmaus. Faith and Sacrament in the American Culture* (New York: Crossroad, 1995) 11. This definition takes into account the much cited definition of culture by Clifford Geertz as "an historically transmitted pattern of meanings embodied in symbols, a system of inherited conceptions expressed in symbolic forms by means of which people communicate, perpetuate and develop their knowledge about and attitudes toward life" in *The Interpretation of Cultures* (New York: Basic Books, 1973) 89.

[9] D. Bullough, *The Age of Charlemagne* (New York: G. P. Putnam, 1966) 25.

Germanic Cultural Identity

Cultural identity continues to be a much controverted subject among anthropologists and historians. In contrast to nineteenth century convictions that ethnic identity and grouping were identified by racial, linguistic, and cultural profiles, more recent approaches consider such identification simplistic.[10] One approach, influenced by field studies, would strongly challenge the assumption that cultural traits invariably identify social groups. The operative question in this approach is: "What identity did individuals claim, and what identity was recognized in them by others?"[11] Varying cultural traits represent the result, not the cause of social boundaries. This approach, while retaining the importance of the group, favors a more fluid and situational view of ethnic identity. A second approach underscores the importance of the physical, social, moral, and historical inheritance that firmly identifies the individual within the group. And it is this varied inheritance that prevents the individual from easily opting out of her group. This latter approach differs from the nineteenth century theory which emphasized group identity rather than the individual's relationship and reaction to the group.

Both of these approaches require a more nuanced and complex reading of a particular group, something similar to Geertz's "thick description." Labels such as Ostrogoth, Visigoth, or Goth cover highly variated sub-groupings of peoples that were in an historical and cultural melting pot for several centuries, eventually interacting not only with the Roman empire but among themselves. This precision is important since Jungmann specifies "the early Middle Ages" in his title, i.e., beginning with Boniface's evangelization among the Germanic tribes. But the socio-cultural context in which Boniface worked was much more complex. A glance at the map of Merovingian and Carolingian Gaul shows not only the "christianized" areas of present-day France, Belgium, and Northern Italy but also the North German areas of Frisia and Saxony that other Anglo-Saxon missionaries as well as Boniface had begun to evangelize. None of this discussion dismisses Herwegen's cultural characterization of the Germanic peoples but a contemporary interpretation would have at its disposal a great deal more data to examine and a more complex methodology to use.

One example of such an interpretation can be found in James C. Russell's *The Germanization of Early Medieval Christianity*.[12] After reviewing Jungmann's thesis, Russell questions its validity: "given the generally low level of the perception and significance of doctrinal subtleties among the Germanic peoples in the early Middle Ages, it seems more likely that these developments were the expression of

---

[10] I follow P. Heather's discussion in *The Goths* (London: Blackwell, 1996) 3–7.

[11] Ibid., 4.

[12] J. C. Russell, *The Germanization of Early Medieval Christianity. A Sociohistorical Approach to Religious Transformation* (New York: Oxford University Press, 1994). Russell's work is generally a synthesis of others' work and does not regularly use primary sources.

a Germanic ethos and worldview."[13] In other words, Russell is asserting that the reason for these liturgical changes is more likely a cultural rather than an heretical one. What Russell seems to forget, however, is Jungmann's qualification, noted above, that the anti-Arianism of the early medieval period was an indirect "recoil" originating in Mozarabic and Anglo-Saxon liturgical influences.

In order to substantiate his critique, Russell summarizes some of the extensive literature not only on Germanic cultural history but also on the interpretation of the socioeconomic background of early Christian communities by biblical scholars such as A. Judge and W. Meeks. Russell notes the pervasive concern with collective security among the Germanic peoples.[14] This concern helped to shape both the family and kin group and the personal lordship within groups. Familial and communal solidarity provided the overriding moral and cultural criteria for the notion of honor among the Germanic peoples. Honor, in turn, led to communal advancement and to assurance of wealth. Russell sums up these cultural attitudes: "the coalesence of honor, wealth, influence, and power within Germanic society inhibited the spread of status inconsistency and its potentially anomic effects, and served to further reinforce Germanic group solidarity."[15]

As with all such generalizations, a certain caution is in order. The Germanic peoples, as already noted, were involved in a series of highly fluid historical and cultural situations over a lengthy period in which subgroups were, to one degree or another, being assimilated.[16] Therefore, in one sense, Herwegen's description of the Germanic peoples is not so much incorrect as it is less concerned with other cultural and historical dimensions.[17] These cursory remarks on the cultural profile of the Germanic peoples, in turn, serve to emphasize the importance of qualifying the meaning that is given to their "conversion" and, ultimately, to the application of the *lex orandi lex credendi* axiom in their case.

Jungmann searches for the sense of conversion implicit in the evangelization of the Germanic peoples by examining the process of catechizing that was employed and briefly comparing it with that same process in the early Church. In

[13] Ibid., 42.

[14] Ibid., 107–33. In summing up the overriding characteristic of the law codes of all the different Germanic peoples of this period, K. F. Drew says: "This common feature is the development of a concept of collective security. This was closely related to two Germanic institutions: the family and kin group on the one hand and personal lordship on the other." K. F. Drew, "Another Look at the Origins of the Middle Ages: A Reassessment of the Role of the Germanic Kingdoms," *Speculum* 62 (1987) 803–12.

[15] Russell, *The Germanization*, 120.

[16] Peter Heather's warning is well taken: "Continuity in group identity cannot be measured by the persistence . . . of individual cultural traits, therefore, but by the transmission over time of a perception of difference: the claim to a particular identity on the part of a number of individuals and the recognition of that claim by others." *The Goths*, 6. The creation of a written language (Ulfila's translation of the Bible) and of other cultural artifacts do point, however, to such identity in some of the fourth century Germanic groups but see Heather's qualifications, Ibid., 85, 313–17.

[17] Russell (*The Germanization*, 99–100) also acknowledges Herwegen's remarks are useful even though their interpretations and methodology do differ in some important ways.

speaking of one Germanic collection of catechetical writings, he notes that it "never touches any nearer upon the mystery of Christ but simply demands a renunciation of the devil in favour of Christ whose commandments must be kept. . . ."[18] In brief, evangelization seems to have consisted of convincing the candidate to be baptized and observe the commandments—certainly not the catechumenal process of the early Church.

This approach, Jungmann adds, encourages a "suppression of Christ's humanity" and a resulting "coalescence of God and Christ." Within such a context, the necessity of Christ's mediation is called into question and the veneration of saints becomes an attractive alternative. This trend to mute the human nature of Christ finds a congenial analogue in the Germanic hero-ideal—Christ as the omnipotent leader-hero. The earlier notions of Church as the Body of Christ and *mater ecclesia* are now understood as a hierarchical institution in which the clergy are separated from the laity—an idea which Germanic peoples would find familiar.[19]

In ecclesiological terms, then, we would say that reception of worship and doctrine by the Germanic peoples, at least in their initial conversion, was apparently minimal. Is this to be explained by the purportedly anti-Arian concerns of their evangelizers that shaped the conversion process of these peoples and favored a muted Christology? This concern brings us back to an earlier question: From what or to what were these peoples converted? That question cannot be answered without acknowledging the cultural and political contexts within which the call to conversion was heard.[20]

The Cultural Dimensions of Conversion

Ramsay MacMullen, in an influential though controversial thesis, has argued that conversion cannot be properly understood apart from the sociocultural and political contexts from which pagans were converted. In one sense, this is not a new thesis. It has long been part of the general wisdom, for example, that the catechumenal process began to break down in the post-Constantinian era, in part, because of insincere conversions tainted by economic and political opportunism. Ambrose and Augustine are certainly eloquent on this issue. But MacMullen takes these

[18] Jungmann, "The Defeat of Teutonic Arianism," 42; for his remarks about the "suppression of Christ's humanity," see Ibid., 44.

[19] Ibid., 59 and C. H. Talbot, *The Anglo-Saxon Missionaries in Germany* (London: Sheed & Ward, 1954) xiv. See also Jungmann's reference to the article by Iserloh in which he finds that Boniface only seems to know of a moral bond between Christ and the Christian ("The Defeat of Teutonic Arianism," 31, n. 42a referring to E. Iserloh, "Die Kontinuität des Christentums beim Übergang von der Antike zum Mittelalter im Lichte der Glaubensverkündigung des hl. Bonifatius," *Trierer theol. Zeitschr.* 63 (1954) 193–205.

[20] Ramsay MacMullen has pointed out that economic factors also play an important role in the way in which conversion is understood and accepted in *Christianizing the Roman Empire A.D. 100–400* (New Haven: Yale University, 1984) 52–58.

non-Christian contexts more seriously than most. He suggests some questions to sensitize the modern person to these contexts of conversion from paganism:

> What items of experience were people talking about and passing on to their neighbors? What impinged on a person's settled universe of ideas, disturbing it and preparing him to question his previous beliefs and even to abandon them? What made news? . . . The prevailing close social and economic relations did not allow non-Christian people to shut out this noise of Christian exuberance, this din of defeat.[21]

Although MacMullen is dealing with conversion within the Roman Empire, his cautions could help us to answer the question: From what kind of life, worship and belief system were the Germanic peoples being converted? Whether that conversion process was initiated by Arian or orthodox missionaries, the question remains valid. Furthermore, we regularly assume that conversion is prompted by a desire for some sort of salvation but is this necessarily so? James Russell thinks otherwise: "Neither the cohesive social structure nor the Indo-European ideological heritage of the Germanic peoples predisposed them to desire salvation."[22]

But that same cultural argument can be phrased in a different way: the cohesive Germanic social structure and its cultural valuing system would make it susceptible to accepting any god that could prosper the group more than their current gods. This seems to be the point of H. Wiedemann's remark, quoted above, about the Germans accepting Christ as a stronger deity. As in even more sophisticated societies, Germanic cultures tended to use gods as insurance against calamities or assurance of help. One funerary plaque, possibly from the seventh century, depicting Christ as the divinity of the Germanic warrior aristocracy "armed as a soldier, scaramax (Frankish battle-axe) in belt and lance in hand . . . He has a long phallus, there are beasts round him and a snake under his feet; and he wears a headdress not unworthy of a pagan god. It has points of resemblance to the figure on a brooch from Finglesham in Kent which is now thought to be Woden."[23] The very fact that Christ could be artistically rendered in this way would seem to indicate the cultural accessibility of Christ as God-hero.

In the frequently cited letter of Bishop Daniel of Winchester to Boniface on the best method of evangelizing the Germanic peoples, the bishop suggests, among

---

[21] Ibid., 66–67. A sobering example of the many meanings of conversion is offered by the Franks who had just slaughtered the Gothic civilian population in an Italian city. A contemporary remarks: "These barbarians though they have become Christians, preserve the greater part of their ancient religion; for they still make human sacrifices and other sacrifices of an unholy nature; and it is in connection with these that they make their prophecies." E. Jones, *The Franks* (Oxford: Basil Blackwell, 1988) 96–97.

[22] Russell, *The Germanization*, 102. Russell's carefully argued theses are influenced by the work of G. Dumézil in comparing the basic social and ideological structures of proto-Indo-European society. See especially Dumézil's *Les Dieux souverains des Indo-Européens* (Paris: Gallimard, 1977). Dumézil's theories have not been universally accepted.

[23] J. M. Wallace-Hadrill, *The Frankish Church* (Oxford: Oxford University, 1983) 28.

other things, that he should point to Christians whose lands abound in wheat and wine while the pagans are freezing in hostile environments. Such an argument, he adds, proves that the Christians have the right god (Letter XV). In other words, while the Germanic peoples may not have felt the spiritual void that some scholars have presumed necessary for conversion, there were other sociocultural arguments that could make the Christian God appear attractive. We will return to this question of evangelization and conversion later in the chapter.

On the other side, from what kind of sociocultural context were these missionaries to the Germanic peoples evangelizing? The Christianity of the early Middle Ages, after all, had inherited the sociocultural disarray resulting from the barbarian invasions. An interesting point of comparison might be the pessimistic reactions of Augustine of Hippo and the prophetically optimistic view of his Spanish disciple Orosius when faced with the disintegration of the empire already precipitated by these invasions and its implications for the future of Christianity.

Boniface came from a very different kind of church than he found in the Frankish kingdoms. In contrast to the Irish missionaries on the Continent and in the north of England, Augustine had reestablished the Church in southern England under the intelligent guidance of Pope Gregory. While insisting on strong ecclesiastical structures and a strict Benedictine monasticism, Gregory eventually gave Augustine great cultural and liturgical leeway. Compromise and adaptation were to guide Augustine's work, allowing him to transform certain pagan feasts and sites, and to use Christian rituals, already in place, if at all possible. Anglo-Saxon missionaries, like Boniface, came from monasteries that were as noted for their outstanding scholarship as they were for their religious lives. Boniface's heritage is seen in his consulting with Rome in questions of morals and canon law. He rarely asks about cultural questions since he feels free to deal with these situations much as Augustine had done in the English Church.

In marked contrast, the Frankish Church under the Merovingians was in a pitiful state due to the theological illiteracy of the clergy and the barely christianised awareness of the laity. As one scholar charitably put it: "All the sources would indicate indeed that the hold the Christian faith had within Merovingian society was somewhat shaky, confined in many instances to the outward observances whose nature and spread undoubtedly possessed close affinities with the old Franco-Celtic paganism of the countryside."[24] Boniface found himself constantly hampered in his missionary efforts by this "Christian" culture.[25] Did Boniface and

[24] R. McKitterick, *The Frankish Church and the Carolingian Reforms, 789–895* (London: Royal Historical Society, 1977) xviii. For a somewhat more positive assessment, see J. M. Wallace-Hadrill, "A background to St. Boniface's mission," *England Before the Conquest*, ed. P. Clemoes and K. Hughes (Cambridge: Cambridge University, 1971) 35–48. For an overall summary of Boniface's reform movement, see P. Riché, *The Carolingians. A Family Who Forged Europe*, trans. M. I. Allen (Philadelphia: University of Pennsylvania, 1993) 53–57.

[25] See, e.g., Boniface's letter to Pope Zacharias in 742, Letter XL (*Letters of St. Boniface*, 78–83) and Karlmann's publication of the synod decrees of 742 and 743, Letter XLIV (Ibid., 91–94).

the other Anglo-Saxon missionaries simply adapt doctrinally and liturgically to the Germanic mentality of the Frisians and Saxons or were their evangelization methods shaped, in part, as a reaction to the type of Christianity they saw among the baptized in Frankland? Or should more weight be given to the argument of the "germanization" of the Christian culture, doctrine, and liturgy?

The adaptive interpretation is succinctly stated by H. Mayr-Harting: "Adaptations were required of Christianity; biblical colours had to be matched to Germanic ones . . . Another Germanic epic, the Old High German *Heiland*, presented Christ the Savior as a great Germanic war-leader with the apostles as his followers in battle."[26] Jungmann's argumentation seems to follow this line. While not denying the eventual Germanic influence on the Western Church, precisely in such liturgical matters as the ordination rites and forms of address to God, he ultimately faults the heretical character of the Germanic peoples to which the missionaries had to adapt. Jungmann is too fine an historian to oversimplify this complex situation but he does seem to underestimate the power and complexity of the Germanic cultures which were evangelized.

J. Russell and other scholars prefer the "germanization" interpretation of this same history. This interpretation allows some importance to the doctrinal dimensions of the situation (in this case, the Arian persuasion of the Germanic peoples) but insists on the decadent sociocultural situation *from which the missionaries evangelized*! The social attractiveness of Christianity as a perduring society within the disintegrating empire offered little to Germanic peoples whose familial and communal solidarity was the envy of many outsiders. Once the minimal evangelization of these peoples was accomplished, they were gradually able to transpose culturally what was received in such a way that it was eventually recognized and welcomed as a development of the tradition.

I have no intention of defending the "germanization" interpretation against the adaptation approach on this specific question. Not only do both interpretations have considerable merit, they are in agreement on the importance of sociocultural contexts while differing on the weight to be given those contexts. Ultimately, it seems to me, we are dealing with the complex ecclesial question of "reception," understood not only as the acknowledgment and appropriation by one local church of some aspects of the faith and praxis of another local church but also an awareness that such an appropriation will lead to an enhanced gospel life. But one cannot discuss "reception" in a cultural void without misinterpreting it.

I am not as persuaded as Jungmann of the importance of the Arian persuasion in the "give and take" of the evangelizaton of the Germanic peoples—a point I will return to in discussing their ongoing catechesis. His liturgical argument seems more cogent during Alcuin's period of influence under Charlemagne. In any case,

---

[26] H. Mayr-Harting, "The West: The Age of Conversion (700–1050)," *The Oxford Illustrated History of Christianity*, ed. H. McManners (Oxford: Oxford University, 1990) 107.

I do believe that if Jungmann were writing today, he would take full advantage of the sociocultural riches of current scholarship as he had the historical scholarship of his own day and that his final judgment on the "revolution in religious culture," inspired by the Germanic imput, might have been a more complex and rich one.

Lex orandi lex credendi is always an operative principle but, as with "reception," it always occurs in a sociocultural context. What options would Jungmann have chosen among the complex and often conflicting theories and methodologies of cultural research? And are some of these approaches more congenial to liturgical research than others? To answer such questions, we turn to some of the current insights on the question of cultural interpretation.

The Cultural Turn

One of the many reasons that liturgists have reason to be grateful for the work of the *Liturgy Digest* was its issue on liturgy and culture. The whole issue might serve as a general introduction to the state of the question in cultural anthropology and to the possible theological models for any discussion of liturgical inculturation. In that issue John Witvliet puts his finger on the overriding concern of the liturgist: "The goal for all thoughtful liturgists is not simply to arrive at an apt description of culture, but rather to discern how particular cultural traits both enhance and obscure the nature and purpose of liturgy, and how liturgical reform can capitalize on the unrealized potential of contemporary cultural traits."[27]

I have already suggested that an appreciation of the complex and interactive nature of culture is a safeguard against an overly facile or an historicized interpretation of the Germanic situation with which Jungmann deals so perceptively. But such an appreciation is only the beginning of the task: "The sense of culture is then one thing; actual social interactions and intentions and participants in them is another."[28] Clifford Geertz and others have convinced us of this by their penetrating studies of specific cultural situations and actions. This reminder is particularly pertinent to the work of the liturgical theologian. Jungmann instinctively knew this as is evidenced by his questioning the underlying notion of "conversion" that was operative in the Germanic situation. In examining the catechetical sources of the period, he was attempting to uncover just such a definition. Both the cultural anthropologist and the liturgical theologian have something to learn from the actions and thought patterns of participants in a given cultural context about the operative meaning of conversion.

But the difficulty of just such an enterprise has been highlighted by the debate occasioned by Ramsey MacMullen's thesis that I cited earlier. Robert Markus in a provocative examination of the notion of "secularity" demonstrates the complexity

---

[27] J. D. Witvliet, "Theological and Conceptual Models for Liturgy and Culture," *Liturgy Digest* 3:2 (1996) 5–46, here 40, as well as the following report, "Cult, Creed and Culture," Ibid., 47–63.

[28] Tanner, *Theories of Culture*, 42.

of distinguishing religion and culture by asking how tightly was Christianity linked to particular cultural forms.[29] This distinction is crucial if "conversion" is to be discussed in a particular culture. His own task, as an historian, is not only to consider "the completeness or otherwise of conversion, but also the extent of unnecessary change inflicted on the convert in the name of Christianity."[30] But such a task entails acceptance of the relative character of such terms as "completeness": "Just how much renunciation of the old does conversion to the new require?"[31] ("Renunciation of the old" is culturally synonymous with a radical change of some thought patterns and participation.) In other words, the scriptural description of "conversion" does not do away with the difficulty of its application in a particular culture.

One aspect of this difficulty is revealed in distinguishing a religious way of life from secular customs. The history of the "foreign missions" is replete with examples.[32] At this point, Markus cites MacMullen at length, ending with the latter's question: "what difference did conversion actually make anyway in the various zones of life?"[33] Markus points to the assumption that seems to underly MacMullen's approach and methodology: ". . . that the boundary between what is 'religion' and what is not is fixed and unambiguous."[34] Since MacMullen sees the opposite situation in the non-Christian world where everything is affected by religion, Markus draws the obvious conclusion to MacMullen's position: if everything is religion in the non-Christian world, then everything must be changed in Christian conversion.

Since Markus obviously does not accept this position, what is his own solution? Two valid but very different approaches, he suggests, are possible: either delineate the processes by which society has or has not become "christianised," whatever one means by that term, or trace the "shifting boundaries" as worked out in late antiquity by which a society was considered "Christian."[35] What Markus is calling for, in contrast to what he believes is MacMullen's methodology, is a more nuanced reading of such terms as "pagan," "Christian," "conversion," and so on. The practical way in which to take such a reading is, he argues, to inquire how Christians of an historical period distinguished the sacred from the secular within their culture rather than to distinguish religion from culture. Therefore, one must investigate not only the cultural institutions and patterns of living but also the ways in which the participants interpreted these realities.[36]

[29] R. Markus, *The End of Ancient Christianity* (Cambridge: Cambridge University Press, 1990) 1.

[30] Ibid., 3.

[31] Ibid., 5.

[32] To illustrate this, one has only to think of the Chinese rites controversy. For a description of the cultural complexity of that situation, see G. Minamiki, *The Chinese Rites Controversy* (Chicago: Loyola University, 1985).

[33] Markus, *The End*, 7, cited MacMullen, *Christianizing*, 74.

[34] Markus, *The End*, 7.

[35] Ibid., 8–9.

[36] Ibid., 13–15.

It might seem odd to the reader that both MacMullen and Markus refer to Clifford Geertz's seminal conception of culture approvingly and yet seem so separated in their respective historical methodologies by the application of this concept. I suspect that their approaches are not as inimical to one another as Markus maintains. MacMullen insists on the sociocultural ramifications of conversion that should be discernible in an historical situation: ". . . the readiness and capacity to attract attention, such as could be found among Christians much more than among non-Christians. Thereby the former seem to me to have enjoyed far more historical significance than their numbers alone could explain."[37] Markus is more concerned with what characterizes a particular society as "Christian" and understands "secular" as that part of life that "is not considered to be of direct religious significance."[38] The strengths of both approaches are needed if an adequate understanding of "conversion" within a given sociocultural and historical situation is to be achieved.

Is Liturgy Always an Expression of Conversion?

With this in mind, if we turn one last time to Jungmann's interpretation of the Germanic conversion, what might that scholar have reconsidered in light of the current cultural discussions? If MacMullen were discussing Jungmann's paper, I suspect he would ask whether the non-Germanic evangelizers' conception of conversion was not a highly inculturated one that allowed a rapid and superficial admission of Germanic tribes into the Church. Accommodation as a missionary strategy would seem to imply, at first glance, a weakening of the notion of conversion at the same time that it acknowledges cohesiveness of the host culture, no matter how that is described ("pagan," etc.) But are these suspicions actually borne out in the data about the conversion of the Germanic tribes?

Jungmann indirectly provides an answer to such a concern in his examination of the preparation of Germanic candidates for initiation, a preparation that was primitively catechetical but certainly not catechumenal. He attributes such preparation "to the primitive spirituality of these people and their less than sketchy instruction."[39] If these Germanic candidates were of an Arian persuasion, then this would presumably affect their formation for initiation with a greater emphasis on doctrinal rather than on moral questions. There is a question, however, among contemporary scholars as to how deep the Germanic understanding of Arianism actually was. I find Maurice Wiles's argument persuasive: "If, as evidence certainly seems to suggest, distinctiveness of doctrine was not a matter of primary importance for the Gothic church, it is not surprising that the transition to Catholic Christianity at the instigation of a ruler such as Reccared did not prove too difficult

---

[37] MacMullen, *Christianizing*, 84.
[38] Markus, *The End*, 15.
[39] Jungmann, "The Defeat of Teutonic Arianism," 41.

a process. *Doctrinal purity was not as central as the social role of the shared faith.*[40] This was as true of the Germanic peoples as it was of the Visigoths.

Jungmann's pastoral remarks on baptismal preparation certainly have a socio-cultural dimension. The Germanic peoples had a strong cultural heritage of social integration based on the clan system and their allegiance to their leaders. This Germanic heritage in some respects would have been highly appreciative of a cate-chumenal ecclesiology (such as still evident in Augustine of Hippo's own catechu-menal experience as well as his later teaching). This classical catechumenal process had a strong ecclesial context which not only focused its doctrinal and moral teaching but also provided a penetrating challenge to the sociocultural values and priorities of its people.

By contrast, the Anglo-Saxon missionaries' own ecclesiology no longer saw the church as sacrament as, it seems, their predecessors, the Irish missionaries did,[41] but rather as the carrier of God's salvation. Boniface and his compatriots came from a land that had experienced some of the political and cultural chaos engendered by the gradual disintegration of what had been the Roman Empire, though certainly not to the degree that the Frankish countries had. Although some of that same so-ciocultural anomie might also describe the situation of the Germanic peoples, it appears that they had sufficient resources to deal with it.[42] The Graeco-Roman cultural heritage of respect for the rule of law that had directly or indirectly supported the moral tone of Christianity, if not its specific moral positions, was becoming increasingly difficult to maintain in the social and cultural confusion of the aftermath of the barbarian invasions. These observations might make one wonder if the Germanic peoples were in a culture, Arian or not, so inimical to evangelization or rather, if the harassed Anglo-Saxon missionaries who were struggling with the severely damaged Frankish culture as well as the Germanic cultures found themselves in a much more difficult position to evangelize than Augustine and his monks had encountered in the British isles. Certainly Boniface's own Roman-centered ecclesial orientation, a unique heritage from Augustine in refounding the British Church, provided the unifying cultural as well as theological heritage that was needed.[43]

---

[40] See Wiles, *Archetypal Heresy*, 50, my emphasis; see also, T. S. Burns, *A History of the Ostro-Goths* (Bloomington, Ind.: Indiana University, 1984) 158–62. E. A. Thompson has speculated that Ulfila's fourth century translation of the Bible into the Gothic tongue (an important cultural achievement), explains why there was no perceived need to use Latin or Greek which would have provided access to a larger theological world; see Thompson, *The Visigoths in the Time of Ulfila*, 117–19.

[41] Russell, *The Germanization*, 154–60 presents some of the background to this earlier evangelizing movement.

[42] For a description of the non-Germanic anomie, see J. Le Goff, *La Civilisation de l'Occident Médiéval* (Paris: Arthaud, 1967) 59–64; for its subsequent effect on the church, see J. H. Lynch, *The Medieval Church: A Brief History* (New York: Longman, 1992) 72–87.

[43] Y. Congar is certainly correct in emphasizing the importance Boniface attached to local synods and their historical importance in his evangelizing efforts which Congar interprets as showing a "very vivid awareness of being united by an identical faith and formed as one body under one head" (133) but I wonder if this is also explained by another point he mentions: Boniface was the first non-Italian

Boniface's task was also complicated by the unappropriated faith of the Frankish kingdoms, a missionary obstacle already alluded to. When Boniface describes the pastoral difficulties of preparing candidates for the sacraments of initiation, he singles out the bishops and priests *in situ* as being "erring fakers *(erroneos simulatores)* . . . who do not preach the catholic faith to the pagans nor do they have a correct faith themselves," and then goes on to enumerate some of the catechumenal steps (renunciation of Satan, the signing of the Cross, the teaching on the Triune God) that are necessary to achieve the Pauline goal that "they might believe in their heart to justification and the confession of their mouth might effect salvation in them."[44] In other words, Boniface recalls the Pauline description of ongoing conversion with all its sociocultural implications. He had enough experience of the Frankish notion of culture that had too often been equated with Christianity.

The proof that Boniface and his missionary contemporaries took the long view of Germanic conversion is their establishment of monasteries as both religious and cultural centers. When Pope Zacharias replied favorably to Boniface's petition to establish a monastery under the rule of St. Benedict in the wilderness of Fulda that was to enjoy the privilege of being directly under the Holy See, he sanctioned a missionary strategy to deal with the cultural and moral remoteness of the Germanic peoples as well as with the need for ongoing doctrinal formation.[45] This hybrid form of missionary monasticism (originating either in Irish monasticism or more probably, in Pope Gregory's innovative use of missionary monks) "brought together evangelization, the spread of culture and a strong attachment to an aristocratic family corresponding better . . . to the social, religious, and cultural givens of Europe at the end of the barbarian invasions."[46] These monastic centers would also play a crucial role, in the time of Alcuin, as centers of lay as well as monastic education and culture, and the development of that most important of cultural artifacts, language. When the reform regional church councils in the late eight and

---

bishop to take an oath of profession of faith and promise of obedience to the pope on the occasion of his episcopal ordination in Rome (197); see *L'Ecclésiologie du Haut Moyen Age* (Parish: Cerf, 1968). For the text of the oath, C. H. Talbot, *The Anglo-Saxon Missionaries in Germany*, 70–71.

    [44] Ep. 80, *Monumenta Germaniae Historica* Epp. 1:176, the Latin text as cited by G. Kretschmar, "Die Geschichte des Taufgottesdienstes in der alten Kirche" in K. F. Müller and W. Blankenburg, eds., *Leiturgia* V (Kassel: J. Stauda, 1970) 1–342, here, 309. Kretschmar points out that Boniface is not employing the term 'catechumen' as in the early Church's usage but rather as someone who has been taught the doctrinal and liturgical meaning of what is celebrated in Initiation.

    [45] Letters LXX, LXXI and LXXIII (the papal charter for Fulda), in *Letters of St. Boniface*, 157–64, 165–66.

    [46] J. Paul, *L'Eglise et la Culture en Occident. La sanctification de l'ordre temporel et spirituel* (Paris: Presses universitaries de France, 1986) 109–10. Paul's discussion of monasticism in this situation is quite thorough; see ibid., 103–21. C. H. Talbot gives an even more enthusiastic assessment: "The consequent foundation of the Abbey of Fulda resulted in a complete transformation of cultural conditions in Germany, and spreading of its sphere of influence was as remarkable as it was extensive." (*The Anglo-Saxon Missionaries in Germany*, xiii–xiv).

ninth centuries legislated the translation of homilies into the vernacular (the Ale-
mannia, Rhine-Frankish, and other dialects), these monasteries were cultural centers for this important task as they were for the liturgical developments and its
literary dissemination of the Carolingian era.[47]

Jungmann was perfectly justified in his conclusions about the lack of breadth
and depth in catechesis of the Germanic tribes as represented in the extant writings
of the time. On the other hand, the monastic centers that Boniface set up, no doubt
in imitation of the same system set up by Gregory and Augustine in Britain, assured a long-term catechesis as well as cultural clearing houses for an ongoing exchange between the host culture and Christianity.

Charlemagne's Sociocultural Context for Conversion

The sociocultural dimension of conversion and its expression in initiation
were transposed into a new and more intense key in the following generations with
the accession of Charlemagne to the throne and his retention of the Anglo-Saxon
monk Alcuin as his adviser. In 789 Charlemagne issued his *Admonitio generalis*
which represented his vision of how a Christian society should function. He expressed this vision in legislative language suited to the actual situation of the empire and the various cultural groupings within it. The extirpation of pagan superstition
and practices, the observance of Sunday, the reception of the sacraments, the re-
sponsibilities of the clergy to teach, preach, and give good example were all part of
Charlemagne's *utilitas publica*.[48]

Despite this enlightened Christian policy, Charlemagne saw no problem with
the forced baptism of some Germanic tribes (the Saxons of Northwest Germany
and the Avars). In his mind this practice, no doubt, was also part of the *utilitas publica*. But Alcuin's famous pastoral reaction to such a practice was trenchant: "How
can someone be forced to believe what he does not believe? Someone can be compelled to baptism but not to faith."[49] In that same letter, he comments on the do-
minical command to teach and baptize by noting that Christ says "teach" twice and
"baptize" once because after baptism there is again the need for instruction in the

---

[47] An intriguing question, of course, is what languages or dialects did Boniface himself evangelize in. Latin was not universal among the less educated clergy in Frankland. See *Letters of St. Boniface*, 122–23, letter LIV for just such an incident and Pope Zacharias's reply to Boniface on its
sacramental consequences. Some scholars point out that there is no mention of Boniface using translators in his missionary preaching. Whatever Anglo-Saxon dialect Boniface was reared in may have been
of some help.

[48] R. McKetterick gives an excellent analysis of this legislation and its applications in the episcopal statutes in *The Frankish Church*, 1–79.

[49] Alcuin, Ep. 113 to Arno of Salzburg in 796. The Latin text is given by Kretschmar, "Die
Geschichte des Taufgottesdienstes," 309, n. 43. For an overall description, see Riché, *The Carolingians*, 102-09; for more detail on Alcuin's reactions and correctives to the forced baptism issue, see
also Bullough, "Alcuin and the Kingdom of God," *The Carolingians*, 42–45.

gospel precepts.[50] Alcuin, no more than Boniface, had any illusions about restoring the ancient catechumenate but was insisting on the realistic formation of converts within their own culture and time.[51] Involved as he was in the ecclesial reforms of the kingdom, Alcuin had some idea of the cultural and as well as theological obstacles to an appropriated faith.

There are two indications that Alcuin's warning about an unappropriated faith, to some extent, was heard: the number of baptismal instructions extant from this period and Charlemagne's insistence on regular and effective vernacular preaching throughout his lands.[52] The existence of such instructions, however, are no indication of how often and how well they were used. There are certainly enough indications that some of the Frankish clergy did not know Latin (or could not even read) and would have benefited very little from such instructions.

Pastorally effective preaching has always been a problem in the Church as witnessed by the constant references and canons in synods and councils. Reform councils attempted to implement Charlemagne's insistence on preaching by encouraging it in the dialect of the region in which the diocese was located.[53] As already noted, language is a primary cultural creation and its development and use is tied to a number of other important cultural values. An effective and lasting evangelization in any epoch has always depended on the availability of adequate translations of the essential Christian texts and understandable vernacular commentaries on those texts. Yet, as Rosamond McKetterick has pointed out, the Church in the east and west Frankish areas was almost apologetic in their use of the vernacular in contrast to the clergy "in the dioceses and monasteries established by the Anglo-Saxon missionaries who encouraged the use of the language of the people they lived among and produced these translated texts and glossaries."[54]

---

[50] Again, the Latin text is given in Kretschmar, "Die Geschichte des Taufgottesdienstes," 310, n. 47.

[51] For a discussion of the Carolingian baptismal rituals, see Ibid., 311–23. For the importance of the baptismal and other creeds in Alcuin's fight against Adoptionism, see D. Bullough, "Alcuin and the Kingdom of God: Liturgy, Theology, and the Carolingian Age," *Carolingian Essays*, ed. U-R. Blumenthal (Wash. D.C.: The Catholic University of America Press, 1983) 1–69, esp. 37–67.

[52] Particularly interesting among the list of incipits of baptismal instructions that Susan Keefe has documented, is Alcuin's ordo for baptism and a baptismal questionnaire from Charlemagne based on that ordo. See S. Keefe, "Carolingian Baptismal Expositions: A Handlist of Tracts and Manuscripts," *Carolingian Essays*, 151–237; here 184–86 (Alcuin's ordo) and 189–91 (the incipit of Charlemagne's questionnaire). For the text of the questionnaire, see *Monumenta Historiae Germanica*, capit. I, 125 (246).

For a discussion of some of the copied responses to the questionnaire on the question of baptism and its rituals, see Kretschmar, "Die Geschichte des Taufgottesdienstes," 323–27 and T. Maertens, *Histoire et Pastorale du Rituel du Catéchuménat et du Baptême* (Bruges: Biblica, 1962) 210–11 where he speaks of the bishops' responses as an attempt "to conceal the sad reality of the time" (211).

[53] See McKetterick, *The Frankish Church*, 14, 73, and esp. 84 where she cites the canon from the council of Tours in 813.

[54] Ibid., 204. Her whole chapter on the vernacular is a fine summary of this important cultural development (Ibid., 184–204).

Jungmann, in his brief discussion of catechetical texts and missionary sermons, constantly points out "this same careless interchangeability of Christ and God."[55] His point is well taken. But there is a great deal more in the Carolingian sermon collections and homiliaries. These collections were meant to support the reform councils' demands for effective preaching in the kingdom. McKitterick makes an important distinction between two types of ninth century Carolingian collections: one destined for private devotion of the literate theological reader and the second, for reading during the liturgy that might also serve as sermons to be preached to the people.[56]

The point of mentioning these collections is that the ideal of ongoing conversion would seem to have been generally well served by the preaching they contain. Hrabanus Maurus, for example, compiled a collection of seventy homilies while at Fulda (814–826).[57] The tone of his homilies is reminiscent of those of Caesar of Arles in the sixth century—pastoral, hortatory, direct, and relevant in their examples.[58] The cultural implications of this type of preaching are fairly obvious: appropriation of initiation in the culturally and politically turbulent ninth century was difficult but possible if the Christian virtues guided social life and cultural expression.

Conclusions

Jungmann essentially employs two types of argumentation to support his "Arian" thesis: the one cultural, the other liturgical. As already noted, his liturgical-theological argument which constitutes a major part of the article (9–46) traces the Spanish Visigothic Arianism to its liturgical refutation by Alcuin and others. I find this argument convincing but are we dealing here with *Teutonic* Arianism?

Jungmann's cultural argument with its leit-motiv furnished by Herweggen is another matter. Both writers used the best available scholarship of the day. But in the light of current historical and cultural resources I believe that they might have argued their cultural points with greater precision and more respect for the Germanic cultures. Not to make too fine a point, was the fairly decadent Merovingian Church that still had remnants of the classical culture to be preferred to what the

---

[55] Jungmann, "The Defeat of Teutonic Arianism," 45. I wonder if some of that carelessness might not also be attributed to the reaction against Spanish Adoptionism beginning with the council of Frankfort in 794 and Alcuin's very active role in the orthododox response. For the background, see Bullough, *The Age of Charlemagne*, 112, 162–65 and L. Wallach, *Alcuin and Charlemagne: Studies in Carolingian History and Literature* (Ithaca: Cornell University, 1959) 147–77.

[56] McKitterick, *The Frankish Church*, 92.

[57] Hrabanus Maurus, *Homeliae*, PL 110, c. 13–136. Although the texts are in Latin, I assume that they were given in the vernacular for the reasons cited earlier. It was customary throughout the medieval period that such collections destined for popular preaching were written in Latin as a source for vernacular preaching.

[58] McKitterick gives a good summary of this collection, *The Frankish Church*, 102. Her chapter on preaching is detailed and fairly comprehensive, Ibid., 80–114.

Germanic cultures brought to the faith? In a sense, Jungmann gave more balance to his cultural argument when he introduced the questions of conversion and their expression in the theology and praxis of initiation. But I feel sure that he would have developed this argument differently in view of what we know today about the cultural contexts of evangelization and conversion.

One practical way to do this is to reevaluate the mission of Boniface and the other Anglo-Saxon missionaries. Their own cultural background and ecclesial heritage from Gregory helped them to evangelize more effectively than they have perhaps been given credit for. The foundation of monasteries in the Benedictine tradition reinforced their cultural and ecclesial approach for the long term. If I have given more attention to the Anglo-Saxon missionaries than Jungmann did, it is because they supply the necessary cultural contexts for assessing the liturgical reactions of Alcuin in the Carolingian Church.

There is a wonderful set of miniatures in a Fulda sacramentary from the early eleventh century that shows Boniface, in one scene, baptizing and, in another, being martyred.[59] Peter Cramer has pointed out that when artists wished to picture the life of Boniface and other missionaries, they usually chose the scenes of their baptizing and of their martyrdom to sum up their lives.[60] At the moment of his martyrdom, the Anglo-Saxon Boniface holds the book of the gospels before him (not to ward off marytrdom, as some have asserted) but to summarize the meaning of his mission and his martyrdom. The ultimate success of his mission owes as much to his cultural strengths as to his committed witness.

Some Pastoral Corollaries

More than once in this paper, I have asked how Jungmann would have approached his topic today. Since his concerns were both academic and pastoral, I believe that his contemporary endeavors would also be in those areas. Jungmann was professor of pastoral theology at Innsbruck for half a century. Perhaps his wide-ranging concerns and his less restricted methodology were as much the result of preparing seminarians for the complexities of pastoral ministry as they were a response to the varied interests of his many doctoral students.

The first corollary that I would draw from Jungmann's rich legacy is that the pastoral praxis of the local Christian Church should benefit more consistently from the cultural implications of current interdisciplinary liturgical research. To cite but one example, it is now more than two decades since the publication of Paul VI's *Evangelii nuntiandi* [1976] and its insistence on the importance of cultural con-

---

[59] There is an excellent reproduction in Mayr-Hart, "The West," *The Oxford Illustrated History of Christianity*, 100.

[60] P. Cramer, *Baptism and Change in the Early Middle Ages c.200–c.1150* (Cambridge: Cambridge University, 1993), 203. Cramer comments on a similar set of miniatures of Boniface's baptizing and martyrdom but finds there the theme of humiliation.

texts for evangelizing and preaching. There is a growing body of interdisciplinary studies that could assist the Church to train more adequate preachers who are attuned to the cultures and sub-cultures in which they work. Charlemagne seemed to have been more concerned about this issue than we sometimes appear to be.

The second corollary that Jungmann's work suggests is the American Church has as much need to be concerned with cultural evangelization as Boniface and Alcuin in their day. The contemporary equivalent of the struggle of those earlier evangelizers with language and other cultural communication is the seeming irrelevance of much preaching and teaching to American teenagers and young adults. Perhaps part of the reason for this situation can be found in a rephrasing of the question raised by MacMullen: from what are our young American Catholics being converted?

Our American culture and its sub-cultures seem more successful in their direct and indirect advocacy for cultural values in the areas of life-goals, sexual and public ethics, and life-styles with their implied definitions of happiness than is the American Church. If our cultural analysis is superficial, then how can our religious challenge in preaching and teaching be relevant? If our language, a cultural product, does not make effective use of the images and expressions of our culture, then is it any wonder that we cannot be "heard" by younger Americans? These questions suggest a third corollary.

A final pastoral corollary is the need for identifying "centers" of cultural evangelization in our own American situation. The genius of Boniface's monastic centers of evangelization was the "translation" of the gospel message not only into texts but their necessary precursors, the discovery of the cultural images that spark a cultural language. This cultural imaging is probably more obvious, e.g., in the Spanish-speaking or Haitian cultures within the American Church than it might be for middle-class white Catholics.

But all these cultural groups, especially their younger members, seem to draw on television and videos as an important source for their ideas, values, and images. Although professional competence in cultural and communication issues is important, the "centers" of cultural evangelization I am suggesting are informal groups within sub-cultures who have a "hands-on" expertise. The Young Catholic Worker movement, particularly active in the earlier part of this century, is an historical example of such a "center." Working class youth were reevangelized so successfully by this movement because other committed young workers knew its cultural milieu and its symbols, images and language and were able to employ them in evangelizing their peers. Such informal groups already exist in parishes, on college campuses, and in professional and business circles. To identify such "centers" entails some consciousness raising and an empowerment to this special mission of helping the Word to be clothed in the appropriate cultural signs of the times.

Among the suggestions that Bishop Daniel of Winchester offered Boniface to convince the Germanic tribes of the benefits of conversion to Christianity was the challenge that pagan lands were cold and barren while Christian lands were "rich in oil and wine."[61] Although Bishop Daniel expected these tribes to understand the image in its most literal sense, the reference remains highly symbolic for Christians of every age. Boniface, Alcuin, and Jungmann, though separated from each other by time and task, were united in their conviction that a "new creation" would be built on God's first creation with all its cultural overtones. For each of them instinctively understood and lived the norm that Vatican II offered the contemporary evangelizing Church: "it must implant itself among all these groups in the same way that Christ by his incarnation committed himself to the particular social and cultural circumstances of the people among who he lived."[62]

---

[61] Ltter XV in *Letters of St. Boniface*, 49–50.

[62] Vatican II, Decree on the Church's Missionary Activity (*Ad gentes divinitus*), *Vatican Council II. The Conciliar and Post Conciliar Documents*, A. Flannery, ed. (Northport, N.Y.: Costello, rev. ed. 1988) 824–25.

Bibliography

Important Works in English by Josef A. Jungmann, s.j.

Bibliographic and Biographical Material about Josef A. Jungmann, s.j.

Section I provides an alphabetical list of Jungmann's books in English, followed by the German title and date of the original (if any). Section II presents a chronological list of Jungmann's articles in English. Section III includes a selected list of important sources for bibliographical and biographical material on Jungmann; some selections are in English and others are available only in German.

A more comprehensive bibliography of Josef Jungmann can be found in Balthasar Fischer and Hans B. Meyer, eds., *J. A. Jungmann: ein Leben für Liturgie und Kerygma* (see section III below). Items found among the numbered entries on that bibliography (abbreviated as **L**) are noted in { }. In addition to literature searches some material has also been taken from the entry on Jungmann in Anthony Ward and Cuthbert Johnson, eds., *Orbis Liturgicus* (see section III below).

I. Books by Josef A. Jungmann

Announcing the Word of God. London: Burns & Oates, 1967; New York: Herder and Herder, 1968. [*Glaubensverkündigung im Lichte der Frohbotschaft*, 1963] {**L 206**}.

Christian Prayer Through the Centuries. Mahwah, N.J.: Paulist, 1978. [*Christliches Beten im Wandel und Bestand*, 1969] {**L 280**}.

The Early Liturgy: to the Time of Gregory the Great. Notre Dame: University of Notre Dame Press, 1959. {**L 166**}.

The Eucharistic Prayer: A Study of the Canon of the Mass. Chicago: Fides, 1956, 1964; London: Challoner, 1962. [*Das Eucharistiche Hochgebet. Grundgedanken des Canon Missae*, 1954] {**L 113**}.

The Good News Yesterday and Today. New York: W. H. Sadlier, 1962. [*Die Frohbotschaft und unsere Glaubensverkündigung*, 1936] {**L28**}.

Handing on the Faith: A Manual of Catechetics. New York: Herder & Herder, 1959. [*Katechetik. Aufgabe und Methode der religiösen Unterweisung*, 1953, 1955] {**L 99**}.

The Liturgical Movement. Derby, N.Y.: St. Paul's Publications, 1966.

263

Liturgical Renewal in Retrospect and Prospect. London: Burns & Oates, 1965. [*Liturgische Erneuerung. Rückblick und Ausblick*, 1962] {**L 198**}.

Liturgical Worship. New York and Cincinnati: Frederick Pustet, 1941. [*Die liturgische Feier. Grundsätzliches und Geschichtliches über Formgesetze der Liturgie*, 1939] {**L 41**}.

The Liturgy of the Word. London: Burns & Oates, 1966. [*Wortgottesdienst im Lichte von Theologie und Geschichte*, 1965] {**L 231**}.

The Mass: An Historical, Theological and Pastoral Survey. Collegeville: The Liturgical Press, 1976.

The Mass of the Roman Rite: Its Origins and Development. 2 vols. Westminster, Md.: Christian Classics Inc., 1986 (reprint of New York: Benziger, 1951–55). One-volume abridged ed. London: Burns & Oates, 1959; Westminster, Md.: Christian Classics, 1959, 1980; New York: Benziger, 1961. [*Missarum Sollemnia. Eine genetische Erklärung der römischen Messe,* 1949, 2d ed.] {**L 69**}.

The Meaning of Sunday. Notre Dame: Fides, 1961. [*Sonntag und Sonntagsmesse. Sinn der Sonntagsfeier,* 1959] {**L 167**}.

Pastoral Liturgy. New York: Herder; Tenbury Wells: Challoner, 1962. [*Liturgisches Erbe und pastorale Gegenwart,* 1960; a collection of updated, previously published articles] {**L 179**}.

The Place of Christ in Liturgical Prayer. 2d rev. ed. Staten Island, N.Y.: Alba House, 1965; Collegeville: The Liturgical Press, 1989. [*Die Stellung Christi im liturgischen Gebet,* 1925, 1962] {**L 4**}.

Public Worship: A Survey. London: Challoner Publications, 1957; Collegeville: The Liturgical Press, 1958. [*Der Gottesdienst der Kirche auf dem Hintergrund seiner Geschichte kurz erläutert,* 1955, 1957] {**L 123**}.

The Sacrifice of the Church: The Meaning of the Mass. Collegeville: The Liturgical Press; London: Challoner, 1956. [*Vom Sinn der Messe als Opfer der Gemeinschaft,* 1954] {**L 114**}.

II. Articles by Josef A. Jungmann (Chronological order)

"What is Liturgy?" *Ecclesiastical Review* 96 (1937) 584–610. {**L 32**}.

"The Pastoral Effect of the Liturgy," *Orate Fratres* 23 (1948–49) 481–91. {**L 80**}.

"We Offer," *Orate Fratres* 24 (1949–50) 97–102. {**L 86**}.

"An Adult Christian," *Worship* 27 (1952) 5–11.

"Father Jungmann's Answer," *Worship* 29 (1954) 58–62. {**L 116**}.

"Problems of the Missal," *Worship* 28 (1954) 153–57.

"Church Art," *Worship* 29 (1955) 68–82.

"Holy Church," *Worship* 30 (1955) 3–12. {**L 131**}.

"The Pastoral Liturgical Idea in the History of the Liturgy," *Worship* 30 (1956) 608–22.

"The Sense for the Sacred," *Worship* 30 (1956) 354–60.

"The Liturgy in the Parish," *Worship* 31 (1957) 62–67.

"From Tradition to a Pastoral Liturgy," *Hibernia* 4 (1958) 5–20. {**L 163**}.

"*Pia exercitia* and Liturgy," *Worship* 33 (1959) 616–22. {**L 173**}.

"Liturgy on the Eve of the Reformation," *Worship* 33 (1959) 505–15.

"The History of Holy Week as the Heart of the Liturgical Year," *The Furrow* 10 (1959) 287–309. {**L 172**}.

"Religious Education in late Medieval Times: Shaping the Christian Message," in Gerard S. Sloyan, ed., *Shaping the Christian Message: Essays in Religious Education.* New York: Macmillan, 1958, 1959, 38–62. {**L 175**}.

"Eucharistic Piety," *Worship* 35 (1961) 410–20.

"The Eucharist and Pastoral Practice," *Worship* 35 (1961) 83–90.

"What the Sunday Mass Could Mean," *Worship* 37 (1962) 21–30. {**L 204**}.

"Vespers and the Devotional Service: Liturgy for the People," in William J. Leonard, ed., *Liturgy for the People: Essays in Honor of Gerald Ellard.* Milwaukee: Bruce Publishing Company, 1963, 168–78. {**L 211**}.

"Liturgy in the Missions after the Council," *Teaching All Nations* 4 (1967) 3–14. {**L 262**}.

III. Bibliographic and Biographical Publications about Jungmann (English and German)

Coreth, Emerich, and others. *Sonderheft zur Vollendung des 80 Lebensjahres von J. A. Jungmann. ZKTh* 91 (1969) 249–516; bibliography 510–15.

Fischer, Balthasar, and Hans B. Meyer, eds. *J. A. Jungmann: ein Leben für Liturgie und Kerygma.* Innsbruck: Tyrolia Verlag, 1975; bibliography (= **L**, see above) 156–207.

Fischer, Balthasar, and Johannes Wagner, eds. *Paschatis sollemnia: Studien zur Osterfeier und zur Osterfrömmigkeit.* Freiburg: Herder, 1959. (*Festschrift* for Jungmann's seventieth birthday.)

Hofinger, Johannes. "Jungmann, Joseph Andreas," in *New Catholic Encyclopedia* XVII: *Supplement, Change in the Church.* Washington, D.C.: Publishers Guild, 1979, 312–13.

"Jungmann, Josef," in Peter Fink, S.J., ed., *The New Dictionary of Sacramental Worship.* Collegeville: The Liturgical Press, 1990, 635.

"Jungmann, Josef A.," in Kathleen Hughes, R.S.C.J., ed., *How Firm a Foundation: Voices of the Early Liturgical Movement.* Chicago: Liturgy Training Publications, 1990, 151–59. (Brief selections from his writings in English.)

"Jungmann, Josef Andreas," in Anthony Ward, S.M., and Cuthbert Johnson, O.S.B., eds., *Orbis Liturgicus: Who's Who in Contemporary Liturgical Studies.* Rome: C.L.V.–Edizioni Liturgiche, 1995. No. [985], 703–705.

Klöckener, Martin. "Jungmann, Josef Andreas s.j.," no. 1123, pp. 320–21, in idem, "Bio-Bibliographisches Repertorium der Liturgiewissenschaft," *ALw* 35/36 (1993/94) 285–357.

Meyer, Hans Bernhard. *Eucharistie: Geschichte, Theologie, Pastoral: Zum Andenken an den 100. Geburtstag von Josef Andreas Jungmann sj am 16. Nov. 1989.* Regensburg: Pustet, 1989. [*Gottesdienst der Kirche: Handbuch der Liturgiewissenschaft*, Teil 4.] (In commemoration of the centenary anniversary of Jungmann's birth.)

———. "Das theologische Profil von Josef Andreas Jungmann, s.j. (16.11.1889 bis 26.1.1975)," *Liturgisches Jahrbuch* 39 (4/1989) 195–205.

Peiffer, Robert. "Josef Jungmann: Laying a Foundation for Vatican II," in Robert Tuzik, ed., *How Firm a Foundation: Leaders of the Liturgical Movement* (Chicago: Liturgy Training Publications, 1990) 58–62.

Rasmussen, Niels K., o.p. "Jungmann, Josef Andreas," no. 35, p. 217 in idem. "Some Bibliographies of Liturgists," *ALw* 11 (1969) 214–18.

———. "Jungmann, Josef Andreas," no. 71, p. 169 in idem. "Bibliographies of Liturgists: A First Supplement," *ALw* 15 (1973) 168–71.

———. "Jungmann, Josef Andreas" no. 118, p. 136 in idem. "Bibliographies of Liturgists: A Second Supplement," *ALw* 19 (1978) 134–39.

Vass, Georg T., and Hans Bernhard Meyer, eds. *Zum 100. Geburtstag von Josef Andreas Jungmann, s.j. ZKTh* 111 (1989) 257–359.

Contributors

Gerard Austin, O.P., teaches at the Rice School for Pastoral Ministry in the diocese of Venice, Florida. He taught for thirty years at The Catholic University of America. A past-president of the North American Academy of Liturgy, he has published widely about the sacraments of initiation and ministry.

John Baldovin, S.J., is professor of historical and liturgical theology at the Weston Jesuit School of Theology. He is on the advisory committee of the International Commission on the Liturgy (ICEL) and on the council of the international ecumenical *Societas Liturgica*. He is a past president of the North American Academy of Liturgy.

Nancy A. Dallavalle is associate professor in the department of religious studies at Fairfield University. Her "Revisiting Rahner: On the Theological Status of Trinitarian Theology" appeared in *The Irish Theological Quarterly*; and her work on Catholic feminist theology has been published in *Horizons* and *Modern Theology*.

Michael Downey is professor of systematic theology and spirituality at St. John's Seminary in Camarillo in the archdiocese of Los Angeles. Editor of the award-winning *New Dictionary of Catholic Spirituality*, his most recent books are *Understanding Christian Spirituality; Trappist: Living in the Land of Desire;* and *Hope Begins Where Hope Begins*.

Regis A. Duffy, O.F.M., is scholar in residence, The Franciscan Institute, St. Bonaventure University. He has authored *Real Presence; A Roman Catholic Theology of Pastoral Care; On Becoming a Catholic; An American Emmaus;* and *The Liturgy in the Catechism*.

Peter E. Fink, S.J., is professor of sacramental-liturgical theology at the Weston Jesuit School of Theology, where he has taught since 1975. He is author of *Worship: Praying the Sacraments* and editor of *The New Dictionary of Sacramental Worship* and two volumes in the *Alternative Futures for Worship* series. He is a past president of the North American Academy of Liturgy.

Balthasar Fischer studied liturgical theology with Josef A. Jungmann at Innsbruck from 1933–1936 and subsequently taught that subject in the university at Trier from 1950–1980. He was a participant at Vatican II and headed the commission that revised the rite of Christian initiation for adults. He received the Berakah Award from the North American Academy of Liturgy in 1989.

Kathleen Hughes, R.S.C.J., is professor of liturgy at the Catholic Theological Union where she served as academic dean from 1992–1995. Her recent works include *Saying Amen: A Mystagogical Reflection on the Sacraments* and *Finding Voice to Give God Praise.* She is a past president of the North American Academy of Liturgy.

John K. Leonard is associate professor of religious studies at Edgewood College. Publications include (with Nathan Mitchell) *The Postures of the Assembly During the Eucharistic Prayer*; (with Eleanor Bernstein) *Children in the Assembly of the Church*; and the video *Leading the Community in Prayer: The Art of Presiding*.

Nathan D. Mitchell is associate director for research at the Center for Pastoral Liturgy at the University of Notre Dame. His books include *Cult and Controversy, Mission and Ministry*, and *Eucharist as Sacrament of Initiation*. He received the Berakah Award from the North American Academy of Liturgy in 1998.

John Allyn Melloh, S.M., is the director of the John. S. Marten Program in Homiletics and Liturgics at the University of Notre Dame. Past president of the Catholic Association of Teachers of Homiletics and Liturgics (CATH), he is widely published in homiletics. A forthcoming book will deal with preaching at sacraments and funerals.

Joanne M. Pierce is an associate professor in the department of religious studies at the College of the Holy Cross (Worcester, Massachusetts), where she teaches historical and sacramental/liturgical theology. A specialist in medieval liturgy, she has published articles in collections and journals and serves as a member of the Anglican-Roman Catholic Consultation in the U.S.A.

Marjorie Procter-Smith is LeVan Professor of Worship and Preaching at Perkins School of Theology, Southern Methodist University. She is author of *In Her Own Rite: Constructing Feminist Liturgical Tradition,* and *Praying With Our Eyes Open: Engendering Feminist Liturgical Prayer*; and co-editor, with Janet Walton, of *Women at Worship: Interpretations of North American Diversity.*

Thomas P. Rausch, S.J., is professor and chair of theological studies at Loyola Marymount University. A specialist in ecclesiology, ecumenism, and the theology of the priesthood, his books include the award-winning *Catholicism at the Dawn of the Third Millennium.*

Don E. Saliers, Parker Professor of Theology and Liturgics, Emory University, also teaches during summers at the University of Notre Dame and St. John's University (Collegeville). Among his recent publications are *Worship Come To Its Senses,* and *Worship As Theology: Foretaste of Glory Divine.* A past president of the North American Academy of Liturgy, he received its Berakah Award in 1993.

Kenneth Stevenson, Bishop of Portsmouth, England, is an Anglican scholar who has written extensively on areas of liturgical history and sacramental theology. His books include *Nuptial Blessing*; *Eucharist and Offering*; *Covenant of Grace Renewed: A Vision of the Eucharist in the Seventeenth Century*; and *The Mystery of Baptism in the Anglican Tradition.*

Karen B. Westerfield Tucker is assistant professor of liturgical studies at the Divinity School, Duke University and an assistant editor of *Studia Liturgica. She* commissioned and compiled *The Sunday Service of the Methodists: Twentieth-Century Worship in Worldwide Methodism* (1996) and is the author of *American Methodist Worship* (forthcoming).

Mark E. Wedig, O.P., is assistant professor of theology and chair of the department of theology and philosophy at Barry University. He writes in the areas of liturgy, culture, and the visual arts.

Index